ISHTYLE

TRIANGULATIONS
Lesbian/Gay/Queer ▲ Theater/Drama/Performance

Series Editors
Jill Dolan, Princeton University
David Román, University of Southern California

Associate Editors
Ramón H. Rivera-Servera, Northwestern University
Sara Warner, Cornell University

ISHTYLE

Accenting Gay Indian Nightlife

Kareem Khubchandani

UNIVERSITY OF MICHIGAN PRESS

Ann Arbor

Copyright © 2020 by Kareem Khubchandani
All rights reserved

For questions or permissions, please contact um.press.perms@umich.edu

Published in the United States of America by
the University of Michigan Press
Manufactured in the United States of America
Printed on acid-free paper

First published July 2020

A CIP catalog record for this book is available from the British Library.

ISBN 978-0-472-07421 1 (hardcover : alk. paper)
ISBN 978-0-472-05421-3 (paper : alk. paper)
ISBN 978-0-472-12581-4 (ebook)

For my mother,
my ishtyle icon.

Contents

Digital materials related to this title can be found on the Fulcrum platform via the following citable URL https://doi.org/10.3998/mpub.9958984

Acknowledgments
A Playlist

Thank you for sharing pleasure, performance, politics, queerness, brownness, nightlife, dance, critical thought, and ishtyle with me. Here's a playlist for a perfect night out with you.
Listen along at bit.ly/IshtyleAcknowledgments.

"Aben Wo Ha," Daddy Lumba
You, the reader.
"Sissy That Walk," RuPaul
University of Michigan Press; LeAnn Fields; Anna Pohold; Marcia LaBrenz; Jasjyot Singh Hans; Richard Isomaki; David Luljak; Heather Dubnick; David Román; Jill Dolan; Sara Warner.
"Together Again," Janet Jackson
E. Patrick Johnson; Ramón Rivera-Servera; D. Soyini Madison; Martin Manalansan; Gayatri Reddy.
"Mighty Real," Sylvester
Shane Vogel; Jyoti Puri; Clare Croft; C. Winter Han; Sharmila Rudrappa; Laura Gutierrez; Naisargi Dave
"Finally," CeCe Peniston
Joshua Chambers-Letson; Nitasha Sharma; Ji-Yeon Yuh; Nick Davis; Lane Fenrich; Mary Weismantel; Sandra Richards; Susan Manning; Héctor Carrillo; Steven Epstein; Shalini Shankar; Jinah Kim; Harvey Young; Alan Shefsky; Dina Walters; Emily Gilbert.
"Sun is Shining," Funkstar De Luxe vs. Bob Marley
Neville Hoad; Ann Cvetkovich; Sue Heinzelman; Lyndon Gill; Xavier Livermon; Tarek El-Ariss; Jackie Salcedo; Pat Heisler.
"Mast Kalandar," Mika Singh & Yo Yo Honey Singh
Yamuna Sangarasivam; Anita Mannur; Svati Shah; Priya Srinivasan;

Chandan Reddy; Nayan Shah; Hari Krishnan; Stanley Thangaraj; Anjali Arondekar; Jisha Menon; Royona Mitra; Parmesh Shahani.

"Mera Piya Ghar Aaya," Kavita Krishnamurthy

Judith Hamera; Robin Bernstein; Patricia Ybarra; David Getsy; Eng-Beng Lim; Juana María Rodríguez; Patrick Anderson; Brian Herrera; David Eppel; Berta Jottar; Sandra Burton; Regina Kunzel; Sarah Bay-Cheng.

"Juice," Lizzo

Lisa Lowe; Kris Manjapra; Lee Edelman; Heather Nathans; Noe Montez; Sarah Pinto; Kendra Field; Nancy Bauer; Rita Dioguardi; Adriana Zavala; Hope Freeman; Nino Testa; Cynthia Sanders.

"Aap Jaise Koi," Nazia Hasan

Gowri Vijayakumar; Joshua Williams; Dwai Banerjee; Nidhi Mahajan; Bijoy Desai; Robert Ramirez; Jesus Valles; Johnny Estrella; Nick Harkins; Alex Cho; Chris Lloyd; Nikki Yeboah; Mbongeni Mtshali; Kemi Adeyemi; AB Brown; Munjulika Rahman; Meiver De la Cruz; Pavithra Prasad; Jeff Roy; Summer Kim Lee; Christine Goding; Moses Tulasi; Gautham Reddy; Vyjayanthi Vadrevu; Ajay Cadambi; Tejas Pande; Rohini Malur; Nanju Reddy; Sanjay Vaswani; Samyuktha Varma; Nisha Thompson; Geraldine Shen.

"Chura Liya," Bally Sagoo

Mum and Pap; Archie, Diana, Miki, Sofia; Rishi, Farzana, Layla, Anaiya; my very beloved extended family.

"Oo Mungda Mungda," Usha Mangeshkar

Rekha Malhotra; Surabhi Kukke; D'Lo; Fawzia Mirza; Ashu Rai; Shazad Hai; Waseem Shaikh; Amita Handa; DJ Dynamite; Rohan Sheth; Arshad Khan; Samir Narang; Arnish Thakore; Brenden Varma; Mohammed Moiz; Yasmin Nair; Jaishri Abichandani; Meera Sethi; Alok Vaid-Menon; Kazim Ali; Brendan Fernandes; Zulfikar Ali Bhutto; Kiran Rajagopalan; Tara Ali Asgar.

"Ring Ringa," Devi Sri Prasad, Priya Himesh

Ronak Kapadia; Durba Mitra; Natasha Bissonauth; Anna Cruz; Alexandra Shraytekh; Aymar Jean Christian; Lilian Mengesha; Greg Mitchell; Lisa Biggs; Kelly Chung; Eddie Gamboa; Jonathan Magat; Justin Zullo; Rhaisa Williams; Jasmine Mahmoud; Kantara Souffrant; Elias Krell; Patricia Nguyen; Victoria Fortuna; Colleen Daniher; Faith Kares; Melissa Olive Minor; Linde Murugan; Jennifer Tyburczy; James Zarsadiaz; Tom Sarmiento; Ian Shin; Sony Bolton Coráñez; Vanita Reddy; Anantha Sudhakar; Rumya Putcha; Angela

Alghren; Anusha Kedhar; Jasmine Johnson; Brian Horton; Elliot Powell; Debanuj DasGupta; Rohit Dasgupta; Alpesh Patel; Ashvin Kini; Naomi Bragin; Jade Sotomayor; Armando Garcia; Joanna Dee Das; Lakshmi Padmanabhan; Rushaan Kumar; Nishant Upadhyay; Ani Dutta; James McMaster; Aaron Thomas; Joseph Cermatori; Lindsay Brandon Hunter; Victor I. Cares; Zirwat Chowdhury; Patrick McKelvey; Sucheta Kanjilal; Akhil Kang; Dhiren Borisa; Hemangini Gupta; Vikram Aditya Sahai; Iván Ramos; Christina Léon; Micah Salkind; Leon Hilton; Tupur Chatterjee; Claire Pamment; Ramzi Fawaz.

"Diva, Diva," Kailash Kher, Priyadarshini
Rumi Harish; Sunil Mohan; Gee Semmalar; Karthik Bittu Kondaiah; Danish Sheikh; Ratna Appnender; Dhruv Dody; Abhishek Smurthy; Joshua Muyiwa; Namita Malhotra; Nitya Vasudevan; Nithin Manayath; Arvind Narrain; Harsh Bargotya; Varun Kumar Nair; Henry Prashant; Kartik Konchada; Ramkrishna Sinha; Sandeep Mahajan; Narendra Kumar Sinha; Seshadri Iyengar; Natasha; Sowmya Reddy; Siddharth Swaminathan; Srini Satya; Manas Modi; Sagar Vidya; Mahesh Natrajan; Rovan Varghese; Vinay Chandran; Siddharth Narrain; Abhishek Agarwal; Nakul Yash Sharma; Kiran R; Alex Mathew; Shyam Konnur; Alex Victor; Madav; Aditya V.S.; Yogesh Mishra; Partha Randir; Amrita Chanda; Daman Singh Arya; Dolly Koshy; Jayprakash; Parul Sharma; Manish Gaur; Rajiv; Anindyo Gupta; Rōmal Lāishram; Aditya Kini; Ravi Jain; Radhika Shastry; Manjunath.

"Call Your Girlfriend," Robyn
Michelle Fire; Hal Kolsky; Kyle Wood; Big Chicks; Amit Shah; Neeral Patel; Amit Patwardhan; Dheeraj Upadhay; Deepa Patel; Naomi Anurag Lahiri; Jay Nair; JJ Williams; Siby Easow; Mayur Patel; Ejaz Ali; Prerna Sampat; Imi Rashid; Sloka Krishnan; Shruti Kannan; Sal Salam; Ifti Nasim; Viru Joshi; Sarwat Rumi; Vikas Punjabi; Jai Sanghvi; Krishna Raghavan; Jackie Carmen Guerrero; Sachin Gupta; Erik Roldan; Nevin Hersch; Eks Pii; Manoj Dimri; Nabeela Rasheed; Arun Gulrajani; Ashish Arun; Tanay Dubey; Syam Reddy; Michael Elyea; Vidur Bandhari; Lovish; Mahi.

"Mr. Loverman," Shabba Ranks
Natasha Nyanin; Eli Pearlman-Storch; Justin Wynn; Victor Matos; David Depeña; Rhonda Jewels; Sabel Scities; Patrick Aitcheson; Marcela Villada-Peacock; Joel Williams; Arif Smith; Isabelle Holmes; Kat Gurley.

"La vida es un carnaval," Celia Cruz

> Harry Hoke; Teri Incampo; Seçil Reel Sen; Javier Hurtado; Emma Youcha; Caleb Luna; Al Evangelista.

"Work," Rihanna feat. Drake

> Gay Bombay; Alternative Law From; Good As You; Swabhava; We're Here and Queer; Sangama; Coalition for Sexuality Minorities Rights; Trikone-Chicago; Trikone-Bay Area; Khush-Austin; Boston MASALA; Mustard Seed Film Festival; 3ʳᵈ i Film Festival; Mississauga South Asian Film Festival; Asia Society; Rasaka Theatre; DesiQ; Sholay Events; Pink Nation; Rangeela; Invisible to Invincible; Besharam Toronto; Kitty Su.

"Million Dollar Bill," Whitney Houston

> Embrey Family Foundation; Andrew W. Mellon Foundation; Northwestern Buffett Institute for Global Affairs; Sexualities Project at Northwestern; American Society for Theatre Research; Dance Studies Association; CLAGS: The Center for LGBTQ Studies.

"It's Not Right, but It's Okay—Thunderpuss 2000 Club Mix," Whitney Houston

> Women's, Gender, and Sexuality Studies Program (Boston University); Gender and Sexuality Studies (Princeton University); Program in South Asian Studies (Brandeis University); Performance and Culture working group (Texas A&M University); Anthropology Colloquium (Rice University); Simpson Center for the Humanities (University of Washington); Department of Theatre and Dance (Colorado College); Dance Department (Williams College); South Asian Studies Program (University of Iowa); Gender, Sexuality, and Women's Studies (Bowdoin College); South Asia Center (Syracuse University); South Asia Program (Cornell University).

Preface

In Search of a Desi Drag Queen

The Queen's Labor

I fucking love drag queens. As emcees in gay nightlife spaces, drag queens welcome us: "You look so good tonight!" and, "You are all sluts!" Some welcome us in multiple languages, some acknowledge gender variety in the audience. When the show begins, we orient ourselves toward the stage and prepare ourselves for performances of racialized and classed femininity; in doing, so we recall our own attachments to those embodiments. Individuals and small groups are suddenly one audience, invited into shared experience. In hypersexualized club spaces, those of us who rarely receive attention await her eye contact, touch, or even kiss as she takes a currency bill from our hand—giving *her* a few dollars makes *us* feel valuable.[1]

Drag artists assemble cultural meanings of race, gender, and class on their bodies, relocating us to worlds beyond the club. They make apparent tools—dress, makeup, hairstyle, body modification, comportment, gesture, pose—we can use on and off the dance floor, in and out of the club, to reinvent ourselves, our worlds. Drag offers respite from the night, giving us instruction, emplacement, and orientation in the darkness and din. To suggest that queens do this on their own is to forget that gender is set into motion and secured through "communal performance labor,"[2] through our whistles, yaaaases, snaps, stares, and dollar bills. By facing her, tipping her, whistling for her, we come into relation with her, become gendered subjects of her address, ritualized witnesses of her song and dance, fellow travelers through time, space, and feeling. For those of us who traffic in her aesthetics, she affirms our right to be there, to reinvent gender, to exaggerate dance, to commit fully to the emotions and breaths of a song.

We continue to cruise while she performs, but her splits and lip-quivers fight for our attention, ask us to praise and honor her transfemininity in spaces where naturalized masculinities—jocks, bros, and bears—carry so much cultural capital.[3]

Between 2002 and 2008, I regularly traveled from rural New England to attend *Desilicious* parties in New York City, quarterly queer nights that featured Bollywood music and a predominantly South Asian crowd, primarily gay men. I was vigilant not to miss the queens' performances, especially because their show times were never announced. Like my favorite aunties, they were a source of desi cultural capital, training my ear, eye, and body to what nostalgic and contemporary songs could be mined for queer potentials: lewd jokes, transgressive femininity, self-exhibition, seduction, and innovative intertextualities. Their dances eventually led me to graduate school to explore how heteronormative Bollywood tropes, narratives, and choreographies were queered in South Asian nightclubs, particularly through the drag queen. When I moved to Chicago in the fall of 2008 to begin my graduate work, there was no queer desi nightlife scene, nor queens I could follow, and upon my return to *Desilicious* after 2010, those queens didn't perform regularly any more.

Though scores of South Asian queens across the world now network with each other via Facebook and Instagram, this wasn't the case during the primary years of fieldwork (2009–13). The apparent absence of drag did many things to shape this book, requiring me to look away from spectacular stages to more implicit pedagogies of nightlife citizenship. In the absence of drag, I turned to social dance floors to examine danced styles, what I call "drag labor," that engendered the socialities described above. Like staged shows, moments on the dance floor invite an audience to look, and ask bar patrons to pause and be together. Like the performances of queens, social dance reorients desires and pleasures. Theatrical eruptions that looked and felt *like* drag required me to think more capaciously about gender systems, identities, and performance in the club. Also, in the absence of drag queens, I became one. Because I circulate in the academy and nightclubs *as* a drag queen, people expect that drag is my object of analysis. But drag was hard to find when I started this project. This preface describes how I arrived in new spaces, lays out the gender landscape and social histories of queer South Asian nightlife, and demonstrates how drag became a research method.

Where Have All the Drag Queens Gone?

In the fall of 2008, the LGBTQ South Asian support group Trikone-Chicago was just coalescing. Following on the coattails of recently defunct organizations including Sangat, Khuli Zabaan, Rangeela, and SALGA-Chicago, Trikone desired a more sustainable model of organizing, and this required fund-raising. Arriving with fresh memories of *Desilicious*, I suggested a queer Bollywood dance party that included a drag show; planning fell on me. I inquired among Trikone's constituency about desi drag artists in Chicago, and the only lead pointed me to Ifti Nasim. Ifti, a multilingual Pakistani poet and luxury car salesman, cofounded Sangat in the mid-eighties. Though Ifti's Pepto-Bismol-pink apartment living room occasionally doubled as a performance salon, he bluntly explained that for his friends, doing a show in a *gay* bar—where drag performers were assumed to be men—would discredit the quotidian feminine gender they labored to establish. This concept is echoed in Adnan Malik's short documentary *Bijli* (2003), in which the title subject Bijli, while dancing at *Desilicious*, describes her desire to be seen and desired as a woman, not a man in drag, not a gay man.

I assumed drag was integral to queer desi nightlife, but when I returned to *Desilicious* in 2010, there was no guarantee of a show. Resident DJ Ashu Rai explained that queens I saw in the early 2000s were rarely booked to perform; several were migrant trans women, some undocumented, whose performances were last-minute additions at the parties, if not spontaneous improvisations. Additionally, several of those *Desilicious* queens enjoyed a Pakistani house party scene in the boroughs of New York and, like Ifti's friends in Chicago, were more likely to choose those parties over clubs and bars where patrons and performers are presumed gay and male.[4] Categories unraveled quickly; house parties promised sanctuary that the liberatory club could not, and desi queens in New York that I adored were, by and large, not "drag queens" as we typically define them.[5] However, the embodied cultural work of these dancers served as "drag labor," that is, the work we associate with drag queens to orient bodies in the space, to create relationships between those present, and to invoke identities, histories, and geographies not immediately apparent.

Jai Ho!, Trikone-Chicago's first queer Bollywood night, was arriving quickly.[6] In this city of thirty-six gay bars with a thriving drag community and over a hundred thousand South Asians, I could not locate a desi drag queen. In this absence, I became one. I adopted the stage persona LaWhore Vagistan, a name gesturing expansively to the subcontinent and embracing femininity and sexuality. I am diasporic Sindhi, born in Gibraltar and raised in Ghana, from a family of transnational Hindu merchants who originate from what is now Pakistan but were displaced into India and beyond the subcontinent under the 1947 partition. In Ghana, I was raised to think of myself as Indian, with little attachment to India save for the heavy-handed nationalism of Hindi films.

Upon moving to the United States, I found comfort in terms like "South Asian" and "desi" that did not require me to articulate myself as "Indian,"[7] and as a drag queen I employed the name "Vagistan" to embody a more expansive image of the Indian subcontinent. This book centers gay *Indian* nightlife precisely to interrogate the Indian nationalism, normativity, and nostalgia that have been used globally to manage many South Asian bodies. The collusion between India and the United States' national projects produce monolithic sexual and gender discourses that I and other artists seek to dislodge in fabulating more expansive and less violent geographies, like Vagistan, Discostan, Queeristan, Womanistan, Kalalabad, or Gaysi.[8] The critical motif of my stage name was, however, the deepest thought I put into LaWhore's debut at *Jai Ho!* Everything about my first act was cheap: makeup verging on whiteface, thrift store-assembled outfit, shake-and-go wig, unrehearsed choreography, and rough audio mixing of the sexy Hindi film song "Beedi Jalaile" and diasporic Sri Lankan pop star M.I.A.'s "Paper Planes." Despite my unpolished presentation, *Jai Ho!*'s audience was enthusiastic for more LaWhore. Desi drag, even my cheap desi drag, fulfilled desires and pleasures.

In developing *Jai Ho!* into a quarterly party with a signature midnight show, I simultaneously created a research field site. However, the culture of the event was not solely the result of my curatorial labor. I certainly used dance, dress, and music to orient the audience, but "co-temporal witnessing" made clear that culture, identity, and meaning were made *between* the spectators and myself.[9] Watching me provided the audience opportunities both to validate my performances and to stage their own cultural affinities, by circling money around my body before tucking it into my waist, removing the evil eye from me as I danced by drawing knuckles to temples, or sliding imaginary thousand-rupee notes off their palms toward LaWhore. My drag has also frightened away newcomers to the community; desi queens who facilitate community and pleasure can experience the abjection caused by collusive forces of diasporic respectability, gay men's femmephobia, ubiquitous transphobia, and South Asian hijraphobia. But nevertheless, my reputation as a drag queen extended to Bangalore, where I was invited to choreograph for friends, providing one more way to learn about their dance, bodies, and histories.

My own dances—on stage, in rehearsal with friends, in the club—were essential to being fully present during my fieldwork. Coperformative witnessing, asserts performance studies scholar D. Soyini Madison, derives its urgent politics by requiring that "we do what Others do *with* them inside the politics of their locations, the economies of their desires and their constraints, and, most importantly inside the materiality of their struggles and consequences."[10] I strive to be transparent about how my queer performances and desires enter my fieldwork and interpretation, and attend to "invasions" that my diasporic queerness performs.[11] Drawing on the work of Black, feminist, and queer researchers, I embrace and honor ethnography as a means of uplifting minoritarian ways of knowing.[12] Describing how I approached and was encountered in the field, I mobilize reflexivity to resist colonial and patriarchal tendencies to efface the (presumably objective) researcher: "Revealing the pathways of our analyses as we represent others is an important step toward integrity in research."[13] Like performance ethnographer Aimee Meredith Cox, I understand that though "this ethnography is not about me," by accounting for my experiences, I can illuminate some of the politics governing my interlocutors' lives.[14]

Though desi drag queens in North America have been referred to by some New York–based scholars as "staple" and "fetishized,"[15] perhaps because of their popularity in South Asian visual art and literature,[16] they had no consistent public venues until *Desilicious* in 2002. But I wasn't alone in feeling that queer desi nightlife *needed* a drag queen. At the 2011 *Kulture Kulcha* LGBTQ South Asian gala in Oakland, California, queer Punjabi DJ Rekha Malhotra and trans Sri Lankan emcee D'Lo wondered to each other, "Why wasn't there a drag queen in the lineup?" The performance roster was diverse, but Rekha, D'Lo, and I, gossiping behind the DJ booth, felt that an activation of the night was missing. Rekha looked at me and asked, "If I put on 'Salaam E Ishq,' will you dance?" At that moment, the event hall's security signaled for them to cut the music—closing time. At *Kulture Kulcha* two years later, DJ Rekha did not miss their opportunity to play "Salaam E Ishq," and the stage filled with many Rekhas (the Hindi film actress): nonbinary, trans, lesbian, and queer Rekhas seducing a desi dance floor in Lata Mangeshkar's shrill voice.

Desi drag was simultaneously legendary and elusive, and *Jai Ho!*
became an exceptional space that normalized the practice.[17] It became a
ground for other Chicago desis—women, trans folks, nonbinary friends,
and men—to experiment with gender. Deepa and Anurag performed as
the infamous Bollywood father and son Bachchan duo, and *Jai Ho!* gave
a platform to several young queens: The Salamander, Sakhina Kaki, Alisha Boti Kabab, and Masala Sapphire. Ehmad, a young, working-class,
Indian, Muslim college student came to a Trikone support-group meeting
one afternoon looking for advice about parental marriage pressure.[18] We
invited him to *Jai Ho!,* where he was swept up in the familiarity of dance
and wanted to be part of the drag show. It was Ehmad's dance—graceful
wrist flourishes, zooming spins, overexaggerated lip-synch—that always
made him the night's most memorable queen, even without makeup or
wigs; living with his parents, he could not risk coming home bearing the
telltale traces of glitter or blush. True to the model minority stereotype,
Ehmad's parents placed pressure on him to succeed in medical studies,
and this meant that he had to lie about being at late-night study groups
when he was in fact dancing for an admiring audience. Constrained by
these standards of respectability and parental discipline, Ehmad and my
other interlocutors capitalized on dance's ephemerality to take pleasure in
gender play.

No Drag Rules

When I started this project, opportunities in North America to regularly
stage desi drag in public were limited to infrequent parties. Queer desis
rely on a network of organizations and friendships to find out about scenes
in other cities; *Jai Ho!* regulars would invite friends from across the Chica-
goland area and Midwest to the parties. Those with the money would even
travel from Chicago to *Desilicious* in New York or *Kulture Kulcha* in the
Bay Area. In an essay in the pioneering 1993 queer South Asian anthology
Lotus of Another Color, Kim observes that "even gay Indians settled in the
U.S. are surprised that there is a massive, vibrant, and exciting gay scene
in India."[19] I too became wary of rhetoric among US-raised and immigrant friends that suggested these social and performance possibilities
were uniquely available in the diaspora and not the subcontinent, and I
obtained a research grant that allowed me to explore queer nightlife and
drag performance in India. The queens in Sridhar Rangayan's *Gulabi Aina*

(2006), Parmesh Shahani's account of courtesan-inspired performances by transgender dancers, and gay travel guides describing vibrant sexy nights at Voodoo Lounge in Mumbai suggested some semblance of drag culture.[20] What I found instead were queer and trans communities deeply segregated by class, sporadic house parties nostalgic for drag opportunities, and bars and parties where gender binaries were tightly policed.

Mithun, an acquaintance from Chicago, introduced me to his gay friends in Bangalore in the summer of 2010. At a small house party hosted by Mithun's friends, I asked whether there were drag queens in town. The men quickly recalled house parties where they "dragged" for each other: "We haven't done a drag night in a long time!" A year later, I was with Mithun again, at a Sunday afternoon party at Misha's house. Misha pulled out transparent plexiglass heels and catwalked through the living room, subsequently lending the heels to several others to model until they snapped under wobbles and weight. At Pallav's house another night, Misha wrapped Ravi in a sari, Ravi's first time "in drag." That night, Pallav said to Misha, "Let's do the 'Nimbooda' choreography you showed me," and Misha adjusted Pallav's choreography as they performed together for us. These were intimate moments of gender and sexual pedagogy in which the party's buzz paused for a moment to look at, learn from, and love these queens.

But intimate labors in domestic contexts were not limited to this Bangalore friend group. Moses, who co-organized *Jai Ho!*, hosted a party at his home in Hyderabad that erupted in Kathak *mujras*, Salman Khan routines, and Sridevi realness. At *Jai Ho!*, when I arrived as LaWhore Vagistan, Raja asked, "Can we go in the back? I want to retie your sari." Minor shade. "I learned in Bombay, at house parties. My sisters showed me." While retucking the sari into my waistband, he explained how he learned from gay sisters to swivel his hips when walking through the alleys of Bombay to cruise straight men—another subtle jab at my poorly executed desi femininity, but also a moment in which LaWhore elicited performance and commentary. After losing track of Raja following his departure from Chicago to enroll in a graduate program elsewhere in the United States, I unexpectedly ran into him at a Bangalore *Heatwave* party three years later—such serendipitous transnational encounters braid India and North America, Chicago and Bangalore, into each other, across this project.

The queer auntie labor of Misha and Raja who cultivate a space for the transfer of culturally situated knowledge between community and across generations is increasingly lost in the infrequency of house parties and tendencies toward club nights in Indian cities.[21] I don't have a clear answer as to why queer house parties, opportunities to "find home," have dissipated into such infrequency and nostalgia.[22] One possibility is the increasingly diverse "Indian middle class" employed by multinational companies; while more people find economic and geographic mobility, cultural capital still segregates new and old money. Elite men in the United States and India who opened their homes and liquor cabinets for private parties in the 1980s and 1990s—sometimes risking police raids—can no longer regulate who crosses their threshold, as cities fill with migrants. Migrant men, many living in single-room occupancies, paying-guest residences, shared accommodations, or extended family homes, struggle to find spaces to host sex partners, let alone house parties. Also, for Indian men seeking to perform class mobility as they cross geopolitical borders, clubs and bars symbolize cosmopolitan futures and offer larger audiences to witness their economic success (new clothes, hairstyles, dance moves) in ways demure house parties cannot. The few queer house parties I attended in Bangalore were beautiful, filled with joyful improvised performances, physical intimacy, shared food, dancing; they were also much more uniform across class lines than what one would typically find at Saturday night parties at nightclubs.

A weekend party circuit—*Pink Nation, Heatwave, Club Time*—run by a handful of enterprising men, expanded in size along with Bangalore's urban development. The city's cosmopolitan ethos motivated freelance entrepreneur Akshaye to start *Pink Nation*, Bangalore's first gay party held in a commercial establishment, and other organizers followed suit. Weekend parties attracted between one to three hundred men each Saturday, shifting venues across Bangalore, and featuring DJs spinning all night. On occasion, there was other entertainment or programming alongside the DJ—a fashion show, go-go dancer, singer, competition—but rarely was any kind of transfemininity staged at these parties. Also, depending on the venue, Bangalore parties disallowed cross-dressing and drag, limiting and discouraging gender diversity.

In Bombay's scene, prohibitions against drag stem from the 1999 raid of a farmhouse party on the city's outskirts that effectively eliminated the relatively private but frequent house party scene. During this raid, "The police selectively targeted men who were in drag, and the ones who were found indulging in any sexual activity in dark corners."[23] To resuscitate gay nightlife, the social/activist group Gay Bombay conceded to a cover charge at the nightclubs they booked, and enforced the "no drag" rule in order not to rouse police harassment—some Bombay parties have since scrapped these policies.[24] Party organizers in Bangalore attributed "no cross-dressing" rules to the demands of bar managers. While bouncers often did the bulk of sartorial policing at these establishments, party promoters selectively admitted gay boys in cosmopolitan femme-chic fashion: heels, bangles, bangs, painted nails, and so on. In such ways, selective gender policing and class discrimination work coconstitutively to establish a cosmopolitan ethos at gay parties.[25]

In addition to "no drag," there were generally no women at Bangalore's Saturday night gay parties. Some straight women see gay bars as safe havens to enjoy nightlife free of heterosexual rape culture.[26] However, some men at *Heatwave* parties in Bangalore were not solely attracted to men; they enjoyed fun (sex, dancing, company) with men, while preferring sex and long-term relationships with women. Different from a bisexual *identity*, sex and desire between some men is play and indulgence, and not in conflict with being "straight" or "normal."[27] The presence of "straight" men meant that women, straight or queer, could not enjoy escape from unwanted heterosexual attention. It also suggests that these parties could be affirming spaces for transfeminine people to feel sexy and desirable, if they were regularly welcome. Some Bangalore gay parties provided free admission to women, not necessarily to be lesbian-inclusive but to balance gender ratios and thereby protect the bar's reputation from any gay stigma.[28] Despite limited options, queer women in Bangalore innovatively capitalized on "Ladies' Nights" at various bars—usually held in service of heterosexual men's enjoyment—to take advantage of the free entry, free drinks, and cover of women's public homosociality.[29]

While "no drag" rules at Saturday night parties alienated some feminine, cross-dressing, and trans middle- and upper-class folks, the combination of steep cover charges and sartorial codes actively excluded working-class trans folks. Indian transfeminine identities such as *hijra*, *kothi*, *aravani*, *thirunangai*, *durani* are often differentiated from gay men not only by gender but also class position, though there are multiple ways these seemingly fixed identities bleed into and borrow from each other.[30] At the same time, India's LGBTQ movement has relied heavily on working- and poor-class transfeminine people to perform at the front lines of visibility for the movement, most literally by dancing in the streets during pride marches.[31] In several of my research interviews, gay men's coming-out stories included clarifying to families and friends, "I am not a *hijra*."[32] This iterative speech act performatively abjects hijra identity to secure gender, class, and caste privilege.[33] In these "disavowed homosexualities," my friends' speech acts relied on the hypervisibility of poor-class transgender communities to make gayness palatable to middle- and upper-class families.[34] Hijras do drag labor for queer India, dancing publicly at marches and performing item numbers at *melas* and pageants during pride month, reinterpreting film songs for our entertainment and nostalgia, but never at the club. I name these disavowals—material barriers to club entry, as well as intimate speech acts—because even as I argue that transfeminine performance matters in orienting the night, and that gender performance in gay nightlife is more diverse than the hegemonic masculinities it prioritizes, some cultural workers are never given the opportunity to participate in the scene at all.

These fissures in the queer community—entrenched by class hierarchy, English-speaking privilege, transphobia, and caste—eliminate social contact between working-class and subordinate-caste hijras and middle- and upper-class dominant-caste gay men, even though they all convene during annual pride marches and are spectacularly photographed for global dissemination. While in Bangalore, I was informed of a unique space of cross-class intimacy, a bar where gay men, trans women, *kothis*, and cross-dressers gathered to cruise, trick, dance, and drink: Chin Lung. When I went there, not only were transfeminine people banned, but so was dancing. How were we to orient ourselves without queens, without dance? It was at Chin Lung that I learned to look elsewhere for drag labor, to think more carefully about how performance crafts sociality even within limits.

The Queen Is Dead, Long Live the Queen

Trained by gay clubs in the United States, I was attuned to anticipate drag shows as the night's ultimate punctuation. Even when there were no drag queens, I entered gay spaces awaiting theatrical exhibition. These exhibitions presented themselves, in flashes of fun that quickly subsumed themselves back into the pulsing crowd of *Heatwave* or the seated stillness of Chin Lung. These unsanctioned performances reorient pleasures of the night in ways that drag queens do. These drag labors manifested through bodily manipulations—dance, pose, gesture, contact, choreography, what dance scholar Naomi Bragin calls "corporeal drag"[35]—that revealed "the mutability of the body to perform many genders."[36] Attending to corporeal drag allows me to look for choreographic summonings of displaced queens and transfeminine performers, "surrogations" of performers who are no longer present.[37] Attending to dance can show that the queen was never not there. Throughout this book, danced gender reconfigures social and political arrangements in the club and "affectively binds its audience,"[38] essentially doing drag labor: invocations of belonging, copresence, and kinship; purposeful transfers of gender repertoires; generous enactments for the pleasure of onlookers; intimate transactions for those who feel negated in the space and outside.

Though dispersed in the crowd and not elevated on stage, flashes of drag labor reveal alternative pedagogies in nightlife spaces. Drag queens serve as the gay club's most didactic instructor: "Tip your bartenders!"; "Do you, girl!"; "Don't grab my ass without my permission!" Such spectacular forms of pedagogy in gay nightlife obscure implicit cultural instructions already present. Approaching nightlife *as if* I were searching for a desi drag queen led me to attend to the performative value of nightlife's less spectacular contours, which could recalibrate affective citizenships in the space. Becoming a drag queen and occupying the stage literally reoriented my position in the club, requiring me to look at audiences as performers. LaWhore's fans made clear that they too were in search of a desi drag queen, someone who would reconfigure relations in the space, to shape their sense of belonging and presence, especially when they felt anxious about being there. Watching *them* lip-synch during my numbers, seeing who reacted to what gestures, helped me understand what cultural knowledge we shared.

In this project, I think about "gay nightlife" as clubs, bars, and parties that privilege desire between masculine cisgender men—not all people in the spaces identify as gay or as men, but hegemonic masculinities are privileged in the space, promotion, music, and dance styles. Many people capitalize on these spaces as opportunities to indulge in raced and gendered practices not welcome elsewhere, or even there. I am eschewing identity politics, attending instead to aesthetics and performance, to ask: what styles are given value; what are the politics, histories, and circulations of these styles; how do people perform in line with and against dominant stylistic codes; what new forms of relation are made when performances grind against the dominant aesthetics of nightlife? I ask how nightlife—architecture, invitations, entertainment—iteratively orients bodies and engenders tendencies, close-reading moments in which social dance (re)orients the party, or even just me, in unexpected ways.[39] Without the drag queen to give me bearings, to work as "a beacon for queer possibility and survival,"[40] I gravitate to spontaneous performances that do her work, that wield the force of history to hail me, to offer an orientation, a starting point to look outward, elsewhere, and askance. In these moments of reorientation, nightlife looks into the everyday: home, activism, festival, protest, bed, and classroom.

Drag Boom

If the desi drag queen was nowhere to be found during my primary fieldwork years, she is everywhere since: emceeing weekly drag nights at high-end hotel bars and annual pride festivals in Mumbai, Delhi, Chandigarh, Chennai, and Bangalore; performing in mainstream gay bars (not just desi nights) in San Francisco, New York, Chicago, Philadelphia, Toronto, London, Cape Town, Montreal, Miami; offering TEDx talks; modeling at Indian wedding expos; glowing up across Instagram; and writing this book. We can attribute the global boom in desi drag to professionalization of the art form by now-mainstream TV show *RuPaul's Drag Race*;[41] but before the queens inspired by *Drag Race* were hijras at pride marches and *kothi mujras* at NGOs, trans women at *Desilicious*, and amateur dancers at house parties.

This drag boom in the public sphere does not mean that desi queens enjoy legibility, respect, or even safety. The policing of transfemininity in gay nightlife spaces, the "phallic masculinization" of India's global workforce,[42] and the model minority pressures of migrant heteronormativity require me to nuance my interlocutors' genders as they intersect with race, coloniality, caste, migration, and economic development. As postcolonial subjects and people of color moving across national borders and other geopolitical thresholds, they anyways have tenuous relationships with dominant notions of gender. The gay nightlife spaces I arrive at prioritize hegemonic maleness and masculinity, but the people I dance with hold and perform a variety of attachments to dominant genders. Gender transgressions that blossom inside the club are defiant and ethical practices that open up possibilities and models for other performances, identifications, and pleasures in nightlife spaces, and the world at large.

Sub-*kulcha*

The Meaning of Ishtyle

Hearing Myself

Accents—inflections, dropped consonants, lilts, melodies, alternate emphases—enable recognition. Accents allow us to see someone like ourselves in an other. They also make us illegible, even when speaking the same language. They carry evidence of communities that raised us, and signal our classed, racial, and regional origins and attachments. We rehearse accents out of our bodies to neutralize these valences—though neutralizing is never neutral—but against our will they emerge when we're angry, drunk, or on the phone with parents. In the company of others like us, accents thicken. Accents come into relief as the body speaks in new spaces.[1] They can be appropriated by cultural insiders and outsiders, but to different ends and consequences.[2] Accents make us strange and intelligible, foreign and familiar.

The first time I heard an accent like mine was on the answering machine of the South Asian Lesbian and Gay Association (SALGA) in New York City in summer 2001. I was eighteen, fresh out of the Godrej cupboard, arriving from Ghana the year prior for undergraduate education. At that age, my accent was trained by my multilingual diasporic parents, my British Ghanaian drama teacher, and an unhealthy preoccupation with *Friends*. But, out of desire, isolation, and naivete, I heard a semblance of myself on the other end of the phone. It was comforting to say, "I have a gay desi accent!"

With SALGA's generous mentors I attended a queer South Asian party in summer 2002, Sholay Events' first *Desilicious* night.[3] At *Desilicious*, the movements I already held in my body, learned from variety shows at temple and high school performances in Ghana, translated effortlessly onto the dance floor. I was equipped with lyrics, lip-synch, facial expressions, wrist flourishes, weight shifts, hip thrusts, and pivots to flirt through Bollywood songs with other dancers. Amitabh songs, a favorite of my uncles, brothers, and cousins, were my forte. When the floor suddenly cleared for performance, I watched in awe as a queen danced "Maar Daala" into life with vigorous twirls, passionate lunges, and muscularly feminine gestures. Mildly perplexed that her white *ghagra* was soaking up gray beer muck on the floor, I reveled in this *mujra*, this filmic courtesan performance set in a decadent *kotha* of green laser lights conjured mere inches from my body, and the collective pause clubgoers took to orient themselves in a circle around her dance.

I would commute six hours to this dance space every few months, but I wanted to be fully transformed by queer South Asian community— research was very much part of a personal journey motivated by "my interest in finding a place for myself."[4] Inspired by visits to *Desilicious* in New York City from rural New England between 2002 and 2008, I imagined a project about the transference of dance between Bollywood screens and diasporic drag queens in nightclub venues. As ethnography unfolded, I was reoriented away from the queen's spectacular stage to the social dance floor; Bollywood dance receded to but one form of vernacular performance that I describe as "ishtyle," accented style.

Ishtyle: Accenting Gay Indian Nightlife is an ethnographic study of performances of cultural difference, dance in particular, in gay nightlife spaces in Chicago, Bangalore, and other global cities. These spaces (and times) are populated primarily by migrant Indian men, transnational subjects of global economies who work as flexible surplus labor in multinational industries. Though they are impelled in workplaces and nightclubs to perform as appropriate cosmopolitan subjects, their ishtyle enables alternative affective, erotic, and social transactions by accenting the night with vernacular articulations of Indianness. Studying their improvised aesthetic practices in the erotic nightclub, *Ishtyle* stages this globalized professional class, whose lives are discursively overdetermined by their identity as rational and scientific laborers, as creative and sexual subjects. Attending to how global laborers interface with the aesthetic regimes of bar and club spaces, *Ishtyle* argues that the unlikely site of nightlife is a productive venue to explore how political economies live in and on the body. Following the itineraries of people, music, and dance into, at, and out of the club, I show how out-of-place aesthetics engender affective, erotic, and social frictions, frictions that lay bare the politics governing party spaces and my interlocutors' lives beyond the bar. By staging brown queers through nightlife performance, a perhaps unorthodox object of Indian study,[5] this book invests in political forms of queer life other than rights-based appeals to the nation-state and teleological narrations of identity, which have become dominant rubrics of research and representation.[6]

According to Saidiya Hartman, racial capitalism obscures sexual and gendered contours of workers' lives and subjectivities;[7] but she also argues that pleasure and dance can be harnessed by racial capitalism to placate and subjugate minoritarian bodies.[8] I am eager to show the subjects of this global class in pursuit of aesthetics, sensations, and pleasures not immediately available to or expected of them. However, my intention is not to give a better or more whole account of workers and their pleasures that makes them vulnerable to further management. Rather, following Kelly Chung's approach to studying global Asian workers, I rely on the ephemeral, obstructive, and messy conditions of nightlife to render "representations of and encounters with the worker as always abstract, partial, and indeterminate."[9] Global Indian workers are repeatedly described in simplistic terms: caught between East and West, struggling to preserve Indianness in the face of globalization, cogs in capitalist and national machinery. Asking them about parties and sex, dancing and flirting with them, cochoreographing protests and performances, I amass data that points to creative and sexual labors that run parallel to and are insinuated into our professional lives. Drawing on Ramón Rivera-Servera's exploration of "quotidian utopias," I point to small opportunities for radical inclusion, pleasure making, and self-fashioning that dancers at the club "fight for" in the face of the systemic exclusions that nightlife colludes with.[10] Exclusions may be as material as cover charges or accessibility for wheelchair users, but also operate as dominant aesthetics and emotions in the space, an "affective grid [and] microphysics of colonial rule."[11]

Ishtyle argues that the unlikely site of nightlife is a productive locus for the study of global politics—in this case the historical and contemporary displacements of people across and out of South Asia under liberal capitalism and its collusion with US and Indian nationalisms. In the public imaginary, nightlife constitutes exceptional space and time: titillating, dangerous, utopic, transcendent, adventurous, risky; it is all of these things. However, *Ishtyle* extends Celeste Fraser Delgado and José Esteban Muñoz's formulation of "everynight life" to demonstrate that nightlife traffics in quotidian politics.[12] Nightlife is proximal to and enmeshed in global labor, home, activism, and family as well as mundane embodiments of gender, race, class, and caste. The club is already shaped by and imbricated in the elsewhere and the everyday.

A heavily aestheticized environment for the staging of social contracts,[13] nightlife offers unique opportunities to see politics at play, to see how power sutures itself into our muscles and psyches, how it is apprehended and recast by the body. Dance in particular, Victoria Fortuna argues, "as a nonverbal and non-textual form, can be understood as a privileged site for fleshing out how (violent) social orders are both historically instilled in and negotiated at the level of the body in motion."[14] As Anusha Kedhar demonstrates, global working conditions require South Asians to not only be flexible corporate laborers, but to be flexible in their emotional attachments, physical bodies, and dance practices.[15] Queer dance at nightclubs and parties then is not merely an escape from politics, but a chance to revel inside them, letting power, meaning, bodies, aesthetics, and affects collide and find each other in new ways, inventing alternative realms to inhabit through sweat, sways, gestures, jatkas, and matkas, driven by the pursuit of beauty, sex, friendship, and intimacy.

Nightlife scholarship is expected to demonstrate how the party lingers into the everyday,[16] and even enables institutional change. In the public sphere, this appears as the primacy of the 1969 Stonewall Riots, incited by police antagonism of patrons at a gay bar in New York City, as the inception of a global LGBTQ movement. Representations of gay nightlife often cast the systemic threat to sanctuary and community as outside the bar's ecology— religious and educational institutions, law enforcement, parents, and so on. Sylvia Rivera and Mama René testify that even inside the Stonewall Bar, class, race, gender identity, gender performance, and immigrant status shaped access to safety, pleasure, and desire, memories erased from the dominant narrative.[17] The nightclub is not a space of exception; as Jafari Allen suggests, "To carry on at the club . . . is in fact to carry on—that is, get on with the stuff of life."[18] It is by "lingering" in nightlife, dwelling in it and relishing its textures and inventiveness, that I acquire insight into its sociocultural, geographic, and economic milieus.[19] Nightlife is not outside of politics; politics are inside of it. Across *Ishtyle* I document the many ways gay nightlife, represented and celebrated as inclusive and ecstatic, capitulates to mundane exclusions—built into the infrastructures and institutions that constitute nightlife—of dissident genders, gestures, styles, and bodies. These figures and figurations haunt the nightclub, facilitating affective transactions and requiring critical reconsiderations of nightlife's utopic discourses. Attending to performance inside of these contexts, I demonstrate that what happens in nightlife is important, is political, because it happens *there* and *then*, in what Kemi Adeyemi articulates as "the cobbled together *now* as the site where radical queer and trans narratives are actively shaped."[20]

I analyze dance to evidence the travel, appropriation, and creative reconstitution of cultural practices by migrant subjects—practices that reify and respond to political hierarchies and hegemonies entrenched in music, decor, architecture, norms, and patronage. Intimacy, pleasure, space, sex, community, and individuality that nightlife promises are predetermined across a range of political scales—transnational, national, regional, urban, spatial, and bodily; no single scale of geopolitical analysis is sufficient to accommodate the multiple epicenters from which governance is exerted and affinity is foreclosed.[21] I therefore take the "inherently comparative" accent as an analytic.[22] The ability to shift registers across geography—for an elite, English-educated, Delhi accent to read only as North Indian in Bangalore, and only as ambiguously foreign in the United States—makes accents a useful lens to explore performativities across scales of geographic and classed contexts.

Dances, with their own geopolitical histories and kinesthetic efforts, are performative tools to manipulate and recalibrate politics, to try on new (or old!) modes of relating to one another or oneself. In their movement and stillness, in their verticality and leans, "by the body's placement in a space,"[23] dancing bodies conform to and riskily disturb "a larger system (state sovereignty, the nation state, the body politic)."[24] Dance keeps time and holds time; as a chronotope, with its own archaeologies dance recalibrates the temporality of the night, and ghosts the space with dancers who won't or can't enter the club.[25] Heeding Jack Halberstam's call to study how queer and trans people *use* time, space, and their human capital, can we document transactions on the dance floor that do not passively submit to the tentacular forces of heterocapitalism?[26] What tools do my friends and fellow dancers wield to critique, survive, and play with the economies that bind them?

In this introduction, I offer ishtyle, accented style, as a useful rubric to consider performances of cultural difference across geopolitical scales while also demonstrating the historically politicized nature of Indian accents and habitus. Discourses around Indian accents lead me to scholarship on India's "new middle classes," multinationals, and global labor migrants—a rich body of work that thinks extensively about labor, culture, and gender, but rarely centers sexuality, pleasure, or performance. Finally, I discuss how both Bangalore and Chicago offer novel contributions to studies of activism, urban politics, and gay nightlife.

The Meaning of Ishtyle

Ishtyle is a playful and common South Asian (more particularly North Indian, and even more specifically Bombay) accenting of the English word "style." It is sometimes used as a catchall for Mumbai's fashion industry,[27] but I grew up hearing the term among Indians in Ghana in the 1980s. My cousins and I would mock each other's style: tight jeans too adult for our tween bodies, dance moves too referential to films we borrowed them from, embroidered tops too blingy for the everyday, exposed muscles that suggested we aspired to look like film heroes instead of ourselves. Calling something "ishtyle" lays bare its aspirational qualities; it makes apparent that we haven't yet gotten "there." The mock dictionary samosapedia.com captures ishtyle: "used when someone is attempting to do something out of the ordinary to differentiate themselves but is caught in the act."[28]

Some of my South Asian readers already know to bring their tongue closer to the roof of their mouth to make the "t" sound, instead of using the front of their teeth. Some will punch the "ish," onomatopoeically performing the theatrical excess this term describes. Regional vocalizations of "style" also sound like "style-u" or "esstyle"; ishtyle is a distinctly North Indian idiom and cannot alone capture the nuances of cultural difference. I mobilize ishtyle to work beyond its vernacular use and serve as shorthand for "accented style." Thinking broadly with accents allows me to analyze difference across borders and scales, but also to ask how brown bodies, regardless of cultural performance, are rendered accents.

Accents are a useful rubric to study performance in the interstices of empires and between regimes of culture, drawing our attention to "the sensorial logics of imperial governance and its manifold resistance."[29] Accents engender both emplacement and displacement[30] and are thus fickle and precarious, but at the same time nimble tools to think queerly across scales of analysis. Like other culturally situated aesthetics of the everyday—Filipina *puro arte* and *biyuti*; Latinx *chusma* and *rasquache*; African American *boojie*—"ishtyle" names South Asians' mimetic, improper, aspirational, "unmastered," and unassimilated embodiments of dominant sensibilities.[31] For my interlocutors who enjoy varying levels of geographic and class mobility, modernity and cosmopolitanism remain insecure projects; the stakes of performance are always high. Like Fanon's postcolonial subject, "the black man who swallows his r's," we overperform by using too many r's and in the wrong places.[32] Poet Shailja Patel argues that the excess effort put into rehearsing modernity is tied as much to style as it is to work, and imperfections and mistakes "cost us jobs, visas, lives."[33] Aesthetic and sensorial excesses are mapped onto minoritarian bodies precisely because they are surplus populations produced under racial capitalism.[34]

I do not describe ishtyle as failure or imperfect performance to dismiss the critical labors of people I write about or to laugh at them[35]—in my belly, body hair, and brown skin, my love of prints and jewelry, my very desi and dated drag influences, I too get gay citizenship wrong. I'm instead interested in a "reparative" project that contemplates the humor, possibility, and pleasure of cultural frictions produced in risky stagings of the body in difference, particularly in the moral and cultural milieu of dominant hegemonies.[36] Failure, Della Pollock tells us, "becomes something else altogether—it is the excess, the surplus, the off-screen, the stumbling translation, the untranslatable translation, the way another language . . . 'captures' an idea more exactly and less explicably than its 'original' English."[37] Such a "queer art of failure"[38] allows us, as Marcia Ochoa offers, "to honor the fact that sometimes riding the razor's edge between our perverse existence and the perversions of modern institutions—like the police state, democracy or science—is part of the fun."[39]

Centering the accent in this project on gay nightlife brings into focus embodied resources we are often asked to *leave behind* as we enter the nightclub, and how they suture themselves to new spaces we are initiated into. Sometimes we choose to show off perversions; at other times accents reveal themselves involuntarily. The scenes of ishtyle I document do not traffic in a "currency of fabulousness."[40] They are earnest hybridizations that, unlike disidentifications that queer of color artists engage in, are uncurated and improvised;[41] disidentification, according to Thomas DeFrantz, is "not . . . a very sustainable way of life."[42] Critically distancing oneself from the entrapments of identity is exhausting work; accents expose identity and reveal attachment—studying ishtyle becomes a way of cataloging the possibilities and consequences of such exposure.

Performances that are unmodern, excessive, accented, or failed congeal through repetition into familiar and useful gestures that do more than the "original": English turns of phrase ("like that only," "do one thing," "slept off"), onomatopoeia ("dichkyaon," "dishoom," "dhak dhak"), embodied gestures (exaggeratedly biting a lower lip; pulsing the chest as a heartbeat), and accented pronunciations ("wover," "luw," "fraaand-ship," "fillum," "hep"). These waning modes of earnest expression are unique forms of cultural capital because global nightclubs traffic so heavily in whiteness and/or oriental tropes that uphold whiteness. My first encounters with nightlife were as a teenager in the 1990s attending winter weddings in Bombay. We had to change out of saris and kurtas and into close-toed shoes, button-downs, slacks, and dresses to go to nightclubs. Some of those bars mimicked the opium den chic of the French Buddha Bar, while simultaneously restricting Asian performance. These trends have persisted in the venues I frequented: in Bangalore, weekend gay party fliers advertised hip-white-Western sartorial and sonic environments, and in Chicago I was disoriented by Orientalist decor, visuals, and performances in commercial gay bars that rendered brown bodies marginal. What kinds of social, erotic, and affective transactions can ishtyle facilitate, even if, or precisely because, it is the wrong cultural currency?

Style, and its association with clothing, is widely mobilized to think through the challenges of modernity, difference, and power. In the chapter title, I am riffing on Dick Hebdige's landmark study *Subculture: The Meaning of Style*, which explores relationships between fashion, music, and national politics.[43] Queer Asian studies scholars draw on sartorial idioms—"epistemology of the pocket" and "unfurling of the cape"—to show how style negotiates sexuality in the public sphere, particularly for minoritarian bodies who do not have the privilege of privacy.[44] Attending to dance and gesture, I bring motion to style studies; my fieldsites were filled with gestures that costume the body: curling an imaginary mustache, flipping absent hair, crowds parting to accommodate the flaring of a nonexistent *ghagra*, fingers fluttering in place of lengthened eyelashes.

Style also references individuality: "She has such excellent style!" I think of style this way to mark my interlocutors' intentional efforts to render themselves beautiful on their own terms. But to be received as such means having purchase in unmarked forms of normative representation. According to Vanita Reddy, minoritarian bodies live in a conundrum: performing past their difference (assimilating), or performing their difference (self-exoticizing) to have purchase in unmarked, but still racialized and caste-based, categories of beauty.[45] Minoritarian bodies are, as Dorinne Kondo argues, subject to greater scrutiny in their style: "After all, who can afford to be unconcerned about appearance? Who is *allowed* to ignore it with impunity?"[46] Accented style accounts for how attempts at liberal individuation are burdened by the residue of cultural difference mapped onto racially marked bodies, difference entrenched by colonial, casteist, regional, multicultural, and nationalist projects. As I show, people experience accents that may not even be there because of other racialized markers.

Accents point us to habitus, acquired "dispositions," embodied scripts, tendencies, and tastes we accumulate as a result of daily exposure to, and rehearsal of, cultural norms.[47] They are body knowledge, ingrained in the musculature of mouths, throats, ribcages, and tongues, "sensual specificities that overflow verbal content."[48] Where Tom Boellstorff's "cultural dubbing" underscores situated subjectivities of *gay* and *lesbi* Indonesians interfacing with mediated identity categories, my turn to "accenting" focuses on embodied practice, as well as transnational flows of media *and* human capital.[49] Accents are epistemologies too, ways of discerning; fashion designer Sanjay Garg says, "When I say *Rani* pink to you, you get it. I don't have to explain this shade to you. Your *dadi* or your *nani* would have passed it on to you."[50]

The performativity of accents, their ability to effect and impact nightlife, is multiple. The weight that Indian accents gather through iterative representations—colonial mimicry, outsourced labor, Islamic terror—allow them to wield historical force in their efficacy.[51] Similarly, particular dances conjure masculinity, femininity, hypersexuality, and queer intimacy because, through discursive and embodied repetition, they are associated with gender, ethnicity, region, class, and caste. Accented sound also acquires efficacy in its ontological difference, in the different ways it strikes the sensate body to produce pleasure.[52] I'm interested in how particular dances, as accents in the nightclub, not only wield the performative force of history they have acquired in repetition to conjure gender, race, and class, but how their kinetic force physically "punctures" space and time to bring bodies into new proximity and relation.[53]

The Indian accent is its own curious cultural formation. Since the mid-1990s, Indian accents have come under scrutiny within neoliberal outsourcing industries that locate call centers in India to provide technical support to global customers. India's English-language education system, a vestige of British colonialism, makes the country a prime source for flexible labor. However, call centers perceive Indian accents as an impediment to efficient delivery of phone-based support.[54] "Accent neutralization," the coaching of British or US accents, is integrated into call center trainings and has even become its own business alongside other lifestyle trainings for India's increasingly mobile middle classes.[55] Tracing the genealogies of mediated Indian accents from *The Party* to *The Simpsons*, Shilpa Davé also argues that brown bodies can function as accents, as "cultural artifacts," ornate embellishments to decorate white masculinities.[56] Theories of colonial mimicry argue that to perform like the other both blurs boundaries and confirms differences between colonizer and colonized.[57] These performances-with-a-difference secure white supremacy because "To the Westerner . . . the Oriental was always *like* some aspect of the West."[58] In colonial contexts, the difference that accents conjure are not only racial, as Mrinalini Sinha reminds us: "The accented speaker, the babu, is the effeminate but also classed."[59]

Accents are not complete departures from dominant forms of communication, but perform in an excess of registers: "'short-circuits in language," "minor language," or "interruqtions [in the] genericized ontology of the language."[60] These excesses enable queer theorists to imagine how phonetic alterations such as "quare," "qwir," "quia," or "cuír" articulate a different set of political urgencies in studies of gender and sexual dissidence.[61] These projects give me permission to ask, "What else can queer sound, look, or dance like?": practicing homoeroticism through bhangra, koothu, or the gestures of qawwali singers; seducing through kathak; performing divahood via Madhuri Dixit and Sridevi; or exhibiting femininity by turning a T-shirt into a *choli* (cutoff blouse). When so much of global queer popular culture is coded as white, and communities of color and non-Western nations are discursively rendered dangerous for LGBTQ people, accented style helps me think about a variety of "embedded" South Asian symbols, practices, objects, and affects that activate queer collective memory.[62]

Attending to accents textures articulations of gender and sexual dissidence across global contexts. Iterative abjections of gayness as un-Indian by governments, families, religious leaders, psychologists, and teachers,[63] alongside regulatory fictions of gay citizenship, requires queer desis to style their lives with care and intention. Also, non-Western and nonwhite subjects are designated as sexually perverse and gender nonconforming. As such, purposeful attempts to be sexy or to cross gender boundaries are rendered mute: "We're not queer, we're just foreign."[64] Accents thicken in the company of others like us, as Richard Fung realizes when he arrives at a Toronto gay club with other Asian men: "The doorman was genuinely unsure of our sexual orientation." The thickening of cultural difference in this grouping of Asian men undid gayness, implicitly coded as white.[65] Sometimes, the threshold of a gay bar functions more as an imperialist checkpoint than an entrance to queertopia.[66]

Ishtyle is a dialogic method for critical performance ethnography. Accents come into relief in multidirectional encounters of classed, raced, gendered, national subjects who perceive each other through situated epistemes. In this way, ishtyle involves listening for "frictive encounters" in the nightclub,[67] a "disobedient listening" that allows us "to move through and beyond preoccupations with authenticity by listening against and beyond dominant discourses" of racialized performance and "to identify their impact, their *doing* in the world."[68] Sometimes my ishtyle incited others to perform with me. At other moments, I was hailed by strange familiarities of others' dances, knowing them not from trips to the nightclub, but from my participation in South Asian cultural communities. And of course there are accents I couldn't hear, performances I didn't identify as Indian because of my diasporic upbringing in West Africa, because I had not read the appropriate scholarship, seen the right movie, learned the proper language, or spent time in the relevant ethnic/regional/caste/class community. "Bringing experience to the field," I find particular meanings and makings on the dance floor, but inevitably miss others.[69] I substantially supplement my experiences with theorizations from my interlocutors whose narration of attachments, identities, and intimate lives help me see the possibilities and politics of the dance floor, even when I do not experience them through my own phenomenologies.

Queering India's New Middle Classes

I had heard that Vaibhav from Bangalore was moving to Chicago for work, but didn't know when. Running into him unexpectedly in Boystown, one of Chicago's gay neighborhoods, on a Saturday night was a pleasant surprise, and we sent a selfie to friends in Bangalore. They immediately responded via WhatsApp with a picture at Sunday brunch. Gays love brunch. Technology recalibrates time to compact geographic and affective distances between diaspora and subcontinent.[70] Technological developments also reorganize labor geographies such that migrations of temporary workers such as Vaibhav are accompanied by "virtual migrations" of workers in India delivering real-time services to US clients while staying put.[71] In these spatiotemporal reorganizations, leisure and labor come into new proximities.[72] Friends in Bangalore left parties at midnight to start work shifts, and friends in Chicago would forgo a night out, or step out of a bar, to take calls with India- or China-based offices. Many men I met worked in software industries, business process outsourcing (BPO), and other multinational companies (MNC). A common answer when I asked them about their profession for the first time was, "Same thing. IT. Boring." They assumed this was boring to me, but when software engineers met each other, they always had lots to discuss: potential employers, negotiating travel requirements, and fields of specialty.

In transparency, this project did not begin with questions of labor and class. During fieldwork in Bangalore and Chicago, many people I met worked in multinational corporations, and their migration and career trajectories resembled scholarly accounts of new middle classes. "India's new middle classes" is a self-fulfilling idiom that, though curiously undefined in the public sphere, generally refers to postliberalization emergence of professionalized workers in transnational private corporations. Studies home in on software sector and outsourcing industries, although other professions have burgeoned to complement these businesses: English-language training, leadership consulting, self-help, content experts for software development, and diversity training.[73] The kind of fun I had with queer MNC-types at nightclubs, activist rallies, support group meetings, cafés, and house parties is rarely accounted for in other scholarship. But while I prioritized pleasure and performance in my fieldwork, I came to realize that work structured my friends' lives in ways that I was not attentive to. At the end of our interview, Hari insisted, "You're a teacher! Please tell your students, 'Don't go into biotech!'" and proceeded to explain the challenges he had securing a job. This was one of several moments where I realized that labor and education were central to my interlocutors' lives, and their relation to me, in ways I was not always seeing from the vantage of the dance floor.

What we refer to as new middle classes in fact occupies a numerically insignificant proportion of India's population, but an outsized role in global, national, and urban imaginations.[74] Even still, the analytic lenses brought to this overdetermined category remain limited. As an ethnography of "India's new middle classes," *Ishtyle* approaches this population obtusely, meeting them at the nightclub instead of the office—although some gay parties actually took place on corporate campuses—and meeting them in the diaspora *and* subcontinent. Indian participation in nightlife burgeons with the growth of the middle classes. Where discos were once exclusive, elite, and expensive venues hidden in high-end hotels catering to Non-Resident Indians (NRIs) and celebrities, postliberalization middle-class growth saw the proliferation of newly affordable commodity leisure venues: malls, multiplex cinemas, bowling alleys, and of course bars, lounges, and nightclubs. Leela Fernandes notes that aesthetic labors offer purchase in this emergent class category,[75] encouraging me to divert attention to the creative and sexual labors of new middle classes. Across the book, these creative and sexual labors don't look like fucking, kissing, or groping, but appear as stagings of the body in sexy, beautiful, entrancing ways. I also expand the notion of nighttime labor—mostly understood to reference to MNC night schedules—to study "the trying work involved in the pursuit of pleasure" in nightlife spaces.[76]

Middle-class transformations are attached not singularly to 1990s economic liberalization, but also racialization of Asian labor under British colonial expansion and US neoliberalism; caste-based nepotism and economic mobility; histories of technological education and development within India; and diasporic investment in India. Since the early twentieth century Bangalore has prioritized engineering and technological innovation, and in the 1970s and 1980s, the city was regarded as a global leader in software development.[77] As the United States looked abroad for IT labor, India's ubiquitous English-language education made delivery of services and products more efficient.[78] An IMF loan in the 1990s required deregulation of India's economic borders to international trade and investment. Foreign injections of private capital into the Indian economy included software and outsourcing industries, as well as factories, natural extraction, media expansion, and tourism. India's recovery from economic depression since the 1990s to become a global economic, education, and military power was accompanied by a rise in Hindutva governance across the country that has fueled communal violence against Muslims, oppressed castes, and migrants from within India, other South Asian countries, and Africa.

In addition to private foreign investment postliberalization, India courted diasporic wealth through "intimate economies"[79] by creating an official NRI category, which Ashvin Kini notes relies on distinctly heteronormative logics of nation and diaspora.[80] This privileged category also favors recent upper- and middle-class migrants with travel records, and not descendants of indentured laborers in Africa and the Caribbean. NRIs could more easily buy land in India, spiking real estate prices in Bangalore even before major tech booms.[81] Diasporic entrepreneurs sourced skilled IT labor pre-1990s through "bodyshopping" (hiring temporary workers into the United States for third-party employers) as well as opening small outsourcing operations in India.[82] While some scholars idealistically describe the software industry as meritocratic,[83] diasporic recruitments and migrations function nepotistically (within families and education institutions) to reify class and caste hierarchies.[84] Bodyshopping continues today through third-party contractors who secure H-1B visas to keep labor flexible and disposable, requiring migrant men to live with each other in less-than-desirable conditions,[85] ostensibly "employed," until actual placement arises with a third-party company.[86] Internal shifts in US industry and economy, such as the 2000 dot-com bust that displaced migrant Indian workers from California to Texas, force further migrations across the diaspora.

US demand for tech labor was made explicit in the 1990 creation of H-1B visas, which allow skilled temporary workers to convert to permanent resident status while on the visa. Precedent to the H-1B, the 1965 Hart-Cellar Act, which scrapped early twentieth-century immigration quotas based on national origin, was an indicator of the United States' willingness to grow its surplus pool of racialized immigrant laborers, who could be paid less. Racist epithets that call center workers in India regularly endure because they are supposedly "stealing" jobs remind us that surplus labor (bodyshopping, immigration, offshoring) is explicitly racialized.[87] Increased militarization of US borders post-9/11 couples with regulations of global labor supplies to render migrants doubly suspicious. This was always clear to me when I renewed visas and had to declare that I was not coming to the United States to engage in terrorism or human trafficking. The severe limits placed on H-1B visas following terrorist attacks, or accompanying the Trump administration's Muslim ban, remind us that regulations of global surplus labor is tied to border militarization.[88] Deracination of call center workers through "accent neutralization" does not simply lubricate delivery of service; obscuring racial/national difference, it masks from clients the economic stakes of offshoring and various "threats" that racialized labor supposedly poses. A seemingly benign cultural difference, the accent, carries the weight of international trade *and* global warfare.

In addition to English-language capacities and specialized skills, Indian bodies are made palatable to global workplaces through a variety of performances. A gay friend in Bangalore scoffed when I asked if he aspired to work in the United States. Referring to Islamophobia, he knew as a turban-wearing Sikh that the United States was "not for people like me." The coding of IT and other H-1B workers in the United States as "curry" signals multisensorial ways racialized bodies are interpreted and discriminated.[89] Olfactory disciplining appears in India too, where workers are invited to use gel instead of hair oil, and deodorant instead of talcum powder.[90] Like workplaces, bars too feature "sanitized sensoriums"; Chicago friends described how body smells and grooming were disciplined to make them legible and desirable.[91] Ubiquitous etiquette, intercultural, and soft-skills training integrated into IT and BPO industries remake Indian habitus and neutralize embodied accents, in service of delivering virtual services from India or in person abroad. Western (distinctly white!) pop culture referents such as *Friends* and Billy Joel songs are used to train accents, tastes, and desires.[92] Even affective dispositions are managed when women are asked to smile during calls because smiles can be "heard."[93] The chronic and temporary illnesses that workers endure in these industries[94] evidence that their bodies are intensely regulated and reorganized by changing working conditions in order to "extract surplus value."[95]

Quotidian refashioning is coupled with cultural performance in the workspace. A friend working in human resources at a technology MNC invited me to offer a theater workshop in preparation for his team's annual variety show. My first time on an MNC campus, I was surprised first by the overwhelming security measures, and upon entry, by the pristine campus: meditation huts, swans in ponds, glass architecture, and roads with no potholes. Architecture too "provides software workers with cues to appropriate behavior."[96] Workplace variety shows are not uncommon: I choreographed for friends representing their office at Google's global summit, watched a Hindu mythological skit my friend directed at his IT workplace in Chicago, and danced at an Austin IT firm where members of my dance troupe also worked. Heeding dance scholar Priya Srinivasan's argument that creative contributions of migrant populations are understudied and forgotten,[97] I pay attention to how migrant workers creatively configure their quotidian lives. While creativity is part of the ethos of entrepreneurial global workers,[98] my focus on social dance examines forms of creativity that are not as easily commodified by multinational corporations.

Sanjay Srivastava argues that "the idea of 'middle class' becomes a key site for discussion around sexuality,"[99] but I also find that the MNC in particular is a complicated and underinvestigated site that regulates and propagates LGBT identity and performance. At the MNC performance workshop I delivered in Bangalore, my chaperone for the day greeted the friend who invited me: "Hello sir. Sir, I saw your picture in the newspaper from this weekend. It was very nice." He dismissed her compliment with a mutter, embarrassed by the picture of him at Bangalore's queer pride march and the implications it had for his work persona. While some friends in Bangalore's MNCs were not out at work because of potential discrimination from coworkers, others celebrated their workplaces' LGBTQ protections, affirmative actions, and support groups. Regardless of the official inclusivity work at MNCs, queer people navigate the corporate campus differently. Some friends used location-based networking apps to find friends at their campuses to eat lunch, rent apartments, and go to parties with. While mingling at parties, I've listened as men asked new acquaintances about job opportunities at their companies. Dating profiles on gay networking sites regularly state "working at MNC" as a marker of desirability.

The relationship between MNCs and queerness is fraught and impinges on my friends' lives in many ways. In Chicago, friends on H-1B visas stayed in the closet at work, unsure of how immigration status might be affected by employer's or colleague's attitudes. One friend reported enduring homophobic abuse from an employer and colleagues, unable to leave because the company was sponsoring his green card and had him under an extortive contract. Alternatively, a friend working in IT described coming out to his white, straight boss, who excitedly took him to Chicago's drag shows. Meanwhile, he could only afford to live with straight Indian colleagues in the suburbs who "like to talk about bikes. They say my shoes are gay, and make fun of me. They want to know what bars I'm going to." On the dance floor in Chicago, I met someone whose Indian employer recruited him to the United States via PlanetRomeo. Both men were married to women, and the employer, holding the visa and gay identity over this man's head, extorted labor and sexual favors. I prioritize the complicated, risky, and pleasurable intersections between migration and sexuality as they manifest in the rearrangements of human capital to, from, and within India,[100] because as Nayan Shah asserts, the sexual lives of migrant workers go understudied precisely because of their transience.[101]

Studies of Indian middle-class professionals often assume the worker to be heterosexual or invested in heteronormativity, and intimacy, sexuality, and gender are taken up primarily in reference to women.[102] Women working at call centers are demonized as "women of the night," or else vulnerable figures to be protected as they commute without safe or efficient public transportation at night.[103] Highly publicized assaults on middle-class women traveling at night symbolize the precarity of women's bodies within shifting political-economic conditions. The attention they have received also reveals the disproportionate value placed on middle-class professionals as darlings of India's global growth, and not on transgender, working-class, oppressed caste, African, Muslim, Northeastern, and Kashmiri women who routinely endure spectacular brutality traversing public space.[104] In the US diasporic context, scholarship focuses on challenges women face living on H-4B spousal visas that do not allow them to work, and the vulnerability they endure without access to personal income, community, or redress in cases of abuse.

Scholarship on Indian women and MNC work engenders a rather singular narrative of women as only vulnerable in their sexuality.[105] What else might we learn about labor, migration, and sexuality if we listen to LGBTQ subjects? How might we queer presumed effects of neoliberal globalization? A couple of queer women I interviewed in Bangalore talked about their MNC jobs as important sources of income that enabled them to live away from biological family, and thus date other women, openly identify as queer, have sexual partners over, film queer movies and install art studios at home, and host parties and activist meetings. They quickly made connections between professional identities, migration, sexuality, and creativity, and evidenced different relationships to home, family, community, pleasure, intimacy, and nostalgia. Ethnography can nuance "the meanings of middle classness,"[106] but what my queer friends discussed with me looks very different from what ethnographers of IT and call center workers print. Scholars discuss the alienation of workers from their biological families and spouses and from a situated sense of Indianness due to migration, frequent travel, or night shifts,[107] but queers have different relationships to nation, home, family, travel, and the night.

What if we approach this transnational population through queer and aesthetic lenses, not solely through their labor? What if we, following Zora Neale Hurston, take quotidian practices such as social dance and dress *as* art, acts of discovery and invention?[108] What if we take seriously their creativity and sexuality as labor, as effort they expend to manufacture worlds they want to live in, worlds that accommodate their complexities and multiplicities more capaciously? If middle-class Indians are taught to sound, smell, look, and move in ways that service global markets and state interests, to what other ends do they make use of their bodies? What happens when they refuse or fail to execute global styles not only in workplaces, but nightclubs too? Nightlife as a site for exhibition and travel of bodies tells a different story, evidences different pursuits and entanglements. How do my interlocutors' performances, especially their ishtyle, engender other ways of experiencing the night? Like the coconut hair oil left on the call center worker's headset, accented dance too leaves unsettling residues in the nightclub that reorient desires, emotions, and pleasures.[109]

Queer Activations, Global Circuits

The opening twang of "Aaja Nachle" winds out of the speakers at Big Chicks, a gay bar in Chicago, and the South Asian crowd cheers. It is summer 2009, we are at *Jai Ho!*, a queer Bollywood dance night organized by Trikone-Chicago, an LGBTQ South Asian activist and support group. I am dancing on a slim bench that borders the crowded dance floor, feeling my Madhuri oats. An Indian man dancing next to me is living his Mohini fantasy. We lock eyes. He grabs hold of both my hands and in panicked pleasure tells me, "I love this song!" Months later, we are reintroduced on the streets of Boystown by another friend. I learn his name is Mithun, and that he has to return to Bangalore, having recently been laid off from his IT job following the 2008 economic downturn. Mithun promises to show me gay Bangalore that summer. He brings me to meetings of the support group Good As You (GAY), which meets at the sexual health nonprofit Swabhava, through which I eventually learn my way into Bangalore's gay bar and party scene. My encounters with Mithun in both Chicago and Bangalore are more than serendipitous. Labor and economy imbricate diaspora and subcontinent, and Mithun's multidirectional migrations fit the trajectories of global traffic. Also, in both sites, it is via LGBT activism (Trikone-Chicago and GAY) that I come to nightlife.

Here, I explore how US Midwestern Chicago and South Indian Bangalore matter to each other, as do activism and nightlife. I could list on end the times I've run into the same people in both countries if not both cities, especially *at* parties. These queer South Asian global circuits are constituted by transnational labor routes, but also religious pilgrimages, family weddings and funerals, tourism, sexile[110] (including seeking asylum for better HIV and gender transition care), long-distance relationships, education, online friendships, and more. These parties, as the site of serendipitous transnational encounter, reveal not only the iterative displacement and mobility that undergirds middle-class Indian life, but the affinity for clubs and parties, the magnetism of nightlife, that draws queer desis to dance with each other. Why, if you are visiting New York from Bangalore for work, would you come to *Desilicious* bursting with Bollywood music and brown men, and miss out on a more "all American" (whatever that is) night out? I ask this facetiously, hoping that this book charts productive possibilities and pleasures these particular parties afford. At a *Heatwave* party in Bangalore, a British Indian man in town visiting his family asked what kind of research I do; he proceeded to list all the queer desi parties he knows about and has attended in the United States, Canada, and United Kingdom. These parties are their own niche circuit for those who can travel, or are required to travel—a different kind of "circuit party." Focusing on Bangalore and Chicago, with relevant detours to New York, San Francisco, Toronto, Hyderabad, Mumbai, and Delhi, I center two second cities in queer South Asian scholarship not simply to fill geographic voids, but because both cities pose curious contexts to explore relationships between sexuality, globalization, and urban politics.[111]

Initially, I imagined exploring nightlife in New York City, where the vibrant *Desilicious* parties thrown by Sholay Events were integral to my queer coming of age. My preference for New York was informed by coastal biases that influence queer scholarship, and the city's place in the imaginary of queer liberation, that is, as the site of the Stonewall Riots.[112] The San Francisco Bay Area occupies importance in the narrative of queer Indian diaspora not only as a global queer center, but also where engineering student Arvind Kumar started the still-vibrant LGBT South Asian organization and magazine *Trikone* in the mid-1980s. My arrival in Chicago in fall 2008 coincided with the creation of a new queer South Asian organization, Trikone-Chicago. Franchising the San Francisco organization obscured rich histories of queer South Asian activism *in* Chicago, initiated in the late eighties by Sangat and Khuli Zabaan. Chicago and the *Jai Ho!* parties are an important destination for queer South Asians across the Midwest who drive in from Ohio, Michigan, Wisconsin, and Indiana to find community and to dance. Despite its importance as a transnational Asian and queer capital in the American heartland, I was reminded of its second-city status when Chicago friends paid pilgrimage to New York's *Desilicious* parties, or lamented Chicago's incomparability with San Francisco's expansive desi gay scene.

Chicago has only recently received the public and scholarly attention as a queer capital that New York and San Francisco have, even though it has long been a stage of national queer politics and civil rights activism.[113] The city boasts several "gay neighborhoods" (Boystown, Andersonville, Rogers Park, Uptown), but its novel geographies are actually residues of moral policing, race-based ghettoization, migration, gentrification, and urban multiculturalism that ethnicize and differentiate neighborhoods to stimulate tourism.[114] In the chapters focused on Chicago, I explore how South Asians experience gay neighborhoods, and how commercial gay bars interpellate race. Focusing on *Jai Ho!*, Trikone-Chicago's Bollywood night in the Uptown neighborhood, I ask how its aesthetic inventions reorient race and desire in the club and in Chicago's gay geographies. Just as New York and San Francisco are the sexier cities to be queer in, Boystown has an appeal that Uptown simply can't compete with. However, Uptown locates the party in closer proximity to Devon Street, Chicago's historically Indian-Pakistani area located in Rogers Park.

The density of Indians in Chicago skews to the suburbs, given the relocation of IT companies, pioneered by Motorola's move to Schaumburg. Like Bangalore, Chicago's urban geography shifts with the expansion of India's new middle classes, owing exponential growth in Indian populations to the increased export of tech labor.[115] Despite the growth of Indo-burbs, Devon Avenue maintains its South Asian ethos with grocery stores, restaurants, and boutiques. Devon, named after the English county Devonshire,[116] is now pronounced as "de-vaughn" or even "dee-waan"; South Asian accents have indeed left their residue on the city. Historically working-class neighborhoods proximate to Devon (Rogers Park, Edgewater, Uptown) house many South Asian migrants.[117] These urban geographies place queer life in proximity to South Asian enclaves, allowing for strange intimacies that include an Uptown Pakistani restaurant selling CDs of Ifti Nasim's queer poetry, desi cab drivers knowing exactly where the leather and bear bars off Devon Avenue are, fully clothed desi families skirting around sunbathing muscle queens in Speedos during summer walks on Hollywood Beach, and a remarkable number of *Jai Ho!* attendees living within a ten-minute walk of the party location. These urban geographies make Chicago an exciting site to think about how the city choreographs race and sexuality.

My detour to Chicago resembles my elision of Bombay and Delhi for Bangalore. I had a specific interest in Mumbai's notorious, now-closed, Voodoo Lounge, located not far from the Gateway to India monument, an infamous cruising strip.[118] Master narratives of India's gay activism center Mumbai, home of the efficiently staffed Humsafar Trust NGO and well-documented Gay Bombay online/offline community.[119] Delhi, as the epicenter of backlash against Deepa Mehta's *Fire* and battleground of India's legal fight to decriminalize sodomy, is fleshed out in Naisargi Dave's *Queer Activism in India*.[120] The South Indian city of Bangalore, popularly known as India's "Silicon Valley," does not enjoy global visibility as a queer political center despite housing the radical legal services organization Alternative Law Forum, expansive NGO Sangama, which serves hijras, *kothis*, and working-class queer and trans folks, several English-speaking LGBT groups, including Good As You, We're Here and Queer, and Queer Campus, and an exceptionally cruisy bus depot and movie theater. As Chicago is to the Midwest, Bangalore is to South India, a regional urban haven for queer and transgender migrants on account of its urban and economic development and its sophisticated NGO/nonprofit complex.

Bangalore's rise as "Silicon Valley" has occluded the visibility of its sexual cultures and progressive movements. However, it is precisely its growth as a tech center that creates interesting and complicated nightlife geographies. Bangalore's gay geographies through the 1990s were clustered around the city's historic center: small bars and pubs around Mahatma Gandhi Road and Church Street that didn't harass gay patrons, movie theaters that showed "blue films," and cruising in Cubbon Park.[121] Recent moral policing of public intimacy, even between straight couples who look to the park when home is not an option,[122] has driven out the queer convening that characterized Sunday evenings at Cubbon Park in the 1990s and early 2000s.

Bangalore's gay sex cultures have been dispersed by the fast rise of tech-burbs, initiated by the growth of MNCs such as Infosys and Wipro in Electronic City in the mid-1990s. Migrations to live and work in Bangalore's suburbs meant more men living away from familial homes, and in close quarters with each other. Web-based networking tools such as PlanetRomeo and Grindr served as informal mapping tools while I was in Bangalore, and evidenced concentrations of gay men beyond the city center, and around tech suburbs: Marathahalli, Electronic City, Whitefield, and so on. While "bachelors" in older neighborhoods such as Malleshwaram, Fraser Town, and Indiranagar lived with family, men closer to tech campuses had their own places to invite lovers over. Also around tech campuses were several nightclubs that did not enjoy the regular patronage city center bars and clubs did. As such, they were easier to rent for gay parties and evade police scrutiny; they were discrete enough to keep open until one in the morning when all other bars closed at eleven. That said, when party organizers found more central locations, they not only relocated parties, they advertised the change: "party in central for all our guys." Despite the convenience, discretion, and unique aesthetic possibilities of suburban locations, centrally located parties were more appealing to aspirational tastes. Charting Bangalore's gay geographies demonstrates possibilities and prohibitions that come with changing economic, labor, and urban landscapes.

As a second city, Bangalore is deemed a less desirable place to be queer. At Bangalore parties, visitors in town for work from Bombay and Delhi deemed the crowd, music, location, and decor unsophisticated. Though Bangalore developed the moniker "Pub City" following the flourishing of bars in the mid-nineties,[123] the regional government's approach to vice legislation has been perceived as highly draconian with nighttime breathalyzer checks, bar raids on suspicions of drug trafficking and sex work, strict closing time, and a ban on social dance.[124] These policies and practices reflect not only nationwide Hindutva efforts to regulate gender and sexuality in service of casteist heteronormativity, but also regional anxieties in the state of Karnataka to preserve "local" cultures in the face of rapid globalization.

In *Ishtyle* nightlife reveals itself as a place where global, national, regional, and urban politics are enacted and contested through embodied and representational discourses. I want to make explicit connections between nightlife and activism because so much scholarship on queer South Asian diaspora and queer India focuses on cultural entities more legibly read as activist/political: support groups, marches, protests, NGOs. Additionally, popular discourses in India and the diaspora suggest that party gays are not as "political" as those who attend marches, parades, potlucks, or organizing meetings. These discourses intimate a break between the pursuit of pleasure that cruising and partying afford, and the work of critical social change. However, Deborah Gould and Sara Warner have argued that pleasure, sexiness, and humor have been central to mobilizing queer criticism and social change, and David Román has emphasized the important nature of entertainment fund-raisers in and as queer activism.[125] Performance, affect, style, choreography, and pleasure are central to social and political transformation.[126]

Queer activism and gay nightlife bear on each other in my field sites. Ifti Nasim, founder of Sangat in Chicago, described dancing almost naked on bar tables in the late 1970s with the same bright enthusiasm that he talked about rallying against Islamophobic violence in the wake of 9/11. Akshaye, founder of *Pink Nation*, Bangalore's first public gay party, discovered queer community first through cinemas screening softcore films, then public cruising in Cubbon Park, which led him to Good As You, where he found out about farmhouse parties, and subsequently conceived of parties in Pub City's fabulous bars. In his story, public sex, activism, and parties are proximate *and* mutually constitutive. Activist Vinay Chandran described to me how the founders of GAY conceived of this safe space after being perpetually displaced from bars they convened at. Bangalore's Coalition for Sexual Minorities Rights (CSMR), which hosts a variety of performances, panels, and protests for pride every November, relied on substantial contributions from *Heatwave* parties. Similarly, Trikone-Chicago amassed its operating budget through *Jai Ho!* parties. Trikone-Chicago has sent *Jai Ho!* proceeds to support pride in India, including in Bangalore. These anecdotes confirm Monisha Das Gupta's argument that South Asian LGBT activism is a distinctly transnational formation made through intimate connections, as well as violent ruptures that engender displacement: partition, colonization, militant dictatorships, and neoliberal flexibilization of global labor.[127] In the travels of people, money, and expressive practices, activism and nightlife, subcontinent and diaspora, are intertwined.

I am not asking my reader to think about nightclubs as sites of queer activism per se, but rather to know them as political sites materially and affectively bound up in and working parallel to nonprofit industrial complexes and social movements to consolidate, police, and liberate gender and sexuality. Much like what we might call queer activism, nightlife molds and shapes its participants into political subjects, and those subjects participate through debate, resistance, refusal, and consent. Nightlife traffics in a different set of political tools, relying less on the didactic verbiage of systemic and social change, instead orienting its subjects and patrons through a variety of sensorial instruments. Dancers at the club too debate, resist, refuse, and consent to the beat. While my interlocutors do not vocalize rhetoric that articulates radical queer political positions, their accented styles produce productively queer configurations in the nightclub. Strange moments of ishtyle demonstrate that nightlife is a critical site for producing political selves and worlds; they signal the urgencies of pleasure, worldmaking, and redistribution of resources in and beyond the club.

Ishtyle, in Three Acts

Ishtyle demonstrates that nightlife is proximal to and implicated in spaces it is assumed to be exceptional to. In this way, nightlife becomes a productive place to study global, national, regional, and urban politics as a means of understanding how macropolitics insinuates itself into bodies and communities. My focus on performance foregrounds how people resist, consent to, and confound the politics, the style, they are asked to subscribe to in nightclubs and elsewhere. My interlocutors are queer, gay, lesbian, bisexual, trans, or unsure; they identify as Pakistani, Bangladeshi, Indian, South Asian, desi, mixed race, immigrant, Canadian, and American. I frame the book around "gay Indian nightlife" to acknowledge the dominance of "gay" and "Indian" identities and aesthetics in the spaces I study, but also to unmoor and nuance globally constructed hegemonies of these categories. The forthcoming chapters take you to a variety of parties, bars, nightclubs, and gay neighborhoods, asking how queer South Asians perform in pursuit of citizenship, community, sex, and beauty. Each chapter uses ishtyle to make apparent the stakes of enacting minoritarian difference at various geopolitical scales. As detailed in the preface, I attend to "drag labor," microperformances that teach party patrons how to be with each other. These moments emerge in frictive circumstances as ishtyle, which reorients me in the club to look out toward home, work, ritual, childhood, law, street, and film screen, and to see them as always already in the club.

In the first section, I invite my reader to Bangalore. The city's rise as "Silicon Valley" transfers on to its residents, often generalized as "techies." In chapter 1, "techie" identities trap middle-class gay men in discursive dichotomies: global/local, gay/straight, techie/artist, culture/art, and Indian/Western. I show how weekly Saturday night parties in Bangalore called *Heatwave* replicate binaries through invitations, themes, DJ sets, and even US corporate sponsorships. The party's ethos is modeled on white, masculine, and Western aesthetics of gayness that aggravate already existing suspicions around categories like "gay" and "techie." But party attendees, "gay techies" and others, refuse Western codes dictated for them, and I detail small but perpetual rejections of party decorum that accent "global gay" cultures. Rather than reading these rejections only as resistance to hegemonic expectations, I show how they create open-ended possibilities for self-expression and intimacy in spaces where style is rigorously predetermined.

Where chapter 1 positions my interlocutors in transnational imaginaries of India's globalization, chapter 2 focuses on national and regional politics, with specific attention to law. The queer Indian movement has, since the late 1990s, centered heavily on decriminalizing consensual sex between people of the same gender by repealing Section 377 of the India Penal Code in the Supreme and Delhi High Courts. Centering a different legal issue, the ban on social dance enforced in Bangalore between 2006 and 2014, I expand conversations on law and sexuality to think across genders and sexualities, and to include women and trans people. This chapter focuses on bars that are not necessarily gay, but allow queer people to convene and sometimes dance despite a ban on social dance. Ishtyle, in this chapter, describes muted and inventive ways my interlocutors insinuate dance into the stillness of the dance ban, dances that don't *look* like nightlife, but still conjure its pleasures.

In Part II, we travel to the United States, and specifically to Chicago's gay neighborhoods. The first chapter follows my interlocutors as they describe social and erotic pursuits in the city's gay neighborhoods. Relying on interview transcripts, I trace how their bodies and identities become desirable in this multicultural city, often functioning as ornamental accents that complement and reify whiteness. I broaden extensive scholarship on interracial desire to show that in addition to recalcitrant colonial stereotypes, India's recent rise on the global stage as an economic power renders new discourses that make South Asians performing racialized labor attractive homonormative partners. This chapter reveals performance as an especially productive approach to theorizing racialized desire: attending to oral narratives as performance, exploring the performativity of South Asian bodies, and detailing how race/accents intensify in proximity to other bodies and objects.

Chapter 4 juxtaposes Chicago's commercial gay nightlife with Trikone-Chicago's quarterly Bollywood party, *Jai Ho!* Commercial bars orient citizenship in their venues via decor, entertainment, visuals, promotion, music, architecture, and labor; whiteness is distinctly ascendant in all these forms, and orientalia uplifts whiteness and abjects Asian Americans. To invite in and entertain a primarily South Asian queer audience, *Jai Ho!* accents instruments of commercial gay nightlife, in ways that unsettle the night. A variety of accents—Bollywood music videos, desi drag performers, Punjabi, Hindi, and Tamil music—encourage choreographies that reorganize orientations in the bar, and I focus on how bhangra choreographies enable alternative homosocialities.

Part III studies how mediated cultures shape nightlife choreographies, for while global economic change has displaced bodies across borders, it has also facilitated rapid transformation and travel of media. In chapter 5, I demonstrate how institutional transformations in the Hindi film industry since the 1990s have shifted the quality of Bollywood music and choreography. These changes make certain sounds, choreographies, and affects less available on screen and in nightlife. I document my interlocutors' nostalgia for the dances of Sridevi and Madhuri Dixit. Sridevi's snake dance and Madhuri Dixit's breast pulse are not simply campy relics of the 1980s and 1990s; my interviewees' narratives about home, childhood, and nightclubs reveal complicated intimacies associated with these feminine gestures. Accenting club choreographies with these nostalgic gestures facilitates a reparative labor for many men who have been disciplined into respectable masculinities.

Chapter 6 traces the itineraries of *dappankoothu* music and dance, from Dalit (oppressed caste) ritual communities, to Tamil film, to a gay party called *Koothnytz*. Asking how Indian street dance facilitates queer intimacies in the nightclub, I center categories of region, class, and caste. *Koothnytz*, I argue, provides an important opportunity for my interlocutors to express regional sexualities and performances that are otherwise elided in Bangalore's cosmopolitan bar spaces. The tagline for *Koothnytz* is "Lose your couth!" a phonetic-play between "couth" and "koothu" that invites middle-class, predominantly dominant-caste, attendees to refuse propriety by dancing *dappankoothu*. The pleasure of rejecting respectability at *Koothnytz* is made possible by effacement of the dance's Dalit roots. This chapter makes clear how middle-class queer pleasures are predicated on class, region, and caste in ways that often go unmarked.

Ishtyle celebrates strange eruptions of accented dance in cosmopolitan, gay nightlife spaces. But across the book particular people are estranged from pleasures of the night: oppressed castes, bar dancers, queer women, trans men, working-class folks, non-English speakers, feminine men, Muslims, hijras. Drawing on queer-of-color theorizations of the stranger, my conclusion asks who becomes strange in the nightclub, and what our responsibilities are to dance with strangers and to dance strangely. Drawing on a visit to *Besharam*, a party in Toronto that attracted a queer crowd but became mostly straight, I think through the unique problems and possibilities of curating queer nightlife. I argue that studies of nightlife must take seriously performance as method, analytic, and object in order to account for the breadth of political projects and possibilities in these spaces.

This book critiques hierarchies that gay nightlife reproduces; these spaces should aspire toward being more capacious. But I am not ambivalent about nightlife's transformative possibilities; I regularly find myself in awe of complex ways people inhabit parties, clubs, and bars: guiding each other to move in tandem, making space for themselves and others, and finding friendship and sex with strangers. I have been transformed by nightlife, and by my fieldwork. I learned of new old divas to worship, ornate ways to adorn my body, expansive approaches to inhabit and interpret gender, situated styles of cruising. I developed new intimacies with places I already called home, made new friends, and fell in love several times over. Nightlife, proximal to and imbricated in spaces of work, home, protest, and violence, feels present all the time. Politics negotiated in nightlife matters not only because performance leaves residues that extend beyond the space and time of its emergence, but because the club is already inside systems and structures of politics and not exceptional to them. Spaces of music and social dance are opportunities for embodied invention, chances to be with others (or oneself) purposefully and pleasurably, to be more than the sum of our identities, to dance new relations into being. Nightlife has saved lives, made new genders possible, facilitated institutional organizing, and been a site of healing and mourning. Queer nightlife spaces in particular—house parties, boats, clubs, bathhouses, artist co-ops—have been vulnerable to raids, fires, and massacres. In the wake of such violence, some of it fatal, this book honors the fortunate moments of nightlife, the opportunities for eroticism, emplacement, and emergence, and the many cultural workers who make them possible.

PART I

ONE

B1nary C0des

Undoing Dichotomies at Heatwave

N.U.D.E.

On December 31, 2011, two party promoters, *Heatwave* and *Pink Nation*, collaborated to host simultaneous gay parties in Goa and Bangalore.[1] Akshaye hosted the Goa party, which was a flop because the bar owner changed its name without informing anyone, and so attendees couldn't find it. The Bangalore party was held at Seven Hotel, in the tech-burb of Marathahalli. Seven, a boutique hotel owned by a white French gay couple, was always amenable to parties, usually held in the rooftop Pink Sky Bar decorated with fuchsia floral wallpaper. When the French couple sold their boutique hotel to an Indian family in 2013, *Heatwave* could no longer host parties there. This New Year's Eve, the gay party was relegated to the basement bar, The Box, as a straight DJ had booked Pink Sky Bar for a higher price. Mihir's ad for the party read:

> N.U.D.E. 2012: N-ew year's eve U-nderground D-ance E-xtravaganza
> | Our party's called NUDE but v wont b rude if u dress in nothin.
> HAHA! | But wen v call it a NUDE party, do v really take u fr
> granted? | Here v r stripping it down 2 bare essentials u must hv fr
> the party mood. | 1) MEN'S LINGERIE SHOW: Hunky models in
> International brand lingerie! | 2) DARK HOUR frm 11PM til stroke
> of midnight. | . . . | Cum the way u were born—not NUDE but
> UNINHIBITED!

Gay party invitations, not just this one, are loaded with detailed explanations of what to expect. "Hunky models," "International brand lingerie," and "the way you were born" signal preferences for masculinity, foreign consumer products, and US pop culture like Lady Gaga's gay anthem "Born This Way." The overtly explanatory nature of this advertisement, clarifying that nude does not necessarily mean naked, for example, alerts us to the organizer's curatorial intentionality. The text is littered with text-message style abbreviations: "we" as "v" mimics Indianized pronunciation of the English word, and "come" as "cum" evokes "ejaculate." This invitation is simultaneously hypersexual and modest, international and local, formal and colloquial. It also generates several expectations for the party while still leaving one unsure of what interpretation of "nude" to arrive with.

The promise of the "men's lingerie show" had us excited, and there was an eager buzz among the sweaty crowd when the ugly fluorescent lights turned on. With great difficulty, Mihir clears the five-by-five-foot stage of sweaty dancers, and escorts in two men draped in long white terrycloth robes. Neither cracks a smile. One pulls at his belt and his robe opens to reveal a smooth muscular, fair-skinned body, and leopard-print underwear. Gaining confidence from the cheering audience, the other removes his robe completely and smiles. More screams and cheers. In under sixty seconds, robes are back on and tied, and models are gone. Craning necks wonder, "Is that all?" Suddenly gleeful cheers erupt as Subodh, skinny and dark-skinned, scampers from the bathroom to the stage. He mischievously mounts the stage in a red women's one-piece bathing suit and wiggles his exposed ass; his cock is dangerously close to falling out. After a minute, he is gently guided off stage by Mihir, who brings back the models; they have new underwear to show off. Again, they flash their bodies for less than a minute and disappear. Their departure is quickly followed by several men rushing on stage to dance, removing and unbuttoning their shirts to show off muscles, jiggling bellies, tattoos, and hairy chests while bright lights still light them. The room darkens, and the party continues.

In lieu of a disappointing show, partygoers prompted by the recently released item song "Chikni Chameli" claimed the stage and became their own go-go boys, strippers, and item-girls. Their enthusiastic dances became models of achievable sexiness that the hired models could not offer. Subodh and the "Chikni Chameli" dancers seized the stage, riffing on the party's invitation to be "nude," while also refusing decorum generally expected of partygoers. Their skinny, fat, hairy, feminine, and dark bodies contrasted with both the fair-skinned, masculine, muscular, hairless models, and the white beefcakes on the party invitation. The upscale boutique hotel, high-end tech-burb, party promotion, and event aesthetics invited guests into a globalized ethos, one that goes unmarked as Western, white, North Indian, savarna, light-skinned, and rich. However, embodied practices in the space worked with and against the parties' environment to confound cultural expectations. Attendees negotiated pleasures of language, choreography, music, and intimacy in ways that refused, ignored, or misinterpreted the party's pedagogy; in these aesthetic breaks is the accenting of dominant gay style, ishtyle.

Extending the introduction's discussion on discursive and material ties between multinational corporations and gay life, this chapter explores how technology industries, and technology itself, bear on gay nightlife by producing urban geographies, professional identities, and channels of communication. Tech parks become party venues, phone apps become integral to socializing, techno becomes the sound preferable to outdated Indian instrumentation, and the diverse queer Indian middle classes become "techies." While many of my fellow partygoers work in IT and its proximate industries, I am more generally concerned with the IT industry's "disproportionate influence . . . given its actual size" to calcify rigid cultural discourses.[2] I therefore draw on the lingua franca of information technology, using "binary codes" to gesture to the reductive logics produced under ongoing globalization. Under rapid economic, political, and infrastructural change, categories of difference are entrenched to quell cultural anxieties and manage bodies; binary codes become fixed: modernity/tradition; masculine/feminine; gay/straight; public/private; mind/body; West/East; immoral/moral, and so forth.

In this matrix, club culture, already too proximate to gayness, falls into a nexus with criminality and Westernness, rendering gay nightlife particularly suspicious. It doesn't help that gay party organizers collude with this binarized logic; the party invitations, like the one above, cultivate white Western sensibilities. But in party patrons' habitus, their messy improvisations, we find a less binarized code for enacting desire and pleasure.[3] They arrive with repertoires of dance, style, and fun that are not in accord with or do not achieve global gay modernity. I chart how party aesthetics capitulate to cultural binaries that render gayness un-Indian, and I honor my interlocutors' small refusals, misfires, and elisions as accents that undo the binary codes of inhabiting global gay nightlife, not resistance per se, but politically inflected acts "that remain outside of the field of political action properly conceived."[4]

Cultural imperialism perceived in new development projects requires national subjects—particularly urban, middle-class workers—to suture moral codes and cultural practices of state-sanctioned Hindutva with tenets of neoliberal globalization in order to remain "appropriately Indian."[5] I am interested in ishtyle that is *in*appropriately Indian, that refuses the decorum expected of the heteronormative techie, while also not complying with white gay aesthetics. Leading my reader into parties held in various bars and clubs across Bangalore, I detail the inappropriately Indian ways that partygoers perform gayness, playing with and tripping over the interpellations of the night, enjoying alternative habitations of the party.

Notes on a Scandal

Indian nightlife's nexus, its embroilment with criminality and queerness, became clear to me via friends in Chicago, not Bangalore. In February 2011 I received an email from Gautham, a graduate student at the University of Chicago at the time, with the subject line "AJ in hyd gay scandal." He translated the linked YouTube clip of a Telugu news exposé by Hyderabad's TV9 channel:

> an alarmist report on telugu newschannel tv9 about the rise of gay culture. they do a focus on planet romeo and the burgeoning private party scene (note the scary music). AJ's profile is fixated on and analyzed. the whole thing is weird b/c they keep emphasizing how "students, children of wealthy families, and software people" are entering into this "perverse lifestyle."[6]

This infamous and widely denounced "sting" by Hyderabad's TV9 features surreptitiously recorded phone conversations with users of a popular gay networking site called PlanetRomeo. Without consent, the news feature unapologetically displays profile pictures of men seeking sex with men, while playing audio clips of their phone conversations with a journalist who was masquerading as a possible date.[7] Blurry footage from an illicit camera shows silhouettes of men dancing in swirling disco lights.[8] AJ, featured prominently in the exposé, had recently arrived in Chicago to visit his partner. He was a popular figure in Hyderabad's gay party scene, and his PlanetRomeo profile picture, shirtless and flexing, repeatedly appears in the news feature. The anchor purposefully notes AJ's profession: "The picture that you see is of Arjun who happens to be a software engineer who has taken sexy pictures of himself and uploaded on the site to attract other gay men." Given the widespread notoriety he earned through this scandal, it is no wonder AJ decided to stay in Chicago, finding creative ways to parlay his short-term work visa into permanent resident status.

In September 2013, AJ texted me a link, "One more police raid in Hyderabad gay club."[9] In this sting, cameras repeatedly zoom in on men's faces, which they cover with hankies, hands, or T-shirts. Coverage of this raid makes the scene seem more decadent by underlaying news narration with peppy Bollywood tracks and ambient "nss nss" techno music. Cameras zoom in dramatically on clusters of empty beer bottles and ashtrays, as if capturing the space's unique degeneracy. These journalists fold excess, gayness, criminality, Westernness, North Indianness into one another, colluding with police by capturing sensationalist footage that shames partygoers and portrays police as paternalistic heroes.[10] Like the 2011 TV9 scandal, coverage of this 2013 raid highlights partygoers' professional backgrounds— "Most of the guests were students, software employees, and from the business community"[11]—and describes the event as a "gay party from western culture."[12] Gay party raids in Hyderabad and Bombay have ripple effects across the country, inciting both protest (demonstrations outside TV9 offices) and caution (a Bangalore organizer texted us to cancel his event the night after Mumbai police raided a gay party). The mobility of unmarried, middle-class, migrant workers becomes a source of anxiety when not properly inscribed into the familial Hindu household.[13]

"Scandals reveal clues to dominant attitudes toward social boundaries,"[14] and the language used in these news clips provides important insight into anxieties around new middle classes. Education and professional migrants are often described as "techies," a term that conveniently lacks specificity and mobilizes ambivalence around the IT worker—the star of India's global economy, but also a new and volatile identity category. Journalist Ben Crair suggests that "techie" is a pathologizing moniker in news media that emphasizes scandal and crisis—adultery, suicide, murder—in the wake of economic redistribution, infrastructural change, and migration: "The stories can read like morality plays . . . suggesting that a tech worker's material wealth conceals a deeper poverty."[15] A headline like "Infosys Techie Booked under Sec 377 after Wife Filmed His Gay Encounters" forgoes "employee" for "techie," capitalizing on the capacious, ambivalent, and sinister implications of the category.[16] Ostensibly friendly coverage of Bengaluru's pride march is naively titled: "Techies Reveal Their Colours." "Reveal" implies that middle-class workers have repressed truths underlying their professional identities. Further, this generalization flattens the professional diversity of middle-class queers, and disappear working- and poor-class *kothis* and hijras dancing and chanting at the march, as well as Dalit musicians who heralded the demonstration.[17]

Gross conflations of the software worker, gayness, and nightlife too, are made possible by the proximities they acquire in a discursive "nexus."[18] Lawrence Cohen, writing in the wake of the murder of an elite gay man and his working-class lover, makes clear that the stakes of exceeding the ambivalent though generally undefined "style"—the acceptable limits of aspirational performance and desire under neoliberalism's moderniz-ing conditions—can be dire.[19] In contrast to style is "fashion": feminine, unaffordable, studied, extraordinary, cosmetic, un-Indian, "over style."[20] But these scholarly frameworks too work in binary codes (style/fashion; men/women; aspirational/excessive) that can't accommodate the fric-tions between the fashionable party curation, feminine performances, masculine expectations, and playful improvisations I witnessed. My use of ishtyle centers the unpredictable modes of performance that muddy these formulas as my queer interlocutors move across global aspiration and everyday fun in gay nightlife spaces.

Gayness has perpetually been positioned as un-Indian, "other" to the nation;[21] an especially public incident at a 2011 HIV/AIDS conference in New Delhi saw the health minister claiming homosexuality to be an unnatural disease from the West. Political moves to consolidate hetero-sexual Hindu masculinity construct homosexuality as a Western colonial import, while also ascribing gender and sexual deviance to religious and ethnic others within India.[22] Given the repeated claim that gayness is un-Indian, performing queerness in India becomes "a series of moral calcu-lations" that mediate the pressures of appearing as a good minority.[23] In response to homophobia from state and family, my friends discussed with me moral calculations they engage in, detailing ways to Indianize queer-ness, often by valorizing classical Hindu imagery and mythology that features same-sex desire and nonbinary gender. This is not an unsurpris-ing turn; Giti Thadani's careful excavation of desire between women in ancient India, along with her visibility and vocality about such same-sex traditions, made space for the flourishing of lesbian activisms.[24] However, justifying queerness through historical examples of same-sex desire estab-lishes false equivalences that cannot accommodate shifting hierarchies of gender, sexuality, race, age, caste, and class. Also, relying on Hindu mythology to claim queer ancestry renders Hinduism an exceptionally liberal and inclusive religion, further marginalizing Muslims and Muslim queers in India.[25]

In addition to the suggestion that same-sex desire is rooted in Indian culture, another popular argument among my friends is to claim that homophobia is imported, specifically by citing colonial origins of India's antisodomy laws. What this argument misses is that the retention of Section 377 in the IPC after independence conveniently consolidates multiple and localized strains of sexism, heteronormativity, casteism, and transphobia, not just Victorian conservativism.[26] Following Anjali Arondekar's productive problematization of the search for sexuality's truth in the archive,[27] I explore embodied tendencies to accent queerness that draw from quotidian repertoire instead of sanctified archive.[28]

Gayness is rendered a Western import, but so too is nightlife. Club and bar cultures in India emerge from elite social clubs known as gymkhanas that are vestiges of colonial leisure practices; postcolonial cabarets and discos housed primarily in expensive hotels; and electronic dance music scenes fostered in Goa by white tourists and settlers.[29] Indian nightclubs mark themselves as Western, or *not* Indian, in decor, music, and dress codes. Pubs and microbreweries show a penchant for rustic British exposed red brick, while nightclubs and lounges feature futuristic white leather, glass block accent walls, glowing bars, and polished metallic surfaces.[30] I was delighted when a gay party was held in my parents' neighborhood at an obscure nightclub in a small hotel in Malleshwaram that was unironically decorated with a thatch awning over the bar and vividly colored hoarding-style murals of men and women in languid sexy poses—a brand of Indian kitsch. Once it became a regular party venue, however, these lovely artworks were painted over.

Bangalore is a curious city in which to study nightlife. It has a long-standing reputation as the "science city,"[31] but following liberalization it has had to compete with other Indian cities to keep its "Silicon Valley" title by improving local infrastructure and attracting private investment.[32] Rapid change has brought not only technology parks, but entertainment structures such as multiplex cinemas, malls, and nightclubs that choreograph gendered and classed citizenship. The city simultaneously acquired titles of "Silicon Valley" and "Pub City," and yet nightlife is regulated quite stringently by early closing hours, liquor licenses, nighttime breathalyzer tests, and dancing laws. In a police memo sent to bars in the trendy Indiranagar neighborhood of Bangalore in 2012, "loud Western music" was cited as a source of nuisance.

Cultural anxieties around infrastructural and cultural change, characterized as "anti-Western sentiments," are incited not only by rapid globalization following the opening of the nation's economic borders, but at other geopolitical scales. Bangalore as a historically multilingual migrant city gets characterized in film as a cosmopolitan and risky urban center within Karnataka.[33] Further, Karnataka's competition over natural resources and cultural production with bordering state Tamil Nadu fuels regional chauvinism.[34] During my fieldwork, xenophobia in Bangalore spectacularly erupted as violence against African migrants, and online threats against Northeastern Indians.[35] Cultural conditions that appear broadly as anti-Western sentiments then are not produced merely through anticolonial or antiglobalization anxieties, but also through recalcitrant and overlapping dichotomies: urban/rural, north/south, Tamil Nadu/Karnataka, and nation/region. Within this matrix, gay nightlife is rendered a cipher for antagonism and suspicion.

What follows is an exploration of stagings and eruptions at *Heatwave*, one of a handful of weekly Saturday night parties (including *Club Time*, *Pink Nation*, *Divalicious*) that operated during my fieldwork. These parties, organized by entrepreneurial men motivated more by profit than community building, take place at any bar that will allow a gay crowd. Sutured into the expanding leisure options that accompany India's liberalization, these Saturday night parties accompany and largely replace a network of sporadic house parties (see preface). The organizers show preferences for bars in upscale commercial areas such as central Bangalore and Indiranagar. Often however, the more amenable bars are at the peripheries of the city, newer neighborhoods built to accommodate Bangalore's rapid growth as a hub for global labor. I engage the impressively written weekly invitations to show that, much like the multinational corporations that cultivate a cosmopolitan habitus, *Heatwave*'s invitations dictate appropriate embodiments even before arrival. Inside the club too, music, decor, fashion, and dance regulate gender, class, and comportment.

My Sexy Valentine

Anti-Western sentiments often show up as moral policing that enforces the expression of "traditional values" in the public sphere. In addition to police harassing and arresting couples in parks, 2009 saw a high-profile campaign by right-wing Hindutva activists against Valentine's Day, claiming the holiday to be against Indian culture. Vigilante activists threatened to marry off unmarried couples out on dates and at bars on February 14. These right-wing projects and creative responses to them such as the 2009 Pink Chaddi Campaign and the 2014 Kiss of Love nationwide kiss-in have rendered Valentine's Day curiously politicized.[36]

In a 2012 Valentine's Day feature, *DNA* newspaper printed a picture of two Indian men leaning against each other, both their right hands clasped around a rose stem, captioned: "Love knows no bounds: IT professionals Kiran and Elen have known each other for the past four years and are looking forward to celebrating Valentine's Day."[37] This quick caption makes gayness respectable by centering love and long-term commitment. Highlighting their professional backgrounds, it inscribes them into the state-sanctioned professional identity of IT worker, a category that grants greater license to cross romantic and sexual boundaries.[38] Another Valentine's Day feature in *TimeOut Bengaluru* features four queer and trans couples, including the founder of *Pink Nation* parties, Akshaye. *Pink Nation* is described as a "queer event management firm," eschewing the sexual or licentious undertones of nightlife and parties for the more modest "event management."[39]

In stark contrast to respectable images of same gender love was the gay party hosted by *Heatwave*, *Pink Nation*, and *Divalicious* that same weekend advertised via the gay social networking site PlanetRomeo.

> COSMIC VALENTINE'S PARTY-SINGLES IN THE CITY . . .
> Saturday 11 Feb 2012 from 8PM—1:15AM. | It's Valentine's Day, the holiday beloved by Bacchus, the god of safe sex and organic wine. So come hither, where we will have games, libations, and general merriment. As an offering to the gods, please don a costume that evokes the spirit of love. (For example: a nudist, Bacchus, Dr. Ruth, a flower child, Heidi Fleiss, a flasher, a celebrity couple, a bride, Venus, the Marquis de Sade, Romeo and Juliet, a j-date employee, or your sweet self in red or white!). Sample the Nectar of the Gods. Devour the strawberries dipped in chocolate. Spin the bottle. Watch the hot men sizzling on the ramp. Unlock the lock of someone's heart. Form a pair on the musical chairs. Listen to the glorious music by DJ Sunny & DJ Lopez. Spend 5 hours in heaven!

Unlike the news articles, this invitation encourages hedonism and indulgence, but through decidedly Western and white markers culled from internet searches: Heidi Fleiss, J-Date, Bacchus, Dr. Ruth. Marketing and curating gay parties through white and Western tropes is instructive to some partygoers, exciting to others, and alienating to many. These party invitations cultivate cultural expectations that might be quite estranged from partygoers' quotidian desires, pleasures, tastes, and identities, but they also engender new kinds of fun as partygoers accent these party instructions with what they already know and like.

The overwrought curation reveals its own excesses and makes possible other kinds of habitations of the party. For example, the party did in fact stop for a game of musical chairs, a strange scene of men vigorously grappling against each other competitively, jealously, childishly, and sexily. They took the game very seriously; someone's jeans were even torn. The potential for childish behavior in the nightclub, I argue in chapter 5, has the potential to be both erotically charged and reparative. In the discord between invitation description *and* improvised performance is ishtyle, as the organizers aspire toward modern, global gay style and attendees accent these practices with their own situated epistemologies and bodies. Ishtyle moves beyond dichotomous frameworks to interpret how global gay style and quotidian tendencies are rendered in the body simultaneously. Partygoers interact with gay pedagogies prescribed to them, but the overstyled parties themselves reveal a gaudy localized sensibility that exceeds Western referents.

I am critical of the white, Western, and hypermasculine imagery used to frame gay parties, but I have also had a lot of fun on these Saturday nights. The creative labor of party organizers Akshaye, Mihir, and Kirti, who emerge from finance and IT professional backgrounds, is phenomenal. The truths they bend to acquire party spaces, scouting they undertake to find amenable bars and DJs, time put into assembling elaborate invitations, meticulous record they keep of partygoers, and slick fliers they produce to make us feel like we're getting a new experience each week are a fraction of the weekly labor they expend in manufacturing an alternative world for us to enjoy. In Bangalore's start-up spirit, they demonstrate excellent entrepreneurial and managerial skills: diplomatically negotiating police regulation and homophobic bar ownership; raising funds for queer events such as the pride march and queer film festival; recruiting patronage via online venues; and cultivating privacy and anonymity at their events. Mihir, Akshaye, Kirti and the few others who organize parties do a substantial amount of creative labor in imagining their events. It is with "critical generosity" that I approach their parties, with an eye toward the limited resources with which they program as well as the limits their curation places on patrons.[40] Sareeta Amrute writes, "The cultural branding of Indian programmers [and other urban professionals] inclines towards conceiving of them as spiritually motivated, able to work long hours with little recompense and incapable of doing creative work, except in exceptional cases."[41] My ethnography of aesthetics focuses on how partygoers, who are also global workers, break with the prescribed ethos of parties in order to mark their creative choices, expressions that are "more forceful and beautiful" than dominant or prescribed styles.[42] Their critical refusals of dominant pedagogies of gayness are creative practices that escape the corporatizing tendencies of the neoliberal city.

Hot Night, Crazy Party, Olé!

An e-flier from *Heatwave* featuring two matadors and a man dressed as a bull arrives in my inbox on PlanetRomeo. The accompanying text reads:

"NOCHE CALIENTE, FIESTA LOCA" @ SEVEN HOTEL on November 19th, Saturday from 8PM—1:15AM hosted by HEATWAVE & PINK NATION

A Pride Fund Raiser Party!
====================================
Noche | Caliente | Fiesta | Loca
These are the words which can be associated with any rocking party. But what are they? Don't say they sound Greek to you! They are certainly not Greek but Spanish!
 Spanish is a sexy and romantic language! And so are Latino men. Spanish music is equally sensual.
 Well "Noche Caliente, Fiesta Loca" means "Hot Night, Crazy Party"! So now you know what we are talkin' bout.
 Get ready to gyrate on the erotic Spanish tunes and other club numbers this Saturday as The Dirty Trio spin their best tracks.
 Bring out the Spanish in you by dressing up as a matador or a bull!:-)
 Or just dress up in a cool outfit and party like the Spanish for they sure know how to party big!
 The best outfit would win a cool prize.

Enjoy the night and get tipsy with Mojitos, Margaritas and Sangrias.

Also, feel good coz this party is for a cause. A portion of the entry amount would be donated towards this year's Bangalore Pride Funds. So make sure you bring all your friends along and party in style and contribute to the cause and say "Hola"!

We also have a special discount for students if they bring their IDs. Hasta pronto amigos!

DATE: November 19th 2011 Saturday

TIME: 8PM—1:15AM

VENUE:

Pink Sky Bar, Seven Hotel, 4th Floor

Beside new total shopping mall, Outer Ring Road, Between Marathahalli & KR Puram Bridges, Doddanekundi, Bangalore

ENTRY: 299/-

DEAL:

1) 250+ crowd 2) Great ambience 3) 2 party groups together 4) Great crowd 5) Gay-friendly venue 6) Cool Spanish theme 7) Prize for best costume

Like most party invitations, that for Noche Caliente offers a heavy dose of pedagogy about how to be a cosmopolitan subject, alongside reassurance that paying the entry fee will guarantee fun. The invitation implies that the hosts have novel knowledge to share with those invited. Promoters capitalize on the "economies of passion" associated with Latin America and Spain,[43] while also failing to differentiate between (American) Latino ethnicity and (European) Spanish nationality. Noche Caliente rides on the coattails of 2011 Hindi film *Zindagi Na Milegi Dobara*, which exposed Indian publics to Spanish spectacles such as the Running of the Bulls and Tomatina festival. The message promises drinks that were unavailable at the bar, and music that is "erotic" and "sensual" but was unfamiliar to partygoers. That night, the only person who seemed particularly at home in the club was a local salsa instructor.

The overwrought quality of these invitations reveals at once the dominant aesthetics of gay nightlife, as well as the playful possibilities of ishtyle. The flier itself features an image—one quickly found with a Google Image search of "gay matador"—of white muscular men against an abstract, sparkling background. With rare exceptions, every model featured on gay party fliers, like the matadors in this one, is white (or white-passing), mus cular, and seemingly masculine; even "Pink Diwali" and "Desi Glamour Nyt" fliers feature white, hairless men. Encouraging patrons to dress as a "matador or bull," organizers buy into clichéd notions of Spanish culture while also inviting strange and exciting sartorial styles. A flier for the Hipster Ball in 2011 explains: "[Hipsters] can be found in the Williamsburg, Wicker Park, and Mission neighborhoods." This presumes a well-traveled patron, creates aspirational desires to visit specific US neighborhoods, and alienates readers who do not know where these neighborhoods are.[44] Then again, it also scripts a queer nostalgia or even a queer brown migrant futurity into these increasingly gentrified and heteronormative upscale US neighborhoods.

Meredith McGuire argues that middle-class performance is not simply cultivated through quotidian consumption practices in new commercial spaces such as malls, coffee shops, and pubs, but is actively taught. She describes how call centers and IT firms instruct and cultivate bodily disposition through trainings called "Personal Development and Enhancement modules" to match globalized standards of professional comportment and self-fashioning.[45] Like PDE modules, gay party invitations offer sartorial and performance scripts that engender and regulate class and racial performance. The regularity of party themes structured around style—"The Hipster Ball," "Umbrella Party," "Black Tie Edition," "Ripped Jeans Party," "Raincoat Party," "T-Shirt Party," "Waistcoat Party," "Lockets and Jackets," "Dudes in Boots," "Uniform Party"—invites patrons into shared global fashion sensibilities through lengthy descriptions about the appeal of these garments and styles. Fashion statements are not only cultural capital at these parties, but a material incentive to participate in these sartorial economies, as they sometimes get you a discount at the door.

Much like Hector Carrillo's account of a "skirts night" in Mexico City, inspired by a gay US trend, at *Heatwave* parties "the original theme had given rise to a multiplicity of interpretations. In US gay mainstream communities, a party of this kind would have resulted in a fairly homogenous look."[46] Despite rigorous style instructions, most attendees flouted the invitations' recommendations and wore what they felt like. Eventually, *Heatwave*'s elaborate dress codes included "or just dress hot!," succumbing to patrons' refusals, laziness, or lack of access to these very specific fashions. Even when partygoers conform to high-end aesthetics that organizers cultivate, they may not be to everyone's liking. One PlanetRomeo user writes on *Heatwave*'s message board:

> Most of them were Hi5 [hi-fi, hi-funda, an Indianism meaning
> upscale] people from rich families. . . . Most of them looked like
> Models!! Slim body, White skin, Black Dress [clothing] (Black dress
> was the dress code), very height [tall] and they had every qualities
> to be a models in Fashion TV. There were also muscled men, but I
> did not like their faces . . . I don't like such people.. ;) I like Mass!
> [variously meaning popular, local, regional] . . . There was a guy
> standing next to me who was sexy too. Oh he was too "south-Indian-
> ish" which I love.

This user's reflection about his party experience suggests that while the upscale crowd conformed to both Western and North Indian standards of beauty and style promoted in the party's theme, he was more interested in South Indian men with a local flair.

This PlanetRomeo user's desire for the "south-Indian-ish" man resists a dominant desire for light-skinned, North Indian, and westernized men, but it is not void of politics and hierarchy. Over the course of my time in Bangalore, friends and anonymous Grindr profiles named their desire for "Northeastern boys with smooth assholes," "cut Muslim dick," "pretty Kashmiri boys," "Mallu tops," and so on. In his reading of underground sexual comics in Banaras, Lawrence Cohen shows how sexual metaphors of penetration, weakness, and genitalia are used to stage discourses of communalism, mobility, and modernity; he makes clear how race, region, and religion become politicized axes of desire.[47] While Bangalore-based interlocutors were not as forthcoming about the contours of desire as some of my diasporic friends (see chapter 3), it is worth noting that it is often minoritized and regional identities that are fetishized over unmarked dominant ones. Fetishistic desire for minoritarian subjects reifies their supposed (phenotypical, moral, bodily) difference, and renders them abject from (sexual) citizenship. At the same time, difference and power can be mobilized in sexual play, inventing other forms of citizenship, subjectivity, and relationality. This one blogger's desire for a "south Indian-ish" lover lives inside pliable boundaries of power hierarchies, but it gathers its critical capacity in the context of *Heatwave*'s hegemonizing aesthetics.

Pink Passports and City Limits

Akshaye's desire to start *Pink Nation* came from his admiration of Bangalore's thriving nightlife in the early 2000s, as well as his disdain for gay farmhouse parties that took place at private residences, far from the city's center: "Why these parties have to be done in secluded places? Why can't they be done in mainstream venues?" His vision for the parties was cosmopolitan, and he conceived of a conceit to create this ethos:

> I came up with the concept of a Pink Passport. It had exactly the same number of pages in an actual passport, but the size was of credit card size so that people could put it in the wallet. Everyone had to fill in whatever, put their photograph in that, and they had to bring that along to the party. Only if you bring the pink passport you get a free entry.

Several of my interviewees fondly recollected their Pink Passports and the perks they provided. Around 2009, Akshaye chatted with Krishna on PlanetRomeo, telling him about his parties; Krishna reminisces, "I wanted that Pink Passport, but I didn't want to give out my name or number." While the party's brand and passport gimmick gesture to escape from the mundanity of Indian work life, Krishna expresses concerns about such forms of documentation even while desiring inclusion in this "Pink Nation." He describes the material complexities of arriving at his first *Pink Nation* party: the bouncers kept asking whom he knew at the party but Krishna only had Akshaye's online pseudonym to go by; there was a Bachata dance lesson going on when he arrived, so he wasn't sure he was in the right place; the presence of women made him unsure whether this was a gay party; and he was relying on buses to commute, so he couldn't stay for more than an hour.

Despite the organizers' resourceful planning, the party experience is mediated by a variety of material conditions: what patrons can afford, getting to or from remote party locations given limited transport options, police regulations, and so on. The promise of escape from realms of heteronormativity and respectability that the club affords is tempered by material contexts. Bangalore's geography, infrastructure, and politics shape the night: sometimes patrons arrive to a shuttered door because the bar fears a police raid; liquor service stops early because of citywide religious observances; a power outage ends the party early; or the music and lights must pause for ten minutes because police have arrived to take a bribe. These material limitations are most apparent in the location of a party. Events would take place primarily at the city's peripheries, Marathahalli, Domlur, and Bellandur, shifting locations when bars became mainstream or fancier spaces became available. The many party locations serve as markers for a gay geography.[48]

For example, one PR user adds on his profile that he can host sex partners at his apartment "very close to Shah," a little-known restaurant in Bellandur where parties were often held. Sometimes parties were scheduled at nightclubs inside highly manicured tech parks. At one of these, I wandered into the proximate but shuttered food court in search of a restroom, and a sweet man offered to show me the way: "It's difficult to find, but I work in this complex so I know how to get there." For this man, labor and leisure overlap, as gay nightlife comes to the tech campus.

While bars in these areas, proximate to multinational business campuses, were convenient to some men who live close to work, they did not offer the trendy cachet of central Bangalore, nor the upscale spirit of Indiranagar. When Mihir secured a club in Indiranagar or Brigade Road, he made sure to advertise: "Party in city central for all our guys." Often these parties shared space with straight clientele, and bouncers—reading our gender, style, and cruisy glances—were present to direct traffic to one side of the club or the other. Sometimes organizers were not invited back to first-time locations when bar owners realized that there was a gay party on their premises.

The limited access to bars also meant renting out hotel multipurpose spaces for parties. Such indecorous make-do locations, with white, fabric-covered chairs along the walls, peanut snacks on side tables, and makeshift bar and DJ station, led Piyush to comment, "Are we at a fucking wedding?" and later and more incredulously, "What is this? A Texas high school party? I came out for real urban life, not for a night in Phoenix." Similarly, Amar comments at the same party, "This is like being in Iowa!" Comparing this party to the US Midwest, South, and Southwest, as well as the pageantry of a wedding, Amar and Piyush evaluate the party's success through a model that ascribes proper gay modernity to coastal urban America.[49] For elite and elitist patrons, organizers' failure to stage the trendy aesthetics developed in their party invitations becomes doubly disappointing. Often they stand on the periphery, drinking and judging instead of dancing. For elite men with global mobility, the elsewheres that party organizers curate might seem trivial and unsophisticated, but for those bound to Bangalore, Pink Passports and other creative instructions allow them to inhabit the city as playful global subjects.

Stuttering Soundscapes

Like the PDE modules of multinational workplaces, party invitations script modes of performance that cultivate an urbane comportment.

MNCs train workers' bodies, tastes, and pleasures by shaping architecture and environment, designating noisy spaces for table tennis and quiet conference rooms and meditation huts.[50] So too, party patrons are primed for the party not only through the online fliers, but inside the space by the club decor, soundscape, and even giveaways. As we leave Pink Sky Lounge one night, Akshaye hands all patrons a CD mixed by the night's DJ; the CD remained in my car and became my turn-up music on the way to the parties. The first mix was American Top 40s: Katy Perry, Kesha, Pitbull. The second mix was all electronic music. No Indian tracks.

I asked Mihir how he secures DJs:

MIHIR: Through contacts. Just friends. I change a lot of DJs.

KAREEM: Do they care about the gay crowd?

MIHIR: As far as they get money they don't [care about] anything. If you don't say anything, they play "straight" party music. Not "our" party music. Our people like more commercial. [It's a] divas music crowd: like Lady Gaga, Shakira, Jenny [Jennifer Lopez]. This kind of music our people like, like Pitbull, Akon. Straight party is only House music type. That music I'm sure our people don't like. People keep coming out [of the party to the lobby], "Mihir change the music."

KAREEM: What about Bollywood?

MIHIR: Fifty-fifty. If in case DJ is playing his own music, I tell him directly people don't like it and immediately they change it. You remember sometimes [you have seen me] come inside and talk to the DJ?"

Music at gay parties is contested and negotiated between the organizers, straight DJs, and queer partygoers. The frequency with which gay parties rotate DJs means that a queer subcultural sound, produced in a sustained conversation with attendees, does not develop at these parties.

The classification of electronic dance music as classier than Bollywood is evident in mainstream DJs' preference for these forms. When they played Hindi music, it was heavily remixed; a "Choli Ke Peeche" remix only sampled the chorus and never escalated into the verses, edging the dancers but never offering relief. Attempts to vary the music, such as spinning Spanish tracks at Noche Caliente, quickly cleared the dance floor. As Mihir explained, he has to constantly regulate what DJs play given the varying tastes present. In addition to the DJs who prefer playing techno are seasoned clubgoers who travel to Goa and Bangkok and who enjoy the "universal" sound of EDM as opposed to the more local Bollywood—performing one's musical taste becomes an expression of class and mobility.

At a *Retro Metro Party*, the DJ played English-language commercial pop music for most of the time. Only following a white American's request did the DJ announce over the PA system, "We're switching to retro," and played Boney M, ABBA, and Haddaway before switching back to his regular repertoire. Though the invitation called patrons to "Dust off your bell bottoms. . . . Wear your disco threads," songs that elicited the most vocal and athletic excitement from dancers that night were "Bachna Ae Haseeno," "Waka Waka," and the Dropkick Murphys' "Shipping to Boston," which corralled dancers into small circles as they held hands and did an Irish jig. While a distinctly Indian version of disco exists, the music choices and the largely unpurchased party gifts for sale at the entrance— colorful afro wigs, oversized sunglasses, metallic bowties—did not gesture to the gilded opulence of Zeenat Aman and Mithun Chakraborty. The prescriptive taste of party organizers and stubborn preference of DJs for electronic dance music grates against a much less predictable dancing public that takes pleasure in a strange variety of popular global sound. In the gushingly earnest eruptions for these three tracks, the crowd performed a cosmopolitanism quite unlike that imagined in the party's theme.

DJ Grim's announcement, "We're switching to retro," was not unfamiliar. At most parties, DJs actively (over)used the microphone: "OK guys, we're switching to Bollywood now," "We're going back to commercial!" "Come on you guys, make some noise!" and even, "Have a good night! Practice safe sex!" Like the party invitations, these frequent announcements perform a didactic pedagogy that attempts to shape the party experience. At one party the DJ shouted into the mic, "Do you want commercial and Bollywood, or do you want dubstep?" Dubstep, techno, electronica gained popularity via the Goa EDM scene and have become dominant sounds in Bangalore nightclubs. "Commercial" music refers to Euro-American pop and is seen as a concession to these genres, Hindi music is low on the list, and South Indian film music is a virtual no-no. To the chagrin of gay men in the space, the DJ's crowd of straight friends loudly chanted "Dubstep! Dubstep! Dubstep!" while moshing in a circle. DJs would bring along entourages, other straight friends. Sometimes they'd get drunk enough to be seduced by the queerness around them; other times, such as this one, they actively asserted hetero-difference through musical taste. DJs open a dialogue through their (over)use of the mic, but their inability to read a gay crowd's pleasure and response leads to moments such as this, where their straight friends become more legible than queer dancers. This DJ's transition to dubstep led a flock of gay men to leave the dance floor and hang out on the patio.

I became particularly sensitive to Bangalore gay parties' penchant for EDM after visiting other Indian cities. In Delhi and Mumbai, where there are multiple party scenes, some exclusively play Hindi and US Top 40 music, although they are characterized as less classy than those that hire EDM DJs. In Hyderabad, the DJ played gay crowd-pleasers that had no place in a club, but which everyone lived for regardless; "Pinga," from *Bajirao Mastani* led to a diva dance-off, and "Deewani Mastani" from the same movie provoked such joy that the DJ played it in its entirety three times in the two hours I was there. This "queer desi DJing" (see chapter 4) permits dancers to relish the gendered and sexual universe of film songs, as opposed to prioritizing the presumed shared danceability of electronic dance music. Queer desi DJing enables drag labor, inciting patrons to be with each other in performance, as dancers and witnesses.

Driving around Bangalore with Sridhar one Saturday afternoon, we debated whether to go to that night's party. A professional classical dancer, Sridhar has traveled to the United States to teach bharata natyam, and we have been clubbing together both in Chicago and Bangalore. "I just want to dance to Bollywood music tonight. But I know they won't play it. I don't understand! They know people want it, but they won't play it." Knowing that it will not be played, patrons came prepared to demand it regardless. The makeshift arrangement of gay party spaces allowed for proximity and dialogue between DJ and audience. Quite often, DJs were stationed at tables set up on the dance floor instead of in nicely raised and protected booths. This allowed dancers to pester DJs with their requests, which we did with abandon. Where much of Bangalore's elite nightlife sacralizes the DJ as maestro, at gay parties the DJ is irritated into engaging gay desires. This vernacular habitation of the space, treating the DJ like he is your cousin, like he has some obligation to you, is ishtyle; it may not successfully "Indian-ize" the space with Bollywood music, but it does make it feel familiar. Whether or not DJs succumb and play Bollywood, patrons take advantage of the makeshift club arrangement to feel some ownership of the party by badgering the DJ.

Feminine Fissures

With the dominance of EDM sounds comes a masculinization of the dance floor.[51] Expressive and individualizing choreographies are forsaken for head nods, fist pumps, and side-to-side steps. Because Indian music was not the dominant sound in the space—except for Bollywood theme nights—dancers took the opportunity to indulge in short bursts of desi sound. Shubha Mudgal's "Dholna," a nineties Indi-pop hit that mixes Rajasthani folk with pulsing dance beats, unexpectedly bursts through the speakers after a mostly electronic set. Milind's friend whines in urgency, "Indian steps *karo na yaar!*" [Come on and do Indian steps!]. Milind, short, fair, and twinky, switches to a simple and common step—right hand repetitively extends across chest to meet extended left hand, and then reaches behind the right shoulder. His friends join in to make a circle of hands blossoming in and out while right feet softly tap back and forth to keep the rhythm. The circle that forms draws Milind to the center; he wants to queen out but is worried about frightening away the tall, muscular straight boy he brought along as his date. After peering around however, he mouths, "Fuck it," and pulls the bottom of his T-shirt through its neckhole, creating a *choli*. He launches into quick turns, his graceful hands stretching above his head as his wrists turn against each other, much to the glee of the circle.

While such feminine performances are praised, they are not the norm. When such drag labor erupts, it has the capacity to orient others, to invite into the space gestures and selves kept at its margins. Party invitations, in text and imagery, rarely represent, let alone extol, femininity. The fashionable e-fliers feature muscular men, almost always shirtless, and in the long list of sartorial themes I've kept track of since 2009, glitter, nail polish, and makeup never made the cut—once, in May 2018, patrons were invited to a "High Heels Party." Organizers told me that they only disallowed crossdressing—clearly noted on online invitations—when it was the club's policy.[52] However, their preference was for the most appealing space, not the most inclusive—that is, they would choose a club with a great ambience and location over one that permits cross-dressing. The club's ambience was central to their marketing; Mihir often sent images of the "sexy location" over WhatsApp to his patrons when he arrived early on site. The underdefined cross-dressing policies that are "per club rules" also police class at these parties; a hipster with nail polish and heavy jewelry will still be let in, but a hijra in a sari will not be welcome. As I mentioned above, Akshaye started *Pink Nation* parties to be "classy," to capitalize on the city's urbanity. Kirti, a software engineer who organized parties for a couple of years, tells me that English-speaking gay men made fun of him and conspired not to attend his parties for a variety of reasons: his English is not as fluent as theirs, he is married to a woman, he is bisexual, his "crowd" is not English speaking, and he allowed CDs (cross-dressers) at his parties. In addition to Kirti's own failure to conform to global gay standards, femininity at his parties also renders them less popular. Cross-dressing, feminine behavior, drag, and regional languages, approximating hijra and *kothi* performance and eschewing muscular, white masculinity that dominates global visions of gayness, becomes "down market."[53]

Like the short bursts of popular Indian music that dancers reveled in, patrons seize the few opportunities to cross-dress, come in drag, and present as women. Natasha, a middle-class trans woman, who usually presents in masculine wear, was allowed to come to the party in a sari—"because I knew the organizer," she tells me. "That night, I got more attention than I've ever gotten as a guy." Another trans woman explained that she comes to these parties precisely to pick up "straight men." I didn't recognize her when she started talking to me; the last time we spoke at a party, she was in a boy look. When the party location allows her to cross-dress, she does. In a leopard print dress she straddled the hips of a muscular man who had lifted her up by the butt, kicked off her heels, and threw her head back in pleasure, pushing her breasts into the man's face. In his revelry, the man beckoned for a sip of my drink, drank most of it, and handed me back my ice as he kissed the drink into his dance partner's lipsticked mouth.

RuPaul's Drag Race has made drag "classy" in India, and while drag now has a weekly presence in Bangalore's gay nightlife, in 2012 I witnessed an unscheduled impromptu act at the end of the night to "Chikni Chameli." This queen shimmied her heavily embroidered beige sari off her skinny body to reveal a fully bejeweled bikini. The party had ended, but the forty-odd people milling about at the end of the night got to witness it; we made a semicircle around her, whistling, screaming, and smiling, as she *jhatka*-ed in front of the DJ's table. It was "stolen time," in the queer afterward that follows closing time;[54] though the party did not give her a stage during its duration, she found a moment in which she could seize attention.

The faggotry and femininity danced by Milind above are not the kinds of performances that the party anticipates in theme, promotion, or description. Moreover, the party does little to prioritize the pleasure of or even welcome transgender women. But stealing an impromptu drag show, seizing the opportunity to "cross-dress," and capitalizing on short bursts of desi diva sound become a way of finding pleasure in the interstices of the masculine hegemony of gay parties. These moments suggest the possibility of another kind of party, a sexier, more gender-diverse, visually and kinesthetically thrilling night. They also summon the party's ghosts, other feminine subjects abjected from the space because of class and caste (see chapter 2).

Virtually Partying

Party organizers have been innovative in combining technology and parties: "Grindr Party," "Facebook Summer Party," "Selfie Party," and "Bluetooth Party." The description of the Grindr Party reads:

> As all knows, GrindR is a mobile application where you can find your Mate & Date by using this unique GPS application which is specially designed for gay crowd. . . . If you are shy to talk to the person you like, Install GrindR application in your mobile and create your profile with your details and picture, then you will see all guys who are near to you in some feet away those are having the GrindR profile. . . . Its awesome na ;p | then let's chat, share and get the dream guy you required. . . . Not only this, Show your GrindR profile after you entered to the party and get 100Rs discount in the entry fee.

This message is written with Indianisms, typos, emojis, and homonyms that hail Indian users of Grindr and WhatsApp (another phone app named on the e-flier). At the same time, asking patrons to interact via apps regulates class at the party, requiring one to have a smartphone in order to access citizenship in the space.[55] The Selfie Party encourages patrons to send in photographs via WhatsApp so that they can be projected at the party, whereas the Facebook Party asks users to post pictures to the Facebook page, and images with the most likes will win a cash prize.

However, integrations of the virtual into the party space are not perfectly seamless. While Bluetooth and internet-based connections might allow for new forms of mingling at the party, they may not actually result in hookups. On gay websites and apps, it is typical for people looking for a sex date to say whether they "have place" or not, that is, if they live alone, have a place to themselves for some time, or live with roommates who are amenable to hook ups coming over. The living constraints placed on single men—hostels do not allow visitors, apartment buildings don't like to rent to "bachelors," single incomes in a booming city require living with roommates, longtime Bangalore residents stay with parents until marriage—makes "having place" a rarity.

One party attendee posts on *Heatwave*'s PlanetRomeo message board after he tries to flirt with someone at the party who already had a date: "He said that he came with his partner and said that it would be bad if he leaves his partner alone. I understood. :(I learnt a lesson. I now know that I shouldn't go alone!!" I too learned this lesson during fieldwork; many partygoers prearrange their dates, ensuring that someone has place. While I exchanged numbers with many cute men at the parties, they never led to an immediate hookup because neither of us "had place"—I lived with my parents during fieldwork. I once left the party with someone, and with no home to hook up at, we made out in his car, but police rapped on the foggy windows and sent me home alone in an auto-rickshaw. Many patrons simply come to dance, drink, and socialize, knowing that a hookup isn't foreseeable without further negotiations about place; their time at the party is better spent gossiping and boogying.[56] As Shaka McGlotten writes about Grindr, hooking up is not necessarily the primary use for the app.[57] Similarly, parties advertising the possibility of dates and hookups, even those that integrate hookup apps, are put to very different uses.

In 2012, US-based gay social networking site Manhunt.net started sponsoring *Pink Nation*'s parties, sending a large banner and a cardboard cutout of a muscular white man to display outside the entrance. The parties advertised free Manhunt giveaways; the Manhunt lip balm I received was a local brand with a printed MH sticker wrapped around the tube. Similarly, when the website sponsored a hunky Indian model in a Manhunt tank-top to strut around the party, he disaffectedly handed out MH beer mugs, which were locally purchased pint glasses with a tiny paper sticker awkwardly placed on the glass. At the end of the night, the prized Manhunt mugs advertised in the party invitation were left scattered around the bar. Manhunt's attempt to drive traffic to its website reflects a paternalism espoused by other gay websites. Detecting my India-based IP address, PlanetRomeo notified me that my membership would be free because this Netherlands-based company was committed to "furthering the cause of gay rights" globally.[58] Similarly, the location-based networking app Scruff let me know that I was in a country in which gay sex is illegal and to be careful. The discarded Manhunt mugs, like unsold rainbow-afro wigs at the Retro Party and abandoned yellow roses at the Friendship Day Party do not mean that party patrons completely reject Western consumerist modes of performing gayness, but it does signal their discerning engagement with "mainstream White Gay Inc. global movements."[59]

Unruly Silence

In the wake of the 2016 mass shooting at a gay club's Latinx night in Orlando, there followed a global outpouring of grief from people whose queer lives felt even more precarious than they already were. I landed in Bangalore the week of the Orlando attack, and attended a *Heatwave* party at Chili's (an American chain restaurant) in Indiranagar. This felt different from my previous visits; no longer were we relegated to outskirts like Marathahalli and Bellandur, nor to the no-name bars that needed business, even gay business. But the oddities of Bangalore gay nightlife persisted. A makeshift draping of red fabric protected the virtuous families eating quesadillas upstairs from looking down at the debauchery below them. And yet aunties descending the staircase in saris to exit still had to listen to Demi Lovato and watch boys with too much product in their hair locking lips.

The party's Facebook event, "Love is Love: Stop Hatred, Spread Love," advertised solidarity with the victims of the Orlando shooting and mentioned that there would be a moment of silence in their memory. The moment of silence was brutally indecorous. The person trying to get everyone's attention to observe the moment of silence shouted throatily into the faulty mic, "Orlando! We are with you! We remember! Okay now, let's see if we can be quiet!!!" This ritual moment had not been carefully thought out; the buzz of the still-open restaurant and the proximal street traffic made silence unachievable. Moreover, the chatter in the party crowd never stopped. A British-Indian visitor standing next to me fussed, "People here just don't know how to listen." He became further annoyed when the himbo next to him tried to flirt by asking cluelessly, "This is for what? That Orlando thing?"

To me, the lack of silence did not indicate disrespect. Partygoers ignored announcements over the crappy sound system, as they always do. Music turning off was par for the course at a party. Advertised party themes were inconsequential. This unruly moment reminded me that these Saturday night parties in Bangalore engender a habitus different from many global party circuits. Gay subjectivity in Bangalore can and does subscribe to liberal and rights-based understandings of gay similitude; someone on Grindr nearby even had the screenname "v r all orlando." But of course it is precisely "slippages" such as his "v" instead of "we" that remind us that the accent corrupts our ability or desire to perform gayness samely.[60] The accenting of gayness, and more specifically the material habitation of these parties—shitty sound systems, liminal party locations, irregular and overwrought gimmicks—make the staging of a universal gay identity unattainable.[61]

These parties, complicated as they are, are sutured into the laboring lives of my interlocutors, held in spatial proximity to or even in tech parks, and in temporal proximity to work life for those working the night shift. The mundanity of labor and the intensity of the nightclub constitute each other: working and partying become important complements implicated in a shared aspirational ethos. I've documented here a variety of refusals of this aspirational ethos enacted by party patrons: ignoring dress codes, desiring "South-Indian-ish" men, displacing hired go-go boys, discarding party paraphernalia, departing the dance floor, bugging the DJ for Bollywood, dancing like a diva, and preplanning dates. The parties, like multinational workplaces, are invested in bodily comportments that look less and less like the quotidian environments in which many of my friends and other partygoers were raised. Their dissenting habitations of the gay party allow my interlocutors to enjoy a less binarized experience of the weekly events, not necessarily reveling in Indianness per se, but rather pursuing their various bodily pleasures against the will of hegemonic pedagogies of dominant gay citizenship.

TWO

Dancing against the Law
Critical Moves in Pub City

Pub City

My parents moved from Accra to Bangalore in 2002 looking forward to retirement in the "air-conditioned" garden city. But precisely then, Bangalore was experiencing new growth from burgeoning white-collar industries such as information technology and business process outsourcing. The city exploded in size and population in subsequent years to become India's "Silicon Valley." I remember my mum telling me about her cousin's new English-style bar, "The Pub"—a novel idea for the city at the cusp of the millennium that snowballed into many more pubs, bars, lounges, and clubs springing up across central Bangalore. By 2005, Bangalore was branded "Pub City," and a commercial nightlife scene had grown, attempting to match and capitalize on the city's growth.

I learned of the bar Chin Lung in 2008, on a casual visit to Bangalore before starting graduate school. A guy using the screenname "Whisper" sent me a message on the social networking site Gaydar, "Are you from here? New in town?" He invited me to a gay party he was hosting at a hotel nightclub not far from my home. My mother quickly dismissed my request: "What if there's a raid? You'll get arrested. You don't want to end up in jail, you're supposed to go back to the US in two days." Without accurate information about what is and is not legal, and prior to mainstream news coverage of India's LGBTQ pride marches and legal battles, my mother—who remains fairly disinterested in Indian politics—understands that queerness and criminality are bound to each other, and something somewhere justifies police raiding a gay party. Whisper assured me that it was safe. If I needed another option, he said I could check out Chin Lung, a bar in the center of the city that was "gay-friendly." He implied that I probably wouldn't want to go there, though, that the clientele was less than savory.

Chin Lung

On my first visit to Chin Lung, in September 2011, I was taken by how unimpressive the space was. Entering a tiny liquor store on the ground-level first floor, close to the perpetually packed Brigade Road, I ascended a darkened staircase into a restaurant. How could a "gay bar" be located in the center of the city, surrounded by bustling commerce? The middle-aged men sitting at tables watching cricket didn't look gay; they weren't. This second floor, I learned, was the "straight floor." The terrace featured a mix of tourists, hipsters, and college kids in search of a cheap drink. The third floor was the "gay floor": equipped with white plastic garden chairs and tables, minimally decorated with beer posters, and pumping music louder than any of the other floors; the lights were dimmer as well. A blogger reminisces about his college days when he frequented Chin Lung for cheap liquor: "Chin Lung was a bar of three unusable floors with the fourth floor being an open rooftop."[1] On this "unusable" third floor, there was nothing to indicate obvious queerness.

I was disappointed. Online accounts from gay travelers, and nostalgic descriptions from friends who frequented Chin Lung in years prior described transgender women dancing, rent boys working, and raucous socializing—these descriptions ranged from fond memories to disdainful judgment. The scene I arrived upon was more demure: men sitting in white garden chairs, struggling to maintain conversations in the din of music and street noise, their eyes perpetually scanning other tables for a possible flirt or fuck. One blogger calls Chin Lung "the worst bar in Bangalore"—tattered, dingy, stained, hell, shabby, broken, stank, nightmare, "an attack on every sense."[2] In its *suciedad*, its filthiness, it didn't promise Pub City's shining middle-class futures.[3] But my friends never complained about the bar's aesthetic quality; some certainly basked in its inconsequence and filth.

Priyank, tall and dark with an immaculate mustache, hears the opening beats of "Crazy Kiya Re." He pushes his chair back—that signature scuffing noise of wobbling plastic on concrete draws attention—clearing a space for himself between the tightly packed furniture. He dances, much to the delight of the men at his table: sharp and angular arm movements across his torso, wind of the waist, and repeat. The dancing had begun! *This* is the Chin Lung I had heard about. Quickly, the teenage busboy, also the makeshift DJ whom people tip to change tracks on the limited iPod selection, taps Priyank on the shoulder and gestures for him to sit down. As soon as the boy's back is turned, Priyank returns to his Aishwariya-realness. An older waiter, referred to by most as "Uncle," comes over and tells him to stop, gesturing to the stairs, suggesting that someone might see him. There are two threats in this situation. Our dancer may be harassed for his womanish behavior by men who are walking between the various floors; queer patrons are sometimes harassed by others, told to "change their behavior, dressing style, hairstyle and to 'act like a man.'"[4] The other possibility is that any policeman who walks in could shut the bar down for allowing dancing.

Dancing: Against the Law

Prior to the explosion of malls across the city, the central Bangalore district was the commercial heart of the city where bars blossomed—Three Aces, The Pub, Peco's, NASA—to earn the moniker "Pub City." Some of these spaces also offered queer people respite in the city center, allowing, or just tolerating, their presence, sociality, and dance. Gay nightlife hid in plain sight, if you knew when and where to congregate. A ban on dancing in Bangalore bars, inconsistently enforced between 2006 and 2014, came to affect nightlife in general, but gay nightlife in particular. This chapter traces how queer people respond to restrictions placed on them through critical movements: social movements that directly engage the law, spatial navigations that offer a different map of middle-class nightlife, new topographies of the dance floor, and improvised articulations of the body. The moves and movements I explore here are critical in both senses of the word: they offer critiques of regulatory systems of power, and they are urgent labors to survive, live, and thrive. Scholarship about the relationship between law and dissident genders and sexualities in India acknowledges that state-sanctioned homophobia and transphobia is enacted through various laws that police can selectively apply to detain, extort, and rape people. However, scholarship and media discourse primarily center Section 377 of the Indian Penal Code and legal activism to decriminalize sodomy.

My focus on the Bangalore dance ban recalls how music and dance have been used to evidence criminality in the colonial regulation of dissident subjects. As I elaborate with more clarity later in this chapter, colonial and postcolonial management of women's dancing bodies instantiates logics of sexual propriety that persist across a century to bear on dancers at Chin Lung and elsewhere. These histories converged in Bangalore's pubs, colluding with regional and national anxieties around neoliberal globalization. Moral panics around the trafficking of women in 2006 led to raids on dance bars, nightclubs where women (including trans women) danced in sensual, but not necessarily provocative, or even athletic, styles, for seated patrons, primarily men. Without evidence of sexual transactions taking place in these spaces, a variety of dance bans were legislated and enforced, not only on dance bars but *all* liquor-serving establishments. The 2008 ban on dancing and live music in alcohol-serving establishments, officially lifted in 2014, was publicly decried by middle and elite classes as a conservative backlash to westernization—claims were made that music and dance are intrinsically Indian, and even a universal right.

To invoke the "nightlife's nexus" described in the previous chapter, the disdain for dance in nightclubs is tied not only to rapid economic growth and the burgeoning entertainment industries that accompany it, but also to anxieties around women's sexualities, men's performance of proper gender, and class and caste respectabilities. Indeed, pub culture was initially meant to secure middle-class decorum in globalizing Bangalore:

> They played Pink Floyd, offered draught beer, and seated scores of young male software engineers enjoying their beer in small groups. The inauguration of the new pubs was accompanied by another first: the introduction of bouncers to maintain the middle class respectability of spaces that were soon increasingly filled by both young men and women. [Bar owners' attention] to the display and performance of public respectability resonated with the state's own desire to craft a "respectable" cosmopolitan and modern city modelled on Singapore.[5]

More than just an "anti-Western" backlash, as blogs and newspapers narrated it, the dance ban was predicated on protecting gender and class propriety in the global city. There are numerous cases of moral policing in Karnataka and across India in which couples in bars and nightclubs were pulled out, harassed, beaten, or threatened with being forcibly married to their dates by Hindutva fundamentalists.[6] These sexual politics are fueled not just by the threat of licentious and liberated women, but also by anxieties around interreligious and intercaste desire.

Gay nightlife in India is interpreted as a decadent Western import, and "criminal intimacies" emerge in the proximal histories of "criminalization of homosexuality, the policing of minoritarian space, and the discursive maintenance of social pathology."[7] Gay nightlife is already risky; dancing during the dance ban was doubly so. That our dancing bodies were always under the purview of law was most evident when the music would very suddenly lower in volume or cease completely at gay parties. Everybody would instantly stop dancing and talking, remaining still and quiet, assuming police had arrived on premises and were in negotiation for a bribe. In contrast, patrons at fancier "straight" bars and clubs have the audacity to boo in anger and entitlement when the sound or lights cut out. Already feeling like we were doing something illegal, the tense stillness in these regular interruptions to gay parties were a learned bodily response, one that law already produces in queer bodies through not only fear, but shame. The passivity of these moments made me see how laws sit in our bones and flesh, as quotidian affects of vulnerability and anticipation.

One night I am out with my friend Amar at a gay party at Hotel Regalis, in central Bangalore. Amar doesn't go out very often; he doesn't really enjoy it, he says. But today he smiles at me as he watches the dance floor and mischievously muses, "This feels so dangerous. All this dancing." The pleasure of dancing and the way we dance are not only shaped by law, but are means of responding to violence committed on our bodies by law. Joshua Chambers-Letson argues that the realm of aesthetic interpretation—art, theater, music, dance, photography—is an important place to look for critiques of law, because law itself is an "embodied art."[8] Always put into effect by those who interpret it—judges, police, lawyers, or even my mother, who may not know the law but has a sense of it—law relies on their "affects, passions, and anxieties" to take effect.[9] In the bars of central Bangalore, dance achieves collectivity in spite of state and social policing, what Elizabeth Son describes as a performative "redress," which affirms that the performer's alienation is real and that other forms of citizenship are possible.[10] My friends don't merely flout the ban on dance, but also stage gay, queer, transgressive, feminine bodies that laugh at a constellation of laws. In these scenes, they don't recreate the rocking nightclub, the chill pub, cool lounges, or hip raves that characterize Pub City's peak in the mid-2000s; there's nothing trendy about these nights. Instead, they accent the night with qawwali, koothu, and kathak, choosing "unusable" bars such as Chin Lung and after-hour dives such as the Silver Lily to revel queerly in Pub City against the comportments expected of them by the bars, state, and nation.

Section 377 and Its Others

My first research trip to India came not long after the July 2009 Delhi High Court reading down of Section 377 of the Indian Penal Code that criminalizes "carnal intercourse against the order of nature."[11] This moment was one of global celebration not only for queers in India and its diaspora, but other former colonies that continue to retain similar British laws in their penal codes. The decision came after a protracted legal battle, initiated fifteen years prior by AIDS Bedhbhav Virdohi Andolan (ABVA), an HIV/AIDS NGO. Both ABVA, and subsequently the Naz Foundation that filed a petition with the Delhi High Court in 2001, posited that the criminalization of sodomy augmented health risks by preventing proper research and delivery of services by HIV/AIDS NGOs. The Delhi High Court deemed in 2004 that Naz could not prove that 377 affected its work. Naz then collaborated with a coalition called Voices Against 377 to file an appeal, revising its rhetorical tactics to premise arguments on dignity, privacy, and autonomy. Naz's lawyers argued that 377 turned gay, lesbian, bisexual, and transgender people into second-class citizens and violated their right to privacy. The high-court judges heard the case in 2008, and in 2009 issued a ruling that "held that criminalisation of consensual sex between adults in private violates the Constitution's guarantees of dignity, equality, and freedom from discrimination based on sexual orientation."[12]

Several interlocutors declared that their entry into gay communities came on the heels of the 2009 decision. One rushed to a gay support group meeting that very day. A graduate student in the UK returned to Bangalore as soon as his degree was completed, feeling a palpable change back home. If I'm honest, this ruling was probably one of the reasons I imagined research in India. The joy was short lived. In 2009, a coalition of conservative, primarily religious, organizations filed appeals with the Supreme Court to revisit the decision—this case was heard in 2011. Nowhere was the interpretive quality of the law more evident than in the Indian Supreme Court as Justices Singhvi and Mukhopadyay chuckled between themselves like horny uncles as they explicitly discussed what particular acts count as "against the order of nature"—was a man putting his penis in a bull's nostril sodomy? They mused that while they knew *of* LGBT public figures—Martina Navratilova and Vikram Seth—they didn't know any. The courtroom was swarming with queers—lawyers, notetakers, academics, and spectators; none of us dared out ourselves.

The judges delivered a wicked blow to the movement, repealing the high court's decision in December 2013, arguing that the defense did not prove that police use 377 to exploit LGBT people; law should not be amended based on the lives of a "miniscule minority"; 377 did not actually turn LGBT people into second-class citizens, as it criminalized acts and not people; and the defense relied too much on non-Indian precedents and comparisons. A curve ball came in the 2014 National Legal Service Authority judgment that guaranteed transgender people third-gender status and all citizenship rights; this agitated an already tenuous camaraderie between trans folks and gay, lesbian, and bisexual people. Gay, lesbian, and bisexual people felt embittered by the nation's embrace of trans people who can claim ancestry via historical and mythological representation; it seemed even more evident that modern gay and lesbian identities were deemed un-Indian by the courts, by the nation. Further, it quickly became apparent that trans people could still be criminalized under Section 377. Fueled by some of these conflicts, and buoyed by the 2017 Supreme Court decision declaring the right to privacy a right for all Indian citizens, several petitions were filed again with the Supreme Court to read down 377 in 2018. The various plaintiffs in this case *were* LGBT people, and the five-judge bench listened to their case with a sense of sympathy and curiosity. In September 2018, Section 377 was read down by India's highest court; instead of fixating on the nature of sex, this judgment insisted on the dignity, privacy, and protection that LGBT people deserved.

The law's performativity, its capacity to render some people precarious and others good citizen-subjects, is made apparent when people come out of the closet or return to India at these watershed moments of legal change.[13] But it is also evident in mundane cultures, in the times that we stop dancing and wait, without asking questions. Turning to scenes of dance in gay nightlife under the dance ban helps me think through relationships between law, sexuality, and culture. Following the lead of scholars who think about how law impacts LGBT India through dance bars, lesbian desire, and drug patents, I turn to the ban on dancing to decenter 377 as the pivot-point to theorize the relationship between culture, queers, and law in India.[14] This obtuse approach allows me to think more expansively about the policing of sexuality and gender, in ways that arguments against 377 have not.

Important critiques have been launched against the terms on which the reading down of Section 377 was argued. In the 2008 arguments, Naz's lawyers relied heavily on the right to privacy as constitutive of a citizen's dignity and autonomy. Privacy arguments privilege the protection of middle- and upper-class life and intimacy, and cannot accommodate working-class queer and transgender people, especially those engaged in cruising and sex work, or who do not have access to private space. Further, arguments focused on "sodomy" center sex between men and do not pay attention to how queer women's desires—perpetually subject to legal and social surveillance—become impossible under the law. In 2018, one lawyer's arguments insisted that 377 specifically polices "orientations," not "genders"; this argument, perhaps deployed to differentiate this case from the NALSA judgment, obscures the legacies of 377, which has been used to police hijras.

It was in fact a hijra who was subject to the first application of 377 in 1884. In the case of *Queen v. Khairati*, a hijra was detained for wearing women's clothing and singing.[15] As Anjali Arondekar points out, Khairati was not singing at the time of her arrest, but was in the habit of singing, and these tendencies were enough to signal her unnatural sexual proclivities and render her subject to an anal examination.[16] Arvind Narrain and Alok Gupta remind us that hijras were already assumed to be criminal, a prejudice written into law as the Criminal Tribes Act of 1871, which de facto criminalized particular communities:

> Any eunuch so registered who appeared *dressed or ornamented like a woman in a public street . . . or who dances or plays music or takes part in public exhibition, in a public street . . .* [could] be arrested without warrant and punished with imprisonment of up to two years or with a fine or both.[17]

The Khairati case and Criminal Tribes Act remind us that hijras were historically vulnerable, and continued to be so, under Section 377.[18] In the Khairati case and Criminal Tribes Act, we are also reminded that dancing, singing, and dress are given the weight of moral and legal transgression. Law enforcers become arbiters of aesthetics. So perhaps it is in aesthetics, in addition to rational argumentation, communal protests, and material evidence, that we might look for forms of popular public dissent. Dance, bound so closely to public and national discourses of gender and sexuality, becomes a prime field to think about how dissidence is enacted.

In addition to their growing familiarity with 377 as a tool to harass queer people,[19] police have used numerous other regulations, often with specious evidence, to raid gay events and to detain and blackmail LGBTQ folks—indecency, nuisance, harassment, disturbing the peace, trafficking, kidnapping, and so forth.[20] While my interlocutors discussed how deeply affected and subjugated they were by Section 377, they enjoyed a robust gay nightlife well before 2009 and continued to party after the 2013 recriminalization, contradicting their spoken fears of criminality. Gay nightlife is simultaneously defiant and vulnerable regardless of whether sodomy is legal. Queerness has always been regulated by a constellation of laws, and the passions and prejudices of those that enforce them. The ban on dance in Bangalore was one of the ways that gay nightlife could come under greater scrutiny, one *more* tool that permitted police to enter parties and bars and to charge people with any other violation they find: drug use or possession, blowjobs in the bathroom, and so on. The ban gives police the authority to define what dance looks like in order to stop it; it puts into the hands of the law the work of aesthetic criticism. Similarly it puts the onus on bar staff—waiters, DJs, bartenders—to watch for bopping hips and nodding heads, anything that might be read as dance, as was the case at Chin Lung. In contrast to the 2011 legal arguments and protests against 377 that could not verify their urgency because the judges didn't "know" any queer people and considered us a "miniscule minority," dancing against the law was an "activist gesture" that verified its importance through the present and enlivened criminal body.[21]

Dance, in Place

At Chin Lung, I repeatedly witnessed how the ban on dance comes to affect performance, and in turn, social dynamics. The ban on dancing, by the state and the management, created a heightened tension in the bar and required new ways of dancing. On busy Saturday nights, when item songs came on—"Ring Ringa" or "Beedi Jalaile"—eyes scanned the room, trying to predict which queen would get up and show off her *nakhras*. But no one did. For the length of a song, necks flexed and craned waiting for a performance, shoulders bounced itching to get up and dance. But no one did. Alternatively, bar patrons found other ways to dance: in their chairs. When a slower or nostalgic song came on, men gestured dramatically to friends across the space like classical musicians while lip-synching the lyrics. The Kannada song "Yavanig Gothu" was on frequent rotation on Chin Lung's playlist through 2011. When the song came on, friends would close their eyes and lose themselves in the winding verses, exhale dramatic clouds of cigarette smoke at opportune notes, or bop heads in time with the song and each other. The song would animate gestures and communication across tables as strangers looked across to catch each other's eyes at the chorus, extending arms and twisting hands to ask, "Yavanig gothu?" In the music video, Puneeth Rajkumar performs highly stylized popping, krumping, and breaking choreographies, with heavily accessorized and vividly colored fashions. Seated performances at Chin Lung took no referent from the video; instead they were melodramatically emotive, picking up less on the song's boppy beat and playing more into the quirky poetry of its lyrics.

Chair dancing is not simply a consequence of no-dancing policies, but cites also Hindustani, Carnatic, Sufi, and film playback musicians who, while seated, use hand and head gestures to keep rhythm, communicate affects, and accentuate sound. Like these musicians, my interlocutors who dance with only hands and face, gesture and lip-synch, too are "musicking bodies."[22] In a space where dance is curtailed, the performativity of embodied gestures is heightened to allow emotive and social bonds to be made across seated distance. These small movements become so much larger as they stretch across the stillness of the space.

Similarly, lip-synching from one's seat carries more gravitas for femme queens who are not allowed to dance. Gender is a "threshold effect," and for many feminine men, dancing is an important way of staging their body that allows them to be read as feminine through their mustaches, muscles, and body hair.[23] But when dancing is restricted in spaces like Chin Lung, shining one's lips with gloss and mouthing songs, with the potential of catching an eye across the space, becomes a necessary means of exhibiting femininity despite the shackles of the plastic chair. Kiran, often referred to as Karina, stays put in his chair all night; but with his *nakhras* (dramatics), he ensures that even in dim lighting from across the room, no one mistakes him for a man.

Documenting these gestural communications is important given the limitations placed on circulating freely (patrons are asked to always be seated) and on convening (there is no dance floor and no communal bar, as servers come to the table). Except during trips to and from the bathroom, which smells like months of dry urine, bodies are not bumping and hands are not grazing strangers' thighs; bargoers sit in the same room as men they've been chatting with on PlanetRomeo, texting each other within the same space without a serendipitous moment to strike up conversation. But Chin Lung, according to several men I've interviewed, has been an important place of encounter, sanctuary, and community.

Arrivals

My friend Nik moved to Bangalore from a small town a few hours away and was introduced to gay nightlife through Chin Lung. He would come to the bar every other day and drink alone, hoping to meet a partner for something other than an internet-arranged one-night stand. He had heard about the bar and Cubbon Park via PlanetRomeo:

> I've been as a kid to Cubbon Park. It is all bushy bushy. I didn't want to go to that [cruising] scene I'm trying to escape. I came to Chin Lung for one year. [Every other] day I came. I just sat, having beer. I found people very odd, weird. There were transgenders, queenly dancing people. They were looking [at me] and giving like ["come hither" gestures]. Now it doesn't happen what I saw those days. They used to dance in between [the tables, with] people throwing money.

Nik tells me that in the meantime he had met a guy online that was discreet about his sexual liaisons because he was "high profile . . . one of Bangalore's most eligible bachelors." (Several men I met at Chin Lung enjoyed gloating about closeted/straight South Indian actors or other celebrities they had dated or had sex with). When Nik told his lover about these adventures at Chin Lung, he disapproved of Nik's participation in a public and down-market gay scene. Among the middle classes, the performance of class is reflective of social capital; while Nik turns to Chin Lung as a more respectable alternative to cruising in the park, his "eligible bachelor" lover sees public gay collectivity in this no-name pub as déclassé.

During this time, Nik came out to his closest high school friend, who, with several others, beat him up severely to punish him for his homosexuality, or to help him, "or something." Nik kept coming to Chings [Chin

Lung] to find community, to find an entry point into community, unsure how to make an approach.[24] Random straight men forced Nik, who would sit alone, to buy them drinks and food until the servers intervened. As finicky as Uncle may have been about how loud we were talking, our penchant for dancing, or our desire to stand and not sit, he often had our safety in mind. Or, at minimum, he understood the frictions produced between different kinds of clientele. Nik decided to go to Chin Lung "one last time"—there had been several one-last-times prior—before completely giving up on making friends; it was this time that a table of twenty-something-year-olds summoned him over. His sense of inclusion grew quickly, and a year into finding a friend group, Nik became a visible and vibrant queer activist in the community. Where he could not find acceptance in his friends, friendship in the cruising park, or a sense of equity with his lover, Nik found a semblance of all three at Chin Lung.

RK was a permanent fixture at Chin Lung, usually at a table with three to five others. As his friends arrived, they pulled up another chair and joined the table. Between the booming music and wide plastic chairs, it was impossible to have a conversation with others unless you were right next to them. This means that there was often a lot of sitting in the din whispering into neighbor's ears and staring around while drinking, instead of spunky banter and high cackling. RK tells me about his entry into Bangalore's gay scene, a story that resonates with gay narratives not only from my fieldwork, but other published oral histories, interviews, and creative writing.

> I started [with men] when I was in fourth standard, with my neighbor, who was also my classmate. . . . I wouldn't call it love, we just did it when we had the chance to do it. I was at an all-boys school. Fifty in my class, forty-five were doing each other. Even in high school. . . . Only after I came to Bangalore for college I got to know that this is the lifestyle. [My friend and I read about] *Bombay Dost* [India's first gay magazine] through Pearl Padamsi's agony aunt column in *Femina* magazine] and there was Ashok Row Kavi's address, and we gave him a call and we got a post box because we couldn't receive the magazine at home.

The pen pal he acquired through *Bombay Dost* brought him to Cubbon Park for cruising, where he found out about the support group Good As You (GAY), and subsequently ended up going to bars with friends he made there. RK charted for me a series of bars that gay men would go to prior to Chin Lung: Three Aces, Night Watchman, Soul Café, London Underground; none of these were gay owned, nor did they have good service, nor were they actively inviting a gay clientele. Gay men just sort of squatted there and made it their hangout until the bars were closed. Given the overwhelming regulation of bars in the city, those bars inevitably closed. He noted with a laugh that a couple of bartenders at these venues flirted and hooked up with some gay men.

Dhaval, whom I met at the *Heatwave* parties, reminisced to me about Chin Lung: how posh he found this "Chinese restaurant" compared to his village life and to Cubbon Park cruising, how much he enjoyed dancing and hanging out with all the cross-dressers. It wasn't until Dhaval's mention of "Chinese" that I registered the paltry attempts to match this in the decor, specifically glass paneling at the top of the first flight of stairs, backlit, and beveled with bamboo designs. While it might seem that Cubbon Park is the down-market option in comparison to Chin Lung, several other friends remember with fondness Sunday evening gatherings in the park, where couples flitted off to fuck, but the majority of the time was spent socializing in small groups. As police presence grew in the parks and other more private options for socializing expanded in the form of pubs and cafés, the park was a less and less attractive watering hole for middle-class gay men.

For Nik's partner, Chin Lung was down-market. For Nik himself, it was a safety net and springboard. For new-to-the-city Dhaval it was a posh Chinese-themed establishment. For foreign-returned RK, it was a second home. Though Chin Lung meant different things to my interlocutors at different times, every one of them insisted that the bar was not what it used to be, that dancing had stopped and cross-dressers were gone. I asked RK about this discrepancy.

The dancing stopped first, early November last year [2011]. That day, we heard from Uncle that the owner found out from a friend that this was a gay hangout from a website. . . . A friend of mine from the US called Bill, American but used to work in Bangalore, confronted the owner: "What's the problem? This has been a gay joint since '97!" And he [the owner] didn't like that. . . . On that day, on his way out, [the owner] called Uncle and the manager: "If you guys let anyone in [cross-dressers or gay men], you guys will be sacked and fired." He's a new guy, only since July or August last year, pretty new.

In a similar episode, one of Bangalore's queer women's groups, We're Here And Queer (WHAQ), was discouraged from returning to a pub where they held their weekly hangouts after *TimeOut Bengaluru* mentioned the pub as "lesbian friendly" in its listings.

Dancing was discouraged prior to November 2011, as I observed in Priyank and Uncle's interactions. But from November 2011 onward, I heard more and more rules by word of mouth: no cross-dressing, no men in makeup, no *kothis*. Gay men were disinvited and then invited back because of the lost business. Chin Lung was no longer a place to convene. The city's ban on dance colluded with homophobia, femmephobia, and transphobia: homophobic managers, femmephobic patrons, the bar's ban on transgender women, the lack of private bathroom stalls, and so on. Together they displaced queer and trans communities from a space that was, for a time, familiar and intimate.

Dancing in Queer Time

Despite the restrictions enforced by Uncle and other servers, gay men kept going to Chin Lung. And despite the restrictions, they continued to dance. One way Chings's clients navigated restrictions placed on their pleasures was to find "queerer times" to dance. On weekend nights, the bar's staff was extremely stringent about dancing, as they were at risk of a raid, but weekdays were less stressful. On a Tuesday night at Chings, there were about twelve men in their forties and fifties sitting in twos or threes across the space. The bar staff, who usually guide tourists and college students away from the third floor and up to the terrace, were less attentive, practically absent. Three straight boys, in jeans and hoodies, arrived and occupied a corner. They smiled watching from the corner of their eyes as Adi mimed the lyrics of "Apni To Jaise Taise," lip-synching Amitabh Bachchan into a high femme with freshly glossed lips. Karina leaned back leisurely in her chair, eyeing one of the handsome straight boys in a hoodie. She is a drama queen par excellence; her lips pout perpetually and she had recycled bottle caps and other paraphernalia on the table into delicate jewelry to accentuate her hand gestures. Karina too queened out, flipping an imaginary shock of long straight hair to the side and brushing it; this is among several brilliant moves Kiran developed for dancing in his chair.

As one of the hot straight boys returned from the bathroom, someone from our table goaded him to dance. Unexpectedly he began breakdancing, landing in handstands and freezes, capitalizing on Daddy Yankee's "Gasolina" to show off his masculinity; the playlist was always unpredictable! We forced reluctant Karina into the open space as "Munni Badnaam" hummed from the speakers; the boy was open and friendly, and they launched into a number together: a strange duet of break dance and Bollywood femme. The boy clearly didn't understand Hindi, but mimicked the wide-armed machismo of a film hero that left room for Kiran to wind his waist like a sexy damsel, or thirsty bottom. The boy lapsed back into his break dance training, and Karina scuttled back to her seat, unsure how to proceed. This opening of the dance floor inspired the older men to step away from their tables and dance; suddenly the sedated bar was alive with men dancing for just one song. Their movements were restrained—side-to-side steps and little bops of the shoulder—but their revelry was not. The time of the bar was queer not only because we were out there dancing on a Tuesday night, but because of the unexpected intergenerational intimacies on the dance floor, and because of the shifting and unpredictable "musical time,"[25] from reggaeton to Bollywood item song, that inspired handstands, uncle shuffles, and *jatkas* and *matkas*.

The straight boys left soon after the number was done, calling to Kiran on the way out, "Dude, be cool man." On the more popular Saturday nights, I never witnessed such unexpected intimacies where older men got up to dance with each other, and straight boys danced with femmes. But the bar's gay crowd was always on the lookout for a moment, a scene, an orientation: cruising coupled with curiosity in search of beauty, of something wonderful, with the desire to be seen, too. This drag labor could make the night an event, could turn friends into celebrities, strangers into lovers. Gay nightlife at Chin Lung was always improvised, and brief eruptions such as Kiran's interaction with the boys were unpredictable; they went unremarked except for a few comments about whether those boys were straight or not, or how great a dancer Kiran is—"But she knows that already!" The lack of explicit or extended commentary does not mean that these moments did not achieve something for those present. This dance duet suggested the heteroflexibility of straight boys, advertised Kiran/Karina's femme persona, and permitted so many others to boogie in a climate that does not encourage spontaneous social dancing. The dance floor may not exist at Chin Lung, but in such moments of improvisation, it can spring to life for all of three minutes. These moments can help us conceive of dance floors as temporal rather than spatial, "practiced place," following Michel de Certeau;[26] understanding the dance floor as a happening and not a location helps us see dance more often, in the "wrong" place, and in choreographies that don't necessarily look like dance.

Ban-galore

Chin Lung was not the only place in which dancing was policed.[27] On Karaoke night at Loveshack the emcee interrupted a singer to insist that her backup dancers stop dancing. At Couch a sign in the entrance stairwell read, "Strictly no dancing police orders." At F Bar, a manager came up to my white friend, who was unconsciously bopping his hips, and asked him to stop moving as "the plainclothes policeman in the corner over there will shut the bar for the night." Bars in Indiranagar received a police memo that ordered the arranging of chairs and tables in ways that discouraged patrons from dancing. Mihir sent an SMS to his Saturday gay party list asking us to stay home, as there were rumors of a raid expected that night. Blue Ice pulled the shutters down on the gay party one Sunday night because other Church Street bars had been visited by police the same evening. When the police entered the premises of Seven Hotel in Marathahalli, or Hotel Dew Drops in Malleshwaram, all movement at the gay party stilled.

Beginning in 2006, Bangalore police officers intermittently visited and raided bars in which people were dancing. A moral panic around prostitution and trafficking of women in Bangalore led to raids on "dance bars" where women—fully clothed and with no physical contact—danced for men's pleasure.[28] As there was little evidence of sexual transactions in these dance bars, police used unenforced excise laws from the 1960s to proclaim that the presence of live music and dancing at liquor-serving venues was illegal.[29] In 2008, when dance bar owners challenged these raids in the high court, stating that these outdated laws were used selectively, "what they got was the blanket ban"[30] that made lounges, restaurants, and discotheques subject to the same restrictions. Police took creative license in how they enforced the dance ban. They could cite the 1960s laws designed to address the cabaret craze of the moment, they could enforce policies set up in 2005 that require nightclubs to have dance licenses that were distributed slowly, inefficiently, and only to the highest bidders, or they could invoke the broad-based ban of 2008.

When I tell people that dancing was illegal in Bangalore, the first response is often "Like *Footloose*?" But if we consider the impulse to "save" public women, bar dancers, from the terrors of nightlife and men's gazes, the more apparent parallel is the antinautch campaign of the late nineteenth century in which folk dancers, courtesans, and devadasis were identified as performers whose indecent lives and vulgar dances must be reformed. The recent dance ban extends a long history of policing dance in India through the regulation of public women, particularly women from heritage performance communities, and tribal and subordinate castes. Attending to the replication of these sexist logics over the course of a century reminds us that crises produced after India's economic liberalization (such as the antinightlife backlash) are indicative of longer histories of colonial and patriarchal politics invested in instantiating caste and class hierarchy and managing sexual labor.

Bangalore's moral panic around dance bars resulted in a ban on social dance; a contemporaneous panic in Mumbai resulted in a ban on dance bars and has received some scholarly attention. William Mazzarella suggests that the increasingly iconic sexy dance bars did not fit the respectable global vision of India that somehow sutured technological and infrastructural development with bucolic visions of the orient.[31] Further, he argues that dance bars were shut down "vis-à-vis a series of precedents reaching back into colonial times" that include legal designations of public and private space, regulation of proscenium-style performance, debates over obscenity, and contestations over what qualifies as traditional performance. Anna Morcom more explicitly argues that Mumbai's dance bar closures replicate the logics of the antinautch campaign: "The basic arguments were the same. . . . These women were basically prostitutes, leading lives of immorality . . . an insult to Indian womanhood."[32]

Devadasis in South Indian temples and courts performed heterogeneous styles of *sadir* dance, which was eventually reformed into what we now call bharata natyam. Their counterparts in the north, *tawaifs*, were women courtesans whose dance was codified into forms we refer to as kathak, particularly by virtuoso men such as Birju Maharaj. In precolonial contexts, these courtesans were essential guardians of memory, history, and performance repertoires, and were considered important pedagogues in their respective communities.[33] British authorities perceived them primarily as prostitutes. The association of devadasis with Hinduism—some, not all, women had been dedicated at a young age to temples—fueled

Western contrition for the decadence and immorality of Indian religion. In response, reform activists, made up of dominant-caste, educated professionals strongly influenced by Christian morality and religion, began lobbying against the dedication of women to temples through the antinautch campaign ("nautch" is an anglicization of *naach*, which means dance).[34]

Alongside reform movements was also a revivalist endeavor: upper-class, professional Brahmin women, under the encouragement of Europeans traveling in the subcontinent, transformed dance repertoires into respectable traditions by associating them with Hindu mythology, codifying movement for the purpose of replication, and stripping them of explicitly sexual content. Bharata natyam innovators dissociated the form from the decadence and improvisation of *sadir* to develop a seemingly timeless Indian dance. In such postcolonial respectability movements emerge distinctions between high and low art, between dance as labor and leisure, between stage and social dance, between improvised and repertoire-based dance, between erotic and sacred forms. This comes to affect the livelihood of heritage performers who, displaced under reform and revival movements, perform to Bollywood songs in the lounge-style dance bars, a labor deemed "not sophisticated enough to count as a 'skill.'"[35]

The revivals and reforms of bharata natyam and kathak, as well as *tamasha* and *lavni*, and the effects they had on heritage dancers lives, have been central to South Asian dance studies. The persistence of antinautch logics in Bangalore's gay nightlife is an important opportunity to think across dance and queer studies in India. In Bangalore, specious accounts of trafficking appeared in newspaper articles and TV reports about raids on dance bars and massage parlors, supposedly fronts for sex work. News footage often attempts to capture women's faces as they are ushered around by policemen, shaming them even in the process of "saving" them. The media collude with police who invite them to document raids, and act as an arm of the state's moral policing. I am often struck by the very similar visual of men being escorted out of gay parties, in which the news cameras attempt to film men as they shield their faces with whatever garments they have available.

The ban on dancing in Bangalore, as Mazzarella and Morcom suggest of the Mumbai context, is a result of anxieties about the moral and cultural consequences of liberalization as well as of discursive legacies of colonial and postcolonial moral, gender, caste, and sexual regulation. For the working women who danced in bars, the ban on dance meant a loss of income. For many of my interlocutors who have tenuous access to community and pleasure, the opportunity to dance with others was a promise of queer sociality in an alienating city. The injunction against dancing makes the labor of collectivity in gay nightlife, an already precarious space, more difficult. The ban on dancing, as fascist as it sounds, was temporarily a part of a morally rigid landscape that people in Bangalore learned to make flexible. It was ridiculous, but so are many other state-sanctioned regulations, and minoritarian subjects figure out ways to find pleasure every day without feeling completely exhausted.

The Silver Lily

Beginning research in Bangalore in 2010, I felt that I missed out on a golden age of Chin Lung, where queens danced fiercely for everyone to watch. My interviewees told me of fabulous fashion shows at farmhouses. I heard about house parties where expert and amateur *mujras* alike turned living rooms into *kothas*. I learned of Pink Passports that made the gay party-going experience a weekly international adventure. In much of my participation in gay nightlife in Bangalore, the moments where all people in the bar felt that we were in one place together were few and far between. Small groups came and went, rarely did the room burst into unison choreography, or turn to witness the same performance together. That sense of intimacy, of embodied togetherness, was rare.

A mellow Sunday night in April 2012. It is 11:25 p.m. and we are being ushered out of Chin Lung. RK invites me to join him to the Silver Lily, a five-minute walk away. We arrived to a shuttered storefront, and with a bone-shaking rattle the grate is opened; we enter into a basement and are briskly ushered to the second floor. Though other bars closed at 11:30 p.m., here the dance floor is open for performance and flirtation past 3:00 a.m.[36] One police commissioner, responding to rigid enforcement of bar curfews, declares, "Nighttime is for sleeping," clarifying the logics of capitalist, heterosexual, and reproductive time that shape Bangalore's nightlife.[37] Yet "closing time," as Shane Vogel offers, "inaugurates a queer temporality that extends beyond sanctioned possibilities for sociality."[38]

At the Silver Lily, men trickled in, each snuck in past noisy shutters: young skinny boys with feminine demeanors; two tall men in all black, with their shirts unbuttoned to reveal gold chains. I sat with RK's party of five on white pleather sofas waiting for someone to dance. Everyone on the periphery waited. The room was arranged as such, white pleather sofas bordering an open dance floor. Finally someone gets up: a man in khaki pants and an embellished black T-shirt. She pushes the sleeves up to her shoulder, exposing hairless arms she can writhe and angle to create feminine silhouettes. With the catchy beat of "Ring Ring Ringa" from *Slumdog Millionaire* she fills the dance floor with her *nakhras*. Running her hand down the length of her extended leg, she creates an imaginary *ghagra* (skirt). She slips on the shiny, slick white floor, knocking the low table where the two men in black are seated. My friends and I hold in our wicked laughter, releasing only a collective gasp. She recovers from the embarrassment of her fall by rolling on the ground sexily. We watch, mortified by her lack of grace, but captivated and buoyed by her commitment to the dance, as she rotates her hips to each "Ring Ring Ringa."

The music shifts at the whims of the servers and the tips of the patrons. I am pulled onto the dance floor by Krish, whom I was flirting with at Chin Lung earlier in the night, to dance to "Nakka Mukka." I couldn't tell who at his table was single or coupled, so I flirted with the whole group. I had told Krish that I was recently obsessed with koothu music. I try to keep up with his vigorous moves on the slippery white-tiled floor as he hops, feet together, left then right, hips pumping. I am no match for his style. His friends ease my shame, warmly explaining that my style is clearly "North Indian! Bollywood!"

When "Salaam E Ishq" from *Muqadar Ka Sikandar* comes on, Abhay's face whispers with intricate but muted *abhinayas* (facial expressions) in front of me. His fingers, still by his sides, rehearse careful choreography. I can tell he has kathak training and urge him to dance; he feigns reluctance but edges toward the dance floor anyway. Suddenly his whole body springs to life as Lata Mangeshkar completes the song's opening poetry and the quick tabla notes drum into the air. He becomes Rekha, exceeds Rekha, in a gorgeous display of film-style courtesan choreography. I am mesmerized, but so is everyone else. RK leans over to tell me, without taking eyes off Abhay, "He's trained with Birju Maharaj." I am spellbound by Abhay's fierce effeminacy, enthralled by this *mujra* in a public venue. This was the Bangalore I had heard about: the sharing of space together, the coming together through dance and drink and performance and witnessing and effeminacy and affirmation.

Displacements

But as I dug a little further, asking RK about the Silver Lily, things got complicated.

It was quite happening two and half years ago. Exact same scene as right now: they'd let you in and put the shutters down. The cops know what's going on, which is why [the staff won't] let you stand around [outside]. Two years ago the first floor was a straight floor. We had the second, and the third floor was filled with bouncers and waiters who wanted to keep going [after getting off work]. Suddenly after a two-week break, it was a ladies' bar, a dance bar. Every floor. You could go if you want to, but you have to sit there and watch women. You can't dance with them. You cannot! That went on for two years until ladies' bars got banned. [The bar staff] sent out feelers, and they asked us to come back. When the cross-dressers were banned from Chin Lung, they went [to the Silver Lily], only the last month and the half since that's been happening.

Until it was raided two months prior, the Silver Lily had been a dance bar, which explains its layout of low seating facing an open dance floor. For a while after, the staff would encourage transgender dancers to tell their gay friends to come drink and dance after hours in order to boost business following the displacement of bar dancers.

Here at the Silver Lily, the very possibility of a clandestine dance night, in which men dance for men's pleasures in regional, effeminate, and classical styles, exists only because of the dancing women who have been deprived of their professions by police raids. But those gay men were invited there by the transgender women and cross-dressing men displaced by the queerphobia of Chin Lung's manager. More generally, transgender women also feel displaced from the dance bar scene, as those spaces have become more particular about hiring cisgender women and refusing transgender dancers.[39] Further, queer people used to go to the Silver Lily until it became a dance bar; they could still go then but were not allowed to dance. For that time, they only fit there within heterosexist logics that required them to occupy men's roles as spectators. And there I was, watching a man perform in the *filmi* feminine courtesan style, precisely because bar girls had been displaced by the same logic that ousted courtesans from their careers. What is even more complex is that Abhay trained with Birju Maharaj, one of the "fathers" of modern kathak, who displaced the authority of women courtesans in kathak's revival movement.[40] Moreover, I was watching the kinds of intimate queer dances I associated only with house parties, which had become so rare in the age of pubs and clubs. This scene is both haunted and populated by perpetual displacements: house parties, heritage dancers, trans women, effeminate men, bar girls, regional music.

Attending to dance has allowed me to think across different gender and sexual subjects in relation to law; as Treva Ellison offers, turning to praxis, the critical ways we use bodies, rethinks relationships between anatomy, criminalization, and gender justice.[41] The perpetual displacement of gendered and sexual others in the nightlife scene that I have traced here evidences that queer men are not alone in their experiences of social, moral, and legal policing. Following Svati Shah's project of focusing on "the context of articulating a common cause between sexworkers' and LGBTQ movements," turning to the dance ban and its collusion with other kinds of regulations becomes an opportunity to make clear to queer men that they are systemically bound up in the policing of sex workers, bar dancers, cross-dressers, hijras, and *kothis*. The precarious gay spaces where men dance and find pleasure are ghosted by the displaced bodies of trans and cis women who danced in those bars.

Gay nightlife thrived before the 2009 reading-down of 377, and after the 2013 recriminalization. However, since the 2018 Supreme Court ruling, gay nightlife has gained greater visibility in news coverage, and some party organizers have relaxed privacy measures. Diversity and inclusion work in the corporate sphere has also begun to prioritize LGBTQ sensitivity. However, Section 377 of the Indian Penal Code does not alone make LGBTQ people second-class citizens in India—police extortions, hijra rapes, Grindr blackmail, and gay party raids between 2009 and 2013, when sodomy was technically legal, reflect this. Also, in September of 2019, authorities used noise ordinances to close a regular venue for gay parties in Bangalore. Sexual and gendered others are produced not only through directive laws, but through a constellation of scripts, players, and sanctioned aesthetics, brought to life in a violent theater. This record of displacements of effeminate men, bar dancers, courtesans, temple dancers, and transgender heritage performers across India and Bangalore's geographies and temporalities is a reminder that—especially given the vastly different material stakes for those whose livelihoods depend on (public) sex work—our politics must be coalitional, that the logics that oppress middle-class queer men also impinge on women's sexual freedoms and on transgender people's right to self-determination and their access to safety, pleasure, and capital. One way to start mapping these intersections is to ask: Who had to leave for us to dance here?

PART II

THREE

Desiring Desis

Race, Migration, and Markets in Boystown

"The American Gay Way of Living"

Keshav moved from Bombay to San Francisco for an MBA in telecommunications technology in 2001. Subsequently moving to Chicago, he built a reputation as the glue between a diverse social circle of queer men of color. They were a sweet group, always supportive of my drag shows, and regularly inviting me to beach days, rooftop parties, and cocktail evenings. Keshav performs his love of nightlife on Facebook, often indicating which circuit party or gay resort he is traveling to next. He loves wearing as little clothing as possible, and on occasion he volunteers as a go-go dancer. I was interested to know if integrating into this subculture, which seems like a major part of his life, was vital to his US migration:

KAREEM: Did you know America had a gay scene?
KESHAV: Mmm mmm [no]. I [had been] in San Francisco for a year. I was going to Best Buy and the bus drove through Castro, and I was like, "Oh wait! What is this place? There are sex shops and gay flags. Oh my god, it's a gay neighborhood!" On the way back from Best Buy I got off and walked around.

While the San Francisco Bay Area is touted as a "gay Mecca," it embodies other aspirations in the global imagination, including that of "Desi Land," given the large concentration of Indians working in multinational information technology companies.[1] One of the longest-standing South Asian LGBT organizations, Trikone, was founded there in the eighties by engineering student Arvind Kumar. But gay community was not the impetus of Keshav's migration.[2] Instead, his entry point into gay nightlife was serendipitous, a happy accident a year after his arrival. I'm reminded here that gay neighborhoods and cliché rainbow flags, critiqued as symbols of homonationalist capitalism, function differently for migrants. Fraught as they are, they fix gayness somewhere where people new to the city, or curious in their sexuality, can wander into.[3] Queer party cultures, often more trans-inclusive and body positive than gay bars, often have to move around town and find refuge in less accessible locations. Gay bars in commercial neighborhoods, though they privilege whiteness, tend to be where I met South Asian migrant men most often.

This chapter charts my interlocutors' experiences in Chicago's gay neighborhoods, encounters that provide insight into how they desire, and become desirable. Many of the encounters are set in Chicago's Boystown and other commercial gay neighborhoods such as Andersonville and Rogers Park. Boystown emerged as a gay residential neighborhood in the late 1960s, and gay residents staked their claim to the area in 1973 by commemorating the 1969 Stonewall Riots.[4] The area has, since the 1970s, seen a drastic rise in gay entrepreneurship, and there are currently at least nineteen gay bars in Boystown. In 1998 the city acknowledged its gay character by raising permanent, phallic, rainbow pylons along Halsted Street, and 2019 saw the installation of a rainbow crosswalk.[5] The quickly rising value of real estate in Boystown has driven many gay men into Uptown, Rogers Park, and Andersonville, where they have displaced lesbians and people of color.[6]

The racial contours of commercial gay nightlife in Chicago are shaped by city-sanctioned policing and development: decades of gentrification across Chicago's North Side that perpetually displaces LGBT and ethnic enclaves; a public transportation system that makes travel to the North Side from the far West and South Sides difficult; the neighborhood business alliance that privatizes public spaces in Boystown; and police that harass young poor Black and Latinx folks who come to Boystown to access support, health services, and community. So while I praise the possibilities of gay neighborhoods, I realize that those possibilities are sometimes predicated on systemic exclusions and displacements. Many of my South Asian interlocutors have the cultural and economic capital to participate as paying citizens of commercial gay nightlife. But not all South Asians I befriended were affluent enough to enjoy Boystown's aspirational ethos; as I show later in this chapter, a queer Pakistani friend working in service industries found himself in Boystown rather serendipitously, for work and not pleasure.

Keshav caught on quickly to the pleasures of gay nightlife, but also to the regulatory aesthetics of this scene:

KESHAV: I met one guy on campus, Ricardo—you remember Ricardo on the beach? Anyways he lives in Chicago now. I found out he was gay, and I told him, and he took me to the gay clubs. I became addicted to them. I suddenly realized I've lost so many years and I need to catch up. The music, the dancing, the men . . . I made a few friends; I could not hook up because I didn't know how to hook up. I didn't know the American gay way of living: go to the gym, and you cut your nails, and clean your nostril hairs, and keep yourself in good shape and clean.

KAREEM: Did guys hit on you?

KESHAV: No, very rarely.

Coming out and going out are normalized in teleologies of gayness, as Summer Kim Lee argues,[7] and Keshav places club culture in this timeline when he says, "I need to catch up." But he also reminds us that you don't just organically grow into club culture. There are distinct pedagogies, particular behaviors and comportments in bars that one must learn; knowing these repertoires—gym going, trimming nostril hairs—suggests the possibility of sex and romance. But even doing these things did not guarantee flirtations. The bar is a place to seek pleasure—"the music, the dancing, the men"—but it also places limits on those who do not possess the racialized capital being traded there. His mention of the gym as central to gay men's regimens returns me to my own body, to the ways that my own tummy feels accented.[8] A gay white friend once asked if "all Indian men have *that paunch*," and among some desi friends, we joke about having the "rice and chapatti belly" from our mothers' and aunties' cooking; they want us to be "healthy." My brown belly renders me unassimilated into white gay fitness culture, accented, and while I embrace fat positivity, bear culture, and brown pride, the body shame has sedimented deeply.

Keshav's narrative tells us that while the search for queer community is not the only premise under which people migrate, there are distinct contours to the shape of queer migrants' experiences in gay neighborhoods like Boystown and the Castro. They become aware of their accents, the particularity of their habitus, as they come into relief against the conformity of life in gay neighborhoods. Accents make us exotic or abject, and we make choices about whether and how to assimilate. Gay nightlife certainly functions as much more than a site of sexuality and desire, but for those of us who arrive with the hope of erotic intimacies, desirability is premised on the multivalent and hierarchical ways in which our bodies are racialized. The first two chapters cataloged the many ways that my interlocutors in Bangalore used their bodies to navigate the expectations to perform in accordance with various modes of citizenship: global gay masculinity, appropriately Indian heteronormativity, police-enforced expectations of decency. This chapter considers how South Asian migrant men come into knowledge about their desirability, and how they articulate their desire for others in US gay nightlife; exploring the conditions of our desire reveals how macropolitics plays out in intimate realms.

The chapter's title draws on the double possibilities of "desiring" that renders South Asians objects to be desired, but also subjects who can desire. When we are called Aladdin, we are returned to the Orientalist fantasies of colonial conquest. When we trigger the nostalgia of military veterans, we are metonyms of bomb-able territories. When we are desired as engineers or taxi drivers, we are slotted into recent histories of labor migration. The multivalent performativity of South Asian bodies—phenotypically diverse and variably represented in global media—produces a variety of intimate interpellations. I place my interlocutor's voices in conversation with South Asian literature, film, and poetry, as well as critical scholarship on race and colonization, to evidence relationships between political economy and desirability. That we don't meet figures of governance—police, judges, multinational companies—in the same way as we did in previous chapters does not indicate that these migrant men's lives are not being surveilled; rather this chapter demonstrates the insidious and less spectacular renditions of global governance shaping queer intimacies. Nightlife's pleasures remain bound to elsewheres such as the workplace and warfare. AB Brown argues that performance helps us see that racialization is predicated not only on colonial formations of difference, but on ongoing postcolonial negotiations of global power.[9] The interviews I explore show that alongside stubborn colonial formations of gender difference that have structured most analyses of racialized desire, contemporary global political economies produce additional axes through which South Asian men become (un)desirable.

Dwight McBride insists upon the salience of race in the "marketplace of gay desire,"[10] extending E. Patrick Johnson's discussion of "race trouble with queer theory," a field that valorizes sexuality's radical potentials, but fails to attend to how sexuality is constituted by race, and experienced differently by people of color.[11] Queer-of-color criticism understands that surplus populations—produced under labor migration, economic displacement, settler colonialism—are regulated through gender and sexuality.[12] In the process of becoming surplus, their genders and sexualities too become queer. These very genders and sexualities, measured against white Euro-Western norms, are construed as perversions that have been used to justify settlement, extraction, and domination. The iterative Orientalist knowledge production of and about minoritarian bodies turns us into objects and "body ornaments,"[13] or brings us into proximity with objects.[14] We become ornate objects—accents—to decorate white bodies, to both deflect and justify their queerness.[15] That said, objecthood can be its own agentive tactic.[16] Much of the literature demonstrates how the sexualities of people of color have been essentialized as (un)desirable to the colonial palette, but Russell Leong asks us to consider "How . . . Asian Americans figure as the subjects, rather than the objects, of homosexual history and desire?"[17] I listen here to my interlocutors as they name what they desire, but also how they find pleasure amid the limited terms under which they are desired.

The acts that Keshav mentions to describe becoming a good citizen of the nightclub, trimming nails and nostril hairs, are distinctly gendered acts that bring the brown migrant body into a kind of good gay gender. Colonial legacies have affixed race, gender, and sexuality, linking hyperfemininity and Asianness, hypermasculinity and Blackness, and passion and Latinidad—archetypes that manifest in same-gender settings. Studying gay sex tourism in Brazil, Gregory Mitchell demonstrates how sex workers engage in "performative labor" such that "their success or failure depends on constructing certain styles of gender that are often rooted in neocolonial variations of archetypes."[18] Asian men's presumed effeminacy repeatedly casts them as the bottom in gay pornography,[19] though some Asian men deploy feminine performativity to their advantage in drag shows.[20] In pornography, personal ads, and everyday life, Black men are iteratively positioned as the hypermasculine penetrator in gay sex.[21] These genders are perpetually constructed in relation to "unmarked" whiteness.[22] Eng-Beng Lim's transnational study of Asian genders and sexualities explores iterations of the brown man–white boy dyad; the "boy," whether forever young, effeminate, and acquiescent, or wild and aggressive, confirms and confers white paternalism.[23] Lim extends Edward Said's claim, "In a quite constant way, Orientalism depends for its strategy on this flexible *positional* superiority";[24] white men can be feminine, masculine, bottom, or top, remaining superior regardless of social or sexual position.

South Asian genders have been interpreted as various and contradictory. South Asian men are gendered via historical discourse and contemporary media as the asexual Gandhi-like ascetic, the virile courtesan, the hypermasculine Sikh/Muslim, the effeminate Bengali.[25] Colonial suppositions of South Asian effeminacy have engendered backlash over the last two centuries that has instigated a flourishing of fitness cultures and muscularity; communal violence and rape; and emphases on rational thought and self-control. In addition, gender shifts under migration and displacement: despite the symbolic masculinity it acquired given Sikhs' association with martial orders, the turban of Sikh laborers in California in the early twentieth century was characterized as feminine,[26] and now, since 9/11, turbans tip toward the queerly hypermasculine given their association with Osama bin Laden and the Taliban.[27]

That desire is shaped by political economy becomes particularly evident in associations between South Asian migrants' sexuality and their work, as IT guys, engineers, cab drivers, and Kwik-E-Mart workers. In this multivalent landscape of race, gender, and sexuality—inflected also by class, caste, religion, and the performance of these identities—all of which are set into motion by transnational migrations, my interlocutors are well aware of how discourse shapes their desirability. Further, queer South Asian's identities and desires, even when cultivated within a US racial framework, are, as Afzal Ahmed argues, inflected by unmistakably transnational epistemologies.[28] What I hope is evident is that the terms of desire are never straightforward. In their theorizations, my friends evidence a pursuit of intimacy and pleasure, sometimes clambering ungracefully through their commentary, to make sense of difference and marginality, to rhetorically secure a sense of hope, to believe that they deserve to be desired. The hesitations, repetitions, retractions, and trailed words of their interviews evidence the effort they put into making sense of uneven landscapes of desire. They offered me "theories in the flesh" that I print here at length so that their theories live alongside, confirm, expand on, and contradict critical race and gender studies scholars.[29]

This chapter deploys performance to explore the politicized dimensions of desire, drawing on the interview as site of performance, mobilizing performativity as a useful analytic, and accounting for the shifting meaning and value of South Asian bodies on a variety of social stages.

Their interview performances, with and for me as witness and audience, are "definitional ceremonies," ritual scenes of subject making—whether or not they are desired out there in the gay neighborhood, here in the interview they can be desiring subjects.[30] Performance also accounts for the brown body's mutability. Like the accent, the brown body has the capacity to transform through and past the historical discourses in relation to surroundings and contexts: blending into Latinidad, darkening in proximity to other accented bodies or artifacts, becoming racially ambiguous when alone. "Performative labor," the body's capacity to activate history and discourse, to mobilize desire by playing into and resisting situated archetypes, is another way that performance becomes central to theorizing racialized desire.[31] Color, smell, muscle, hair, dress, taste, work, and accent coconstitute the brown body, and we need performance to account for the multiple ways we manipulate them, and "uncertain" ways they work with and against each other to make us (il)legible, and (un)desirable.[32]

"Either a Doctor or Engineer"

"*Trade*," Dwight McBride asserts, "is not what you 'marry' or 'take home'—it is what you 'hook-up with.'"[33] Hiram Perez probes this bias to ask, "What is the relationship of trade to *trade*?" arguing that varieties of *trade*, hypermasculine ideals that inform and titillate a Western gay imagination—"rough trade, tearoom trade, military trade"—acquire their intrigue at the nexus of "multiple [imperial] routes of international trade."[34] If we consider South Asian men's relationship to trade, how we are inscribed into global markets, we perhaps appear as desirable commodities for gays in pursuit of homonormative domesticity; we are *trade* you might actually marry. As India becomes a global economic and military power in alliance with the United States, Indians—and not other South Asians—gain greater visibility, becoming more attractive, or at the very least, less threatening. Trade makes Indians less like *trade*, and performing one's Indianness might signal economic security; as Shilpa Davé says, "Indian accents imply one type of an Asian model minority [that fits] the image of entrepreneurs, computer engineers, and successful immigrants in general."[35]

Keshav indicates how model minority myths of the good working migrant are placed on his body, particularly in the context of India's rise on the global stage. However, as he expands on these ideas, the ability for racial difference to secure desirability seems like less and less of a guarantee.

> KESHAV: For years I kept wondering if I was the only gay Indian. In a way it was really nice: I'm the only weird one. . . . When I left [San Francisco] in 2006, I started seeing maybe one or two. That time I wouldn't say I'm Indian, but I was not very happy identifying myself as an Indian. I just thought it wasn't cool.
>
> KAREEM: Is it cool now?
>
> KESHAV: Oh god yeah! It is. Now I always make sure I tell them I'm from India, because suddenly India's become this powerful country where everyone wants to go to, visit, and everyone wants to see it, and everyone wants to dance to Bollywood tunes, and everyone wants to know more about the country. I mean the outlook to India has changed in the last ten years. . . . Today it's on everyone's radar. . . . It's the richest ethnic community in the country [United States] today. When I'm on a plane, and people sit across, the first thing they say is, "Oh! You must be smart, either a doctor or an engineer." I just smile. What am I supposed to say? It's like an ego boost to say I'm Indian.

Over his time in the United States, Keshav has enjoyed a shift in attitudes toward Indians, one he attributes to shifting political economies, and "techno-orientalist" perceptions of Indians as model minorities, as doctors and engineers.[36] He manipulates these assumptions with a smile; he enjoys being "cool" after not having access to such social capital. In global trade, model minority queer Indians become the homonormative alternative to *trade*; a Filipino man says to me at a Trikone event, "If you like brown men, date Indians; they're successful and hardworking. Not like my people." But, as I show below, the Indian migrant remains a suspicious character, a new and incomplete citizen of gay modernity, whose commitment to homosexuality/homonormativity is always in question.

Labor comes to bear on our desirability in other ways. While living in Chicago, I would sometimes search for "Indian" on Craigslist personal ads, for research and for myself. A recurring post read:

Keep The Meter Running (Rogers Park) I want a young Indian, Middle Eastern or Latin Cab Driver to pick-me up in West Rogers Park. I am at the end of a dead end street, dark, quiet, no traffic. I get in the front seat of the cab and see you sitting there with your cock hanging out. . . . You sit back and laugh calling me names and tell me how you deserve to be worshipped by a white faggot bitch while the meter is running.

In addition to the approximations between Indian, Latino, and Middle Eastern, which I take up later, I am intrigued by the requirement for the meter to be running. Not only does he want his brown lover to be a cab driver, he wants him to be doing that labor during their encounter. In addition to white-collar jobs, then, South Asian migrants also become (un)desirable in relation to service work as well. In Ghalib Shiraz Dhalla's novel *Ode to Lata*, an Indian man worries that his white lover picked him up at an L.A. nightclub thinking he was Latino, and in the morning sun now sees his Indianness in full, and that this visibility will conflate his body with Apu, accents, and curry: "All those images of 7-Eleven salesmen and heavily accented sing-song dialects would have come flooding to his mind and he would have cringed. He'd realize his exotic passion flower was just the model for a *Simpsons* character."[37] The *Simpsons* character Apu, who incidentally moved to the United States to pursue a PhD in computer science but now runs the Kwik-E-Mart,[38] has instantiated the supermarket worker as an iconic trope through which South Asian men become legible and (un)desirable. While shows such as *The Big Bang Theory* and *Outsourced* desexualize the accented IT-guy, Keshav helps us see some of the ways that he becomes attractive, if not exactly sexy, as a homonormative partner. Most importantly, in conversation with Perez's treatise on *trade*, and the Craigslist ad in search of a taxi driver, Keshav's theorizations help us understand how labor becomes central in theorizing desire for South Asian men.

"This Country Has Indianized Me"

Keshav and I move on to talking about *Jai Ho!* parties:

I love them, I love anywhere there's Indians. Today I'm a very proud Indian. Like Bollywood movies—I never used to watch Bollywood movies in India. [Gesturing to the rack in his living room] I have this collection of Bollywood movies. I almost want to see every movie that's produced. I never used to listen to Indian music. [Now]

I go to Devon [an Indian and Pakistani enclave with restaurants and stores] more than I used to. This country has Indianized me.

Keshav's repeated interpellation *as* Indian makes him *more* Indian than he was in India. Cultural expressions that signify a certain race and ethnicity are not naturalized in bodies, but can be appropriated to make oneself politically and culturally legible, and perhaps also desirable.[39] Despite coming from Mumbai, it is in the United States that Keshav turns to Bollywood objects, the literal DVDs in his living room, to accessorize his life with something legibly Indian. Given the perpetual expectation for his body to stand in for India, he turns to Bollywood, which has spectacularly captivated the multicultural Western imagination.

KESHAV: It's an ego boost to say I'm Indian.

KAREEM: In terms of guys, is it also . . . ?

KESHAV: I was always attracted to Indian guys.

KAREEM: No, no, do guys think it's an attractive quality?

KAREEM: Yes. Ummm, I dunno. Depends which kind of guys you're approaching.

KAREEM: Do you approach guys at bars or do guys approach you?

KESHAV: I approach guys.

KAREEM: And what do they say?

KESHAV: The ones I approach, they generally, once I say I'm from India, yooooooow [sound of a plane nosediving with accompanying hand gesture], they kind of walk away. I'm kind of generalizing. Not everyone walks away. Maybe 60 percent walk away. . . . Today morning I was chatting with someone on Grindr. He pinged me [initiated the conversation]: "Blah blah blah. Where are you? Are you going to work? What's your name?" The last question he asked was, "Where are you from?" I said, "India." That was the end of the conversation [laughs]. And I've seen that, the moment I say I'm from India . . .

The negotiation of sexual capital in cyberspace is instructive in understanding how race produces erotic value; it concretizes many of the felt but unconfirmed experiences in gay bars.[40] Any user of online dating websites or phone-based hookup apps will be familiar with the exclusionary politics of gay desire, often captured in refrains such as "no fats," "no femmes," "no Blacks," "no Asians," "be clean" (STDs and STIs), "masc4masc," "looking for same," and so on. Regardless of whether his Grindr inter-locutor simply forgot to follow up or was turned off by Keshav's ethnicity, the repeated experience of being turned away based on Indian identity becomes a frame for interpreting that morning's interactions. He follows up quickly with a caveat:

> But I know guys who are into Indians. Like most of the [social club I'm part of] is into Indians. They're all into brown boys. When I say Indian I mean Indians, Pakistanis, maybe Arabics; they are sort of Indians. All the guys are into Indian guys. They tell us, "These sexy brown boys. Find me a brown boy." White guys. White guys tend to like Indians. Asians, they don't tend to like Indians as much. I run after the Asians, the Asians run after the whites, the whites run after me. Why else do you think I'm single for the last four years? Apparently I don't look Indian, I look Latin.

While he draws generalizations, Keshav remains aware of the multidirec-tional nature of desire, mapping a matrix beyond a white man–Asian boy dyad, and uses himself as an example of a brown man attracted to other men of color. My conversations with Keshav expose even more ways that Indian bodies acquire value: through (mis)recognition as Arab or Latino, or through appearing appropriately Indian by watching Bollywood. In proximity to Indian objects such as Bollywood, our accent becomes thicker, but in isolation from those signifiers we might be Latino or Arab. Keshav makes apparent the tools available to stage Indianness, but despite his expert dramaturgies of desire, he cannot be sure of the outcome; in a gay marketplace of desire, the ways that Indian bodies acquire value are multivalent and unpredictable.

"White People, They're Not Trustworthy"

Iqbal is a skinny, gregarious, working-class Pakistani guy in his mid-twenties. I met him at the *Jai Ho!* queer Bollywood nights that I orga-nized. He attended the parties even when he was sober during Ramadan, and even though he was sure that he would never meet his preferred demographic—older white men—at this party. I asked him the reasons for such rigorous commitment to the event, and he responds in his enthusi-astic nasal voice, "To meet my own people, feel connection to them. They are my people. We shall be in touch. We shall help other desi people who are not comfortable with them[selves]. There's a lot of desi people who come to *Jai Ho!* but still wanna get married." Though he is Pakistani in a primarily Indian space, he subscribes to an inclusive diasporic vision of "desi people." Iqbal offers a critique of heterosexual marriage pressure in the South Asian queer communities, even as he expresses deep attachment to the community. At first blush, his critique of gay South Asians seems harsh, but throughout our interview, he offers exceptions and alternatives to the generalizations he makes, providing for a rich theorization about race, normativity, and desire.

Iqbal prefers to date white men, especially men much older than himself. While this appears as purchase into the formulaic white man–brown boy dyad, he is astutely aware of how this desire falls into paternalistic colonial formations, and he is critical of men who assume his availability.

> IQBAL: There is only one type since I was a baby: older, mature. When you talk about gays, you think about young cute twink boy: Brad Pitt, Leo DiCaprio. I like bald men: Piers Morgan, Jason Bateman [neither is bald]. To society [that] will look really weird. People will call me: "Oh, he's a sugar daddy [chaser]. Gold digger. Money hungry." That was really weird to me. [Two years ago], I went on a date, Touché [a bar in Rogers Park catering to a bear clientele]. I didn't know about Touché [that it was a gay bar]. This was my first bar actually. I was sitting with him; he was older. There was one guy showing me money [soliciting him as a prostitute]. I got fucked up in my head. I walked out. I told the guy I was with, "I wanna go home." After that I didn't go to bars, I was really fucked up. I was feeling really awful. How [are] people going to treat me? And [when] they find out I'm gay, and [like] being with older guys? [They will ask,] "Why you have to go double your age?"
>
> KAREEM: So you're only attracted to white guys?
>
> IQBAL: Physically I find them very good looking, but emotionally, and so many other levels, I would prefer desi, who understand me, who I don't have to explain about Eid, Ramazan, you know, stuff like that.

Iqbal worries how people will interpret his deeply sedimented desire for older men as having ulterior motives; even consensual intergenerational relationships are burdened with moral regulation.[41] This excerpt describes his attraction to white men, although he elsewhere mentions lusting after hairy, older Arab men in the Middle East where he grew up. Iqbal also wishes he didn't have to explain himself to white men, giving specific examples of Muslim rituals and holidays that are so commonly misconstrued in the United States. Additionally, though he loves older white men, he is aware that being seen in public with them places him squarely in the paternalistic dyad, rendering him a sex worker.

It is not uncommon for my friends, such as Arun below, to be approached as sex workers, as *trade*.

> Every guy I've hooked up with or dated is convinced I'm an escort because I'm not a doctor or engineer. How else am I going to afford the jeans I have on or the cocktail in my hand? That happens a lot. I'm pretty much convinced I'm the only person that happens to. I don't know what it is. I've been verbally told that several thousands of times.

Arun imagines he is the exception, but this has happened to me and my friends before. I was with three South Asian men at a bar in Chicago known for picking up *trade*; when we visited the restroom over the course of the night, a white man approached each one of us, "How much?" How quickly, and far, we fall from the homonormative ideal when we aren't the doctor or engineer, when we are seen with older white men, or when we are in a *trade* bar. On the right stage, we just as easily become the sexually available brown boy of white men's "porno-tropical fantasies."[42]

Intrigued by Iqbal's complex theorizations around dating and desiring white men, I asked:

KAREEM: Have you thought about these questions [of race and desire] before? Is this something new to you?
IQBAL: A lot of white guys I went on a date with, they ask me the same questions: "Your family accept you?" etc.

He links my ethnographic curiosity with the skeptical interrogations of white men he meets. Gregory Mitchell describes how some gay sex tourists arrive in Brazil desiring sex with straight men, having read scholarly publications about Latin American models of masculinity and sexuality.[43] Bobby Benedicto too explains how white gays approach Filipino men with generalizations that suggest an expert knowledge on Filipinos.[44] Dating white men can feel like being an ethnographic subject; not only is there a sense of curiosity in their approach that renders you an other, but critical and anecdotal research also informs that approach.

Implicit in white men (or ethnographers) repeatedly asking Iqbal the question "Does your family accept you?" is the underlying assumption that South Asian families are less likely to accept their queer kin. C. Winter Han notes that for his gay Asian interlocutors, explicitly coming out to family was not a priority, and they were eager to dispel assumptions that white men have of Asian families as more homophobic.[45] We must refuse the narrative that communities of color are exceptionally homophobic, and recognize that homophobia and transphobia are endemic to Americans' obsession with capitalist reproduction, and that historical racisms engender these kinds of phobias in minority communities.[46] As Nayan Shah explains so succinctly: "The urge to make gender and sexual diversity invisible in their own communities is a survival strategy to deflect decades of white suspicion and state persecution that insisted that Asian, black and Latino communities were the source of sexual perversity."[47]

In the recurring refusal to allow the South Asian Lesbian and Gay Association (SALGA) to participate in New York City's India Day Parade, we see a manifestation of the exclusionary logics minoritarian subjects engage in to earn incorporation into the state.[48] On the one hand, rightwing Hindutva conservatism disavowed homosexuality as properly Indian (in addition to disavowing Muslim nations like Pakistan and Bangladesh in the umbrella of "South Asia"), and on the other, Americanness had to be displayed through heteronormativity. The model minority myth may make gay South Asians attractive homonormative partners who will have secure incomes and cosmopolitan mobility. However, those very model minority expectations make desiness and queerness incompatible too.

The heteronormativity expected of brown men by their communities, specifically "arranged marriage pressure," is perceived as more oppressive than heteronormativity in white families, rendering brown men undesirable lovers. Iqbal maps out the consequences of arranged marriage pressure, but as always, offers insightful exceptions that never lets white men off the hook.

> Some people really wanna date [someone] who is comfortable with their life. If they see any brown guy, desi guy, they wanna date, they think [he is] gonna dump him [because the desi guy will eventually get married]. I met [a] few [white guys who think like this]. I met one white guy, he was dating a desi guy, living [together for] four

years. [Due to parental pressure the desi guy] went and got married. That's why white people, *they're not trustworthy*. That was in his head, [an] image about brown people. I was thinking, "Why he did that?" Those desis, I really kind of, I don't feel bad [for] them. I hate them and I feel bad for them too. . . . One of my friends, white guy, he's gay, he got married. Day before his wedding he called a gay guy, drunk call. He still got married, which I find really weird. . . . See, other people, Ravi and Rakesh, they both look normal. They've been together for some time. Even for girls too now. Deepa and her girlfriend. And Promita and Sulekha.

As Iqbal argues, when South Asian men with same-gender desires marry women, it gives white men the impression that we will all do the same—not only are our communities assumed to be more heteronormative, but we are also perceived as not strong enough to stand up to heteronormativity, too acquiescent, too traditional. Many white men I've met have a story about a gay South Asian friend, or coworker, or former lover who "gave in to the whole arranged marriage pressure thing." One such story makes us all undatable, untrustworthy. South Asian men too have similar stories, but they don't dismiss other South Asian men outright. Iqbal also gives us an example of a white man who, in a drunken spell on the eve of his wedding to a woman, reaches out to a gay trick for one more encounter. He goes on to list a number of gay South Asian couples, calling out the reductionist logic of white men who, burned by one South Asian man, deem us all undatable.

Iqbal says, "White people, they're not trustworthy." In the context of his comments, it seems like he wanted say that white people do not trust South Asians. However, I keep the language as he said it because I think this slippage captures some of the suspicions he has of white men, having dated so many. Iqbal's expansive knowledge about white men deserves revisiting what I said before: sometimes, dating white men is like being an ethnographer.

"He Smelled of Chicken Biryani, with Onion"

Manolo Guzman insightfully posits that "an exclusive focus on interracial erotic relations in a discussion of sexualized racial ideals prevents us from acknowledging one most important fact: *intraracial erotic relations are, no matter how unremarkable, also racially marked."*[49] Representations of gay intra-Asian desire, as Cynthia Wu argues, offer an opportunity to reckon with "Asian America's internal factions" as they disavow and collude with a variety of imperial projects.[50] Indeed, Indian migrants to the United States might already be arriving with gendered archetypes that are based on caste, region, and religion, epistemes that inform and color their experience of multiracial Chicago.

In spite of Iqbal's obsession with white men, he describes a date with a South Asian guy, "He smelled [of] chicken biryani. With onion! I didn't want to say anything about it. I picked him up from Devon [the Indian-Pakistani neighborhood] and he was just coming from eating. I had to give him a chewing gum or something." Iqbal reminds us that race is made and multiplied through the senses and discourses attached to them, and is not merely intrinsic to the body. This man's Indianness was amplified by biriyani and onion, and the Devon neighborhood, these excesses drawing him even further away from Iqbal's white ideal.[51] As Anita Mannur argues, culinary idioms are often used to stage Indianness,[52] and like the aural accent, olfactory, and gustatory markers of Indianness too render our bodies (un)desirable. The use of food to articulate racialized gay desire is not uncommon, as we hear in terms such as "bean queen," "sticky rice," and of course, "curry queen."

Iqbal helps us understand how the performance of race, the intensification of race through olfactory accents, shapes how South Asian bodies become (un)desirable, even to each other. But again, he slips between his generalizations playful exceptions that offer a more complex vision of intradesi desires.

> That's how I met Sahir. He was living right there, and he was coming into Bites [the fast-food chain where Iqbal worked]. That story is exciting! That Bites was in Boystown. Used to be open until 5:00 a.m. in the morning, so I see all the crazy drunk people going there. I didn't know what was going on there at all. Until my first three months I didn't know it was Boystown. When I start working at night, I saw a couple guys kissing. One of my straight friends [told me] Boystown [has] so many clubs. Then one of the coworkers, I asked him, "Where is Boystown?" and [he answered], "*This* is Boystown." Now I wonder why my straight friends was telling me about Boystown! Sahir used to come [to Bites], but we never talk there. [He] was kind of a character. Whenever he comes [I wondered]

"Who's he?" First *Jai Ho!*, I saw him there. Sahir looks American-ized. He didn't look like a FOB ["fresh off the boat"], and that time I didn't want to talk to a FOB. Maybe Americanized desi, they will be better to talk to. I was like, "Hey you remember me? I used to make sandwiches."

Iqbal learns that his workplace is located in the center of a commercial gay neighborhood from his immigrant Pakistani co-workers. Given the unexpected source of this information, Iqbal playfully "wonders" about *their* sexual knowledge and proclivities. And so while he deems the "Americanized" Sahir a more valuable gay interlocutor, he does not script out the possibility of his coworkers' queer tendencies, desires, and knowledge.

Iqbal repeatedly derides FOBs—"fresh off the boat"—throughout our interview, even as he seeks out a South Asian queer community, and even as his own accent and English grammar evidence his FOB identity. In her study of South Asian teenagers in suburban California, Shalini Shankar develops FOB not only as a nuanced vernacular category that describes unassimilated immigrants, but also as a mode of performance that, like ishtyle, connotes desiness without a cool or hip sensibility.[53] Notions of FOB-ness function inside of South Asian communities to regulate performances of Indianness in ways that differentiate class and cultural capital. Friends have claimed that they've stopped going to desi parties because of the "FOB crowd," and others—queer and straight alike—refuse to date "FOBs" even if they themselves are migrants. In diaspora, accents, that is, cultural enactments of difference across a range of senses, differentiate South Asians not only from white people, but from each other as well.

"Terrorist Cock Is Really Hot"

Prior to the proliferation of independently filmed pornography featuring South Asian men circulated via OnlyFans, Twitter, and unauthorized captures of webcam exchanges, I struggled to find commercial gay pornography that featured desi men. Little did I realize that a South Asian porn performer lived in Chicago. Nirmalpal Sachdev, who has performed in two films, was the general manager of Steamworks Bathhouse in Chicago. He was easygoing and chatty, but our conversation was cut very short by a plumbing emergency at the bathhouse. Luckily, Nirmalpal had given a dynamic interview to Fausto Fernos and Marc Felion, hosts of the *Feast of Fun* podcast. They introduce him as a "hunky Indian man," but also note that he acted in *Arabesque*, Middle Eastern–themed porn, styled with harem pants, unbuttoned vests, turbans, and Persian rugs. In an extended scene that transitions from orgy to couples, Nirmalpal plays a carpet salesman who both fucks and gets fucked. The podcast hosts ask how he identifies given the film's racialized premise; he says, "Brownie-hound, that's what I call guys who like anybody below the equator. . . . I'm a brownie." His consumable, even edible, body comes to stand in for a host of other races, an entire hemisphere. Nirmalpal's theorization of these racial conflations capture what Anne McClintock describes as the porno-tropical fantasies of white imaginations that regard nonwhite, non-Western men as "libidinously eroticized."[54] When the conversation focuses on his ability to suck his own dick, he makes a predicable quip about yoga coming naturally to him.

Nirmalpal continues, "I fulfill the fantasy for anything South East over there. Terrorist right now is really in." Fausto quips, "Terrorist cock is hot!" and presses the question of identity, "You're seen as an exotic man. But culturally you're American." Marc interjects, "Being a person from there is difficult right now." Between them, they gesture to the diasporic conundrum of living in the "9/11 everyday"[55] while looking like you're "from there." Nirmalpal follows up by talking about being self-conscious during airport travel just after 9/11, and also about having a goatee. Beards, like turbans, worn for ritual and fashion alike, potentially render brown bodies too terrorist-y. He continues, "The terrorist is really in right now. A lot of guys hope that I'm Iraqi or from that area." Importantly he adds, "I have an American accent, which diffuses the situation," reminding us that we use performance to regulate the intensity of our racialization.

For these three brown men—Fausto and Marc are Latino—making grotesque jokes about "terrorist cock" is a way of laughing at white fantasies for their "libidinously exotic" bodies. The conversation moves in and out of politically incorrect humor about the desirability of terrorist cock and hyperflexible yogis, as well as more earnest theorizations about non-Western homoeroticism, racial identification, and post-9/11 surveillance. Nirmalpal is quite aware of the capacity of his body to read as terrorist and be subject to Islamophobic surveillance. Racial difference—Persian, Arab, South Asian, North African—is consolidated into a surveillable "Muslim" category,[56] it is through such conflations that Nirmalpal can be both the (Muslim) terrorist cock and the self-sucking (Hindu) yogi. Porno-tropical and Orientalist fantasies (of the simultaneously hypersexual and repressed Muslim) and militarized projects of racial surveillance are mutually implicated.[57] Jasbir Puar has argued that presumed backwardness of Muslim sexuality—including knowledge produced by political scientists and psychologists working for the state, as well as "a centuries long Orientalist tradition"—is used to justify profiling, detaining, torturing, and killing Muslims (or those presumed to be so), as well as invading and bombing the Muslim world.[58]

The terms under which we become (un)desirable as brown folks in gay US spaces are sometimes predicated on militarized logics that have been used to justify torture. A white man once messaged me on Grindr, "Are you Pakistani? I'm very good at differentiating. I used to be stationed in Afghanistan." The recognition techniques of global warfare translate into the discerning tastes of online cruising. Though he doesn't expand on its implications, Nirmalpal says, "A lot of guys hope I'm Iraqi," suggesting that a fantasy in which raced bodies stand in for nation, warfare, rescue, and power can play out. But as Juana María Rodríguez offers us, "In fantasy we can rewrite scripts of sexualized objectification, subjection, and racialized violence."[59] In fact, Mehammad Mack argues of French *beur* porn that features hypermasculine, working-class Arab men from the banlieue, the genre provides performers opportunities to redefine stereotypes of the "macho delinquent" while inhabiting them.[60] But while Nirmalpal jokes that "terrorist is really hot right now," I haven't found any commercial gay porn that actually plays out these fantasies, and I'm wary of building an internet search history that fishes too hard with these words. And sadly, the several times I've been called "terrorist" at gay bars and on gay networking sites have certainly not been flirtatious.

"You're Not Mexican?"

When Moses, my co-organizer for *Jai Ho!* parties, and I were initially building our friendship, we would play the game of finding and befriending other desis in the gay bar. This was not an easy game, as desi men often refused to make eye contact with us.[61] We would approach them anyways. When desis are alone in a club, we can "modulate" our racial ambiguity;[62] but accents thicken in the presence of others, and you might lose erotic currency hanging out with us. This conundrum primarily arises in predominantly white spaces where we're worried about sticking out. Kaushik finds an alternative means of "fitting in" within the visual/racial economy of Chicago's bars.

I've been to the clubs a couple of time with my friends I work with. Roscoes, Hydrate, Scarlet, Circuit for Latino night [these are all bars in Boystown]. For Circuit [where they hosted Latino nights twice a week] it was different, so obviously I fit in perfectly, all the time. They come up to me all the time, and they're like, "You're not Mexican?"

By frequenting a predominantly Latino night in Boystown, Kaushik deploys his racial ambiguity in order to feel less out of place.

These Latinx–South Asian proximities are recurrent in *Ode to Lata*, in the Craigslist personal, in Keshav's story, and in Kaushik's. Vikram Sohan, the only other gay Indian commercial porn actor I've found, acquires roles through Latino castings since his Indianness is so unintelligible in the ethno-visual landscape of the industry.[63] The physical proximity of South Asian and Latinx neighborhoods on the North Side of Chicago enable other intimacies: in Rogers Park, a primarily Mexican Catholic church faces the Hare Krishna Temple; on Devon Street, Latino workers at restaurants and grocery stores banter in broken Hindi and Gujarati with Indian bosses; a Mexican guy I hooked up flirted with me saying, "I know one Pakistani guy. He was my boss."

So much of the literature on racialized desire has privileged the desiring gaze of white men. Moreover, the internet is ablaze with articles about sexual racism and unrequited desire from white men. While we can maintain that people of color can harbor colonial epistemes, it is imperative that we conceptualize desiring economies without centering white people in order to understand how we collude with white supremacy; translate internal hierarchies (such as classism, casteism, communalism) into racism; compare the ways that white supremacy works to police our various communities; and share liberatory resources.[64] What other, more dynamic (but still historically situated) axes of desire come to bear when we center queer interracial intimacies?

Vishnu is an India-based researcher and is often invited on visiting lectureships to the United States. Given his regular move between the subcontinent and the Americas, he has an especially insightful perspective on the various and shifting axes through which he desires and is desired. Unfazed by the irony of academia, he speaks earnestly about bodies, flirtation, and dating.

VISHNU: Darker-skin men I've always found more attractive than lighter-skin men.

KAREEM: And is there a specific type of man that's drawn to you?

VISHNU: Well, most of the men I dated in the US were Latinos, largely because of my own attraction to Latinos. I mainly would be in Latino bars, or even where I was living [in Southern California] was predominantly Latino, Mexican. . . . I think that Latino men were probably attracted to me because I was not as macho as them, even in my own mind. I don't know—maybe I was characterized as a particular type that they found attractive? So I don't know. It's not something I have maybe analyzed about what *they* found interesting in me.

KAREEM: What did they think about you being Indian? Had they had the cultural exposure to . . .

VISHNU: No, not at all. Interestingly, there was no cultural interest in the sense of "Where do you come from?" The commonality we shared was the fact that we were both immigrants. There were a couple of [undocumented] immigrants from Mexico as well. It was not someone who was in a PhD program or anything; one of them was a construction worker who just happened to live on the same street as I am, had just come from Mexico. . . . The fact that I was culturally different was a source of novelty, I guess [he thought], "He's not American." But a lot of the Hispanics who were there also thought of themselves as American [and] I was the foreigner. [They'd say,] "You have a funny accent."

Vishnu ambivalently maps citizenship, migration, documentation, race, skin color, class, geography, masculinity, and accent—all of these imbricated in each other—as axes of desire and compatibility that came to bear on his relationships. He helps us imagine other axes of power in theorizing desire, especially in "diaspora space" where South Asian migrants encounter other diasporas,[65] where intersecting imperialisms force black, brown, and indigenous people into physical and discursive proximities.[66] Vishnu's intimacies with working-class Latinx men could point us to the (emotional and geographic) flexibility required of him by a global academic industrial complex, the militarization of the US border that renders his undocumented partner precarious and his visas temporary, and histories of gentrification, displacement, racism, and migration that produce Latino neighborhoods and Latino gay bars. But in addition to structural conditions that produce these brown-brown intimacies is the will to thrive, play, and find pleasure *through* intimacy. Centering and obsessing over a brown-white axis, we obscure other positionalities, histories, and aesthetics that bear on inter- and intraracial desire, and tropes that are also playful resources for flirtations, friendship, and fucking.

Conditions of desire shift as we move across national borders. Vishnu had moved from India to Southern California for graduate school, and I asked him about his social life in the United States:

> I was in an environment which was not so caste or class bound [referring to an earlier mention of casteism in Chennai, where he grew up in an elite Brahmin household]. You realize it is class bound when you start working. In graduate school, class distinctions are not so great. We were all poor, working in the library, washing dishes, putting muffin batter into those trays. . . . I've discovered when I've come back here [Bangalore], it's kind of coming back ["it" refers to his class and caste positions]. There was this really cute auto guy [auto-rickshaw driver]. I was really attracted to him [but] I didn't proposition. I didn't. I was afraid. I was afraid of the class difference between the two of us.

Migration produces shifts in sociopolitical position that allow Vishnu to date working-class Latino men in the United States, while a return to India "brings back" entrenched regulations of interclass and intercaste intimacy.[67] Like Iqbal, who desired Arab daddies in the Middle East and prefers white men in the United States, Vishnu's desire too transforms as he travels back and forth for work. Identity and desire shift across national borders, and recalibrate according to the sociopolitical contours of our locations—race, caste, and class are never the same, but they accent understandings of each other as migrants move across geopolitical borders.

"But You Look White"

At Bucks, a dive situated on the commercial strip of Halsted in Boystown, my friend Suraj and I are having a quiet weekday drink at the bar. A very sexy, tanned, older white guy comes up to the bar and orders a drink without acknowledging the bartender; his eyes are fixated on Suraj. This man is drunk, horny, and clearly into Suraj. Suraj likes older white men; they are also his primary clients as an art dealer, so he handles them with a rehearsed smoothness. I nudge him to initiate a conversation. The man quickly places his hand on Suraj's thigh, and leans in to whisper loudly.

WHITE MAN: Can we get out of here? How do we make *him* [referring to me] go away?

Suraj ignores his shameless advances.

SURAJ: What's your background?

Asian Americans are repeatedly asked to account for national and ethnic origins in social spaces, particularly with the seemingly benign: "Where are you from?" White people's ethnic origins regularly go unmarked. Rephrasing the question to "What's your background?" Suraj offers an alternative open-ended prompt that still requires the man to mark his whiteness.

WHITE MAN: You mean like my professional background? My education?
SURAJ: No, like what's your ethnic background?
WHITE MAN: Guess!
SURAJ: Italian? German? Polish?
WHITE MAN: Good old Irish Catholic boy.

He says "boy" despite his age, invoking an archetype of virility and perpetual innocence.[68]

WHITE MAN: What about you?
SURAJ: I'm Indian. [Suraj gestures to me; I'm sitting silently with a sour look.] We're both Indian.
WHITE MAN: But you look white.

I realize I'm stating the obvious, but South Asians are phenotypically diverse. Some of us are very light skinned and can pass as white; Suraj does, I don't. More importantly, South Asians in the United States have a complicated historical relationship to whiteness. Bhagat Singh Thind, an Indian man who migrated to the United States to pursue a university education and who fought for the United States during World War I, lost his case for citizenship in the Supreme Court in 1923. Thind's argument for citizenship was premised on being, as a dominant-caste Hindu North Indian, Caucasian.

SURAJ: Well I'm Indian.

WHITE MAN: [The man's tone takes a turn and his lip snarls in sarcasm.] So you can charm a snake with a flute? [He puts his hands to his mouth miming a flute to mock us. Suraj remains unfazed.]

SURAJ: Yes, I can.

WHITE MAN: Well, where's your magic carpet?

SURAJ: I valeted it at Sidetrack [a bar two blocks away].

Suraj closes the conversation by turning away from him to talk to me.

Even though Suraj passes as white, revealing his Indian ethnicity suddenly challenges the good old Irish Catholic boy's unmarked desire for him. Similarly, when call center workers with well-trained accents reveal that they are in India, that they are not white, they suddenly encounter vitriolic racism from previously patient customers.[69] The "fact" of our Indianness produces an accent where it is not, turning us into an ornamental carpet-riding cartoon, a mythic character among a thousand tales.

"Touch Me Like Border Patrol"

When Iqbal and I wrap up our interview, he says, "I need to ask your advice about something." He tells me about his challenges as an undocumented immigrant, how a woman who had agreed to marry him for papers fled with his money. When we run into each other in a gay bar in Boston seven years later, in 2018, he is married to a preppy white man, a former military officer. He is all set with his papers now. Iqbal's white fetish is bound up not only in psychic and bodily desire, but in material consequences too; it has the capacity to grant him citizenship.

White bodies are not merely representational, but performative. They have the power to do things that change us, change how we see and feel about ourselves, how we value our own lives. Sandip Roy writes:

As the only brown-skinned man in a [Midwest] bar, I became acutely conscious of the color of my skin, in a way I had never been in India. No one had to throw eggs at me. No one had to hurl racial slurs at me. I would just see those eyes look at me and through me and away from me, and I would feel put in my place. What I needed most at that time was attention. If any white man had come along then and offered it to me, I doubt that I could have refused him. All I wanted was to see myself reflected in his eyes as attractive, as desirable. He would make my long journey to America seem worthwhile.[70]

The trope of being desired by, and even having sex with, a white person is a common plot point in diasporic writing and film. But what Roy gestures to is the unmarked capacity for white men's desire to perform, to do, to "make my long journey to America seem worthwhile."

Dwight McBride reminds us that "whiteness is a valuable commodity in a fundamentally racist culture."[71] Such a critique of whiteness is important in holding accountable those white men who "perceive their fascination with our Otherness as a confirmation of their progressive politics."[72] Just as our bodies performatively conjure carpets, cabs, curry, and call centers, white bodies too rely on their iterative invocations of meaning and history to stir desire. In their poem "Tryna," diasporic artist Alok Vaid-Menon details their challenge to decolonize their desire for white men. They don't perform this poem any more, but hearing them perform this poem at an open mic in Bangalore, I was taken by such an excellent articulation of white men's performativity:

Touch me like border patrol
Grant me your amnesty,
Fuck me like patriotism.
Embrace me so I can feel American again.

Alok implicates the white body itself as the grantor of naturalization in erotic, sexual, and affective transactions within quotidian contexts.[73]

Susan Koshy's theory of "sexual naturalization" explains that intimacy with white men has been central to securing citizenship and capital—both paper and cultural—for Asian immigrant women. Queer migrants are sometimes granted legal citizenship via fickle asylum processes that position the United States as an exceptional and benevolent nation.[74] But, following Armando García, can we imagine more robustly the role of desire, affect, and creativity in resisting "the urge to reduce human life to the *legal* parameters of citizenship"?[75] In ugly ways, desire from white men can and does grant citizenship. For South Asian migrants in the United States, desiring and enjoying desire from white men is not simply a vestige of British colonialism embedded in the racial psyche, but an ongoing negotiation of belonging amid overlapping imperialisms and tightening national borders.

"I Don't Smell Like Curry All the Time, but It's Been Known to Happen"

My friends theorize the multiple ways their race and racial performance, as well as other axes of identity, come to bear in romantic and erotic transactions. Certain kinds of desiness are literally less palatable than others because they smell of biryani. At other times, Indian bodies are desirable because they can pass for other ethnicities. Indianness becomes desirable alongside India's rise on the global economic and military stage. At the same time, the Indian body comes to be read as improperly gay because of assumptions of South Asian heteronormativity. Desiness intensifies in proximity to older white men, other South Asians, Indo/Pak neighborhoods, or Bollywood objects. The wish for brown bodies to be Iraqi or Pakistani reminds us that erotic desires are informed by militaristic gazes. Whether my interlocutors subscribe to a monogamous homonormative model of gay couple-hood, or whether they just want to get laid, through repeated encounters they have become aware of how fictions of race and culture land on their bodies and function as sexual capital. They calibrate how to bring their body into fields of desire—bars, nightclubs, mobile dating apps, cruising scenarios, gay neighborhoods—knowing that the multivalent performativity of brown bodies does not always guarantee the pleasures of gay nightlife. To study gay South Asian desire then requires us not only to locate bodies in histories and discourses of racialization and colonialism, but also to pay attention to performance, to the ways that histories are activated in inter- and intraracial embodied encounters, how they are theorized through oral performance, and how they are intensified and aestheticized on and around brown bodies.

Toronto-based queer South Asian outreach organization Dosti launched an online campaign to combat stigma in inter- and intraracial desire titled "Brown N Proud." Dosti commissioned a set of graphics styled as Grindr profiles, featuring a variety of brown men. All have marked their ethnicity as "South Asian," but each articulates desires and identities differently: "You gotta love hair because I got lots," "Bangladeshi bear," "#imnotracistbut #yesyouare," and "brown boy who loves his Bollywood Divas." This visual campaign underscores the variety of attributes that brown men are both fetishized and reviled for, attributes we often feel shame about. It makes sexy so much of the ishtyle we are embarrassed to embody. I conclude this chapter with "Brown N Proud" because these imagined unapologetic performances of ishtyle undo the cultural shame of being accented and diversify desi desirability. As Kantara Souffrant argues, art-making provides an opportunity to circumvent diasporic pedagogies of quotidian respectability and rehearse tools to become shameless.[76] Placing these tastes and styles in the erotic milieu of a dating app, "Brown N Proud" acknowledges and expands racial capital in the "marketplace of gay desire," making both curry and antiracism sexy.

FOUR

Slumdogs and Big Chicks
Unsettling Orientations at Jai Ho!

Uptown Chicks

"Predictably, the expatriate Indian's gay revolution has begun from San Francisco," writes an *India Today* journalist in 1989,[1] describing the 1986 founding of Trikone, based in the Bay Area, by IIT-Bombay graduate Arvind Kumar, and the launch of a magazine that circulated to a global readership. Trikone's longevity—it runs till date—renders it an originary site of queer South Asian organizing across North America, followed by Khush Toronto (1987–98), SALGA NYC (1991), and Boston MASALA (1994), as well as the publishing of *Shamakami* newsletter (1990–97) for queer South Asian women. These organizations, and many like them, have published widely circulated newsletters, offered sexual health education, done outreach to parents, launched emergency hotlines, and held festivals, potlucks, and parties. North America's queer South Asian diaspora story, and even narratives of India's queer activism, often begin with Arvind Kumar, the savvy IT guy who mobilized queer organizing.[2] However, queer South Asian women's magazine *Anamika* had started publishing in 1985. Also, in 1986, poet Ifti Nasim, with his friend Viru Joshi, created the organization Sangat in Chicago.[3] Nasim arrived in the United States as a law student, a career he quickly abandoned after his father's passing two years later. Nasim's story isn't told as often, perhaps because it doesn't align as well with the migrant narrative; unlike Hindu, Indian, IT guy Arvind Kumar, the Muslim, Pakistani, poet, and car salesman Nasim does not fit the model minority narrative as well. Add to this the coastal bias of queer history, the story of Chicago's many queer but now defunct organizations—Sangat, Khuli Zabaan, Rangeela, SALGA, akabaka—is hardly archived, let alone written.

In 2009, I emailed Michelle Fire, owner of Big Chicks, a gay bar in the Uptown neighborhood of Chicago, to ask if Trikone-Chicago, a novice South Asian organization created in the wake of the above organizations, could host a queer Bollywood-themed fundraiser there. Uptown is a racially diverse though economically depressed neighborhood featuring Ghanaian restaurants and shops, a handful of gay bars, and Asian-owned beauty and fashion supply stores that many drag queens shop at. Lingering art deco edifices punctuate the area as memories of its entertainment district days. Post–World War II depression sent wealthy residents to the suburbs, and a wide range of migrants as well as mental health patients relocated by the state moved into old buildings refurbished into single-room occupancies.[4] Gentrification is well under way in Uptown, evidenced by renovated train platforms, Orientalist archways welcoming you to Little Vietnam, a humungous Target store, and a ubiquitous police presence. Michelle primarily runs Tweet, the brunch place adjoining Big Chicks, which she opened at the request of increasingly upwardly mobile Uptown residents, a condition for their support during a dispute to keep the bar open. If Uptown was to thrive as a gay neighborhood, it needed a brunch place. Michelle eagerly passed my information along to the bar manager, Hal, a flirty but no-nonsense bear who gave us a Thursday night to host our first party in June 2009.

I initially suggested the party to Trikone members, "In New York, Sholay Events has the *Desilicious* parties! We should do a queer Bollywood night here." We were but a handful at the time, and so I was delegated the task of producing this event. "We should have drag queens!" I couldn't keep my big mouth shut. With no drag queens to be found, I became one (see preface). Even though we had no nightlife industry experience, and despite a limited queer South Asian attendance, the party did well. Curious and supportive straight desis, nondesi queer friends, closeted and married desis from the suburbs, desi queers new to the city, and regular Big Chicks clientele (otters, bears, chasers, neighborhood queers) filled gaps in the dance floor that Trikone's small contingent couldn't. Queer desis came from Wisconsin, Michigan, Indiana, and Ohio to dance with us. Three parties later, Hal offered us a Friday night, and a year later, *Jai Ho!* was even awarded "Best Sporadic Gay Dance Party" by the *Chicago Reader*.

Michelle, a tall and gregarious white woman with short silver curls, popped in early before the first party started—I hadn't met her in person yet, but she was as vibrant and warm as she sounded on the phone. She expressed genuine delight that we were here: "You know, this is where Sangat used to meet! Ifti, in all his regalia, would hold court in that corner"—she pointed to the industrial fan that I liked to stand in front of and beyoncé—"and call everyone a bitch!" Ifti Nasim was a long-standing, and sometimes controversial, figure in the South Asian community. Ifti would eventually become my queer auntie, shepherding me past *dosa* houses and Indo-Pak grocery stores of Devon Street, pointing out which cab drivers and storeowners he had "had." Ifti founded Sangat in the mid-1980s, a social and support group for queer desi men that grew alongside Khuli Zabaan, a group for South Asian queer women. Prior to dissolving, Sangat moved its meetings from a mile up the street in Ifti's tiny, pink-walled living room in Edgewater to Big Chicks in Uptown. It is no coincidence that Ifti lived so close to Big Chicks—Edgewater and its neighboring Rogers Park feature high densities of Indian and Pakistani residents and businesses. To my surprise, Michelle's welcome to Trikone was premised on a South Asian legacy in the space. But the subcontinent looms even larger in the history of the bar.

Over Ethiopian dinner in Edgewater, Michelle explained the origin of the bar's name.

> I opened Big Chicks in 1986, and it's interesting that you're doing this [research] because the genesis of the name comes from India. I was travelling in Mumbai, this is twenty-six, twenty-seven years ago, I was younger, and there was this group of men across the road, pointing at me, yelling at me, "Big chick, big chick!" And they came across the road and they said, "Where are you from?" and I said, "I'm from America." And they said, "Are all women as big as youuuu?" . . . It's a moment in my life. This is a strange and life-changing moment, so surreal to be there, people shouting "big chick" at me.

This geographic specificity is not explicit in the bar's name, but Michelle's regular retelling of this origin story makes clear that a brown-white encounter haunts the space, and Indian men's fascination with white femininity shapes the bar, regardless of their inability to cross borders with the big chick.[5]

Whether in the name of the bar, or the lore of Ifti holding court in gilded regalia, when Trikone hosts *Jai Ho!* at Big Chicks, our bodies are haunted by and interpreted through phantasms that preceded us. Karen Shimakawa writes, "Asian Americans never walk onto an empty stage . . .

[T]hat space is always already densely populated with phantasms of ori-entalness through and against which an Asian American performer must struggle to be seen."[6] In addition to Michelle's story is the stage of gay nightlife—music, decor, dance, entertainment, publicity—where lingering racial phantasms teach others how to see and desire brown bodies in the space. Following Sara Ahmed, I am interested in how we are repeatedly turned toward particular aesthetics and choreographies as sites of desire, and how those repetitive emplacements sediment into orientations.[7] Gay bars largely turn patrons toward white aesthetics—Bowie's punk, Folies' sequins, Broadway's grandeur—that look away from our diasporic and postcolonial homes. To enter commercial gay spaces is, for many people of color, "to live out a politics of disorientation, of never settling or being fully settled, might involve never feeling fully quite at home, of having arrived, in terms of one's embodied identity or location."[8] The term "unset-tling," Purnima Mankekar suggests, captures both geographic *and* affec-tive unease of globalization, migration, and displacement.[9] In this chapter, I am interested in the capacity for ishtyle to unsettle whiteness and its accompanying Orientalism in gay nightlife, as well as ishtyle's ability to emplace migrant subjects, not as settlers with possessive attachment to land but as performers who have permission to feel at home every once in a while, acknowledging too that home, "a four-letter word," is an ambiva-lent place or idea.[10]

The "staging of urban nightlife"[11] traffics in racial aesthetics, accenting spaces with orientalia to appear more blingy, exotic, fabulous, cosmopoli-tan, and sexy.[12] Like Frantz Fanon, who "can't go to the movies without encountering myself,"[13] South Asians constantly run into desiness in gay nightclubs: Ganesh tattoos on the backs and forearms of shirtless white men, white drag queens doing the eight-armed goddess gimmick, saris draped as decor, and music that samples Bollywood and Bhangra. But the stage, José Esteban Muñoz reminds us, is a site of possibility, an orienting device toward utopian aesthetics, to elsewheres.[14] When we host *Jai Ho!* we manipulate these aesthetics and media to create the stage on which to show off our bodies through and against these phantasms, unsettling stag-nant orientations toward brown bodies. *Jai Ho!* is curated to accent the night with Indian visuals, sounds, and choreographies that draw the ire of some bar patrons, and ishtyle of others. These purposeful accentings—music, visuals, fliers, performances—induce improvised choreographies that engender alternative possibilities for staging queer erotics and beauty at the club. This chapter documents how Chicago's commercial gay bars engender orientations in their spaces through promotion, decor, music, and entertainment, and points to the unsettling phantasms that render Asians abject in gay bar spaces. In parallel, I describe how *Jai Ho!* recalibrates these orienting devices. These tactics do not necessarily result in a deep sense of emplacement even if the club momentarily feels like home; rather these curatorial and improvisatory moves unmoor aesthetic orientations to make the night a little more capacious. This chapter follows the trajectory of the night, beginning with event promotion and the journey to the club, arriving at the club's interior, soundscape, and show, and staying on the dance floor with the die-hard partygoers till the lights come up.

False Advertising

Gautham and I became fast friends after I messaged him on Adam4Adam telling him I liked his profile, in which he called out others' race-based sexual preferences as racist. We found we had more in common too: a deep appreciation for the gay brilliance of Kylie Minogue and shared anxieties as first-year graduate students. Gautham, having prior connections to Chicago, invited me to my first Trikone meeting. We quickly grew fond of going out in Boystown, Chicago's primary commercial gay neighborhood, choosing as our favorite bars Scarlet, for its mid-twenties hip clientele, and Berlin, for its hipster seedy appeal. Boystown bars advertise upcoming events on their exteriors: white and light-skinned muscled go-go boys with backward hats and tongues lasciviously teasing passers-by, twinky boys frolicking in bubbles and foam, sequined drag queens with exaggerated winks, all inviting you in to different classed, sexual, and gendered experiences, a "disneyfied" landscape satisfying multiple tastes for paying customers.[15]

In June 2009, Gautham and I spotted a sign outside Berlin, a poster featuring a psychedelic Taj Mahal silhouette, announcing a party titled *Bollyweird*. We were so excited that there would be a desi night in Boystown, at our favorite club. Berlin, located underneath the Belmont Red and Purple Line El Station, several blocks from the Halsted strip, has a less "commercial" vibe from the slick bars of Boystown. We arrived at *Bollyweird* anticipating a room full of desis and speakers pulsing with Shankar, Ehsan, and Loy—there was neither. The strong pour at Berlin gave us liquid courage to climb up to the booth and relentlessly pester the DJ: "Hey it's Bollywood night. Why aren't you playing Bollywood?" She was confused, but took our enthusiasm kindly and played "Jai Ho!" by the Pussycat Dolls, and "Jimmy" by M.I.A. to appease us. Those songs still felt good, personalized for us, particularly M.I.A.'s sampling of "Jimmy" from eighties Hindi film *Disco Dancer*. It was indeed a weird night.

The next time I was at Berlin, I asked the bouncer for clarification about *Bollyweird*, and learned that the advertised night was the launch of Berlin's new decor. It came together quickly as I examined my surroundings: shimmering saris inelegantly wrapped around pillars and scummy with wet and dry beer spill; metal Islamic plates on walls; random hangings of tinseled fabrics usually used for festivals and rituals. Our nostalgic Bollywood pleasures were reduced to gaudy decor, decorative accents, probably sourced from Patel Brothers—I wasn't sure if I was embarrassed for the bar, or myself. Dangling over the bar were two two-dimensional elephant head profiles; this kind of looming elephant decor cites the early twentieth-century Moulin Rouge cabaret: "The 'elephant stage' presents the heavy, strong powers of the Orient that have nevertheless been conquered by the [French]."[16]

But it should come as no surprise to see Orientalist decor at a gay bar. As Edward Said put it, "The Orient became the living tableau of queerness."[17] In the early twentieth century, white men hosted "Scheherazade parties" to draw on the decadence and excess of Orientalist aesthetics, to perform their own dissident desires, visibility, and pleasure.[18] These traditions continue. The famous annual Black Party—definitely not named for the predominance of black men—in New York City was themed *Passage to India / The Ruined Paradise* in 2014, advertising itself with footage of loinclothed yogis, Hindu death rituals, and pink-powdered ecstatic melas in Varanasi. Madrid-based We Party Group themed its 2018 circuit party *Mantra*, and featured garlanded go-go boys, dancing Shivas, and animated Ganesh visuals.[19] *Slumdog Millionaire*'s success in 2008 incited just one more wave of neo-Orientalist fever in the United States; this faux-Bollywood film, "Bollywood in drag" if you will,[20] (re)invigorated obsessions with spectacles of the Orient, spectacles that occlude the lived experiences—both pleasures and profiling—of brown folks.[21] As we left *Bollyweird*, Gautham pacified me: "Your party will be much better." The first *Jai Ho!* was only a month away.

At the Threshold

Before even entering a bar, we are given cues as to whether or not we are welcome there. Attuned to the representational politics of Boystown fliers, I wanted to mark the racial specificity of *Jai Ho!*, especially because the name of the party so desperately panders to nondesi audiences. Our fliers stated, "All Queer! All Bollywood! All Night!" and featured images of Hindi film actors and themes such as *Jalwa*, *Monsoon*, and *Jungal*. More recently, Trikone's graphic artists have produced original images for the poster that feature darker-skinned, genderqueer bodies, which rarely appear in Hindi cinema.

The fliers included "$5 suggested donation"; though Big Chicks never has a cover—part of its mission to remain inclusive in the face of gentrification—Michelle allowed *Jai Ho!* to request a donation at the door since the party is Trikone's primary source of revenue.[22] Other, straighter desi parties in Chicago charge twenty dollars to enter, and hire upscale venues in downtown Chicago, allowing you to feel like you're "in the city." Queerness too can be found at these parties; Rup shamelessly came up to me at a *Bhangratheque* party in my first year in Chicago, saying, "I like the way you dance. We should dance together sometime." He said it in a way that wasn't phobic in the ways straight desi men compliment my diva dancing while never dancing *with* me; but in a space like this I couldn't be sure. If commercial gay bars in Boystown are filled with phantasms of the orient, hetero-desi parties too are rife with queer possibilities, both the "phobic and the erotic."[23] At one *Bhangratheque* party, Ehmad jumped on stage to queen out to "Baby Doll." Not only did other dancers scatter quickly, but a group of desi engineering bros mockingly pushed a reluctant friend on to stage to dance with Ehmad. Lost in the lyrics, Ehmad persisted dancing, while these men phobically jostled each other, laughing at the faggotry they watched on stage.

The dominant presence of men in South Asian migrant spaces such as these desi parties certainly engenders homosociality that allows some queerness to pass, but when gender transgressions are not a joke, they become the butt of the joke. Several queer desi migrants, especially those living in Chicago's suburbs, who initially took up residence with other South Asian men working in their field or even company, have talked with me about the covering they've had to engage in—avoiding and diverting questions about their sexuality, style, and whereabouts. I was surprised, but not, when Rup showed up at *Jai Ho!* a couple of years after our first meeting. Rup prefers to dance to Bollywood music, so he'll select *Bhangratheque* with his straight desi friends over a night in Boystown; but he makes a point of coming to *Jai Ho!*, a rare opportunity for his flirtations with desi men to go unquestioned, and perhaps prove fruitful.

Hosting *Jai Ho!* at this single-story, wood-paneled, art deco venue, with no cover charge or luxurious futuristic interiors, forgoes the opulent experience that other Bollywood parties, and urban nightlife in general, usually promise. The panhandlers and unfussy restaurants of Little Vietnam do not offer the same fanfare as Boystown's rainbow pylons when walking from the train to the bar. Big Chicks' regular clients are often annoyed by our request for a donation, whereas South Asians who are used to paying large amounts for similar parties are generally amenable to the five-dollar donation. For those men, white bears gentrifying Uptown, who see Big Chicks as *their* neighborhood bar, being asked for a cover at the door brings out a possessive impulse. Often they grill us about what their precious money is going toward before deciding whether to surrender five dollars. Meanwhile, I have watched working-class friends—trans men, people of color—struggle to find the right combination of dollar bills and coins in their pockets to pay the donation, even when we insisted, "It's *just* a *suggested* donation," to let them off the hook. Some straight women used the "I'm just going to the ATM, I'll be right back" trick to escape the transaction. They were not used to paying covers because straight clubs often offer complimentary entry to women; their presence assures straight men that that the club is *not* queer.

My friend Abbas would joke every time he saw me, "Girl! You need to change the name of your party, it's so two-thousand-and-late!" Moses and I arrived at *Jai Ho!* as the party's name because of its cultural currency in 2009 as the Academy Award–winning theme song for Danny Boyle's film *Slumdog Millionaire*; we needed a title with mainstream appeal to fill out this fund-raiser for a fledgling organization. We never expected to do a second party, let alone create an event that has run for ten years. Kosha Patel, in *Shit White Girls Say to Brown Girls*, satirizes the way "Jai ho!" becomes a novel Hindi expression for white people to use. And when the song came on at Minibar one night, a straight white woman whined at me, "Teach me how to Bollywood!" while screwing the lightbulb and petting the dog. Unlike the "ethnically exclusive space" of the subcultural "desi scene,"[24] we anticipated that *Jai Ho!* would be a multiethnic event. It inadvertently became a multicultural space, one that had to stage cultural difference, accent itself, for the pleasures and donations of a multiethnic audience.

Thomas DeFrantz discusses the compromises and complexities in the shift from the generative circles of black social dance, which "protect and permit," to the outward-facing proscenium of concert dance. I too am interested in what happens when we sacrifice the insular desi night for the multicultural queer South Asian show.[25] *Jai Ho!* is very much a fund-raiser, but given its target South Asian audience and location in Little Vietnam, it also functions as a "safe" form of urban cultural tourism—or "slumming"—for white gay men.[26] At Circuit Bar in Boystown, the security checks and classed and raced assumptions that surround *Urbano* hip-hop night with a predominantly black crowd, or *Noche Vaquero* with mostly Latinx patronage and pan-Latinx soundscape, make non-Latinx white men virtually absent there.[27] The upward mobility assumed of Asians in America along with Orientalist fantasies secured by a Bollywood theme make *Jai Ho!* a "safer" site for gay cultural tourism. While the party offers an inclusive experience for some brown folks, it is far from free of racism. Nondesi friends at *Jai Ho!* reported back to me the racisms I was not privy to: "Did you know *this* was happening?" "These Indians smell so bad!" "Do you need me to save you from this conversation [with an Indian man]?" "Don't tip them. They're not real drag queens."[28] Amid the consumerist gaze of multiculturalism and the insidious presence of racism that leave us "stuck" in representation, we use accents to inflect the night with other kinds of sounds, visuals, and choreographies that potentially unsettle the ways our bodies are seen.[29]

Brown Noise

Music can tell us how to dance, and how we respond to the music might tell us whether we belong to "communities of sound."[30] Nightclubs are replete with sonic pedagogies that produce communities. Take, for example, when the DJ mutes "Desi Girl" right after the playback singer says, "Who's the hottest girl in the world?" At that precise moment, the crowd knows to fill the lyrics in; some dancers perhaps even reenact Priyanka's bangle-jingling wrist-knocks from the film. There is joy in catching the right cue with everyone else, knowing we are part of a public, that we share the same tastes. There is also a transfer of knowledge in such moments; the second time the DJ does it, if you didn't know it then, you know it now, and you too can belong. In mainstream US nightclubs, South Asians can also be counterpublicly hailed by the many tracks that sample bhangra, Bollywood, and Kollywood—"Lean On," "Contagious," "Me against the Music (Bhangra Remix)" "The Elephunk Theme"—or the few by South Asian artists—"Beware of the Boys," "Jimmy," "Jai Ho!"[31] We are called forth to sound out "mauth mujhko" in Missy's *Get Your Freak On*, as sonic desiness fleetingly ghosts the club.

Unlike its predecessor parties such as *Besharam, Basement Bhangra,* and *Desilicious, Jai Ho!* is not DJ-led, which poses a challenge to sedimenting shared sonic sensibilities between DJ and attendees. Finding DJs for *Jai Ho!* wasn't easy. South Asian DJs spinning for straight clubs, Indian weddings, and college parties charged over $500 for a night, more than half our door collections. DJs in the queer club and party scenes generally requested half that or less. For a while, I would supply queer Latinx guest DJs with Hindi and South Indian film music, dividing MP3s into Dropbox folders such as "Latest," "Retro," and "Gay Emergencies." One of our desi DJs, the straight brother of a Trikone board member played for us for a while, but we were always in competition with suburban desi events that could pay him much more.

Moses, who worked in Chicago as an IT project manager, supervising and launching new software systems for a multinational company, was my partner in conceiving and planning *Jai Ho!* He had hosted desi karaoke nights in Michigan where he used to live, and eventually taught himself to DJ for *Jai Ho!* After returning to Hyderabad from Chicago, he became a filmmaker working primarily with queer, trans, and Dalit activists and artists. His career trajectory is but one example of the creative lives of global workers that often go unaccounted for (see introduction). Unlike straight desi or queer Latinx DJs, Moses could intuitively appeal to his queer desi audience, though his transnational work travels and eventual return to Hyderabad made him unavailable for *Jai Ho!* Once he played the epic nine-minute title song of *Om Shanti Om* in its entirety, through to the dramatic orchestral crescendo of the final minute. A large circle formed on the dance floor, which elicited dizzying turns from a desi gay boy who eventually collapsed into the arms of a lesbian hero ready to catch the suffering heroine. Like DJ Rekha, who will play the full nine minutes of "Choli Ke Peeche" all the way through its less-spun verses that only the faggiest, FOB-iest, and *filmi*est among us will know, or DJ DynAmite, who will spin "Jiya Jale" and "Roop Suhana Lagta Hai" even though they have no club-compatible electronic beats, this "queer desi DJing" allows us to luxuriate in the narrativity and theatrical gender universes of the song and film. Queer desi DJing invites drag labor, requiring the audience to navigate the music and put on a show in order to make sense of these errant sounds in the club.

Reworking the sonic landscape of Big Chicks has effects on club-goers. You are guaranteed to see a white man press his palms in an overhead namaste, groove his neck from side to side, or squiggle his arms at his body's side. These gestures are relics of Orientalist modern and classical Western dance, from Denishawn to Petipa. But under "Indian" sound, whether inflected by hip-hop, disco, or reggae, the white dancer is turned toward these oriental tropes and gestures. A white audience member, also a drag artist, once complimented LaWhore's performance by mimicking the gestures back to me, including an overhead namaste. "I never did that," I said. As a dancer, he could scan through his recollection of the performance, and sheepishly responded, "You're right." These gestures too are phantasms through which our dancing brown bodies are seen.

The unfamiliarity of language leaves bar regulars unimpressed, and these sonic frictions produce a brown noise, a fuzzy sonic blur, that renders unfamiliar audiences disoriented, disappointed, or distracted. Someone passes our Latinx DJ a note, "When can I request something NOT Bollywood?" So lost in the brown noise, he misses the Rihanna and Katy Perry that had already been played over the night. Hindi music is club ready; nostalgic songs have been remixed with electronic dance beats, and films often release club mixes of slow or folk tracks on their albums.[32] It takes just one more whiskey to get the crowd past the Hindi lyrics or Lata Mangeshkar's shrill tones, and on to the more universal beat. But the accent, the discursive noise of racial, cultural, and linguistic difference sometimes impedes a bodily submission to the beat, and the white crowd is left unsettled.

For nonqueer and nondesi DJs, I created a folder of MP3s titled "gay emergencies": "Hawa Hawai," "Aaja Nachle," "Munni Badnaam," and most importantly "Aap Jaisa Koi." This 1980 track by Nazia Hassan—"the closest Bollywood ever got to Donna Summer"—summons a transnational desi nostalgia for disco femininity.[33] I was always amazed by what this song did at *Jai Ho!*, the sheer joy it brought *so many* desis. While much has been written about the relationships between disco, capitalism, and the gay dance floor,[34] this song's "disco/sexuality" is imbued with other roots and routes of desire:[35] Indo-Pak diaspora as Pakistani-British Hassan sings for Indian Bollywood; changing music industries as Hassan rises as a pop star and not just a playback singer; shifting portrayals of femininity in the seventies and eighties by Hassan as well as Zeenat Aman, who lip-synchs the song in *Qurbani*; and the duality of Aman's performance as she sings it twice in the film.[36] This desi disco song is queer not only because disco has always been queer, but because it resonates across genders, borders, and generations. Its soft twangy percussions refuse the pulsing danceability of contemporary electronic music, inviting us instead to sway and groove, and its simple lyrics rally even non-Hindi speakers into chorus. Surrounded by brown queer voices announcing, "Baat ban jaaye" [It would be so nice!], my spirit was always buoyed.

Screens and Queens

At *Showtunes Night* at Sidetrack in Boystown, I stand with Amit, who had recently arrived from India to Chicago for a graduate degree in engineering. Amit is skinny, rocking a bowl cut and shrunken T-shirts, and has a knack for picking up Eastern European men. When I run into him several years later at Big Chicks on a weekend we both happen to be visiting Chicago, he has filled out his designer shirt with newly made muscles. He tells me that he recently got married to an Indian woman, but I saw that he remained an expert at picking up Eastern European men. At *Showtunes Night* we watch with disinterest video-tracks from American musicals that played on Sidetrack's countless video screens. The crowd sings along, and even ritualistically enacts gestures timed with on-screen performance, the most climactic being a spectacular tossing of thousands of paper napkins at the height of Madonna / Eva Perón singing "Don't Cry for Me Argentina." Amit asks dismissively, "Do you get these songs? It's so shit. I don't know any of these songs, and all these people just stand there and sing along and don't do anything." While standing, singing, and throwing napkins are doing *something*,[37] *Showtunes Night* does not engender the same kinds of bodily engagements that Bollywood music videos do. For an immigrant such as Amit, who has intimate attachments to different kinds of media, they leave him bored and disoriented.

And yet it was also on a visit to Sidetrack that Moses and I came up with the name of our party. Watching the music video for "Jai Ho!" on the screens across the bar, and seeing the face of dark-skinned South Indian playback singer A. R. Rahman, who composed the song, we felt hailed in ways others in the room were not. At a whitewashed bar where desi men perpetually avoid making eye contact with other desis, A. R. Rahman's ten seconds on screen offered an acknowledgment of our brownness that our cultural shame denies us. Visual ghostings such as Rahman's peaceful face on Sidetrack's screens are unsettling orientations that unexpectedly emplace South Asian patrons.

Built into the decor of gay nightclubs are now-essential flat-screen TVs.[38] Used for projecting sports games, music videos, pornography, movies, or live viewings of TV shows considered to have broad queer appeal such as *Pose* and *RuPaul's Drag Race*, these screens have become orienting tools in gay club spaces, representing bodies, genders, and tastes favored in the space. On the walls of Big Chicks, Michelle has famously curated feminist artworks that play with and disrupt traditional notions of gender. At *Jai Ho!* these video screens and paintings are the backdrop against which we stage our brown bodies; the sexy, busty, unapologetically queer figures in the images are, as Michelle herself admits, primarily white. Between the screens, artwork, and decor of gay bars, desiness becomes a phantasmatic presence through and against which we and others encounter our brownness.

At each *Jai Ho!* I would bring DVDs of Hindi film songs that my father had sent me from India, to play on the numerous screens at Big Chicks. Screening Bollywood music videos, even with the sound muted, offered an alternative visual episteme for partygoers to see the brown bodies around them. Like video projections used at many North American desi parties, often professionally mixed by video artists, screening Hindi film music videos at *Jai Ho!* provided an alternative visual orientation that centered brown bodies, hybrid desi dance moves, and Indian home- and landscapes. Rajinder Dudrah, in his study of queer British-Asian nightlife, describes how the projection of film videos provides a repository of movement for desi dancers to replicate, and how queer reenactments in the club unsettle on-screen heteronormativity.[39] These videos potentially offer a different way to know, see, approach, and move with the brown bodies on the dance floor. But Bollywood, a white-/light-washed and upper-caste, North Indian–centric, misogynist, neoliberal popular medium, does not manifest a radical redepiction of brown bodies on screen. A first-time party attendee, a Southeast Asian man, could not take his eyes off the shirtless, hairless, light-skinned Salman Khan dancing on screen, his muscles almost impeding his choreography.[40] "Who are these guys?" he asks me, "I didn't know Indian men were so hot!" Virtual visions of Salman Khan's Indian masculinity, neatly manicured by invisible queer laborers in the Hindi film industry, make desiness sexier within the normative desiring matrices of gay bars, but these kinds of visuals also deflect attention from the live, not-so-buff, shiny, waxed, or manicured, South Asian bodies actually present.

Arriving to *Jai Ho!* on time was always a struggle when in full drag. Amid my rush, I once forgot the Bollywood DVDs. Big Chicks played DVDs from its regular stock of camp and comedy already stacked into its six-disc player. That night, the DJ's desi soundscape was coincidentally accompanied by the visuals of *Team America World Police*. A live action puppet satire, *Team America* centers a cohort of US military professionals combatting global terrorism; an opening scene features the team warring against a group of Middle Eastern, dark-skinned, bearded, turbaned terrorists in Paris. While the US team speaks in English, the terrorists only speak in gibberish mimicking incomprehensible languages of the Orient; that night the subtitles "durka durka durka" were printed on the video screens over the dance floor. The film ostensibly critiques US imperialism and paternalism, or at least laughs at America's role as "world police"; at the same time it revels in the opportunity to characterize Korean and Middle Eastern people as childish, clumsy, and stupid. As global media, sound, and bodies mix at Jai Ho!, multicultural satires of South Asians, Muslims, and Arabs land on brown bodies in the club when the parodic "durka durka" subtitles pretend to sync with Hindi lyrics.

The inadvertent racial collisions of *Team America* at Jai Ho! pale in comparison to drag shows I've witnessed or heard about. Walking into Jackhammer, I hear the parodied lyrics of Oleta Adams's "Get Here": "I don't care how you fuck me / just fuck me right damn now!" I live for a parody, and I was mesmerized by the white drag queen lip-synching. She continues, "You can fuck me in Pakistan / Blow my coochie up like the Taliban!" A rumble of cackles erupt from the enraptured audience, but I feel gross. It was strange to hear "Pakistan" and "Taliban" said out loud in the nightclub, and moreover as a terrorism joke. But then again, these are the homonational and racist logics of gay capitalism—captured so concisely in the vulgarly American pronunciation of both words—that make minoritarian citizenship in nightclubs spaces so trying.

This moment was certainly not singular. In Toronto, South Asian men witnessed white queen Donnarama perform Katy Perry's "Firework" emulating a suicide bomber by strapping fake dynamite to her chest, donning a (Hindu) bindi and (Muslim) hijab.[41] Donnarama has also performed the infamous "Jai Ho!" by transforming herself into an unnamed Hindu deity with six extra hands, performing cliché steps such as the overhead namaste and irrelevant hand mudras.[42] In Philadelphia, Ariel Versace performed a "9/11 themed" number that saw her "[dressed] in Muslim garb . . . adorned with bombs."[43] Publicity for the "Miss Gay Akron 2018" drag pageant advertised the competition's theme as "Indian Bollywood," and accented the poster with Arabic script of "Allah," a Buddhist mandala, and Samarkand font that mimics Devanagiri script. The conflations of Hindu mysticism and Muslim terror consolidated in the "politically incorrect" performances of white drag queens render South Asianness "abject"—a necessary presence that reifies homonational whiteness by performing its perpetual foreignness.[44]

Desi drag artists at *Jai Ho!* labor to unsettle static and reductive visions of brown (trans)femininity, and collectively we stage a more diverse and complex orientation toward the subcontinent, diaspora, and brown bodies present in the space. As LaWhore Vagistan, I performed in saris, culottes, jumpsuits, swimsuits, pantsuits, and ghagras, in my attempts to give life to a sexy, hairy auntie whose style never reads as authentically Indian. Unlike Donnarama's unspecified Hindu deity dancing to "Jai Ho!", Abhijeet's performance of an eight-handed, skull-garlanded, blue Kali dancing to "Bad Girls" by Tamil Sri Lankan MIA intentionally meditated on the empowering potential of the deity for diasporic femmes. Masala Sapphire draws from a variety of media referents, including Walt Disney's Princess Jasmine, Ariana Grande, and Bollywood actress Kareena Kapoor, to style herself. Alisha Boti Kabab crafts recognizable characters such as the well-meaning teacher, Punjabi auntie, and abandoned mother whose husband has gone to war—common tropes from Hindi cinema. If "Asian Americanness must be stable and unified, must provide a solid *not-American* border around U.S. Americanness,"[45] the heterogeneity of performances by desi drag queens, and occasionally drag kings, at *Jai Ho!* unsettles any stable orientation to Asianness in that gay space, revealing brown bodies and desi performance as hybrid and unfixed, poking holes in the "*not-American* borders."

Desi drag in Chicago was quite nascent when *Jai Ho!* started, and the artists who performed were certainly not professionalized. As Trikone members experimented with performance, many for the first time, the midnight show at *Jai Ho!* felt much less like virtuosic exhibitions in Boystown, and much more like the hypersupportive desi variety shows of college campuses and community events.[46] Like the Filipino *bakla* Santacruzan in New York City, or the gay Miss Mexico pageant in San Diego, *Jai Ho!*'s midnight show makes celebrities out of community members, instead of playing on the celebrity cachet of traveling drag queens that Boystown bars do.[47] In this spirit, the partygoers are as important to the performance as the queens on stage, and audience responses revealed counterpublic reception to the show. South Asians in particular *oohed* and *yessed* as the songs transitioned in my six-track medley of Madhuri Dixit numbers. Unlike some people in the audience who might perceive us to just be "performing our culture," desis understood the storytelling, twists, and riffs built into our acts.[48] I heard Amit jealously claim, "That's *my* song!" as "Dola re dola" faded into "Chane Ke Khet Mein." From my raised vantage point, I watched Raja mouth along to "Nakka Mukka" against the back wall, taking a rare opportunity to indulge in the rapid rolls and rhythms of Tamil. Sunny squeezed his little body through the crowd toward the stage solely to play Salman Khan to my Malaika Arora, embodying Khan's phallic muscularity through a puffed chest and clenched fists. These forms of witnessing are structured by language, bodily knowledge, and gender, as are the times older Indian audience members swirl dollar bills around my head before handing them to me, or showing appreciation by removing the evil eye from LaWhore by drawing knuckles to their temples. These dialogic forms of gender labor, enacted through lip synch and gesture, constitute a racialized kinesthesia in the space that facilitates a distinctly queer desi counterpublic in this multicultural gay bar.[49]

Performing as LaWhore Vagistan at *Jai Ho!* taught me that the real stars of the night were the partygoers. A drag queen doesn't just perform, she incites performance, and while I danced and lip-synched, I also watched audience members mouth entire tracks with me, wriggle through thickets of flesh to hand over dollars, and perform private shows for their lovers. But there are the shows we stage, and there are times when our queer brown bodies bear "the burden of liveness,"[50] when our performance of "the racial mundane" are transformed into theatrical spectacles,[51] when we are already spectacles for consumption expected to enact authenticity, realness, and flesh. Whenever I was backstage before or after the midnight show, I could tell simply by the sound whether Ehmad or AJ had mounted the risers to dance. The crowd shouted and screamed for Ehmad's perky prances and AJ's shirtless and slouchy theatrics; they inadvertently became a show. The quickness with which *Jai Ho!*'s multicultural crowd stopped dancing and turned to watch them revealed the need to orient their bodies to cultural signifiers, to something properly brown. This kind of attention was not as conspicuous on other dance nights at Big Chicks, where gay men queening and preening on the boxes were just part of the furniture. But in the multicultural frame around *Jai Ho!*, South Asian bodies became authenticating spectacles for nondesi spectators. But by 12:30 a.m., the show ends, and culture vultures quickly leave. It is now that the dance floor comes alive with the bodies of those who needed this night to last!

Voguing at Frat Night

It's not always easy to find a place to dance; making space for oneself, navigating the microgeographies of the dance floor, house party, and nightclub are political negotiations.[52] Dancing in outmoded fashions or taking up too much space breaks the unspoken rules to not bump each other, especially given the synchronicity of movement that has developed in clubbing cultures.[53] Tim Lawrence historicizes movements away from partnered dances in ballrooms and circular social dance spaces, to solo dancing in crowded spaces through the sixties and seventies, reiterating a defense of disco: "The lack of space was of little concern to most protagonists, whose aim was to participate in a musical kinetic form of individual dissolution and collective bliss."[54] But this synchronicity stills particular kinds of bodies and repertoires. As Thomas DeFrantz notes of nightclubs and other spaces of "worldmaking": "These ephemeral imaginary worlds aren't where i usually dance, drive—carefully, as a black man with dreadlocks."[55] Swinging dreadlocks in the club brings the black body under surveillance, as does driving with them. Performing kathak chakras (spins) in a club almost got me thrown out once, hands extending too far from my body, turns whipping too fast for others' safety. How do we make room to dance in dissidenting ways when there is no space for our racialized choreographies, or when our racialized choreographies make us strange? How do we make space for black and brown dance without being subsumed into the synchrony of the nightclub?

Santosh and I are at Scarlet in Boystown, wallflowers judging the mass of messy gays on *Frat Night*. "Kareem! Quick, look at me." Santosh assumes mudras (codified hand gestures), extending them from his solar plexus outward from his body, never fully locking the elbow as he would if he was doing the dance properly, if he had more space. He quickly puts them back in his pockets and giggles. Though he is a trained bharata natyam dancer, he is not one to fight for space on the dance floor. He knows also that to dance strangely is to potentially lose sexual capital, to become a joke. His sneak-peak gesture is ishtyle, embarrassing and incongruous, and doesn't belong despite our sentimental attachment to it. In spite of the sardine-like conditions of the bar, the dance floor opened for another expansive and virtuosic dance.

Beside us is a group of black men. I was thirsty for the one in a tight pink T-shirt who feigned disinterest, though he was well aware my eyes were on him. A remixed "Rolling in the Deep" thumps through the speakers, and Michael begins to dance. Raising his hand like a preacher, he "blesses" his friends, "Ow!" Each one responds, "Ah-ah." His "witnesses" now pay attention to his presence, and with each performative touch he curates them into a circle of disciples. He spies my lustful eyes and blesses me too; while still behind his circle of friends, I am invited to look inward. In this tiny circle Michael, a seasoned butch queen, is dipping, twirling, and duck walking, despite the congestion around him. Suddenly his strong hand is on my wrist, and I turn scarlet as I am pulled into the center of this communal circle. Michael does not willy-nilly spread people into a circle, but draws on particular church and ball-culture call-and-response repertoires that move his friends and make room for his dance and desires. Once in the circle, embarrassed by the crowd, I am reminded by the complicity, accountability, and copresence that the circle requires: "Black people dance inside the circle. The circle permits and protects. Black dance emerges inside the circle. The circle does not distinguish between private and public."[56]

Bhangra Knights

DJ Sachin beckons LaWhore Vagistan on to the bench he is standing on where he is playing the *dhol*, a large drum originating from Punjab and standard in bhangra music. Sachin was *Jai Ho!*'s first DJ, a straight Indian man willing to take on our event, though eventually unaffordable to us. Standing next to him as he drums is a relief, as there is literally no room on the dance floor. The night's theme, *Madonna vs. Madhuri*, has kept the crowd on the dance floor well past the midnight show. From my lofty perspective, I unexpectedly see a patch of club floor. A circular opening appears in the thick mass of pulsating bodies and swirling colored lights: six South Asian men, hands raised behind each other's shoulders, hopping collectively in a circle. One more squeezes his way in. As if satisfied with the size of the group, or perhaps caught up in the sudden tightness from the new dancer, they lock into each other, arms over necks, hands gripping each neighbor's sweaty shoulders, heads almost touching. If their arms cannot fit over shoulders, they bring them down to hug a neighbor's soft, wet waist. Their weighty breaths coordinate with Sachin's drumbeat, eventually evolving into an audible "Hoy! Hoy! Hoy!" Tightly clutching each other's shoulders and midsections, they brace their turning, hopping circle against the elbows, knees, and shoulders that cramp the checkered dance floor.

Prompted by Sachin's *dhol*, these men turned to the movements and vocalizations of bhangra, a Punjabi dance style that draws from martial movement practices and folk dances of Northern India.[57] It is a distinctly regional sound, not only of Punjab, but also, revived in the diaspora post-partition, a sound of the British midlands.[58] In its contemporary iteration, bhangra is often interpreted as a masculine, homosocial, and heteronormative style.[59] These dancers deploy this masculine homosociality toward queer ends, banding together to carve out an intimate space in which they could articulate their racial and ethnic difference for each other's pleasure, *with* each other, their faces turned toward one another rather than any onlooking crowd. They exemplify Patricia Nguyen's understanding of "disorientation" as "a performative experience and method that carries out an act of refusal to break voyeuristic modes of consuming histories of violence and that reorients the body to theorize [minoritarian] subjectivity differently."[60] As Sunaina Maira describes, these Bhangra circles initiate dance at desi nightclubs and make room for other repertoires too.[61] And while this circular configuration is usually performed with hands raised above the head, shoulders spread wide, my friends transformed the dance into something that could fit the cramped dance floor of Big Chicks. Their dance was intimate—timed breathy chants, sweaty bodies interlocked, external gazes blocked—producing an alternative enactment of racialized homoeroticism in the gay bar. Even if momentarily, they inscribe queerness into the homosocial but distinctly heteronormative imaginations of bhangra.[62]

For Ravi, one of the men in this bhangra circle, dancing collectively was a new sensation, one he did not always associate with gay nightclubs. Now in his forties, Ravi moved with his family from India to Tennessee in his early teens, and called an anonymous gay helpline when he was eighteen. The only suggestion was to go to gay bars. And so he went, on his own, each weekend, too nervous to talk to people there. He just danced. Alone. His story resonates with David Román's narration of "dance liberation":

> Dance . . . was a means in itself, a way for me to begin choreographing my own movements through the world as an openly gay man. I loved dancing because it gave me a way to be in my body and to be around other gay people in a way that was very new for me.[63]

Now settled in Chicago's suburbs, Ravi is not much of a club-goer; but his eager attendance at *Jai Ho!*—he travels in from the suburbs and marks the event in his calendar months in advance—evidences the alternative this party provides to the alienation he has felt as an immigrant, and as desi, alone in gay bars. The *dhol*'s invocation of bhangra reorients brown bodies, calls them to turn to each other, to make circles, and cultivate collectivity so that we don't have to always dance alone.

Aunties at the Disco

From the DJ booth, I'm drawn to the other side of the Big Chicks dance floor by hoots and hollers punctuating the title track of *Bachna Ae Haseeno*. It is less crowded than the *Madonna vs. Madhuri* night, and I quickly weave through the maze of bodies to find a circle of twelve or so people. They stand at the periphery, keeping the beat with bopping hips, shrugging shoulders, or enthusiastic claps. In the middle is Sunny, a short, mid-twenty-something-year-old, fair skinned, boyishly handsome Gujarati medical student, dancing wide legged, macho, shimmying for his audience. His sexy Bollywood ishtyle is accentuated by his fashionable waistcoat, immaculately gelled hair, and uncanny smirk acknowledging the many eyes on him.

An anonymous hand pushes Amir into the circle, and Sunny recedes to the periphery. Amir is Middle Eastern, fair skinned, slender with delicate glossed lips, large, light eyes, straight, loose, dark brown hair, and a light shading of stubble. Unexpectedly in the circle's center, he quickly improvises by lifting one leg just inches off the ground. With steady but gentle hip articulations, he pivots in a circle on one foot, confidently looking out at the watching faces but demurely avoiding immediate eye contact. At the circle's edge, I am strangely anxious, knowing that I may be suddenly pulled or pushed in; in this circle, the audience is always potentially a performer. I delay the inevitable by reaching behind me to pull Vicky into the circle; he is a first-timer at *Jai Ho!* and is enthralled at the sight of so many other gay desis around him. He quickly begins the light-footed toe-touch raver-boy dance that he was doing at Hydrate nightclub in Boystown some months before when he hugged me and said, "Please can we be friends?"

Deidre Sklar reminds us how dance can reignite that which our body already knows: "I slipped once again into the familiar rhythms."[64] I know this circle. It is inevitable at every South Asian wedding I've attended, mostly North Indian or Sindhi weddings. An auntie will see me dancing on the edge, recognize my reluctance to make eye contact, and inevitably pull me to dance in the middle. I feign reluctance, but my spontaneous improvisation will bring her, and me, much joy.[65] And here I am, at a gay bar, feeling that nervous anticipation, my body wondering how to respond—as it did when Michael pulled me in—if and when one of *these* aunties, other queer men, beckon me into the center. Unlike the flirtatious couples or small groups bopping within respectful constraints of a crowded floor, the open circle allows a less restrained, more fully embodied response to the Bollywood sound booming overhead.

The auntie circle not only makes room for choreographies unusual to the gay dance floor, but it suddenly integrates "the sights, sounds and tastes of the family wedding party hall, and the dance moves and aesthetics of Bollywood films" into the nightclub.[66] Alpesh Patel writes of the unexpected smells of pakoras and samosas at *Club Zindagi*, a queer desi night in Manchester, that remind him of his mother's home:

> In many ways, the multi-sensory experience of being at Zindagi felt *more* liberatory than the moment of initially "coming out" did for me that was always tinged with a residual guilt and anxiety precipitated by what I felt was a certain requisite disavowal of my family and ethnic ties.

Like the sounds and smells that return Patel home and reconcile worlds, the dancing circle imports the domestic into the nightclub. Clare Croft implies that the queer club and the intergenerational dance circles, both sites of queer possibility, do not share time and space.[67] But unexpectedly at *Jai Ho!* this FOB-y auntie dance configuration collapses seemingly disparate worlds. Like the food smells for Alpesh Patel, the work these dancing circles do for me is especially reparative. As my family and I are forced to grow apart, and I become less and less legible as a drag queen / humanities scholar / American / queer, it is when I dance this way that I am most like them, that we are still alike. Whether at the club or at a wedding, dancing in the auntie circle makes me feel like I didn't have to leave home to be queer.

Film scholar Arthur Knight draws on African American star dances, in which, much like the auntie circle, dancers take turns in the center with approval and applause of other dancers. Knight uses the star dance as a metaphor to think about African American stardom, how black actors make room for each other to rise in Hollywood, taking turns at fame and thus redistributing capital.[68] As Knight helps us see, the circle has a redistributive ethic to it. It offers a different episteme to be in our bodies, and to appreciate each other's bodies by "loosening" the permissible choreographies: "The looser the space, the more likely it will provide opportunities to imagine or enact alternative structures."[69] It allows a variety of individualized performances, as well as generative audience-performer relationships: claps, whistles, ululations, smiles, and screams. The circle interrupts the sexual economy of the gay club by spreading dancers from knee-knocking closeness, but it permits a *different* kind of sexiness, in which all dances and bodies that enter the circle are affirmed, however brief or "unskilled." The auntie circle reminds me of José Esteban Muñoz's articulation of queerness:

> a mode of "being-with" that defies social conventions and conformism and is innately heretical yet still desirous for the world, actively attempting to enact a commons that is not a pulverizing, hierarchical one bequeathed through logics and practices of exploitations . . . it looks to circuits of being-with, in difference and discord, that are laden with potentiality and that manifest the desire to want something else.[70]

While the rise of electronic dance music in nightclubs has reconfigured social dance away from circular topographies, culturally situated repertoires such as this auntie circle, the ring shout, the star dance, the hora, the cypher, rueda, bhangra, *dabke*, or voguing have the potential to briefly reconfigure orientations in the club beyond "a white spatial imaginary."[71] The auntie circle, as a space-making configuration, is a capacious site for "variation, innovation, and irregularity" that can be staged for collective, assenting, and supportive audiences; for a moment all are valuable for how they dance.[72] Jonathan Bollen maps the politics of the dance floor: "Whom you are dancing near, where you are facing, and to whom you address your dancing: this is how social relations are ventured, negotiated, and sustained on the dance floor. It is how social relations are enacted as party goers manipulate relations by making orientational shifts."[73] The orientations that the auntie circle enacts offer new somatic possibilities, other ways of seeing and being with each other; "movement itself as a way of knowing . . . a transformation of attention"[74] that allows us to see other brown men, just momentarily, as stars. It offers another way to be sexy. I've come to realize that at these queer desi parties, there is only moderate grinding, lip-locking, and groping. But they have never felt nonsexual or even "tame." Sexuality, sexiness, is performed, exhibited, flaunted, and staged in different ways, different directions, different proximities, and even different shapes.

When I've presented research from this chapter, audiences seem anxious about two things: "What if I'm a bad dancer and I get pulled into the circle?" and "But who gets left out of the circle?" When auntie pulls you into the circle, she has every intention of momentarily embarrassing you, even though she will gleefully cheer on the most mediocre dance moves; in the circle, bad dance is good dance too. The circle's ability to include is premised on its ability to close itself off to outside viewers and participants; indeed the relatively small number of women, trans folks, or people with mobility challenges at this party signals some exclusions endemic to *Jai Ho!* and Big Chicks.[75] At a queer desi party in Oakland, two lesbians insistently found ways to break the circle as other dancers tried to form one. It was too FOB-y, too male, too exclusive, too inclusive; whatever it was, these two women were just not having it. At *Jai Ho!*, a group of straight men created a circle as a means of watching effeminate gay men dance without having to dance *with* them. On another *Jai Ho!* night, I watched as a black woman attempted to finagle her way into a circle of desis dancing, but to no avail. While new choreographies such as auntie or bhangra circles unsettle orientations in the club, they can also reify others. The circle is not a universal utopic strategy, but in some instances, it provides opportunities to rehearse new aesthetic, erotic, and social possibilities in the gay nightclub.

Dancing in a club is both a navigation of social relationships within the club, and a rehearsal of socialities, utopian possibilities, that linger beyond the moment of copresence.[76] With nowhere to express their ishtyle in the tightness of *Madonna vs. Madhuri* night, my friends doing bhangra, like Michael voguing at Scarlet, used their dance to make space to dance. For my interlocutors, having intimately felt each other's brownness, unabashedly exhibiting their ishtyle for each other's pleasure and approval, they know what it is like to feel desi and desirable in a gay club. The residue of performance does not just help queers of color survive; it also incites them to find and witness each other's difference, to push or pull each other into the circle, as it were.[77] They email Trikone-board members to ask how they can volunteer, to tell us how much fun they had, or to find out when the next *Jai Ho!* is. These are critical quotidian statements that signal that what they found and how they felt at *Jai Ho!* is not available elsewhere. *Jai Ho!* is not only a fund-raiser, it is an opportunity to dance, and "dance [is] not superfluous to the political mission," it redistributes body, gaze, desire, and attention.[78] That dance persists beyond Trikone's quarterly fund-raiser is evidenced by the generosity queer desis show each other: housing recent asylees and local friends displaced from their homes; bringing new and nervous South Asians from across the Midwest they have met online to their first gay bar; opening homes to strangers by hosting potlucks; and returning to dance at *Jai Ho!*

Since wrapping up this ethnography, I've become keenly aware of how rare spaces such as *Jai Ho!*, or even that momentary circle, are. Unless I am visiting New York, Toronto, San Francisco, or Chicago on an opportune weekend, there is almost no moment in which I have full permission to dance like a desi fag, to express my ishtyle in queer public spaces, without worrying about my safety or feeling embarrassed. In the meanwhile, if I'm lucky, I get to steal a *thumka* when Punjabi MC's "Beware of the Boys"—or even the dreaded "Jai Ho!"—comes on at gay clubs. Sometimes, phantasms are all we have to let us feel present.

PART III

FIVE

Snakes on the Dance Floor
Bollywood and Diva Worship

Signature Moves

In the winter of 2011, *Jai Ho!*, Trikone-Chicago's quarterly queer Bolly-wood party, was themed *Madonna vs. Madhuri*.[1] As LaWhore Vagistan, I offered a tribute to screen legend Madhuri Dixit through a medley of her most popular numbers. Madhuri Dixit quickly rose to fame following her performance as Mohini in the 1988 Hindi film *Tezaab*, gaining immense popularity for her sweet and sassy song-and-dance number "Ek, Do, Teen." The last time I had danced to this song was in my parents' bedroom at age seven. Across Madhuri's fluctuating career, her reputation as a dancer has remained consistent, especially evident in her reprisal of Mohini twenty-five years later for *Yeh Jawani Hai Deewani*. As my medley transitioned from one Madhuri song to another, desi partygoers *oohed* and *yessed* in delight at my very curated choices. Amit protested jealously, "That's *my* song!" about "Chane Ke Khet Mein." During the salacious "Dhak Dhak Karne Laga," AJ jumped on stage to play the Anil Kapoor to my Madhuri.

The morning after the party, I woke up to a Facebook note from Kaushik, a mixed-race desi man working in fashion retail whom I knew only in passing: "[I] have never been in a room filled with so many gay/ straight Indian/Paki Men. It was a dream come true for me . . . and what can I say love Maduhriji a lot. She was my inspiration to why I dance." In our interview Kaushik lists his studio-based dance training in modern, ballet, and tap, but adds that in addition to formal training, he plays with movement vocabulary from the Bollywood screen.

KAREEM: What drew you to Madhuri?

KAUSHIK: Okay, from watching her movies. All of them. I've watched a lot of movies. The new ones, *Devdas*. She's been like an idol to me.

KAREEM: What about her dances?

KAUSHIK: I think I could do it. Maybe. I do it at home every now and then. By myself. Watch those movies. Whatever comes on the TV, I'll just practice the stuff.

KAREEM: Like what?

KAREEM: The day we were dancing [during the pride parade], the signature moves.

In the corner of the downtown Chicago Starbucks café where we were meeting, he extends his hands away from his body, sticks out both thumbs, and seesaws his arms up and down rhythmically, mimicking Madhuri's famous gesture from "Chane Ke Khet Mein."

KAREEM: Would you consider doing drag?

KAUSHIK: No, never. It just doesn't appeal to me. Sometimes someone calls me a drag. But for me, it doesn't really appeal. I could be 'this way" and still be a man. Maybe. If they call it that.

In this interview with Kaushik and his Facebook note expressing idolatry for Madhuri Dixit, domestic and everyday rehearsals of gender performance interact with film texts and gay nightlife spaces. Gestures travel between the screen, home, and nightclub, facilitating pleasure in each of these sites. Across my fieldsites I encountered the signature moves of two especially famous Hindi film actresses of the eighties and nineties: Madhuri Dixit's breast pulse and Sridevi's snake dance. Madhuri Dixit and Sridevi were repeatedly mentioned in my ethnographic interviews, but their dancing divadom also emerges during India's economic liberalization, which they danced across, perhaps even danced into being. Sridevi, starting in the Tamil film industry as a child actor, gained popularity in the Bombay cinema circles following *Himmatwala* (1983) and rose to stardom as the snake-woman in *Nagina* (1986). Like Madhuri Dixit's, Sridevi's career is uniquely marked by her dance.

While performance studies has importantly grappled with the mutually constitutive nature of media and live performance, projects have primarily focused on theatrical and concert-style performance, and less so on the quotidian life of gestural migrations.[2] This chapter follows filmic gestures from screen, to home, to nightclub using film studies, interview analysis, and ethnography to show how Madhuri's and Sridevi's dances enable "touch across time" and medium.[3] Kaushik and others' nostalgic tendencies to cite Sridevi's and Madhuri Dixit's gestures in the club enact ishtyle that circumvents contemporary neoliberal aesthetics of Bollywood dance, as well as highly masculinized club styles, recalling forms of on-screen femininity that were less beholden to commercial interests. In recalling these unruly femininities through performance, they return to their own initial encounters with these dances, earlier embodiments of Madhuri's and Sridevi's gestures, of themselves. These gestures thus become repositories of affect, performatives that activate individual and collective memory on the club dance floor, facilitating alternative forms of sociality, or even of being with oneself.

Bollywood Made Me Queer

Hindi film scholarship has sought to queer the largely heteronormative genre and industry; to draw on Rinaldo Walcott, this kind of research "sexes the political limits of our thought through an ethical politicality of making our sexual regimes open up to that which they resist."[4] But instead of queering Bollywood, I want to ask how Bollywood queers us. How does it give us transgressive techniques to put on to our bodies, style ourselves, move, and desire with? Queer approaches to Bollywood have relied on analyses of gay, lesbian, and transgender characters in Hindi film, of which we are seeing more and more. Alternatively, these studies have tended toward reading practices that give agency to queer viewers to interpret and enjoy gender transgression and homosocial interaction on-screen.[5] This chapter's focus on embodied "reanimations" of Hindi cinema[6] responds to Alexander Doty's famous call for alternative lines of inquiry into queer cultural analysis that engage more complicated and layered routes of identification, pleasure, and desire between audience and text.[7] The *filmi* qualities of Hindi cinema, repeated tropes that have become industry standards, produce excesses that align with failed heteronormativity and unruly femininities. Queer affinities for these excesses solidify into camp knowledge that queer desis share with each other.

The 2012 film *Aiyyaa!* features a goofy protagonist named Meenakshi who styles herself after Hindi film actresses of the eighties and nineties, and is portrayed as a poor candidate for marriage. Similarly, in *Khabi*

Khushi Khabi Gham (2001), the clumsy, effusive Anjali apologizes for being too *filmi*, too much "like film." Anjali's perpetual citations of film dialogues mark her girlish obsession with a fantastic life, lack of taste and grace, and her poor class position, all making her an improper object of heteronormative desire. But distaste with *filmi*ness is not merely a joke in films; Bollywood filmmakers themselves are embarrassed by the masala content they include in their films that panders to audiences they deem unsophisticated.[8] *Filmi*ness exceeds quotidian realism; it is vulgar, ornamental, too much. By *K3G*'s end, Anjali has been carefully stripped of her *filmi*ness to become an upper-class, sari-wearing, husband-respecting, Hindu-nation-saluting woman; her film references are replaced by Hindu devotional songs and national anthems. Anjali's *filmi*ness is a queerness that must be resolved by incorporation into familial normativity of both the Hindu nation-state and its imagined diaspora. If Anjali is too *filmi*, what about real-life fans who relish such aesthetic modes, even adopt and mimic them? How does Bollywood queer its audience by infecting us with *filmi* tendencies? How does it make us too girly, too foreign, too theatrical, too Bollywood? In what spaces can we dispel the cultural embarrassment that comes with enjoying this particularly Indian filmic formulation, read as an aesthetic of delayed modernity because of its indulgence in melodrama, fantasy, and moral narratives?

Filmi does not merely indicate theatrical excess; it draws on the Indian film industry's tendency to capitalize on insider knowledge by communicating through repetition.[9] Bollywood traffics in gestures that are distinctly Bollywood, and that sediment into ishtyle through repetition. They may be verbal: "Bachao!" (Save me!) "Nahiiiiiiin!" (Nooooo!), or "Your honor, I object!" They may be sonic: "Dishoom!" (punch) or "Dichkya-aon!" (bullet fired). They may be isolated on the body: eyebrow lifts, *thumkas* (hip pulses), lip bites. Or they may deploy the entire body: leaning back with hands outstretched, or peeking out from behind an obstruction flirtatiously. Incorporated into the bodies of the genre's audience, these stylizations constitute an alternative vernacular that embellishes our speech, movement, and flirtations, reorienting our social position with those around us, and with those we desire. Homing in on gestures helps us pay attention to how film aesthetics come to inhabit the body.

Juana María Rodríguez meditates on how gestures communicate: "Gestures are always relational; they form connections between different parts of our bodies; they cite other gestures; they extend the reach of the self into the space between us; they bring into being the possibility of a 'we.'"[10] I am interested in this "we" work of *filmi* gestures, their ability to summon sociality. At Sidetrack bar in Chicago, among a group of other desi men, Arvind says to us, "I knew I was gay when I saw Shah Rukh Khan do . . ." He extends his arms outward from his body palms open, bends backward just slightly, cocks his head as if looking into the distance, and smiles coyly. More than just conjuring the neoliberal megastar, Arvind's gesture allows him to claim brown origins to his queerness, to occupy space in a mostly white bar, to draw attention to his lithe body in this libidinal economy, and to stir our own desires for Arvind, Shah Rukh, and other brown men. After the 2012 Queer Aazadi March in Mumbai, participants gathered in a Chowpatty pub to drink and celebrate. A group of queer women launched into their favorite Amitabh songs, ghosting the "angry young man" into the room, but also providing them a cover to smack the table, clink mugs, stand on chairs, and publicly inhabit a playful intoxicated masculinity in ways they are often not allowed. *Filmi* gestures make us queer, even if only momentarily, both by recalling stars and films and by giving us embodied tools to inhabit sexualized spaces.

Stacy Wolf's research on American musicals helps us build on queer Bollywood scholarship's assertions that the ubiquitous song-and-dance sequence offers an important structural entry point for queer viewers:[11]

> Characters in musicals are anything but fully psychologized, and the requisite out-front performance style of musical theater, as well as its various modalities of speech, song, and dance, militates against an identificatory reception and for a kinesthetic one, based on humming along and tapping one's toes. . . . The musical is disruptive, kinesthetic, catchy, and nonidentitarian.[12]

While there are distinct structural differences in the use of song and dance between American musicals and Hindi cinema,[13] Bollywood, as a "cinema of interruptions," offers kinesthetic entry points that can eschew heteronormative narrative arcs.[14] It gives us *more* tools to participate in and draw from the film than simply identifying with heterosexual characters. For example, describing his nostalgia for Meena Kumari, Nithin Manayath, points to the precise gestures that actresses offer queer viewers as models of beauty: "a quiet quiver of the lips or a heavily lifted eye."[15]

The current global Bollywood dance explosion—in fitness studios, festivals, and TV shows such as *So You Think You Can Dance*—might suggest that Hindi cinema is well mined for its choreographic possibilities.[16] However, every time Sharon Osborne says to SYTYCD contestants, "That looked like so much fun! You were just smiling all throughout," I'm reminded that the multitudinous affects of Bollywood dance—the pathos, opacity, seduction, refusal in the quivering lip and lifted eye—are lost in these flattened global mediations. Intimate forms of Indianness, and their affective capacities, are expunged in favor of standardization. When I took classes with Shiamak Davar Institute of Performing Arts in Bangalore, junior instructors were chastised by their seniors for explaining hand movements: "It's like you're making chapatti" or "You're asking why. *Kya*?" The instructors were required to name these movements "jiggy hands" and "Indian hands." Too, instructors perpetually gendered choreographies in binary ways: men ball up fists and swing heads, while women splay palms and swing hips. Outside the standardized studio however, we are free to play with these gendered gestures at will.

Gender is disciplined on the gay dance floor just as it is in these dance studios. However, my descriptions of the ways that femininity is policed across my fieldsites has not allowed me to consider what femininity *can do* in the club. My interlocutors' obsessive engagements with Bollywood divas Madhuri Dixit and Sridevi provides space to think about the productive capacities of feminine gestures. Like Marcia Ochoa in *Queen for a Day*, I trace shared repertoires of femininity across differently gendered bodies, while also acknowledging the unpredictable performative capacities of these gestures in various media and sites.[17] This is not to say that femininity is *not* policed in the sites I explore here—screen, home, and nightclub—but rather that it is femininity's fiery determination to exist that makes possible a "we."

Divas on Screen

Contemporary queer South Asian cultural production often uses Hindi film stars as affective cyphers of alienation, fabulosity, and loss. Novels like *Ode to Lata*, films such as *Queen of My Dreams* and *Sheila Ki Jawani*, and plays like *Miss Meena and the Masala Queens* and *The Gentleman's Club* take up Lata Mangeshkar, Sharmila Tagore, Katrina Kaif, Meena Kumari, and Shammi Kapoor as conduits for queerness.[18] So too in my fieldwork, film stars provided embodied and affective cyphers for my friends. As I approached this project, I—perhaps naively—did not expect to center the two queens I described above: Sridevi and Madhuri Dixit.

And while there are many other dancing divas—Vyjayanthimala, Helen, Zeenat Aman, Rekha—my interviewees perpetually raised the names of these two women. The answer to questions such as "What got you into dancing?" "When did you first start dancing?" and "What songs do you like dancing to?" invoked answers that referenced these two women as diva inspirations.

Prior to the eighties, when Sridevi and Madhuri debuted, dance was used to externalize morality: the marriageable Hindu woman only dances classical forms or doesn't dance at all; the naive dancer is saved from her impoverished labor by the hero; the dancing Muslim *tawaif* (courtesan) is relegated to a life of spinsterhood; and the diasporic/Anglo-Indian/westernized cabaret dancing vamp dies before intermission, is coupled with the villain, or disappears from the plot.[19] Sridevi and Madhuri Dixit danced in both Western and Indian styles, performed both cabaret and folk numbers, and could be both sexy and moral at the same time. Since the seventies, heroines have been given more room to express sexuality in the film's narrative;[20] however, Madhuri Dixit's dances, as Usha Iyer methodically demonstrates, actually draw choreography from both vamps and heroines that preceded her.[21] Madhuri and Sridevi did not choreograph themselves, but widespread admiration for them as dancers is a testament to the excellence of their on-screen labor: their deft execution of the dance director's choreography, their command over *abhinaya* (emotive facial expressions), their embellishment of the playback singer's voice with expert lip-synching. Voices can be dubbed, playback artists can provide songs, stunt actors can be employed, artists and stylists take care of fashion and makeup, but when it comes to dance, only the actor's body can evidence their skill.

While much of the literature on divas centers musicians in opera, musicals, and pop,[22] Alexander Doty's special issues of *Camera Obscura* broaden on-screen divahood to include acting, fashion, and even hairstyles.[23] With the notable exception of Peter Stonely's work on gay men's admiration of prima ballerinas, literature on diva worship has not deeply considered dancers as divas.[24] In Hindi film, the relationship between dance and stardom is also understudied.[25] Identifying the Bollywood diva is complicated by a "dual-star text," a doubling of the on-screen heroine and the playback singer who provides her music but never appears on the screen.[26] If we consider choreographers' contributions to song and dance sequences, we might even imagine a "triple-star text." Madhuri and Sridevi—like Helen and Vyjayanthimala before them—were known *for their dance.* One of the reasons they were not caught in the binds of a "triple-star text" was because the choreographer, until the nineties, did not enjoy publicity. With the rise of the choreographer in the film industry— through new media platforms, recreational dance studios, TV dance competitions, award shows—achieving divahood through dance is more difficult, as the actor-choreographer star texts are further uncoupled.[27] As choreographers become industry stars themselves, artistic originality sticks less and less to the actor's persona, as they did for Madhuri Dixit and Sridevi.

For Madhuri and Sridevi, stardom was premised on their dance—not all dancing stars were beloved *for* their dancing. Anyone who has watched "Tip Tip Barsa Paani" wants to dance in the rain in a marigold sari, but few would actually claim Raveena Tandon as their diva. My interlocutors are not the only ones to confer legendary status on these dancing divas. Sunaina Maira too marks the ubiquity of Madhuri Dixit in her fieldwork with desi youth in New York City: "[She] was an extremely popular film icon and sex symbol at the time I was doing this research, and her picture adorned the walls of several Indian American men's rooms."[28] Similarly, the massive outpouring of sorrow from Indians across the world upon Sridevi's sudden death in 2018 mark her widespread appeal. Immersed in my small queer worlds, I often forget that Sridevi and Madhuri were not *just* queer icons.

The vast reach of these queens' divahood, well beyond queer fandom, suggests that it was not just subcultural appeal that facilitated their rise to fame; their popularity burgeoned within a broader socio-political context. Deborah Parédez's research on Selena Quintanilla and other divas offers clarity on the political-economic contexts in which divas emerge that engender such massive widespread appeal. In her book-length treatise on how Selena has been memorialized, Parédez locates the Tejana singer's skyrocketing popularity amid changes in the American music industry, media representation of Latinx people, and immigration debates around the US-Mexico border.[29] Also, in her reading of Lena Horne's 1963 appearance on *The Judy Garland Show*, Parédez argues that Horne capitalizes on the diva duet format to perform a black feminist rage in line with her civil rights politics.[30] Divas emerge amid political and cultural contestation, while also capitalizing on the opportunities to stage desires and difference, they become "special" alongside and against the sociopolitical hegemonies around them.

Like Selena and Lena Horne, Madhuri Dixit and Sridevi dance across the cusp of significant changes in national economy, mediascape, and moral climate—both challenging the status quo, as well as heralding neoliberal aesthetics. The introduction of MTV India and other TV channels following India's economic liberalization changed the nature of song-and-dance sequences; Madhuri's nine-minute long "Choli Ke Peeche" and Sridevi's "Main Teri Dushman," also nine minutes, are much too long for the fast pace of corporate broadcasting. Liberalization also signaled the demise of the mixed-class cinema hall and the rise of slick multiplex cinemas; Madhuri and Sridevi are the last heroines who danced for "both the classes and the masses," as the expression goes. If in earlier chapters, I situated liberalization to signal new regimes of corporate labor and nighttime leisure, in this chapter political economic change comes to bear on dance aesthetics, women's stardom, and the rise of new forms of leisure such as middle-class dance studios.

Accompanying liberalization were backlashes to globalization and westernization, right-wing-sanctioned communal violence, and a burgeoning Hindutva fundamentalist movement—one that now controls national and many regional governments. Amid these changing media, economic, and moral landscapes, women's mobility was called into question by Hindutva right-wing alarmists, epitomized in the controversies around Madhuri Dixit's performance of "Choli Ke Peeche Kya Hai" in *Khalnayak* (1993). In the film, Dixit plays a policewoman attempting to salvage her lover's reputation by pursuing the villain. She disguises herself as a Rajasthani dancer to seduce him and, under the auspices of this regional performance style, she dances to the bawdy lyrics. Dixit's counterpart in the song lewdly asks in Ila Arun's rough voice, "What is under your blouse?" and Madhuri guilelessly responds in Alka Yagnik's melodious notes, "My heart is under my blouse." The pulsing of her breasts—framed conspicuously by a high-cropped blouse—away from and back into the body to represent a beating heart is the most recognizable, and widely repeated, gesture from this number. The opening, "Ku, ku, ku, ku" notes of the song infectiously invite these bodily pulsations.

"Choli Ke Peeche Kya Hai" was released in advance of its film, as songs always are,[31] stirring controversy across India. As filmmakers played with new styles and sounds, including Ila Arun's regional rough voice and Sanjay Dutt's bad-boy image, *Khalnayak*'s makeover of the eighties masala film pushed too many buttons at once. Appeals to excise the song from the film before its release or to edit out the line "Choli ke peeche kya hai?" came from officials associated with India's right-wing Hindutva political constituency.[32] Madhuri's gesture, the pulse of the breasts as an overexaggerated heartbeat, is associated with her body not only through "Choli Ke Peeche"; it also cites other hit dances—"Humko Aaj Kal Hai Intezaar" and "Dhak Dhak Karne Laga"—in which the eroticism of her chest pulses are emphasized by her exposed midriff, wind-blown hair, rolls on the ground, bitten lower lip, and camera close-ups. The breast pulse, masquerading as a heartbeat, invites the diva into the room. Heaving and pulsing the ribcage conjures many scenarios: seduction of a villain; homoerotic banter between two women;[33] rolling around in a sailor's net; frolicking in bales of hay; and Hindutva censorship.

Sridevi's performance of the snake woman in *Nagina* (1986), which catapulted her to fame, also produces gestures attached to her stardom. In the movie she plays a snake that transfigures into a woman; the film's tension derives from whether she or the snake charmer has ulterior motives for the rich family she has married into. Her climactic performance of "Main Teri Dushman" [I am your enemy], now a camp classic, skillfully embodies a fierce cobra, extruding revenge through her violently intense eyes and vulnerability in her writhing body. She sings, "I am your enemy, you are mine too. I am the snake, you are the charmer." Saroj Khan's choreography culls hip and shoulder articulations from belly dance, cupped hands and bent wrists from the mudras (hand gestures) of bharata natyam, and ground rolls and writhes from folk styles like *pampuattam*. But Sridevi's performance is not a deft demonstration of a classical or codified repertoire. It is instead her vigor that is so captivating: piercing stares, unbroken eye contact, unwieldy ground rolls, whipping turns, and sudden darts. Though classically trained in bharata natyam, across her oeuvre Sridevi performs strange and silly dances such as the aggressive serpent, a damsel frolicking with her invisible lover in "Kaate Nahin," a cabaret-witch surrounded by vampires in "Nakabandi," and even a pantheon of screen queens that includes herself in "Rekha ko dekha." But as we see in *Bride and Prejudice*, and other frequent ironic citations of the snake gesture—hands cupped into the cobra's head—in many contemporary Hindi film songs, the snake dance has acquired kitsch status that empties it of its earnest excellence, and renders it a relic of the embarrassing eighties.[34]

As a political gesture, the snake dance is bound by the control of the phallic flute and actively writhes against this control as the dancer declares her charmer the enemy. Sridevi's embodiment of defiant anger through dance and her willingness to take movement and facial expressions *that* far, to be *that* weird, to be "taken over by the performance," permit us to understand her as a dance diva.[35] In her snakelike rapture, she "refutes the limits of femininity even as her [body is] insistently female."[36] To draw on Parédez again, "The diva's monstrosity is undeniably linked to the ways she troubles gender divides and sexual categories."[37] In this vein, Sridevi performs what Joshua Williams calls "transspecies drag . . . the practice by which women artists test the limits imposed on their political selves by moving 'crabwise' across categories of gender, race, and species."[38] Madhuri Dixit's breast pulse and Sridevi's snake dance are acts of "diva citizenship":[39] they force a dialogue with symbolic, embodied, and institutional patriarchies. These dances are—to paraphrase Lauren Berlant—choreographic moments of emergence, stagings of a dramatic coup in the public sphere, challenges posed to audiences to take them seriously, to identify with the enormity of their suffering.[40]

The diva's appeal need not be just a didactic speech act or earnest testimonial, but also a danced gesture. Sridevi, risking her body on screen through strange and vigorous dance, calls for justice within the film's narrative frame, and makes legible an Indian womanhood that defies dominant dichotomies of wife and whore. At the end of the dance sequence, Rishi Kapoor enters the mansion to snap her out of the trance and back into proper domestic womanhood with one tight slap. Similarly, Madhuri Dixit's disguise as a dancing girl is uncovered in *Khalnayak*, and her sexy dance is mocked by the band of *goondas* (villains) as they reenact "Choli Ke Peeche" back to her. When the heroine involuntarily dances under the phantasmatic rapture of a villain, or in order to seduce him for the purposes of revenge, she is absolved of the moral transgression of dancing publicly, vulgarly, or weirdly—these are just some of the convoluted scenarios manufactured to stage diva dances. But regardless of the normative regimes into which women are restored by the film's or even song's end, within the dance itself they call attention to the regulation of their bodies and psyches, "calling on people to change the social and institutional practices of citizenship to which they currently consent."[41]

Dancing across the cusp of liberalization, Madhuri hails the "gentrification of Bollywood" and the "embourgeoisment of Bollywood dance."[42] Her stardom contributed to the success of *Hum Aapke Hain Kaun . . . !*, which initiated the postliberalization Hindu-family-centered-flick trend that moved away from masala formats of the eighties.[43] Madhuri also stars in *Dil To Paagal Hai*, in which Shiamak Davar's choreography inside of a Western-style dance studio cleans up the chorus line, and represents dance as respectable middle-class labor.[44] Sridevi's eccentric performances have also been tamed. In her comeback role in *English Vinglish*, she plays a timid housewife who is too reserved to dance. Her hypercampy "Hawa

Hawai" has been remade twice since her 1987 rendition, once as a grainy-voiced calypso jam for *Shaitan*, and again for *Tumhari Sulu* as a club track with rap interlude.

Madhuri Dixit's breast pulse and Sridevi's snake dance are thus bound to a different time; to recall them in our bodies is not only to remember our childhoods when we learned them, when we knew gender and desire differently, but to performatively invoke a shifting political, economic, and cultural circumstance. As Julian Carter writes, "Different historical moments can, however paradoxically, coexist in the bodies of dancers who are simultaneously present in performance as themselves and as the (past and future) persons they re/present."[45] To reperform those gestures is to recall both the preliberalization contexts of when we learned those moves and the intimate conditions under which we rehearsed them. Prior to the dance studio of India's new middle classes and the post–*Slumdog Millionaire* Bollywood fitness classes at Gold's Gym were our parents' living rooms, backyards, and bedroom mirrors.

Divas at Home

When I landed in India in February 2019, a friend chastised me, "You didn't even call me when Sridevi died. I was expecting your call." It had been a year since she passed away suddenly in 2018—this is how deeply Sridevi mattered to him. While the Indian media sensationalized the unexplained circumstances around her death, queer South Asian social media melodramatically mourned her loss. Only a handful of news outlets and blogs acknowledged her queer following;[46] however, on my Facebook wall, posts from queer friends read: "An inspiration and a true teacher"; "This song was and still is my queer anthem"; "All of gay south asia is mourning today"; "This song cheered me up through the worst of times"; "Slaying since the 1980s"; "There are only four women in my life, my mother, my sisters, and Sridevi"; "Sridevi was my first Bollywood femme crush; she's owed my essence." Delhi-based poet and queer studies scholar Akhil Katyal wrote in the wake of her passing:

Sridevi
Yours was the first song I ever danced to
in a locked bedroom, singing your line
When the parents, the school, the sibling
worried, you told me femme was fine

The day she died, I was in Riverside, California, offering a dance lecture as LaWhore Vagistan, "Bollywood Divas 101"; Sridevi was built into the presentation as "The Comedy Queen." I'm not one to be moved by celebrity deaths, but as I lip-synched to "Hawa Hawai," my heart broke for the many queer interlocutors who confided in me that Sridevi "told [them] femme was fine," offered them life-sustaining femininity when the rest of the world did not.

Dhaval, who works in business process outsourcing, would always stop me at *Heatwave* parties to compliment my jewelry. During our interview at a Café Coffee Day in north Bangalore, he described butching up his performance to please effeminate boys who had a crush on him; he told me how crushed these men were when they caught him dancing effeminately at a bar. He tells me that he spent many years learning bharata natyam and also did courtesan dances in salon-style settings for the cohort of gay men who mentored him in his little town outside of Bangalore. He talked about the parties on the north side of Bangalore where hijras and gay men danced for each other till the wee hours of the morning, parties that professional and respectable gays would never be caught dead at, parties I was never invited to. As he walked me to find an auto-rickshaw, he unexpectedly recalled what inspired him to start dancing: he went to watch *Nagina*. He told me that when he saw the snake dance, Sridevi took over his body. She entered him and has never left him; she is still inside him. The queer dancer's "love-at-first-sight-story,"[47] one of possession, of irrational fascination with Sridevi and Madhuri, is ubiquitous across my ethnographic field and even in South Asian gay literature and film. And while both screen queens have countless straight male admirers, their methodical emulation by boys and men—and the deeply affecting nature of these dances—is unique to adult queer narrators.

I asked Hari, who works in biotechnology in Bangalore, what brought him to dance.

No training. Television. When I was in school I used to do solo dance, very much the usual freestyle. Anything that I used to see on television, always I've tried to imitate them. . . . So many television channels were not there [at that time]. The music album was released [in advance], only you get to see the song [later] in the movie, or previews which did not [broad]cast the entire song.

Hari's dance pedagogy was shaped in the home, by the very material conditions of film and song distribution and broadcast, limitations that rapidly expanded with the introduction of satellite television. As he continues, his story resonates with Dhaval's.

> I am a big Sridevi fan. She is my goddess. So I have danced on each and every number of hers. I have adored her throughout my life. It was in the year of 1985 that this movie *Nagina* was released . . . the *nagin* dance. Probably I was like—that's what my parents tell me—I was like, uh, I was like three or four. That time there was this cassette system, VCP or VCR. They used to get cassettes and movies. I saw then I was so happy, I was so happy looking at Sridevi. And I started dancing there only. That's what they say. "Every time she was there on the TV, you were so goddam happy, you were so goddam happy." Hehehehe. Every time I see her, my eyes are like [he opens his eyes wide and sucks his teeth in excitement]. I have worshipped her all throughout my life. I have danced on probably all her numbers.

Hari's practice of fandom is not merely pleasure in watching, but embodied rehearsal, a commitment to Sridevi's style and steps. Hari remembers, alongside this domestic setting, the outdated technologies, VCP and VCR, that allowed rewinding, rewatching, and rehearsal. These memories are bound both to a past materiality and a residual embodiment—the wide-open-eyed *abhinaya* of Sridevi's dance was the very face Hari made to reenact his own childhood excitement. Between his performance in the interview, and his description of at-home performances, we see how *filminess* is incorporated into the quotidian body—well before YouTube made dance videos widely available, learning dance from Sridevi via cassette gave Hari not only dance steps, but also facial gestures with which to perform excitement and intensity.

For my interlocutors, imitation is precisely the medium of devotion, and the lack of formal training—as in opera or ballet diva worship—is no bar to an embodied tribute. As Daniel Harris writes of his childhood diva worship, his regional Appalachian accent was queerly trained to sound British by the Hollywood stars he was devoted to.[48] So too were my interlocutors' embodiments infected with the strange gestures of dancing divas; to play the diva is to experiment with gender and to find new forms of self.

Vishal, a friend in Bangalore who has trained with an elite dance school, though he works in pharmaceuticals, says that he got his start dancing by watching Madhuri Dixit films.

> I would do all Madhuri Dixit numbers. I'm a child of [the] nineties. She was my diva. She was a rage at that point of time. I would dance to all her numbers within the four walls of my house. They would be social occasions, *baraats*, veddings, and all. . . . There was this constant need for me to practice those numbers the way she does, to be able to replicate what exactly Madhuri Dixit does. I remember standing in front of the mirror aping what Madhuri does: "Dhak Dhak," "Chane Ke Khet Mein." It's funny. My mother used to be "OK, my god, those small boys experiment with lipsticks and all." I would experiment with Madhuri Dixit!

By drawing choreography directly from the screen instead of mediated delivery through the now ubiquitous dance studio, these queer men bypassed formal economies of Bollywood dance. While Bollywood dance shows in the diaspora and on Indian TV emphasize originality by differentiating from on-screen choreography, Vishal and Hari describe a tributary choreography that relies on mimicry and adaptation.

When Vishal articulates "She was my diva," he draws our attention to the work she has done for him, the performativity of her stardom: "The diva is the unattainably glorious deity we worship and the affective sanctuary in which we seek shelter."[49] Regardless of the representational limits placed on the dancing diva where she can perform only in the permissive space of a dreamscape, we "might utilize her interpellated status as a means for survival."[50] As Brett Farmer writes of proto-queer children in his essay "Julie Andrews Made Me Gay":

> Denied the basic protocols of identity construction furnished other subjectivities through the socializing agencies of, inter alia, kinship, education, and state, queers have had quite literally to invent their own modes of selfhood from the ground up, and the transcendent, value-adding economies of divadom have been a rich resource for this process of queer self-making and legitimation. . . . To say, then, that Andrews made one gay [or that Madhuri was my diva] is no

mere rhetorical gesture, but a performative declaration of the queer subject's right to life, love, and the happy pursuit of divine fabulousness.[51]

These discourses on the resilience of divas and their worshippers remind us that the labor of diva worship provides us with something more than the world wants us to have, including life. Even as representation diversifies in TV and film, unruly divas offer models of gender and sexuality, repertoires of affect and movement, that exceed the sanitized, homonormative LGBT models that neoliberal media wishes we would purchase.

For Natasha, dancing like Sridevi has offered respite from ongoing depression that she experiences as a trans person. A software professional who presents as a man in everyday contexts, is married to a woman, and has two kids, Natasha fulfilled her lifelong dream of dancing in full drag as Sridevi at a pride festival in Bangalore in 2014. In the early years of internet availability in India, Natasha even created a Sridevi fan website, one now lost in the evanescence of the World Wide Web.[52] Sitting at a Café Coffee Day by her workplace, in a white button-down shirt, gray slacks, and corporate ID tag hanging around her neck, she too tells me of being rapt by Sridevi's dance as a child.

> Whenever I used to see her on the screen, I was completely out of this world. It was not like straight guys getting attracted to a woman. She would give me something completely new. . . . I used to idolize her. If I grow up, I will be like that. But I always knew that I can't be like that because I'm a guy.

Natasha explains that every time she danced as a child, she was made fun of for being too feminine. Joining a queer dance group, The Pink Divas, as an adult helped Natasha deal with depression and fat-stigma. These were also opportunities to perform femininities routinely denounced and disciplined in everyday life, in the childhood home, the corporate workplace, as well as the household that Natasha provides for.

We tend to look for dance in the nightclub, studio, and stage, but as Judith Hamera shows, the home too is an urgent and politicized site for "dancing communities."[53] The home is a place to experiment with dance, and thus with gender. As with Hari and Vishal, their diva emulations at home and at weddings were applauded and praised. But Natasha's feminine dancing was laughed at and punished, and she hid it into adulthood.

When Gloria Anzaldúa hears that a lesbian student thought "homophobia meant a fear of going home," she thinks to herself, "how apt. Fear of going home. And not being taken in. We're afraid of being abandoned by the mother, the culture, *la Raza* for being unacceptable, faulty, damaged."[54] Gender nonconformity and nonheteronormative sexualities are perpetually abjected from the home space, but queer people can also practice home—house, family, culture, nation—into being:[55] "I am a turtle. Wherever I go, I carry 'home' on my back."[56] But for the proto-queer child, the home is a primary site where gender is disciplined: "Any boy in America could tell you, if he dared talk about it at all, what he has learned concerning the ways in which a man or man-child ought to move his arms and hands—and, more important, how he oughtn't."[57] David Gere's articulation of "the effeminate gesture" reminds us that gender is learned through example and instruction, but also discipline; aberrant gestures commonly invite punishment, as they did for Natasha growing up.

My drag *beti* Ehmad, a recovering medical student, performs as Alisha Boti Kabab without makeup at the *Jai Ho!* parties in Chicago; he does not want any stubborn glittery evidence left on his body when he returns to his parents' home. Once, when Ehmad came to return jewelry and costumes to me one afternoon, he apologized that he would not be able to return the boobs and wig he borrowed, as his father had discovered them and had thrown them away. When we sit down to an interview, he invokes Madhuri and Sridevi as his childhood inspirations, but his recollection of childhood dance takes a dark turn that explains his relationship with family and home.

> Madhuri, Sridevi, they spoke to me. The first song I remember was "Kali Teri Choti." I put on a *dupatta* [enacts wrapping a scarf over his head and twisting it into a faux braid]. It was then that my mother really became worried. She then started saying, "You need to man up." . . . My father was physically abusive when it comes to trying to get rid of my dance. He had heard about it. It happened when one of my uncles came from Saudi, all of my aunts arranged a get-together. They insisted I dance, to showcase for my cousin. It was almost a comic piece for them. . . . At the end [my uncle] came up to me and said, "Aage se aisi nahin nachna" [Don't ever dance like this again]. I was so insulted. For half an hour I said, I don't want to dance. He gave me a Kit Kat. I did it for a Kit Kat! I didn't eat that Kit Kat. That one episode made me stop dancing. I just quit dancing. It would embarrass my mother.

To embody the screen diva, to allow her into us and disorganize normative regimes of gender, is to make ourselves vulnerable to disciplinary structures of gender. The effeminate gesture will fill a candy bar with melodramatic pathos. Ehmad rounds off this story by saying that he took up dancing again after almost fifteen years, when his mother "gave up" on him, that is, after he came out. Ehmad has since performed several Madhuri numbers at *Jai Ho!* parties.[58] His music choices, often obscure 1980s and 1990s tracks that leave even the most avid Hindi film watchers scratching their heads, indicates his intimate relationship with these songs.

Dance is, more broadly, used to discipline all people into gender; we delegate who should dance at all, what kinds of dance are acceptable, and where and when dance is appropriate. Krishna, living in Bangalore, recounts how gender differentiates who has access to dance at a young age. Girls are encouraged to learn classical forms, while boys must rely on informal sources: "I always wanted to learn classical [but] it was a torture for my sister. I had to pick her back [up from class], escort her. I always wanted to dance that way." While many boys long to learn classical dance, many of my girlfriends, like Krishna's sister, recall the annoyance or even agony of forced dance classes required of them by upper-caste respectabilities. This is why Krishna developed such an affinity for Bollywood dance: it was the only dance he—and many other men—had access to. But, as Sunita Mukhi shows in her description of a young girl's interpretation of "Choli Ke Peeche," it is also risky for young women to inhabit the diva too authentically, to be too *filmi*, and these gestures must be sanitized and tamed.[59] As I presented this work at public talks, South Asian women often divulged the discipline they too incurred in dancing like Madhuri and Sridevi, instead of respectable classical or folk styles. What, then, does it mean to return to diva choreographies in adulthood? Where and when are we allowed to reperform these gestures to praise and pleasure rather than discipline and punishment?

Divas in the Club

Alok, my diasporic drag daughter, and I bonded in Bangalore as two activisty queers from the United States, and I took them to their first gay party there. They were astounded by the uniform heaving of bosoms across the dance floor as the "Ku ku ku" refrain of "Choli Ke Peeche Kya Hai" crept through the speakers. Unfamiliar with this infamous song, they pleaded,

"Teach me, Mother!" The DJ's heavily remixed track never led to the cheeky verses of the song; in fact, despite the popularity of Madhuri and Sridevi, their songs are hardly the go-to for Bollywood DJs. But clubgoers seized the opportunity, and reveled in emphatically pulsing their chests at the mere suggestion of the track. The queer diasporic kinship between Alok and me, and the imitable gesture of pulsing chests around us, permitted a moment of pedagogy and shared embodied practice with the rest of the club. In such infectious, contagious moments, I hear the theorizations of nightlife scholar Fiona Buckland:

> The third space of recreation has often been the only space in which queers could express themselves in ways often not available in the home or the workplace. Second, I believe that the practice of improvised social dance offered ways of teaching queers how to be together.[60]

The nightclub offers alternatives to the home, as Buckland suggests, but what happens when we bring "home" choreographies into the club? The terms of citizenship in global LGBTQ community, Brian Horton shows, sometimes come into contradiction with queer Indians' material, emotional, and cultural attachments to their natal homes.[61] When the club asks migrants, people of color, and postcolonial subjects to leave the "unfashionable" pedagogies of home behind, it becomes imperative to accent the club with dances that feel like home, with ishtyle.[62]

Shazad, a Pakistani-Canadian go-go boy, sexual health educator, and party organizer, sat with me in the hallway outside his office, telling me about his first South Asian queer party.

> I came here [Toronto] on a visit from Calgary five years ago. . . .
> I remember hearing about *Besharam* and the *Queer Indian Mela* [queer desi events in Toronto]—that was my first introduction. I was blown away. All these songs! It was so mind blowing for me. It was really exciting. They were playing all these songs I knew growing up. And everybody's gay. And it's okay to dance to "Chane Ke Khet Mein," I mean how you're supposed to dance to it, and nobody will say anything about it. It was very liberating.

In saying that "it's okay to dance . . . how you're supposed to dance to it," he means like Madhuri. His wonder at these parties implicitly marks the heteronormativity of the domestic space where he grew up hearing these songs that he loved, and of the desi parties he had previously attended where dancing how you're "supposed to dance" is policed if you are not read as a woman.[63]

Despite the masculine muscularity he worked so hard to build into his body through go-go labor—the disaffected side-to-side stomp in fitted underwear and matching hi-tops—this butch-queen cannot help but queen out when the right song plays. "Main Teri Dushman" comes on at a *Rangeela* party in Toronto, and he breaks his heavy left-to-right-to-left stomp, plants his feet, raises his overlapping hands above his head, and marks the three tabla notes with his hips. For a brief moment he is compelled into movement as Sridevi enters him—a precise citation of her on-screen performance as the dancing snake—in much less clothing, of course. He returns to his subdued rhythm keeping but continues to lip-synch the song, unable to fully exorcize Sridevi's rapture.

Shazad's citation of the snake gesture, while in "muscle drag," allows him to access raced and gendered affects that are often kept at the periphery of commercial gay club culture.[64] Muscular masculinity is fetishized in the libidinal economy of global gay clubs, and performances of faggotry are privatized in the asexual camp[65] or drag queen's bodies, or as in the case of Krishna, to the domestic space.

> All these days I thought the way I behave is more feminine. . . . Now when I'm meeting at Good As You [a gay support group], they say I'm the most straight-acting guy out there. That made me realize that what I've been working on all these days has given fruits. Of course, if you ask me how I dance at home, it's altogether different. People will be stunned; if it has to be a competition of all these slutty things [I would win]. I'll be doing all this hip movements. So those were like some shades which people do not know about me.

Krishna is self-conscious of the femininity that has perpetually been ascribed to his body, and so has actively rehearsed a masculinity that is read as "straight acting" and is privileged among gay men. His performance labor "has given fruits," he says. In the privacy of his home, however, he retreats from the gendered economy of public gay space that privileges straight acting masculinity and instead dances "slutty" with "hip movements."

It is not only in domestic or work spaces that we are disciplined into gender; gay clubs, with the excess of video images forced upon attendees, with heavy electronic beats to muffle the high pitch of candy pop, and with restricted space, train our bodies to look and dance in regimes of gendered normalcy. But, like Kevin Aviance's dance at the hypermasculine Roxy nightclub that José Esteban Muñoz describes, the eruption of particular gestures "permit dancers to see and experience the feelings they do not permit themselves to let in. He and the gestures he performs are beacons for all the emotions the throng is not allowed to feel."[66] Aviance stages and makes desirable and nostalgic the corporeality and its associated feelings that dancers around him have purposefully refused or rehearsed away.

In the opening of this chapter, I discussed how my own performance as Madhuri Dixit incited responses from Kaushik, Amit, and AJ. When I lip-synched "Hawa Hawai" at *Jai Ho!*, Wesley, an Indian man who didn't know the event was happening but happened to be at the bar, came up to me to tell me he remembered sitting on his grandmother's lap watching Sridevi in that number. That this dance, or the feelings associated with it, are in the "wrong" place is not necessarily disturbing or disorienting if we understand that "[reparative] practices [are] aimed at taking the terror out of error, at making the making of mistakes sexy, creative, even cognitively powerful."[67] A reparative impulse understands that LaWhore Vagistan lip-synching Sridevi's mumbo jumbo at Big Chicks allows Wesley to be on his Indian grandmother's lap, and surrounded by bears at the same time, and that this can be "sexy, creative, even cognitively powerful" rather than an alienating revelation of the psychic, erotic, and geographic distances between these spaces that often renders queers of color homeless.

As I learned of the camp value of the snake dance through my research, LaWhore Vagistan also decided to perform "Main Teri Dushman" for a pride celebration in Chicago. After I had finished rolling around on the ground and darting aggressively at the audience à la Sridevi, Ashiq came up to me smiling: "Good one! That was a good one! That song used to be a *garba* favorite." Here the song hailed my friend's participation in a specific ethnic and religious community, another "home." Naming the song "a *garba* favorite," he reminds me that the song circulates without its kinesthetic and visual referents, functioning simply as a base beat for the repetitive circular folk dance during Hindu Navratri festivals. But my embodied activation of Sridevi's snake dance inscribes queer significance into his memory of a rather heteronormative ritual. It does a reparative cultural labor by allowing dissonant spaces—the gay club and the religious festival—to meet.[68] Through this diva citation, the body becomes a site of encounter between unlikely sites of sentimentality. Diva worship is a corporeal laboring to dance with one's childhood self again on the dance floor, an opportunity for that child to remind us of the embodied faggotry we have disavowed, that we have been forced to exorcise in our rehearsal of respectable gay subjecthood. As Shazad told us earlier, dancing "the way you're supposed to dance" is "liberating"; it frees movements and affects that have been held at bay in our muscles and psyches by scripts of caste, racial, (post)colonial, heteronormative, and homonormative respectabilities.

But also, when diva worship is danced in the queer desi club space, it is more than the recall of embodied memory; this reperformance is caught in the thickly material sexual economy of the gay club space. At a *Heatwave* party in Bangalore, the hit song "Twist" from the 2009 film *Love Aaj Kal* creeps through a fading song, and immediately hands are up in the air: the snake dance. Four men form a small circle. They lift their shirts up to expose their twinkish stomachs, flat but soft. The bottoms of their T-shirts are held in their teeth, and each has a cupped hand above his head, broken at the wrist: the cobra's head. They body roll for each other: chest-stomach-hips, chest-stomach-hips. Zubair, who occasionally helps to organize these parties and bring in the younger "hep crowd," is just beside them. His stance is wide as he shifts the weight of his hips and points of his cowboy boots from left to right; both his hands are over his head, overlapping and cupped: the cobra's head. Farther away from me, a skinny boy dances for his partner, one leg raised off the ground, one arm extended above his head, wrist bent. His entire body is the cobra. The dance floor is full of snakes, cobras, charmed by the DJ's track.

The opening of "Twist" samples the *beena*, the charmer's flute, in "Man Dole Mera Tan Dole" from the 1954 movie *Nagin*. Dancers sustain their serpentine performance despite other very clear musical referents that build in the song: pop, reggae, bhangra, and the twist. Eliding the twist and bhangra in favor of the snake dance is a dissident listening and a counterpublic performance at a party that generally refuses to traffic in nostalgic Bollywood sounds (see chapter 1). The eruption of snakelike movement—cupped hands, broken wrists—takes its referent not from an actual study or mimicking of cobras seduced by snake charmers but rather from the snake dances of Hindi cinema. The quotidian sexy club dance was accented with Sridevi's gesture, and men performed the snake with deep seriousness. They were fully conscious that their bodies were there to be looked at within a libidinal economy, to be tools of negotiation, and that submitting to the charmer's flute might facilitate their sex appeal or could even out them as too feminine, too *filmi*. Zubair's dance struck me most. His move, cocking his hips from left to right, was identical to his improvisation at a house party just weeks before. He walked into the house, loved the Bangla pop song that was playing, scooped his T-shirt off to show off his muscular, fair-skinned, hairless body, and performed that same dance shirtless for us—sans cobra hands, of course. *This* was his sexy dance. Zubair's butch, muscle dance was accented with a recognizable trace of embodied and anachronistic effeminacy through a performative citation of Sridevi's snake dance.

In light of Kaushik's, Krishna's, Vishal's, Hari's, Ehmad's, Dhaval's, and Shazad's stories, we might imagine how such queer gestures allow a rehearsal of domesticity, femininity, and childhood in the club space both in the body of the dancer who has often had to disavow femininities since a young age and in those who witness this display. The libidinal economy of gay clubs, like the multinational corporation's work environment, disciplines us into gender and guides us to privilege conventional forms of masculinity. It is not only queer and trans people who are disciplined into gender; however, we have been, as Dean Spade demonstrates, institutionally trained to melodramatically narrate our childhoods as dysphoric.[69] The diva's gestures performatively "drag" us through time to remember the mechanics and disjunctures of crafting our genders and bodies over extended periods into state-sanctioned subjecthood.[70] Imbuing the diva's gesture with this potential is a "reparative impulse" in that "it wants to assemble and confer plenitude on an object that will then have resources to offer to an inchoate self."[71] I wish for these gestures to rescue the selves we used to be and the queers we're in the process of becoming from the clutches of normativity and lead us toward the unapologetic sexiness of the breast pulse and the assertive strangeness of the snake dance.

In revisiting a queer childhood, "One may be pricked by, pained by, feelings . . . that, even now, are maudlin, earnest, melodramatic, but understandable pangs of despair or sharp unease."[72] The somatic economies of the gay nightclub too fill us with several pangs of unease—feeling too fat, too femme, too old, too drunk, too brown, too hairy, too trans, too dark— and touching one's childhood through gesture can bring a reparative pleasure, but also a queasy nostalgia. These unsettling feelings are the politics of the nightclub, and dance can recalibrate these politics, these feelings. Diva gestures in the gay desi club excavate the diva's affective and gestural excesses that have been quelled by neoliberal Bollywood. These bold enactments of aggressive femininity appear outdated because they recall a less "sophisticated" moment of Indian filmmaking and film choreography, but in these moments of queer sharing, they are revitalized through earnest tributary reperformances. These gestures bring queerness into visibility through a sincere execution of anachronistic, animalistic, vulgar, foreign dance. The contagious nature of ishtyle—the eruption of snakes on the dance floor—is a sharing of subaltern affects, bound simultaneously to pleasure and shame, a sharing that enables the possibility of a "we."

SIX

Raw and Uncouth

Class, Region, and Caste at Koothnytz

Liking It Raw

Koothnytz was an irregular Bangalore-based party hosted between 2011 and 2014 co-organized by journalist, stylist, and activist Romal. The party draws its name from *dappankoothu*, or *koothu*, a highly percussive style of South Indian music that originates in street-based and ritual perfor-mance, but has been liberally appropriated into high production value popular Tamil film songs with vigorous choreography. The parties were not explicitly queer, but they were often hosted in conjunction with queer groups, or as fundraisers for pride. One online ad for *Koothnytz* reads:

> They say music brings us together and we couldn't but agree—that is a universal truth. And when you're Indian, no music brings you better together than the music that resonates with soul—Kooth! . . . Join us for a party that themes itself around dance, a wild desi beat, courtesy DJ Krish, and that innate need to just lose it all and Kooth like mental!

Another ad announces: ":: couthculture—Enough of the behaving, already! ::" and one more reads: "So get those veshtis and sarees and come and party the night out!"

These advertisements gesture to the universal (innate), spiritual (soul), national (when you're Indian), subcontinental (a wild desi beat), and regional (get those veshtis). Through clever wordplay, guests are invited to "lose their couth"—propriety, politeness, shame—by dancing to koothu music. The liberatory rhetoric around *Koothnytz* looks quite different from many of the highly disciplined spaces I've described so far: it insists on different choreographies, accents, and intimacies in the space. What is it about koothu that lends itself to this kind of discourse? What happens when koothu is played in the club? Whose couth is at stake when dancing to koothu? The appearance of koothu music and dance at *Koothnytz* and elsewhere requires me to think through class, region, and caste in nightlife in ways that other parties and dances do not.

Dappankoothu, shortened to *koothu*,[1] refers to a dance and music genre primarily performed by Dalit heritage artists from the South Indian state of Tamil Nadu that relies on the rapid and distinct percussion of the *parai* drum to produce energetic and pulse-like movements in various parts of the body. Dalit musicians and dancers perform koothu at a variety of festivals and rituals, and the form is notably associated with Hindu funeral processions heralded by these Dalit artists.[2] In popular parlance, "koothu" has come to refer to the genre of energetic song and dance sequences in Tamil cinema, different from "melody," "western," or "village folk" songs, and characterized by high-intensity athletic dance, as well as sexualized movements, camerawork, costume, and voice. *Filmi* koothu draws liberally from folk theater, music, and dance styles, and synthesizes them with rap, calypso, and auto-tune effects. Given the long history of exchange between artists (actors, musicians, directors, choreographers) across the various South Indian film industries,[3] koothu extends beyond Tamil cinema into other regional cinemas. Given its invocation of the street, popular, and public, it is also referred to as "mass."

Unlike film music artists producing "mass," *dappankoothu* heritage performers are primarily Dalit musicians and dancers. "Dalit" refers to people relegated to the "bottom" of the hierarchical Hindu caste system, a system of colonial governance endemic to the subcontinent (predating European colonialisms) that colludes with other forms of domination, and that infiltrates non-Hindu communities too. While Dalits inhabit a range of economic class positions, they are largely confined to forms of manual labor such as making leather, picking trash, and cleaning public sewage facilities. Because of their social status, Dalits can make and play the supposedly "unclean" leather surface of the *parai* and other drums— though the moral and religious implications behind this practice is, as Zoe Sherinian shows, contested and in flux.[4] While caste-based discrimination was made illegal after independence, and education and workplace reservations provided for "scheduled castes" and "other backward castes," caste hierarchy and caste-based violence persist across South Asia. Communal violence is often predicated on "beef eating," considered sacrilegious to Hindus and highly politicized under India's right-wing Hindutva government; tasks that involve handling cow carcasses such as making leather for drums remain risky.

Ethnomusicologist Amanda Weidman documents the emergence of koothu music in Tamil film, and captures its aesthetic qualities in her analysis of the sexy item song "En Peru Meenakumari":

> The distinctive "folk" sound of kuuththu is produce by a "rough" or "raw" voice and a particular pronunciation of the words characterized by a more open mouth and excessive trilling of "r" sounds, a sound produced by "pressing on" and "biting" the words. . . . Kuuththu has become a recognized and compulsory genre of song in Tamil films in the last ten years, often placed in the second half of the film to keep up audience interest.[5]

Weidman's essay focuses on the vocal and instrumental "roughness," but one might also attend to the aggressive choreography and cinematography of koothu songs that variously feature cutlasses against women's exposed midriffs, cameras zooming in on tongue rings and through legs, snarling lips, agile jumps, virtuosic athleticism, and repetitive pelvic pumps. Weidman's precise description of sound shows how accents signals moral citizenship—how vowels and consonants leaving the mouth communicate rawness and roughness, class and region.

When Romal first conceived of a koothu club night, these regional and class implications proved to be an impediment to his programming:

> What I got rapped across my face is that it's too low class, it's too local, nobody will want to dance. There were times people would say, "Anyways, half the time the crowd who comes and parties are North Indian, you know. The money is with all the North Indians."

But why wouldn't a koothu party appeal to middle- and upper-class South Indians in Bangalore? In a sly jab, Romal cynically describes the musical tastes of elite Bangaloreans as limited to classical Carnatic music; we had a good cackle over that. Class, Romal helps us see, is both wealth (the spending power of migrants into the city) and cultural capital (Carnatic versus koothu)—implicit in this is caste too, Carnatic music having devotional content and Brahminical patronage, and koothu being associated with the street and Dalit heritage performers.

Koothu is hardly a prevalent sound in Bangalore's nightlife, despite its popularity across South Indian radio stations and music TV channels. In conceiving this party, Romal struggled to locate a DJ who would willingly play South Indian film music. A few mainstream clubs in Bangalore catering to middle and upper classes play Hindi music once a week at themed "Bollywood Nights," usually on weekdays; none advertise Kollywood nights. The disdain for South Indian music in Bangalore's clubs can be severe; one DJ who agreed to spin for *Koothnytz* said he would keep South Indian music on hand if anyone asked for particular songs, but would really prefer to just play techno and house.

In addition to challenges finding an agreeable DJ, Romal also ran into resistance from police when he needed to get a party license for a newly opened bar that didn't yet have dance permits.

> I was actually told that the police are willing to give you permission to play Hindi music, but not to play local music. And the idea within the cops again is that Hindi music is sober, sane [and] apparently will not bring out any "rowdy elements," but South Indian music is so raw, it will bring out rowdy elements. So the police have this idea if you play koothu, people will start taking bottles and smashing.

Weidman argues that koothu carries a "moral tag"; it is "located near the bottom in the hierarchy of respectability in Tamil film songs."[6] In Romal's opinion, it is the very nature of the sound, "raw beats," he says over and over again, and the passions they incite, that the police deemed dangerous. There it is again: raw. Raw voice. Raw beats.

The word continues to haunt Dalit performance. Writer and scholar Akhil Kang contemplates how his queer and Dalit identities come to bear on each other:

> As I slid inside a guy who I was in bed with a couple of months back, in the middle of changing positions, he suddenly blurted out that it felt good that he finally gets to see my "Dalit rawness." Besides losing my erection, I lost something else that day as well. I lost my desire to be Dalit about my queerness.[7]

Akhil is read by his bottom as revealing an authentic Dalit gender, some essentialized quality to sex with a Dalit person, to having Dalit dick inside him. The erotic essentialization of a Dalit body, whether phobic or philic, invokes specious tropes of predatory Dalit men that threaten the sanctity of savarna Hindus—those inside the varna or caste order system—as well as assumptions about the sexual availability of Dalit women. Extrapolating Anupama Rao's theorizations of caste and sexual violence, we might understand that sexual desire is caste based, is in fact caste desire, almost always rendered unmarked by savarna privilege until eruptions of violence, including microaggressive comments such as the one from Akhil's partner.[8] The performative authenticity of Kang's body, its capacity to invoke unchecked sexuality assumed of Dalit bodies that must be disciplined, is captured in the word "raw."

Raw beats. Raw voice. Raw sex. Dalit rhythms, song, and bodies invoke the unclean, unpolished, unfinished, unrefined, uncooked; raw also captures the "backwardness" associated with Dalits, with region, and with poor classes. Lucinda Ramberg carefully brings queer studies to Dalit studies to ask, "But what might be foregone in the movement forward, away from backwardness?"[9] It is not lost on me that raw sex, particularly between gay men, also refers to condom-less anal and oral penetration. Black queer theorist Marlon Bailey describes the value of raw sex. While acknowledging risks of STD/STI transmission, he argues that raw sex "is a way to deal with or alleviate the alienation and feelings of worthlessness and ultimately to create a livable life," especially for those systemically and perpetually deemed worthless and alien by the state.[10] I offer Bailey's commentary to uphold the value, the intimate possibilities, of desiring and enjoying something "raw." There are intimate possibilities in feeling like we are dancing to raw beats, singing in a raw voice, feeling someone's (or our own) rawness. There are intimate possibilities to understanding and embracing minoritarian positions as raw, base, or bottom.[11] But it also worthwhile asking how such affects become available at all, to whom they are available, and how the stakes and conditions of embodying them vary.

Across this chapter, I am interested in how a "raw" style like koothu is mobilized through performance to produce different effects and affects in the nightclub, as well as the institutions that make these affects available by capitalizing on their association with specific bodies: poor, South Indian, Dalit people. As Sunaina Maira writes of the circulation of "cool" aesthetics among South Asian youth, "Black style travels more freely across racial and class borders than young Black men do."[12] So too Dalit, poor-class, regional aesthetics that engender "rawness" and even "freedom" circulate apart from the people they are associated with, people whose mobilities are perpetually obstructed. This chapter deepens *Ishtyle*'s investment in the role of class, region, and caste in queer critique by tracing itineraries of koothu from Dalit hereditary performers to the nightclub via film, making apparent how gay nightlife spaces reify class, region, and caste hierarchies. Class, region, and caste are not necessarily mutually constitutive, but I engage them together in this chapter because they emerge out of my experiences with koothu and *Koothnytz*.

These issues are urgent not only in the context of *Koothnytz*, but amid larger political economies of Bangalore. In the introduction, I explained how "India's new middle class" works as an aspirational self-fulfilling idiom that maps around labor, mobility, and consumption. These economic and cultural shifts are distinctly evident in Bangalore, India's "Silicon Valley"; however, economic development and class mobility in Bangalore rest very much on the backs of its poorest citizens. As Rajyashree Narayanareddy argues, the tech boom is accompanied by massive increases in waste production that relies on the risky labor of poor Muslims and Dalits.[13] In order to even do this manual labor in urban areas, poor Dalits must carefully traverse the city from the suburbs and chawls they are relegated to, without offending savarnas.[14] Reservations for "scheduled castes" and "scheduled tribes"—forms of affirmative action—in India's higher-education system and corporate sectors has had little effect on recalibrating class inequality for Dalits.[15] In addition to systemic economic disenfranchisement of Dalits is vastly unpunished lynching and rape of Dalits for a range of spurious reasons that include speaking with dominant-caste women and eating beef. The implications of outing or performing one's Dalit identity are dire. Further, casteism, colorism, and classism entangle with other kinds of xenophobia, rendering the many migrants in Bangalore, drawn to its expansive economy, renowned educational institutions, and urban amenities subject to racial profiling and physical and sexual harassment.

I have mentioned that my fieldwork changed me, shifted my politics and rechoreographed my body and gender. But where I had expected to write about Bollywood, a dance genre I grew up with, I did not know that I would fall in love with koothu. Learning to dance from hijras, *kothis*, and trans men at the Bangalore Pride March as Dalit drummers heralded our protest, from Tamil and Kannada film-dance competitions on TV, and from dancing with friends at *Koothnytz*, I found new pulsations, rhythms, and weights in my own body that felt fun, sexy, and relational. But tracking this dance style through online discourse and conversations with Romal and a film choreographer, and following the minimal research on koothu music, also forced me to think about caste, region, and class in ways I was not already seeing in nightclubs. Moreover, during fieldwork I learned from activists, organizers, and friends about the quotidian and spectacular forms of caste-based violence that my savarna diasporic life had shielded me from. Writing in the wake of the 2019 Indian elections, in which India's right-wing government resecured its power by activating a Hindutva political base, it feels especially necessary to think about the everyday/everynight nature of caste hierarchy. Across this chapter, I try to hold this critique in tension with the possibilities and urgency of pleasure for various minoritarian subjects.

Cheap Crowd, Expensive Tastes

In this section, I attend to a manifestation of street-style dance at *Heatwave*, thinking particularly about how class as material wealth is measured and performed at the nightclub. Class analysis has been central in shaping queer Indian studies. In ethnographic and cultural studies, queer India is differentiated into English-speaking neoliberal gay and lesbian subjects, and working-class transgenders, hijras, and *kothis* speaking vernacular languages and who are often tied to NGO organizations. But this class-gender-sexuality-language matrix is murkier than a binary. Gayatri Reddy argues in her ethnography of hijras in Hyderabad that identity categories, epistemologies, and language practices blur across class lines.[16] Gay activist Alok Gupta describes how a group of hijras refers to him as "Englishpur ki kothi," inviting him into their ranks as a *kothi*, but hailing him from the imaginary place of "Englishpur."[17] I am interested in these more messy and situated ways of seeing and doing class, not in the aspiration of interclass utopia, but because rigid identity matrices potentially obscure the sharing of productive solidarities and redistribution of material and cultural resources between identity groups.[18]

Bangalore's relatively small party scene affords complexity in studying India's middle classes given the class diversity at these events. Saturday night parties (see chapter 1), despite the many barriers they posed to entry, allowed for mingling of people from various occupations and class groups. At the parties I met men working as retail associates, call center employees, software engineers, IT project managers, fashion and television creatives, and global consulting executives—each in a more lucrative profession than the previous. This kind of class diversity is certainly not reflective of the metropolis's deep class divides, but it is exceptional to Bangalore's nightclubs that institute class-uniformity through steep cover charges, vigilant dress codes, and drink prices. The modicum of class diversity at gay parties is not utopic, and class is monitored by partygoers who judge each other's style—fashion, friend group, dance—to regulate whom they talk to or flirt with.[19]

In 2003, Akshaye's Saturday night *Pink Nation* parties cost four hundred rupees, which included drink tickets, dinner, DJ, and dancing at bars in central Bangalore. Rishab recalls those events: "Yes, it used to be very expensive, but at the same time . . . where you actually find the crowd which is classy in the sense . . . guys you would not mind going for a coffee first." He suggests that in 2003 men who could pay four hundred rupees were men you wouldn't mind being seen in public with, who were good for more than a fuck. When software developer Kirti started hosting parties under the banner *Club Time* with a lower cover charge and without drink tickets or dinner, Akshaye was forced to lower his prices and forgo the "classy" elements of his party, such as dinner or free giveaways. This also changed the economic threshold of coming to the parties and created greater class diversity. The moderately cheaper entry fee of two hundred to three hundred rupees (four to six dollars) that I paid between 2009 and 2012 was still a bar to entry, and occasional "free entry" parties always saw an increase in attendance. The uptick in attendance at free parties made clear to me that even the lowered cover charge was a high threshold for many people wishing to participate in the gay party scene regularly.

Class is differentiated not only by who can afford to come in, but also by how people perform: "Someone who appears bourgeois may not actually inhabit that socioeconomic position and someone who is materially situated within the middle class might not perform a bourgeois sensibility."[20] Bobby Benedicto writes, "Even under the dimmest of lights, class is read in microscopic ways in the ways shirts are tucked into pants, in the way hair falls at the back of someone's head, in the tone of one's voice, or in the way the smell of cologne mixes with the order of one's sweat," and of course in the way one dances.[21]

At a "free entry" *Heatwave* party at The Fountain on Church Street one Sunday night, Salman sidles up behind me as I watch the dance floor. He is gym-built, dark, handsome, in his mid-twenties; he whisper-shouts into my ear, "Cheap crowd tonight, no?" Although we were watching the same scene, I hadn't registered what he saw; his snobby senses were faster than my ethnographic eye. He was commenting on a group of six men who had arrived together; while they had the stylish silhouette of skinny jeans, slim-fit T-shirts, and Converse-style shoes, they danced with aggressive abandon. Arms flailed and jerked, and butts bumped against pulsing crotches, not in soft pulsations but horny thrusts. One held the other by the shoulders for stability and intimacy, and in order to hop and thrust his hips to the left and right and left and right of his friend. These pulsative movements forced their bodies into each other's space. Though performed to heavily remixed and techno-fied Katy Perry and FloRida tracks, this was street-style dance—fluctuating between Bombay-style *tapori* and Chennai-style koothu. It was certainly not the coordinated soft grooves and even weight shifts that allow for gentle improvisations within the moving mass of the nightclub's limited space. The boys played up the homoeroticism of energetic homosocial street dance, holding hands and jumping in a circle, sometimes turning to sloppily kiss each other. Their revelry epitomized *khel* (play) and *masti* (mischief), distinctly Indian idioms of homosocial play that waiver between eroticism and friendship.[22]

Hindi *tapori* and Tamil koothu song and dance sequences are often filmed in urban street settings, and dancers are costumed in everyday, everyman wear. The "rowdy"—macho, street-smart figure who often does these dances—"is a figure of excessive enjoyment and considerable effort goes into producing him as an authentic subaltern. . . . *The politics of the mass film revolves around the rowdy's excesses.*"[23] Despite their insistent danceability and the breadth of choreography they offer viewers, these genres are not nightclub favorites given their association with the street. For Salman, manifestations of street dance in the nightclub, in friction with US pop music, made this crowd "cheap." Unimpressed with such cheap behavior, he goes on to tell me that he is generally unimpressed with the gay party situation, mentioning that the last time he attended one, there was a police raid. Gay parties' association with criminality and immorality make them "cheap." Moneyed partygoers can frequent fancier bars, bars that can eschew police attention with hefty bribes and don't need the income from gay parties.

Later that night, a Grindr acquaintance introduced me to Navin, one of the young men Salman and I watched on the dance floor; my friend had met Navin via PlanetRomeo. Navin is a handsome boy from Orissa, twenty-six years old, although he looked younger, and had been working in clothing retail in Bangalore for the last three years. The sexual chemistry between Navin and me escalated quickly, and he told me, "I like to get funky." I interpreted his use of "funky" as a linguistic remixing of "kinky." I arrived at this after getting bitten, slapped, grabbed, bruised, and having beer poured over my face and licked off on the middle of the dance floor. He kept grabbing my love handles until I could feel the skin bruise and I had to playfully (but also out of necessity) slap his face to distract him so that he would stop; he would smile mischievously after each slap. With his pulsative koothu style, he danced against and into my body, bumping it with his crotch, hips, and butt; at one point he grabbed my hair at its roots and steered my head until I had two tongues in my mouth—his and his friend's. When we left the dance floor, he told me to go and buy another beer. When I protested that I was done drinking, he said, "No, I want to pour it on your head and lick it off your neck. Like they do to show you have money."

Navin draws on the English term "funky" to describe rough sexualities commonly categorized as "kink" or "BDSM" in internet-accessible pornography; his desires are accented, synthesizing the smell, sex, and mood associated with funk,[24] and inadvertently rhyming with "kinky." His funky pleasures were inspired by global media, and he used the cheaper substitute of beer to recreate the gaudy pouring of champagne over women's bodies, as seen in both nineties rap videos and Bollywood films. Navin's funky play certainly draws from global capitalist regimes of pornography and music television, but as he very purposefully sends me to fetch a beer, he acknowledges the limits of embodying these lifestyles in middle-class gay India, where champagne is overpriced or even unavailable at the bar. Also, his tendency to bite lips, grab exposed flesh, and pull hair reminds me of metonymic performances of sex in Indian song and dance sequences from the eighties and nineties, when depictions of intercourse were highly censored and these intimate gestures were used to denote sex. While making out at *Heatwave* parties is not uncommon, it is usually discreet—lovers find a corner, or lock arms around shoulders to manufacture a sense of privacy. Navin's elaborate foreplay, syncretic pleasure drawn from kinky Western porn and censored Indian cinema, is ishtyle that disrupts pedagogies of the night.

While Navin, working in retail, might be from a lower-class echelon than many party attendees, what renders him "cheap" is his dance. But while class may be surveilled and policed at these Saturday night parties, substituting beer for champagne allows for the accented improvisation of moneyed aesthetics and their erotic pleasures. Attending to performance offers the opportunity to investigate class in India with a different nuance, acknowledging that deeply entrenched class hierarchies exist across the queer and trans spectrums, but also between the middle classes. Even in the face of class hierarchy, the pleasures of wealth can be accessed through performance and play. I extricated myself from Navin. He was a little too funky for me, and my flesh couldn't take any more pain. He did take my number, however, and WhatsApped me a schedule of all the times he was available to host a hookup during the week: when he wasn't working and when his roommates weren't home.

Dappankoothu *Hardcore*

I arrived fashionably late at my first *Koothnytz*, held during Bangalore Pride 2011 at a small bar off the trendy and central Church Street; it was already packed. Romal's networks and expansive advertising yielded some of my friends from *Heatwave* parties, but also many people I'd never seen before. Where *Heatwave* used images of white men on its e-fliers distributed only through online venues such as PlanetRomeo, WhatsApp, and Grindr, Romal insisted on *Koothnytz's* South Indianness via ads on public Facebook groups, online magazine *Pink Pages*, *TimeOut Bengaluru*, and TV9. At the front door, Romal collected my cover charge, to be donated to Bangalore Pride, and misted my face with rose water. Swati, his co-organizer, flirtatiously tied a string of jasmines around my wrist, explaining over the music, "We're trying to create an authentic effect!" The stairwell vibrated with fast percussions, and the nightclub space was thick with sweat and body heat.

Romal professes a romantic and capacious vision of koothu that understands the form as "freestyle"—more on that later—and when he finally connected with DJ Chandru, he encouraged him to include any music with heavy percussion. DJ Chandru played primarily Tamil koothu, but also Kannada, Telugu, and Malyalam tracks; Sri Lankan Baila, Afro-British drum and bass, and chutney soca were thrown in for good measure, along with M.I.A. (a diasporic Tamil Sri Lankan artist) and the Black Eyed Peas (who have sampled Tamil film music). Chandru's signature closing song at the few *Koothnytz* he spun at was always "Wavin' Flag" by Somali-Canadian artist K'naan—the uplifting signature song of the 2010 World Cup.

Some dancers arrived at *Koothnytz* following the brief in the online ads, confidently wearing their *veshtis* and *mundus*, generally unseen garb for the nightclub. As they danced, they pulled the fabric up, and their exposed hairy legs rubbed against each other's. I recognized some of Romal's straight friends, and a few of mine were there too, but the communal nature of dance at this party, the freedom to enter and exit small groups on this crowded dance floor, didn't engender clear distinctions between queer and straight. In a circle of dancers, one man rested his weight on his palms and feet on the ground in a high bridge, pulsing his pelvis upward toward another guy straddling him. A woman in a *salwar khameez*—also not nightclub wear—seemingly tired of the gay-boy groupings or of being bumped around, spread her bent legs and outstretched arms wide to occupy space. She stuck her tongue out of her mouth until it reached her chin, holding the pose until she had attracted some attention, before hopping from one foot to another with arms stretched wide and hands quivering, invoking goddess imagery and repertoires of South Indian folk dance styles such as Yakshagana and Bonalu. Koothu engendered alternatives choreographies of homoeroticism and femininity in the club space.

That night, the crowd went especially wild for "Chammak Challo," a Hindi film song that includes Tamil lyrics and was made in collaboration with Senegalese-American Akon; Kannada item song "Oorigoble Pad-mavathi"; Tamil favorite "En Peru Meenakumari"; and a dance-remix of the global Tanglish (Tamil-English) megahit "Kolaveri," which mixes R & B and Tamil folk rhythms and *filmi* masculine sentimentality. At *Koothnytz*, the crotch-bumping street-style dances that Navin and friends were doing at *Heatwave* would not have been out of place amid the slick nightclub interiors and elite and middle-class crowd. These alternative repertoires are emplaced by the sonic landscape of rapid, high-pitched *parai* drumbeats—different from the low nss-nss of techno—as well as by fresh jasmine fragrances, sweat smells, and sweltering heat that made us believe we were in the street, and vibrating walls that simulated the percussive resonance of live drums.

Koothnytz, in insinuating South Indian music, dance, and languages into a cosmopolitan vision of queer India, offers an opportunity to consider queer region. In the popular US queer TV show *RuPaul's Drag Race*, the show's host, RuPaul Charles, refers to drag forms in the US Midwest, South, and Puerto Rico as "regional," often identifying these queens' penchant for pageantry instead of cutting-edge fashion as the determining difference. In the eleventh season, she specifically equates "regional" drag with a "raw" aesthetic; certain places and their associated styles have not yet arrived, or been cooked, into the queer modern. Gayatri Gopinath theorizes "queer region" as a mode of imagining geopolitical analytics other than the global or national, and the distinct aesthetics of gender and sexuality associated with regions. This analytic permits "an alternative mapping of sexual geographies that link disparate transnational locations and that allow new models of sexual subjectivity to come into focus."[25] The celebratory regional rhetoric in Romal's publicity and curation allows gender and desire to "come into focus" in different ways, to be articulated through different techniques of the body: dancing with goddess imagery, flirting with lifted *lungis*, and so on.

Attending to region links "disparate transnational locations." In Romal's and DJ Chandru's crafting of a koothu soundscape, they produce a sonic South Indian-ness that is inclusive of diaspora and blackness—- M.I.A., Akon, K'naan, Black Eyed Peas. Too, so many koothu hits include rap, reggae, chutney, hip-hop, and R & B. Black and South Asian sonic intimacies have primarily been theorized through the bhangra-hip-hop exchanges out of Birmingham and New York City in the nineties.[26] South Indian popular film, music, and dance afford us another opportunity to engage Black-Asian exchange. The figure of actor and choreographer Prabhu Deva offers an especially fertile case to explore convergences of Tamil mass music and dance with blackness. Ritty Lukose writes of Deva's early film *Kaadalan*, which shot him to fame:

> It reconfigures the young lower-caste male body, in the figure of its star Prabhu Deva, to mediate globalization, the violence of the state, and the demands of tradition. Under the sign of "fashion" in- dicated by his desire for blue jeans and sneakers, the body is refash- ioned as urban and consumerist. . . . Previously, it was under the rubric of the "folk" and the "rural" that the lower-caste body had been configured. This film marks an important moment in which globalization and its signifiers attach themselves to the body of the lower-caste, lower-class male.[27]

Beyond sartorial style, Deva's infamous choreographies, unapologeti- cally citational of Michael Jackson, synthesize koothu and Afro-diasporic dance. In developing choreographies that suggest low caste and class in Tamil film, Deva synthesizes the bodily isolations and pumps of urban- folk *dappankoothu* with those of commercial and global popular black dance: the quick points of locking, crafted jerks of popping, the smooth slides of the moonwalk, and Jackson's pelvic thrust-crotch grab. In the "audiotopia" of *Koothnytz*, as bodies pump and pop toward each other, black and South Indian street dances converge to enable diverse homo-erotics and gender displays.[28]

Thinking South India as a queer region is also important because of how it has manifested in dominant North Indian imaginations, particularly in the depiction of South Indian characters, dance, and music in Hindi film. Blockbuster Hindi films like *Chennai Express* reduce Tamil Nadu to a few signature tropes: dark skin, coconuts, mustaches, *lungis*, and Rajnikanth. One song in *Chennai Express* sexualizes koothu by instructing dancers to "Bootyshake, bootyshake, *dappankoothu* hardcore." In Sachin Kundalkar's Hindi film *Aiyyaa!*, a Maharashtrian Brahmin woman falls in love with a dark-skinned South Indian man, and her daydream fantasies manifest in the song "Dreamum Wakeupum" as caricatured versions of Kollywood dance, Tamil language, and outdated camera effects and instrumentation.[29] The sonic, visual, and kinesthetic imagination associated with Kollywood song and dance allows the filmic lovers to grab each other's flesh, pump their groins into each other, and simulate mutual oral sex. Similarly, the *supherit* Hindi film *The Dirty Picture*, an adapted biopic of Tamil softcore porn actress Silk Smitha, uses the chorus of koothu song "Nakka Mukka"—it is the only Tamil song used in this film about a Tamil woman—to underscore Silk's hypersexuality. The choreographies of "Nakka Mukka" in its original appearance in Tamil film *Kahdalil Viz-hunthen* are athletic, hip thrusting, and vigorous, but not explicitly sexual.

The sounds of *Aiyyaa!* and *The Dirty Picture*, even as they carica-ture South Indianness and equate it with hypersexuality, offer sexual soundscapes—orgasmic panting in "Ooh La La," trilled *r*s and nasal *a*s in "Nakka Mukka," suggestively bulbous trombones in "Dreamum Wakeu-pum," postcoital exhales in "Aga Bai"—with which to play in the dance club. The accent, I've suggested, is not only the discursive manifestation of minoritarian difference, but has performative potential in its sensorial difference too. In these complicated uptakes of South India by Bollywood, the club soundscape gains new sounds and sensations to perform sexual-ity. In her ethnography of a women's university hostel in Chennai, Sneha Krishnan describes a moment when a woman shows her peers the newly released "Dreamum Wakeupum" video on a laptop. While they are disap-pointed at the egregious representation of Tamil-ness in this Hindi film, the song's explicit lyrics and choreography inspire homosocial dancing between the women: "They would touch each other's waists and breasts as the actors in the song do. Imitating song-and-dance sequences, particularly item numbers, was often the pretext and context for much same-sex touching and play."[30] When "Dreamum Wakeupum" came on at *Koothnytz*, most dancers in the room began thrusting hips toward each other. Ram spread his legs and squatted, patting his thighs, suggesting I mount them—I realized he was asking me to replicate sexualized choreography from *Aiyyaa!*

The enlivened choreographies of *Koothnytz* and other queer dance spaces offer a unique opportunity to "reanimate" filmic hypersexuality in ways that other middle-class spaces do not.[31] When writing about reperformances of "En Peru Meenakumari," Amanda Weidman details the ways that the song and its choreographies are made respectable in live performance by deflecting excessive sexuality.[32] Similarly, Krishnan's interlocutors too giggle away the hypersexuality of these songs, as well as any lesbian identification in their homosocial play. Queer parties are one of few middle-class spaces where social dance is as sexy in public as it is on screen; at queer parties, the dancing queens will pump their bosoms and run their hands over their bodies with the same vigor as screen stars. So even in Bollywood's grotesque appropriations of South Indianness, might we imagine how South Indian dancers in the nightclub steal choreography and pleasure back from these appropriative songs, Bollywood tracks that are more likely to be played than actual South Indian film music?[33]

At one *Koothnytz* party, I asked the DJ why he was playing so much Hindi music. He said that he was taking all requests and these were the songs people asked for. He was also spinning only snippets of songs with choppy transitions because of the overload of songs requested. Attempting to pack it all in, he played a Tamil melody track, shrill and sweet and different from koothu songs. I had never heard it before, but the crowd sighed nostalgically at the opening notes. Suddenly, I found myself a Krishna to two Radhas. Vishal on one side, with his bharata natyam *abhinaya* (facial expressions) and mudras flirted shamelessly. On the other, Karan's kathak chakras (spins) and extended open palms beckoned me. For both these classically trained dancers—one working in pharmaceuticals, the other at a sexual health NGO—their deeply ingrained repertoires are kept out of the club space due to DJs' Western biases, but also Brahminical propriety that reserves classical dance for the sanctified stage and studio. But this queer desi DJing, playing a melody song, changed the tempo and offered a rare moment to engage embodied memory through dance, inviting *sring-*

ara, erotic repertoires of classical dance, to function as queer flirtation. It's worth noting that Hindu imagery, particularly the *ched chad* (eve teasing) between Radha and Krishna, is popular in commercial Indian film song. While all club-goers can find pleasure in these danced idioms, Muslims and Christians are less likely to be hailed in their faith by the music the way Hindus are. Queer desi DJing that risks playing courtesan, Sufi, or melody songs potentially invites new choreographies, hails minoritarian counterpublics, and allows "divine communion" in the club.[34]

Such moments of "cultural intimacy"[35] are ever rare in Bangalore's gay nightlife, and *Koothnytz* offers especially important opportunities to be in one's regional difference. At this party, most people had sweat stains on their back, but there was a group of boys in the far corner who were sopping! Rather than dance to every track, they waited for South Indian numbers. They took turns dancing for each other: those who recognized the Tamil tracks lip-synched and played, while those more comfortable in Kannada or Telugu got up and danced to those songs. The intimacy of regional language mattered in hailing patrons to dance differently in the club space. At that party I ran into friends from Bombay and even one friend from Chicago; they all looked rather lost throughout the night, disoriented by unfamiliar songs that queer South Indian patrons celebrated. The young men in the corner, hailing from across South India, came with these languages, musics, and dances well rehearsed in their bodies, capitalizing on them as an opportunity to be sexy, seen, or simply themselves. Centering region, at the party and in analysis, offers other aesthetic tools for practicing queer gender and sexuality, be it Prabhu Deva's suave street cool, bharata natyam's and kathak's effaced erotics, or the intimate pulsations of commercial koothu. *Koothnytz*'s expansive sonic landscape emplaces these aesthetics, and gives us permission to feel sexy inside of them.

Romal no longer hosts *Koothnytz*, but he has certainly choreographed koothu into my repertoire. Returning to Chicago, where I hosted *Jai Ho!* parties as LaWhore Vagistan, I supplied our DJs with koothu tracks. While these numbers did not shift the choreography of the entire club, playing "Ringa Ringa" from *Aarya 2* did give some of my Telugu friends opportunities to dance their femininity and sexiness with abandon and force. These women's familiarity with the song's meaning, affects, and choreography gave them permission to take up space, crouch down and dance on the floor itself, and thrust their hips; this regional song allowed them to vigorously wield their bodies at an event that privileges men and North Indian sound (see chapter 4). In January 2018, LaWhore Vagistan was invited to perform at a new queer club night in Bangalore that regularly features drag artists. I lip-synched a medley of songs that concluded with "Nakka Mukka." I peeled off my long blond wig and kicked off my heels; the song called for this raw treatment, unfettered by the accoutrements of Western femininity. The crowd reacted with screams and applause and even asked for an encore of "Nakka Mukka" in particular; multiple audience members joined me on stage for this last dance. The organizer of the party eventually told me LaWhore's show was the first time any Indian music was played at the party, and that the audience's eager reaction inspired them to host a regular *Koothu Night*. At this upscale hotel nightclub that played only EDM and English music, LaWhore's koothu performance hailed a South Indian counterpublic, revealing their attachment to region and inciting alternative choreographies on stage and off.

Whose Couth?

Over the course of my interview with Romal about *Koothnytz,* he variously cited his attraction to the genre as stemming from the rise of koothu in Tamil film music, the appropriation of koothu by Western musicians, and the role of *parai* drummers in South Indian politics. Realizing that South Indian film music was being sampled by US and French bands, he asked, "Why can't we have this music playing in *our* pubs?" He also recalled the explosion of koothu in the Tamil music industry in the late nineties, accompanied by the popularity of these mass songs amongst his Bangalore college mates. Turned on to koothu by these new film songs, he and his friends would run out of the college gates to join koothu religious and funerary processions, dancing in ways they had once deemed "downmarket." Prior to Bangalore, Romal was also exposed to koothu music in the streets of Tamil Nadu where he grew up, where political parties employed koothu musicians to herald their public appearances.

Romal is particularly interested in koothu's capacity to critique Brahmin supremacy. After India's independence, the state of Tamil Nadu, inspired by the philosophies and leadership of E. V. Ramaswamy (also known as Periyar), insisted upon a Dravidian identity that was consciously anti-Brahminism. The inclusion of koothu musicians, and the distinct visual and sound of the *parai* drum, at the campaigns of C. N. Annadurai and K. Kamaraj signaled a commitment to Dalit inclusion. There is a long-standing collaboration and collusion between projects of Tamil statehood and the rhetorics and stars of Tamil film.[36] And yet the eventual deployment of koothu in Tamil film, as Amanda Weidman documents, while signaling poor classes and subordinate castes as urban subjects, links them to hypersexuality, rawness, and roughness instead of lifting them up as subjects deserving of political dignity.[37]

But is hypersexuality in conflict with sociopolitical dignity? An important debate emerges in Dalit feminism that produces tensions with queer studies.[38] Jenny Rowena argues, it is very much an elitist savarna project to laud representations of hypersexuality such as Vidya Balan's portrayal of Silk Smitha in *The Dirty Picture*, ignoring the material conditions of Dalit, Bahujan, and Advivasi women who are forced into bar dancing and sex work.[39] The consequences of refusing respectability, of "losing your couth," are different based on caste. Lucinda Ramberg on the other hand questions the modernizing impulse of reform that renders "Dalits who perform work designated as polluting [who do not] seek to escape such labor" as having a "false consciousness."[40]

How do we extend these critical debates in Dalit feminism to think about queerness and bodily pleasure?[41] Dalit criticism, from B. R. Ambedkar's manifestos for caste eradication to the self-respect marriage movement, has been implicitly queer in its trenchant critique of caste endogamy, and of heteronormative reproduction of gender inequality.[42] Queer activists and scholars also claim solidarity with anticaste projects, arguing "the queer struggle is naturally also about other forms of transgression such as inter-caste and inter-community relationships which are sought to be curbed by society."[43] But when we listen to Dalit queer and trans folks, we find that some of these theoretical moves to bring sexuality and caste into parallel frames of analysis fail to accommodate the multiple oppressions impinging on their lives.[44] A burgeoning body of journalism and public programming is drawing attention to the contributions and complexities of queer and trans Dalit lives.[45] Blogger Surya extrapolates Dalit-Bahujan contributions to queer politics and sociality prior to widespread NGOization, naming the risky visibility and care work that subordinate caste transfeminine people have been doing for decades.[46] These interventions are especially important because of the continued transphobic and casteist dismissal of hijras and other transfeminine people by elite gay men in LGBTQ organizing.[47]

In middle-class sexualized gay spaces such as online platforms and parties caste is staged and certainly shapes desire. It is not uncommon on Grindr to see the infamous torso shot accessorized with a Brahmin's white thread draped diagonally across the body. In profile names dominant caste identities are exhibited with pride, suggesting a correlation between their caste and desirability: "jatt top," or simply "Reddy" or "Gowda." Sometimes caste discrimination is more explicit, and people announce "no dalits" or call Dalit men "polluted." In the well-publicized case of India's "first gay newspaper matrimonial," activist Harish Iyer's mother published an ad looking for a partner for her son. Not only was caste signified in the desire for a "vegetarian groom for my son," but the ad concluded "caste no bar (though Iyer preferred)." Dalit writers also describe the passing politics they engage to look and feel desirable in middle-and upper-class queer social and virtual spaces.[48]

Casteism also manifests as middle-class gay men's subscription to Hindutva politics. In December 2013, I attended the Global Day of Rage protests in front of Bangalore's town hall, organized to decry the Indian Supreme Court's recriminalization of sodomy. A cardboard structure inscribed with both "377" *and* "Manusmriti" was ritually burned, a symbolic condemnation of both national *and* Hindu laws that impinge on sexual freedom and caste liberation. When some men around me realized that the structure included the Manusmriti, they became uncomfortable. And while they chanted loudly against the Supreme Court, the volume dropped significantly against the Hindutva-promoting Bharatiya Janata Party. It is increasingly apparent that many men in the queer community are ardent BJP supporters, despite its silence on queer and trans rights, as well as its anti-Muslim and casteist sentiments and policies.[49]

In later interviews in my fieldwork, as my own awareness of caste developed, I would ask explicitly about my interlocutors' caste backgrounds. It was difficult to get them to name caste, let alone delve into caste hierarchy. One person admitted that while he doesn't believe in caste hierarchy, he wears a Brahmin thread, and that his mother will not let his Muslim friends into certain parts of the house. Another said he was "just a good Tam-Bram [Tamil Brahmin] boy." This forty-something-year-old's invocation of being a "good boy" signals the intrepid innocence, the impunity, of being from a dominant caste. One more person offered that his family's South Indian Brahmin background, their attachment to privilege and social standing, is what made it more difficult for him to come out and for them to accept his sexuality.

Documenting how caste hierarchies inflect queer intimacy, on Grindr and at protests, suggests that caste also marks pleasure and performance in gay nightlife in ways I was perhaps unattuned to for much of my fieldwork. Queer Dalit scholar Dhiren Borisa draws on auto-ethnography to document how he and other minoritarian subjects deflect stigma through sartorial performance and choreography to fit into dominant aesthetic and identitarian frames of Delhi's gay parties, in order to enjoy the pleasures of music, dance, and community they sometimes provide.[50] Though there are limits to my own epistemes as a savarna scholar, and while I did not deeply engage caste in my research interviews, it is necessary that I explore how caste hierarchy shapes nightlife, through sound, choreography, and discourse.

If I've described elsewhere in this book the many ways that nightclubs regulate and restrict performance, *Koothnytz* offers the exciting opportunity to refuse and reject this decorum. Playing on the homonyms, "koothu" and "couth," *Koothnytz* invites patrons to "lose all your inhibitions" in "music that resonates with the soul." But couth is tied to caste, to the decorum of inhabiting elite social positions, and securing them through performance—take my Brahmin friend above, for whom caste made coming out a challenge. As I've described in earlier sections, koothu cultivates choreographies that are unwelcome in the nightclub, that allow bodies to inhabit space with a sense of play and vigor that other spaces do not. These pleasures are important and urgent and are routinely denied to my interlocutors. But savarnas are able to put this caste-inflected play on their body in the space of the nightclub, and safely return to the rest of their lives without stigma.

How is koothu able to accomplish the kind of liberatory work that it does? Romal narrated the form as natural movements of the body that respond to the "raw beats" of the music: "There is no repertoire." A Tamil film choreographer I interviewed reiterated the same sentiment: "It's freestyle." Indeed, the broader rhetoric around *dappankoothu* is replete with the suggestion that it is "free" movement. One blog suggests: "The Dappankuthu is a very informal form of dance. And there aren't any strict rules to it, per se."[51] Another blog explains:

> This is a form of dance for the common man, a freestyle way of dancing. . . . Yes, Dappankuthu is a "free and open source" form of dancing. There are no dance teachers and no student dancers. Everyone is a beginner [and is] expected to create and learn new steps each and every time.[52]

A YouTube video titled "How to Learn DAPPANKUTHU (Drunken Dance) in 5 Easy Steps" explains that you must (1) get drunk, (2) free yourself, (3) swagger on, (4) feel the rhythm, and (5) go all crazy. A bonus title during the video commands: "Have no SHAME."[53] What is curious is that Romal, the film choreographer, and this YouTube video exhibit similar choreographies that also compare with koothu songs in Tamil films. The upper body and arms pulse in opposition to the knees and feet. The tongue is folded under itself. The lower lip is bit emphatically. The chest is pulsed outward with a hand behind the head. Despite being "freestyle" there is very much a repertoire.

Tamil internet celebrity Wilbur Sargunaraj published an instructional video, "How to Do the Dappankuthu," that interviews professional drummer-dancers about their craft.[54] In the video, Sargunaraj's energetic, hip-swinging choreography contrasts with the more reserved, footwork-oriented dances of the *parai* musicians he interviews and films. The essentialist imagination of koothu as "freestyle" misses the very methodical but unspectacular choreography of heritage musicians, as well as ongoing transformations and negotiations of respectability that heritage performers engage to achieve dignity, moral recognition, and employment. For example, Dalit musicians perform Hindu-inflected rituals that sanctify the *parai* drum to uplift its value, and refuse to play funerals in order to mitigate stigma.[55] Zoe Sherinian's extensive work on the discourse and performance of the *parai* also documents how Christian organizations teach Dalit women to use the drum in activist theater that standardizes and desexualizes the movement.[56]

Sargunaraj's lively and erratic dance contrasts with the koothu troupe's repetitive and regulated choreography. To be clear, neither style is "better": as Dalit *parai* drumming undergoes its own respectability projects that disassociate it from sex, death, and play, popular circulations of the genre via film retain its effervescent, sexual, and fun possibilities. What is at stake is the discursive dissociation of koothu from heritage communities that render it "free": free of form and free for appropriation. The appropriations and reformations of heritage dances performed by subordinate caste communities have a long history: the codification of *sadir* dance into bharata natyam, the desexualization of tamasha dancers, and the exploitation of *lavni* dancers.[57] However the articulation of koothu as "free and open source" stands in contrast to the rigidly codified aesthetics of these other forms, a rhetoric characterized by the neoliberal circumstances under which koothu becomes gentrified. As koothu gains popularity through intricate commercial film choreography and becomes a category of exhibition performance via YouTube, Instagram, and diasporic dance studios, as "the glamorous impersonates the ordinary," its caste-based origins and Dalit protagonists recede.[58]

Thomas DeFrantz documents how black social dances circulate under neoliberal conditions of mass mediation, on shows such as *Soul Train* and *American Bandstand*. These circulations not only capitalize on the free market to sell black dance, but also convey the "feeling" of freedom in black social dance's improvisatory qualities.[59] Casting improvised dance into the free market renders it available to all, "a neoliberal right of access."[60] The revival and reformation of bharata natyam under transition from colonial to postcolonial governance shapes the discourses around it; appealing to Western notions of rationality, it loses its association with improvisation in service of repeatable, teachable, repertoire-based performance. Koothu, invited into the popular imagination in a postliberalization context, is taken up precisely because it appeals to neoliberal sensibilities of freedom in its improvisatory nature. Tamil film's uptake of *dappankoothu* is the vehicle by which this urban Dalit folk repertoire becomes "freestyle," disarticulated from the communities that originate the form, available to all. The language of innovation and individual creativity that surrounds koothu reminds us that "the neoliberal project . . . is not merely one of economics and institutions": its "cultural arm is concerned with individual conduct that spills over from the economic realm."[61]

Ramón Rivera-Servera, describing the arrival of reggaeton in Mexican American queer nightclubs, explores the possibility for new and valuable choreographic habitations of homoeroticism that a different soundscape—tropicalized, black, Caribbean—enables. He argues that queer Mexican dancers' uptakes of these sounds, while certainly relying on "discriminatory caricaturing and the desirious characterization of [Puerto Rican] difference and sexual appeal," offer opportunities for sexual performance in a repressive political, moral, and social climate.[62] "Friction," he writes, "dominates the dance floor."[63] The frictive quality of koothu at the club is what engenders pleasure for many of my queer friends, whose performances of sexual desire and regional identity are curtailed at other nightlife venues, workplaces, and in everyday public spheres as well. At *Koothnytz*, koothu really did change the choreographies of the club; we did indeed lose our couth. We could pump pelvises toward each other unapologetically. We could widen our stance and hike up and knot (imaginary) *veshtis*. We could keep one hand on the head and the other on the hip, and swing our hyperfeminine curves. We had a reason to dance on the floor itself, or climb on each other's bodies. For some dancers, they could sing and dance in languages that felt like home, while also translating these grammars into the erotic landscape of the club.

Film-facilitated circulation of koothu allows alternative habitations of the club, sexy and energetic improvisations that don't center whiteness and North Indian-ness, that allow access to movement that (neo)colonial and Brahminical reformations train out of Indian dancing bodies. In the monotone soundscapes of Bangalore's nightlife, *Koothnytz* was an especially exciting diversification of the city's sonic worlds. But in the viciously casteist landscape of middle-class India and of gay nightlife, it behooves us to assess the stakes of finding freedom in Dalit sound. To draw again on DeFrantz, "We might at least be aware of the terms of this exchange, so that we can, at times, disrupt the seeming inevitability of 'dancing like a black American' [or like a Dalit] in order to feel free: physically powerful, sexually provocative, rhythmically aggressive, and preternaturally cool."[64]

I am not critiquing dancers who enjoy these styles; rather I want to point to the systems of governance that suture particular affects and discourses to various forms of popular dance. Commercial film industries too act as "national cinema,"[65] as an arm of state and regional politics, and their embedded dances circulate choreography, meaning, and affect for global, national, and regional audiences. Across Ishtyle, many of the dances I've written about are embroiled in complicated discourses: bhangra often stands in for North Indian dance in Hindi film in ways that efface both ethnic diversity in North India and Sikh Punjabi claims to separate statehood; Madhuri Dixit's infamous sexy style in "Choli Ke Peeche" relies on bucolic visions of rural Rajasthan; and the pervasive snake-woman in Hindi cinema famously embodied in Sridevi's *Nagina* is co-opted from serpent-worship practices in Indian tribal communities. But these dances, as they are transferred to us via film, family, and friends, have the capacity to activate different kinds of politics when set on the body, and performed in the company of others, in the nightclub.

Freedom improvises inside of form, and to deny koothu its form disappears its Dalit origins. Expanding on Sabah Mahmood, Lucinda Ramberg writes, "When we equate freedom with emancipation *from* custom, culture, and religion, we have fenced off these terrains as potential resources for those who find themselves at the margins of social and political life."[66] Restoring koothu as a *form* of improvisation, instead of simply a "free" style, is one way of enjoying the music and dance that now has such widespread circulation, without voiding it of the heritage artists who originate and sustain the form. Restoring freedom *to* "custom, culture, and religion," we uplift those who originated and sustained this "potential resource." In Bangalore, this seems particularly important because the Coalition for

Sexuality Minorities Rights, which plans the annual pride march, consci-
entiously hires Dalit drummers to herald the march. Additionally, it is
Dalit-Bahujan hijras and *kothis* who koothu vigorously and impressively
with the drummers, spectacularly and publicly staging queer visibility for
the community. Meanwhile they are the folks explicitly excluded from
elite nightlife spaces (see preface).

In *I Want to Be Ready*, Danielle Goldman argues that the stakes of
improvisational dance, and the affective freedoms we access in improvisation, vary based on context and identity.[67] In a blog post, Vijeta Kumar
offers a testimonial of her experience at a Dalit women's conference, and
the ecstatic possibilities of koothu that closed the event. At the end of an
empowering day of events, a Tamil *parai* group entered the hall and the
women responded to the drums in an eruption of dance:

> They danced with the indomitable spirit that only Dalit women
> have. . . . They danced like women who were dancing after being
> chained for a long time . . . as if they'd forgotten their bodies. I had
> seen men dance like this on the road during Ganesh Chaturthis. . . .
> I'd gape at them enviously.[68]

Kumar describes the freedom Dalit women enjoy in dancing in this style,
in a space that is free of harassment and stares. Her articulation of freedom
makes clear that freedom found in dancing to *parai* drums is not simply
in the form itself, but in the binds of propriety and subjugation that these
women's bodies have survived. Further, Kumar's account makes evident
that this ecstatic dancing was contingent on other aesthetics that lived in
the space alongside the drummers: multiple languages spoken and translated, portraits of B. R. Ambedkar and Savitribai Phule on the walls, food
served, and saris of many colors and fabrics. Kumar's account reminds
us that the pursuit of freedom in dance is vital and life giving, particularly for people with overlapping subjugated identities. She reminds us
of the curatorial work—the use of aesthetics to make politics present—
that surrounds social dance, that makes social dance work. Vijeta Kumar's
description of this "zingat" at a feminist conference leads me to ask how
to curate the night so that more people can feel free inside of it, can move
and improvise in ways that don't mask their subjugated identities, strange
bodies, or unique choreographies.

Strangers in the Night

Curating Nightlife at Besharam

In August 2019, Trikone-Chicago celebrated the tenth anniversary of *Jai Ho!*, the party I co-founded during my fieldwork. In response to the militarized (re)occupation of Kashmir by India's right-wing government, Trikone's leadership committed to donating party proceeds to the diasporic organization Stand With Kashmir. Trikone's leadership then had to field messages from gay Indian men who were upset with this decision, and who expressed that partying and politics had no relationship to each other. Throughout this book, I have argued that gay Indian nightlife is implicated and imbricated in politics across a range of geographic scales. Sometimes these politics are not as explicit as the expression of solidarity with Kashmir and material / monetary donations. Sometimes, these politics reveal themselves in the aesthetic, sexual, sensorial climate of the club, in the different ways that gay Indian nightlife vibrates. At the same party, LaWhore Vagistan performed the sexy item song "Jalebi Bai"; the song's protagonist, in response to the question "What country are you from?" names herself Jalebi Bai (jalebi woman), and I of course handed out jalebis (the neon orange, sticky, fried sweets, which I sourced from Devon Avenue) to audience members. Trans Bangladeshi artist Tara Ali Asgar writes on Instagram of this moment, "suddenly I discover a deshi girl is shaking my body and asking me 'do you want a piece of Jilebi?'" This stranger shakes Tara's body into a new sticky, sweet, shared, jalebi geopolitics. Such improvisatory moments do not restore sovereignty to occupied territories like Kashmir, or secure sanctuary for dispossessed queer and trans migrants, refugees, and asylees. But these accented moments of aesthetic and affective collision make other futures conceivable by shaking the body into other states of being, and being with.[1]

The queer South Asian dancers I encountered in gay nightlife spaces in Bangalore, Chicago, and elsewhere are not just dancers. They are also negotiating: work in global economies; immigration protocols and migrant blues; long-distance relationships; family dynamics and imaginations of home; gender, sexual, racial, caste, and class performance and inequity; identification, representation, and visibility; language and cultural difference; HIV stigma and chronic illness; and so forth. While many come to the club to escape the quotidian exhaustion that systemic conditions produce, to "get lost in dance,"[2] the club is already imbricated in and reproduces hierarchies associated with other institutions: nationalism, caste, racial capitalism. Nightlife performance, particularly the unexpected introduction of accented styles that grate against dominant aesthetics, has the potential to redistribute choreography, rearrange affects, and recast the inside's relationship to outside.

Completing this manuscript during World Pride 2019, which celebrated the fiftieth anniversary of the 1969 Stonewall Riots in New York City, I was reminded that how we articulate relationships between nightlife and politics still imagines a hypervisible activism in which the arm of the state—law and police—are explicitly present, and radical action looks like intentional protest and demonstration. But nightlife's politics also manifest in the dominant style of body, clothing, dance, and music at the club, and puncturing hegemony might look like accenting ubiquitous glamorous white femininity or hypermasculine muscularity with our *chapatti* potbellies and bare feet, Ila Arun's and Malathy Lakshman's raw voices, and FOB-y snake and circle dances. Reorienting the study of nightlife to the global South, to diaspora, to the Midwest, to South India, to parties instead of bars, to the second floor of a straight bar, to border crossers and transnational workers, to tech parks and ethnic neighborhoods, brings into view other political matrices that structure nightlife, and regulate access to sanctuary, pleasure, and beauty. Across the book, I have developed ishtyle, accented style, as a tool to name performances of cultural difference, and to consider the stakes of violating the dominant aesthetics and politics of nightlife across geopolitical scales.

The accent, ishtyle, has the potential to render us both familiar and strange. The stranger, according to Sara Ahmed, is not an ontological figure, but is rendered so in encounters, "the surprise of being faced by another who cannot be located in the present."[3] Revealing accents in the nightclub bring into relief others who cannot be, are not supposed to be, in the "present" of global gay nightlife: feminine men, courtesans, aunties,

Dalits, bar dancers, techies, unassimilated migrants, South Indians, transgender people, Bollywood divas, fat hairy brown bodies, queer women, classical dancers, hijras, people who smell like chicken biryani—some of these strangers are more vulnerable to violence, systemic neglect, and death than others. Sometimes strange encounters arise from the presence of those bodies, others from the appearance of the symbols, repertoires, and choreographies associated with those bodies.

Nayan Shah argues for the exigency of both ephemeral and enduring intimacies under the alienation of racial capitalism, which forces minoritarian subjects into new and uncomfortable proximities: "Intimacy among strangers points to how 'strangerhood' is a crucial ingredient for public meeting."[4] Entering the nightclub, we open ourselves to encounters with strangers, and in improvisatory social dance we "reach toward one another, engaging in compositions that remind us that bodies are always stranger (*unheimlich*) than they first appear."[5] Improvisation leaves open the possibility of becoming strange to each other, or maybe finding intimacy with strangers, mutual strangeness. For those of us who cannot participate in the aesthetics of similitude that much of gay nightlife has come to privilege, an aspirational sameness that extinguishes racial and gender difference,[6] making room for stranger intimacies feels even more necessary. But who bears the responsibility of making strangers and strangeness welcome?

Nightlife is a highly curatorial practice, informed as much by its publicity and promotions, built environment, sonic landscape, and geopolitical location, as it is by fleshy encounters with others. Through this curation, nightlife dictates the terms of participation that renders people strange. "Curate," sharing linguistic roots with "care," reminds us that all this aesthetic work to stage nightlife has the potential to offer sanctuary and encounter pasts (ancestors, previous selves, other possible versions of the now).[7] As a space for reckoning with the past, nightlife certainly functions as a venue of return, mourning, and embodied transfer,[8] but one that also relegates some cultural figures to the past, strangers. Jennifer Tyburczy offers "queer curatorship" as an opportunity to "undo the history of sexuality by constructing new epistemological frameworks for understanding and exhibiting sexuality in the public sphere."[9] Nightlife offers so many aesthetic venues through which to encounter and manipulate temporality: decor, screens, invitations, themes, music, drag, and so on. But amid all the aesthetic work done to care for nightlife's patrons and pasts, minoritarian subjects improvise with and against these aesthetics to loosen the space and try on new worlds. The study of nightlife needs to attend to curation, as well as develop an embodied and sustained engagement with improvised performance.

From afar, I have admired the curatorial efforts of South Asian cultural workers who stage a different kind of night. Parties like *Papi Juice* and *Color Me Queer* (New York City), *Hungama* and *Mizery* (London), and *Queer Futures Potluck Party* (Delhi) invite in, care for, and celebrate the diverse pleasures of queer and trans people by producing original visual art for fliers and projection in their venues, advertising in multiple languages, featuring Black, Caribbean, Afro-Latinx, Middle Eastern, Asian, women, and trans DJs, offering alcohol-free spaces, and announcing building accessibility on their event promotion. Though my fieldwork never took me to these parties, I did manage to visit *Besharam*, a Toronto-based party that ran from 2004 to 2019, and that I had long been in awe of. The party emerged from the progressive South Asian arts collective Desh Pardesh, that ran from 1988 to 2001. It got its title, *Besharam*, meaning "shameless," from the organizers' desire to address the multiple axes of shame felt by South Asian Canadians, especially women, in their everyday and everynight lives.[10] The monthly party, which welcomed over five hundred people a night, was organized by queer folks; it had a reputation as a gay event, but attracted a primarily straight clientele. The party saw substantial changes over the years: a move from Church Street (Toronto's commercial gay neighborhood) to a more mainstream venue with heavy security, and from a mixed queer and straight crowd to a predominantly hetero audience. DJ Amita reminisced about *Besharam* with me, how it changed, and whom it catered to:

> At one point there was a lot of "sari queens" that would come to the party; they wanted to pick up guys. Men in saris, so, umm, transgender, crossdressers. Normally they'd be going to the queer parties. [But here] they would get all this attention, and all these straight men would be flirting with them. They [the sari queens] would get quite lucky. But because [some] yucky guys were coming, we had to institute policies; we had to say, "No ass pinching." I swear! We had this slideshow [projected over the DJ booth]: "No homophobia. No ass pinching." The sari queens were really upset: "We want guys pinching our ass." Women are like, "We don't want guys pinching our ass." We tried to institute this policy, "no groups of guys"; but then the gay guys were like ["This is not fair!"], and

we were like, "If we know you . . ." Then straight guys [in order to get in] would [pretend] like, "Oh he's my boyfriend," [but] we could sniff it out pretty quickly.

Amita points here to the curatorial work—door policies, overhead visuals—she engaged in, and regularly reevaluated, to create a sexually permissive but also consensual environment, one that could include men, women, straight, gay, nonbinary, and trans folks, their bodies and their pleasures. Omme-Salma Rahemtullah discusses *Besharam*'s curatorial policy not to allow "stags" into the party unless they are known by the organizers. She demonstrates how this policy complies with "the new anti-homophobic Canadian Nation" to construe straight South Asian men as violent and predatory.[11] While I don't disagree with these arguments, they don't do justice to the many scenarios possible inside of nightlife's theater.[12]

When I visited *Besharam* myself, the curatorial work that both polices and permits was even more evident: security, go-go dancers, and give-aways. But, as always, strange encounters exceed and butt up against curatorial work. In line outside I watch a white man refused entry because he is wearing sneakers. Two South Asian men are refused entry because they do not have women companions. Arriving alone, I wonder if I will get past the bouncers; will I appear gay enough? Zavare, Amita's co-organizer, recognizes me from my YouTube video and tells the security guard: "He's fine, he's fine. He can go in." Inside Fly nightclub I run into my cousin up front; she and her friend are leaning over the low stage reaching for the beads Zavare is giving out, ogling the two go-go boys in metallic red Lycra Speedos dancing on raised boxes. They are among many women dancing up front without men, enjoying the giveaways and watching the dancers. A contingent of four or five gay men are hanging stage left by Shazad, one of the go-go boys. Amita presides over the party in her DJ booth at the back of the stage.

I hang out close to Shazad with the other queers, inadvertently obstructing the path to the women's restroom. We are repeatedly interrupted by long-nailed taps on our shoulders to get past us—these taps contrast starkly with my experience in gay bars, where people maneuver around by hands pressing gently on hips, back, or shoulders. This kind of tactile and intimate travel through the club space is not necessarily sexual, but I realize in this moment that it is not appropriate in heteronormative South Asian spaces. As I head to the restroom myself, I become hyper aware about touching any bodies along the way. Squeezing between a for-est of tall men in business-casual wear, I hear one of them, eyes and nose sneering at the go-go boys, say to his friend dismissively, "What is this? A gay club?" Minutes later, when another boy arrives to our gay corner, he huffs in disappointment, "I thought this was a gay party?" Another DJ takes over after Amita, and his bhangra set-list activates the men clustered to the back of the party into hoots and shouts, reorienting the room's focal point away from the gay go-go boys. The women dancing to and with the go-go boys are no longer the center of the party's pleasure; these (presum-ably) straight South Asian men—discursively denied citizenship at the party through door polices—claim the dance floor through their circular, boisterous dance. The queer boys are bored, and we head to Church Street.

A performance method and analytic that attends to topography, touch, sound, interview, gesture, statements, choreography, and style allows for a more dynamic analysis of "strange encounters" and "stranger intima-cies" at *Besharam*. At the front of the room, women danced with and for themselves, in company with and admiration of the go-go boys. Toward the back, men reoriented the room's spatial configuration with extended limbs, rhythmic shouts, and bouncy jumps that gave them greater vis-ibility and sonic dominance. One straight man read the go-go dancers as a gay presence, instead of perhaps there to privilege women's ocular pleasure. One gay man was disappointed at the lack of other gay men, choosing not to interpret the women dancing with each other as queer. The multiplicity of nightlife makes itself known only inside of it.

In 2016 in Bangalore I attended a party, yet unnamed, that was recently started by two friends closely connected with the NGO world, who were eager to accommodate non-English-speaking, Muslim, feminine, and transgender people. The party was hosted in a suburban mall that had closed at 10:00 p.m., so my friends and I had to enter through the service entrance—far from glamorous. But partying in this empty mall provided an unexpected sense of privacy and safety. Unlike the *Heatwave* party we were at earlier in the night at a fancy hotel bar inside of a tech park, this party played contemporary and throwback English, Hindi, and regional tracks; each song elicited eager choreographies and filmic reenactments from the partygoers. The crowd of about forty included cross-dressers, feminine boys, and trans women coupled with men, among others. Their eclectic sartorial styles included casual shorts and T-shirts; bare feet, shiny black shoes, and open-toed sandals; embellished gowns and little-black dresses; and dhotis and Zara-adjacent menswear.

Our short forty-five minutes in this heterotopic bar off the beaten path were flirtatious, sexy, and ribald in ways *Heatwave* could never compare to, in ways I'd never have imagined inside of a generic mall. A different curation of music, location, and patronage engendered a fun, unpredictable, playful world that I had never encountered in Bangalore nightlife. But while the space was welcoming to trans folks, I was uncomfortable with how trans and feminine people became public bodies, swung from man to man; some looked uncomfortable and harassed by these behaviors, and others seemed to be enjoying the attention.

Watching these choreographies, I became aware that it matters not just where the party is, what music is played, or who has been invited or allowed in, but how we dance with each other, how we *let* each other dance. Public discourses about nightlife meditate on parties' responsibility to patrons, holding organizers accountable to their curatorial choices.[13] But it is also necessary to regard how patrons dance, flirt, make eye contact, and speak with each other in nightlife spaces too. The challenge for both nightlife's curators and patrons "might be an opening of access for anyone who wants to think-move queer; an allowance for more people to understand strategies of queer [black/asian/trans/aboriginal] performance on our bodies, in our imaginations, and among our friends."[14]

In his elegy to Latin Night at the queer club written in the wake of the 2016 shooting at Pulse Nightclub in Orlando, Justin Torres uses the refrain "If you're lucky . . ." to enumerate the urgent magic of Latin Night. He reminds us that promises of queer nightlife are not always kept, though they are in fact powerful: "'Safe space' is a cliché, overused and exhausted in our discourse, but the fact remains that a sense of safety transforms the body, transforms the spirit. So many of us walk through the world without it."[15] The club affords us the possibility to forget that we are strangers, if we're lucky; but the club door is also "an entrance into a particular market economy that might not be so alternative to other public economies" and has the potential to perpetually render us strange.[16] The internal economies of the nightclub, as I've argued across this book, enmesh performing bodies in transnational, national, regional, and urban politics that play out through gestures as mundane as eye contact. It is precisely in this spirit that we must attend to improvised performance, to see nightlife's minoritarian patrons as cocurators or minor curators, cultural workers, who reorder politics, mess them up, and innovate other worlds.

Performance as method, optic, and object of analysis allows us to consider a greater range of axes of power functioning in the space and on the bodies inside. Performance enables us to study the structural frames of sociality embedded in nightlife through curation, as well as improvised style, the fleshy and unpredictable encounters that reify and undo the curated ethos and norms. To do this research, I curated parties and I attended them; though they were often fun, neither was easy work. The labor of nightlife requires us to ask what we can do to create more social spaces in which minoritarian subjects feel cared for, feel strange, feel emplaced by their strangeness, feel at home, feel home. What will be the location, cover charge, timing, publicity, performance, visual backdrop, dress code, community agreements, bathroom signage, and sonic landscape of your next party? How will you invite histories (and what histories?) into the space? Curation is only one part of the labor. For those of us attending the party, how can we dance in ways that invite more people into the circle, do the drag labor that makes others feel beautiful and present, steal movements that don't belong in the space, be the aunties who offer new old ways to dress and dance, feel funky with beer instead of champagne? Nightlife isn't for everyone, but for some of us who feel estranged from dominant forms of life, it offers improvisatory, unpredictable, and risky opportunities to find intimacy with other strangers and with our own strangeness, to hear our own accents sung and danced back to us in (un)recognizable ways that "transform the body, transform the spirit" and give us the capacity to dance a little longer.

Notes

Preface: In Search of a Desi Drag Queen

1. Sarah Hankins, "'I'm a Cross between a Clown, a Stripper, and a Streetwalker': Drag Tipping, Sex Work, and a Queer Sociosexual Economy," *Signs* 40, no. 2 (2015): 441–66.

2. Marlon M. Bailey, *Butch Queens up in Pumps: Gender, Performance, and Ballroom Culture in Detroit* (Ann Arbor: University of Michigan Press, 2013), 45.

3. Stephen Amico, "'I Want Muscles': House Music, Homosexuality and Masculine Signification," *Popular Music* 20, no. 3 (2001): 359–78; Martin P. Levine and Michael S. Kimmel, *Gay Macho: The Life and Death of the Homosexual Clone* (New York: New York University Press, 1998).

4. Alok Vaid-Menon, "Imp Queen and the Perpetually Problematic Erasure of Trans Drag Queens," *Them: Condé Nast*, https://www.them.us/story/imp-queen-trans-drag-queens (accessed October 13, 2018).

5. David Valentine, *Imagining Transgender: An Ethnography of a Category* (Durham, NC: Duke University Press, 2007).

6. I have not changed the names of parties and clubs that are open to the public or that are now defunct. In the case of parties that are private or semiprivate, I have changed event names to maintain the privacy of attendees and organizers.

7. "Desi" is a term meaning "of the land" and has Sanskrit roots and variations in several North Indian languages. It is used as a catchall for South Asian identities including diasporic subjects. Not all people of South Asian heritages embrace the term, but like "South Asia" itself, it functions as a placeholder to imagine a more inclusive geography in the wake of colonial, imperial, and national fracture.

8. David Dasharath Kalal, "Kalalabad Vol I," http://www.davidkalal.net/kalalabad-vol-i.html (accessed June 29, 2019); "Gaysi: The Gay Desi," http://gaysifamily.com (accessed June 29, 2019); "Queeristan: Desi Queered by Queer Desis," http://queeristan.blogspot.com (accessed June 29, 2019), "Womanistan," https://instagram.com/womanistan (accessed October 19, 2019).

9. See Dwight Conquergood, "Rethinking Ethnography: Towards a Critical Cultural Politics," in *Cultural Struggles: Performance, Ethnography, Praxis*, ed. E. Patrick Johnson (Ann Arbor: University of Michigan Press, 2013), 81–103.

10. D. Soyini Madison, "Co-performative Witnessing," *Cultural Studies* 21, no. 6 (2007): 829.

11. Anima Adjepong, "Invading Ethnography: A Queer of Color Reflexive Practice," *Ethnography* 20, no. 1 (2017): 27–46.

12. Esther Newton, "My Best Informant's Dress," *Cultural Anthropology* 8, no. 1 (1993): 3–23; Bryant Keith Alexander, "Standing in the Wake: A Critical Auto/Ethnographic Exercise on Reflexivity in Three Movements," *Cultural Studies—Critical Methodologies* 11, no. 2 (2011): 98–107.

13. Yamuna Sangarasivam, "Researcher, Informant, 'Assassin,' Me," *Geographical Review* 91, nos. 1–2 (2001): 95–104.

14. Aimee Meredith Cox, *Shapeshifters: Black Girls and the Choreography of Citizenship* (Durham, NC: Duke University Press, 2015), 31.

15. Gayatri Gopinath, *Impossible Desires: Queer Diasporas and South Asian Public Cultures* (Durham, NC: Duke University Press, 2005), 86; Jasbir K. Puar, *Terrorist Assemblages: Homonationalism in Queer Times* (Durham, NC: Duke University Press, 2007), 173.

16. *Julpari* (Dir. Swati Khurana and Leith Murgai, 1996); Jaishri Abichandani, "One Night in New York 2003–5," https://jaishriabichandani.net/section/166996-One-Night-in-New-York-2003-5.html (accessed June 30, 2019); Jaishri Abichandani, "Bijli, the Heart of a Drag Queen," https://vimeo.com/20099556 (accessed June 30, 2019); Tanuja Desai Hidier, *Born Confused* (New York: Scholastic Press, 2002); Poulomi Desai and Parminder Sekhon, *Red Threads: The South Asian Queer Connection in Photographs* (London: Millivres Prowler, 2003).

17. The only other regular desi parties at that time were *Club Kali* (London, started 1995, monthly), *Desilicious* (New York, started 2002, about every two months), *Besharam* (Toronto, started 2004, every month), *Club Zindagi* (Manchester, started 2003). Other parties include *Disco Rani* (London, started 2014, approximately quarterly), *Rangeela* (Toronto, started 2012, quarterly), *Jalwa* (DC, started 2012, twice a year), *Hungama* (London, started 2017, monthly). Annual events include *Color Me Queer* (New York City), *Kulture Kulcha* (Bay Area), *MASALA Mela* (Boston), *Satrang Annual Gala* (Los Angeles).

18. A majority of my friends' and interlocutors' names have been changed to protect their privacy and in accordance with institutional review board-approved agreements between us. I have retained the names of DJs, performers, and activists with public profiles. I do not indicate which names I have and have not changed.

19. Kim, "They Aren't That Primitive Back Home," in *Lotus of Another Color: An Unfolding of the South Asian Gay and Lesbian Experience*, ed. Rakesh Ratti (Boston: Alyson Publications, 1993), 92–97.

20. Parmesh Shahani, *Gay Bombay: Globalization, Love and (Be)Longing in Contemporary India* (Thousand Oaks, CA: Sage Publications, 2008).

21. See also Marlon Bailey's notion of "kin labor." Bailey, *Butch Queens.*

22. Sheena Malhotra, "Finding Home in a Song and a Dance: Nation, Culture, Bollywood," in *Race/Gender/Class/Media 3.0*, ed. Gail Dines and Jean Humez (Los Angeles: Sage Publications, 2009), 215.

23. Alok Gupta, "*Englishpur Ki Kothi*," in *Because I Have a Voice: Queer Politics in*

India, ed. Arvind Narrain and Gautam Bhan (New Delhi: Yoda Press, 2005), 135; see also Shahani, *Gay Bombay*, 85.

24. Dhamini Ratnam, "The Party Must Go On," *HT Media*, https://www.livemint.com/Leisure/iim5VoD6CBsWLVMGb5I1tJ/The-party-must-go-on.html (accessed September 30, 2018).

25. Shahani, *Gay Bombay*, 25; Rohit K. Dasgupta, "Parties, Advocacy, and Activism: Interrogating Community and Class in Digital Queer India," in *Queer Youth and Media Cultures*, ed. Christopher Pullen (London: Palgrave Macmillan, 2014), 265–77.

26. Jason Orne, *Boystown: Sex & Community in Chicago* (Chicago: University of Chicago Press, 2017); Suman Quazi, "I Am a Heterosexual Indian Girl Who Went to a Gay Party," *News Yahoo*, https://sg.news.yahoo.com/i-am-a-heterosexual-indian-girl-who-went-to-a-gay-120936996.html (accessed September 30, 2018).

27. Akhil Katyal, *The Doubleness of Sexuality: Idioms of Same-Sex Desire in Modern India* (New Delhi: New Text, 2016).

28. There were infrequent lesbian parties that restricted attendance by men, but not without controversy—gay men's fragile egos were offended at an all-women party during Bombay Pride 2017. Yogesh Pawar, "Cracks Surface in LQBTQI Community," *DNA India*, http://www.dnaindia.com/mumbai/report-cracks-surface-in-lgbtqi-community-2296830 (accessed September 30, 2018).

29. Jacquelyn P. Strey, "Queerness's Domain? Queer Negotiations, Utopian Visions and the Failures of Heterotopias in Bangalore," in *Urban Utopias: Excess and Expulsion in Neoliberal South Asia*, ed. Tereza Kuldova and Mathew A. Varghese (Cham, Switzerland: Palgrave Macmillan, 2017), 247–67.

30. Aniruddha Dutta, "An Epistemology of Collusion: Hijras, Kothis and the Historical (Dis)Continuity of Gender/Sexual Identities in Eastern India," *Gender & History* 24, no. 3 (2012): 825–4; Lawrence Cohen, "The Kothi Wars: AIDS Cosmopolitanism and the Morality of Classification," in *Sex in Development: Science, Sexuality, and Morality in Global Perspective*, ed. Stacy Leigh Pigg and Vincanne Adams (Durham, NC: Duke University Press, 2005), 269–303.

31. Aniruddha Dutta, "Claiming Citizenship, Contesting Civility: The Institutional LGBT Movement and the Regulation of Gender/Sexual Dissidence in West Bengal, India," *Jindal Global Law Review* 4, no. 1 (2012): 110–41.

32. In 2016, the Transgender India collective launched an online photo campaign that circulated via *The Better Indian*, *Buzzfeed*, and *The Logical Indian* in which transgender people held signs that articulated their trans identities, followed by "I am not a hijra." This campaign received important criticism because it precisely relies on the abjection of highly visible and stigmatized hijras to render respectable trans subjects. Durga M. Sengupta, "I Am Not a Hijra: A Damaging Offensive Transgender India Photo Campaign," *Catchnews*, http://www.catchnews.com/gender-and-sex/i-am-not-a-hijra-a-damaging-offensive-transgender-india-photo-campaign-1471618717.html (accessed June 30, 2019).

33. Vishal Tondon, "Exclusionary Masculinities: Exploring Caste, Class, and Gender Bias in Urban Indian Gay Men," *Café Dissensus*, https://cafedissensus.com/2017/05/15/exclusionary-masculinities-exploring-caste-class-and-gender-bias-in-urban-indian-gay-men/ (accessed October 13, 2018).

34. Sofian Merabet, "Disavowed Homosexualities in Beirut," *Middle East Report* 230 (2004): 30–33. See also Bobby Benedicto, *Under Bright Lights: Gay Manila and the Global Scene* (Minneapolis: University of Minnesota Press, 2014), 81.

35. Naomi Bragin, "Techniques of Black Male Re/Dress: Corporeal Drag and Kinesthetic Politics in the Rebirth of Waacking/Punkin'," *Women & Performance* 24, no. 1 (2014): 61–78.

36. LaMonda Horton-Stallings, *Funk the Erotic: Transaesthetics and Black Sexual Cultures* (Urbana: University of Illinois Press, 2015), 201.

37. Joseph R. Roach, *Cities of the Dead: Circum-Atlantic Performance* (New York: Columbia University Press, 1996).

38. Jisha Menon, *The Performance of Nationalism: India, Pakistan, and the Memory of Partition* (Cambridge: Cambridge University Press, 2013), 22.

39. Sara Ahmed, *Queer Phenomenology: Orientations, Objects, Others* (Durham, NC: Duke University Press, 2006).

40. José Esteban Muñoz, *Cruising Utopia: The Then and There of Queer Futurity* (New York: New York University Press, 2009), 74.

41. Cory G. Collins, "Drag Race to the Bottom? Updated Notes on the Aesthetic and Political Economy of RuPaul's Drag Race," *TSQ* 4, no. 1 (2017): 128–34.

42. Madhavi Mallapragada, *Virtual Homelands: Indian Immigrants and Online Cultures in the United States* (Urbana: University of Illinois Press, 2014), 33–34.

Introduction. Sub-*kulcha*: The Meaning of Ishtyle

1. Thomas F. DeFrantz, "Hip Hop Habitus V.2.0," in *Black Performance Theory*, ed. Thomas F. DeFrantz and Anita Gonzalez (Durham, NC: Duke University Press, 2014), 223.

2. E. Patrick Johnson, *Appropriating Blackness: Performance and the Politics of Authenticity* (Durham, NC: Duke University Press, 2003).

3. Far from the first of its kind, *Desilicious* draws on legacies of other queer-oriented parties such as New York City's annual *Color Me Queer*, SALGA's Eid and Diwali bashes, and DJ Rekha's *Basement Bhangra*, Toronto's *Desh Pardesh* festival and *Besharam* parties, and London's *Club Kali*.

4. Sangarasivam, "Researcher, Informant, 'Assassin,' Me," 98.

5. Brian A. Horton, "The Queer Turn in South Asian Studies? or 'That's Over & Done Queen, on to the Next,'" *QED* 5, no. 3 (2018): 176.

6. Menon, Jisha. "Queer Selfhoods in the Shadow of Neoliberal Urbanism," *Journal of Historical Sociology* 26, no. 1 (2013): 100–19.

7. Saidiya Hartman, "The Belly of the World: A Note on Black Women's Labors," *Souls* 18, no. 1 (2016): 166.

8. Saidiya Hartman, *Scenes of Subjection: Terror, Slavery, and Self-Making in Nineteenth-Century America* (New York: Oxford University Press, 1997), 50.

9. Kelly I. Chung, "The Defiant Still Worker: Ramiro Gomez and the Expressionism of Abstract Labor," *Women & Performance* 29, no. 1 (2019): 64.

10. Ramón H. Rivera-Servera, *Performing Queer Latinidad: Dance, Sexuality, Politics* (Ann Arbor: University of Michigan Press, 2012), 135.

11. Ann Laura Stoler, *Carnal Knowledge and Imperial Power: Race and the Intimate in Colonial Rule* (Berkeley: University of California Press, 2002), 7–8.

12. Celeste Fraser Delgado and José Esteban Muñoz, *Everynight Life: Culture and Dance in Latin/o America* (Durham, NC: Duke University Press, 1997).

13. Clifford Geertz, "Deep Play: Notes on the Balinese Cockfight," *Daedalus* 101, no. 1 (1972): 1–37.

14. Victoria Fortuna, "A Dance of Many Bodies: Moving Trauma in Susana Tambutti's La Puñalada," *Performance Research* 16, no. 1 (2011): 44.

15. Anusha Kedhar, "Flexibility and Its Bodily Limits: Transnational South Asian Dancers in an Age of Neoliberalism," *Dance Research Journal* 46, no. 1 (2014): 23–40.

16. José Esteban Muñoz, "Ephemera as Evidence: Introductory Notes to Queer Acts," *Women & Performance* 8, no. 2 (1996): 5–16; Joshua Chambers-Letson, *After the Party: A Manifesto for Queer of Color Life* (New York: New York University Press, 2018).

17. Martin F. Manalansan IV, "In the Shadows of Stonewall: Examining Gay Transnational Politics and the Diasporic Dilemma," *GLQ* 2, no. 4 (1995): 425–38; Sylvia Rivera, "Queens in Exile, the Forgotten Ones," in *GenderQueer: Voices from beyond the Sexual Binary*, ed. Joan Nestle, Clare Howell, and Riki Wilchins (Los Angeles: Alyson Publications, 2002), 67–85.

18. Jafari Sinclaire Allen, "For 'the Children' Dancing the Beloved Community," *Souls* 11, no. 3 (2009): 325.

19. Joshua Javier Guzmán and Christina A. León, "Cuts and Impressions: The Aesthetic Work of Lingering in Latinidad," *Women & Performance* 24, no. 3 (2015): 261–76.

20. Kemi Adeyemi, "Oliverio Rodriguez's The Last Seduction / La Seducción Fatal (2015–)," *TSQ* 6, no. 2 (2019): 273.

21. Martin F. Manalansan IV et al., "Queering the Middle: Race, Region, and a Queer Midwest," *GLQ* 20, nos. 1–2 (2014): 1–12; Anjali Arondekar and Geeta Patel, "Area Impossible: Notes toward an Introduction," *GLQ* 22, no. 2 (2016): 151–71; Gayatri Gopinath, *Unruly Visions: The Aesthetic Practices of Queer Diaspora* (Durham: Duke University Press, 2018); Neville Wallace Hoad, *African Intimacies: Race, Homosexuality, and Globalization* (Minneapolis: University of Minnesota Press, 2007), xxviii.

22. Shilpa Davé, *Indian Accents: Brown Voice and Racial Performance in American Television and Film* (Urbana: University of Illinois Press, 2013), 3.

23. Cox, *Shapeshifters*, 29.

24. Erin Manning, *Politics of Touch: Sense, Movement, Sovereignty* (Minneapolis: University of Minnesota Press, 2007), xvii; Kemi Adeyemi, "Beyond 90°: The Angularities of Black/Queer/Women/Lean," *Women & Performance* 29, no. 1 (2019): 9–24.

25. Judith Hamera, *Dancing Communities: Performance, Difference and Connection in the Global City* (London: Palgrave Macmillan UK, 2007); Susan Foster, "Pygmalion's No-Body and the Body of Dance," in *Performance and Cultural Politics*, ed. Elin Diamond (New York: Routledge, 1996).

26. Jack Halberstam, *In a Queer Time and Place: Transgender Bodies, Subcultural Lives* (New York: New York University Press, 2005).

27. Rachel Dwyer, "Bombay Ishtyle," in *Fashion Cultures: Theories, Explorations and Analysis*, ed. Stella Bruzzi and Pamela Gibson (London: Routledge, 2000), 178–90.

28. Dishoom Dishoom, "Ishtyle," *Samosapedia*, http://www.samosapedia.com/e/ishtyle (accessed June 30, 2019).

29. Ronak Kapadia, "Up in the Air and on the Skin: Drone Warfare and the Queer Calculus of Pain," in *Critical Ethnic Studies: A Reader*, ed. Nadia Elia et al. (Durham, NC: Duke University Press, 2016), 373.

30. Hamid Naficy, *An Accented Cinema: Exilic and Diasporic Filmmaking* (Princeton, NJ: Princeton University Press, 2001).

31. On "puro arte" see Lucy Mae San Pablo Burns, *Puro Arte: Filipinos on the Stages of Empire* (New York: New York University Press, 2012); on "biyuti" see Martin F. Manalansan IV, *Global Divas: Filipino Gay Men in the Diaspora* (Durham, NC: Duke University Press, 2003); Robert Diaz, "Biyuti from Below," *TSQ* 5, no. 3 (2018): 404–24; on "chusmeria" and "rasquache" see José Esteban Muñoz, *Disidentifications: Queers of Color and the Performance of Politics* (Minneapolis: University of Minnesota Press, 1999); on "boojie" see E. Patrick Johnson, "Foreword," in *From Bourgeois to Boojie: Black Middle-Class Performances*, ed. Vershawn Ashanti Young and Bridget Harris Tsemo (Detroit: Wayne State University Press, 2011); on "unmastered aesthetics" see Elliott H. Powell, "Unmastered: The Queer Black Aesthetics of Unfinished Recordings," *Black Scholar* 49, no. 1 (2019): 28–39.

32. Frantz Fanon, *Black Skin, White Masks*, trans. Richard Philcox (New York: Grove Press, 1967), 5.

33. Shailja Patel, *Migritude* (New York: Kaya Press, 2010), 33.

34. Deborah R. Vargas, "Ruminations on *Lo Sucio* as a Latino Queer Analytic," *American Quarterly* 66, no. 3 (2014): 715–26.

35. See also Sanjay Srivastava's concern over the use of "ishtyle." Sanjay Srivastava, *Passionate Modernity: Sexuality, Class, and Consumption in India* (New Delhi: Routledge, 2007), 228.

36. Eve Kosofsky Sedgwick, *Touching Feeling: Affect, Pedagogy, Performativity* (Durham, NC: Duke University Press, 2003); Rinaldo Walcott, "Boyfriends with Clits and Girlfriends with Dicks: Hip Hop's Queer Future," *Palimpsest* 2, no. 2 (2013): 169.

37. Della Pollock, "Failing," *Communication and Critical/Cultural Studies* 4, no. 4 (2007): 443.

38. Jack Halberstam, *The Queer Art of Failure* (Durham, NC: Duke University Press, 2011).

39. Marcia Ochoa, *Queen for a Day: Transformistas, Beauty Queens, and the Performance of Femininity in Venezuela* (Durham, NC: Duke University Press, 2014), 15.

40. Fiona Buckland, *Impossible Dance: Club Culture and Queer World-Making* (Middletown, CT: Wesleyan University Press, 2002); Madison Moore, *Fabulous: The Rise of the Beautiful Eccentric* (New Haven: Yale University Press, 2018).

41. Muñoz, *Disidentifications*.

42. Thomas F. DeFrantz, "Queer Dance in Three Acts," in *Queer Dance: Meanings and Makings*, ed. Clare Croft (New York: Oxford University Press, 2017), 175.

43. Dick Hebdige, *Subculture: The Meaning of Style* (London: Methuen, 1979). Substituting "culture" for the accented *kulcha*, a type of Indian bread, I mean to invoke scholarship that links food, sensorium, performance, consumption, and race. See "Eating the Other: Desire and Resistance," in bell hooks, *Black Looks: Race and Representation* (Boston: South End Press, 1992), 21–39; Martin F. Manalansan, Anita Mannur, and Robert Ji-Song Ku, *Eating Asian America: A Food Studies Reader* (New York: New York University Press, 2013).

44. Manalansan, *Global Divas*, 27; Andrew Leong, "The Pocket and the Watch: A Collective Individualist Reading of Japanese American Literature," *Verge* 1, no. 2 (2015): 76–114.

45. Vanita Reddy, *Fashioning Diaspora: Beauty, Femininity, and South Asian American Culture* (Philadelphia: Temple University Press, 2016). Also, as SanSan Kwan evidences, Asian Americans performing on the Chop Suey Circuit had to fake Asian accents in order to appeal to popular sensibilities, SanSan Kwan, "Performing a Geography of Asian America: The Chop Suey Circuit," *TDR* 55, no. 1 (2011): 122.

46. Dorinne K. Kondo, *About Face: Performing Race in Fashion and Theater* (New York: Routledge, 1997), 15.

47. Pierre Bourdieu, *Outline of a Theory of Practice*, trans. Richard Nice (Cambridge: Cambridge University Press, 1977).

48. Madison, "Co-performative Witnessing," 828.

49. Tom Boellstorff, *The Gay Archipelago: Sexuality and Nation in Indonesia* (Princeton, NJ: Princeton University Press, 2005).

50. Arti Sandhu, *Indian Fashion: Tradition, Innovation, Style* (London: Bloomsbury Academic, 2015), 162.

51. Judith Butler, *Bodies That Matter: On the Discursive Limits of "Sex"* (New York: Routledge, 1993), 226.

52. Juana María Rodríguez, *Sexual Futures, Queer Gestures, and Other Latina Longings* (New York: New York University Press, 2014), 127.

53. Joshua Takano Chambers-Letson, *A Race So Different: Performance and Law in Asian America* (New York: New York University Press, 2013), 137; D. Soyini Madison, "Dressing Out-of-Place: From Ghana to Obama Commemorative Cloth on the US-American Red Carpet," in *African Dress: Fashion, Agency, Performance*, ed. Karen Tranberg Hansen and D. Soyini Madison (London: Bloomsbury, 2013), 218.

54. Kalindi Vora, "Limits of 'Labor': Accounting for Affect and the Biological in Transnational Surrogacy and Service Work," *South Atlantic Quarterly* 111, no. 4 (2012): 681–700; Dale Hudson, "Undesirable Bodies and Desirable Labor: Documenting the Globalization and Digitization of Transnational American Dreams in Indian Call Centers," *Cinema Journal* 49, no. 1 (2009): 82–102.

55. Claire Cowie, "The Accents of Outsourcing: The Meanings of 'Neutral' in the Indian Call Centre Industry," *World Englishes* 26, no. 3 (2007): 316–30; Jisha Menon, "Calling Local / Talking Global: The Cosmo-Politics of the Call-Center Industry," *Women & Performance* 23, no. 2 (2013): 162–77.

56. Davé, *Indian Accents*, 29.

57. Homi K. Bhabha, *The Location of Culture* (New York: Routledge, 1994).

58. Edward W. Said, *Orientalism* (New York: Pantheon Books, 1978), 67.

59. Mrinalini Sinha, *Colonial Masculinity: The "Manly Englishman" and the "Effeminate Bengali" in the Late Nineteenth Century* (Manchester: Manchester University Press, 1995), 17.

60. Tom Boellstorff et al., "Decolonizing Transgender: A Roundtable Discussion," *TSQ* 1, no. 3 (2014), 422.

61. E. Patrick Johnson, "'Quare' Studies, or (Almost) Everything I Know about Queer Studies I Learned from My Grandmother," *Text and Performance Quarterly* 21, no. 1 (2001): 1–25; Mojisola Adebayo, "Everything You Know about Queerness You Learnt

from Blackness: The Afri-Quia Theatre of Black Dykes, Crips, and Kids," in *Queer Dramaturgies: International Perspectives on Where Performance Leads Queer*, ed. Alyson Campbell and Stephen Farrier (London: Palgrave Macmillan UK, 2016); Heidi Minning, "Qwir-English Code Mixing in Germany: Constructing a Rainbow of Identities," in *Speaking in Queer Tongues*, ed. William Leap and Tom Boellstorff (Urbana: University of Illinois Press, 2004), 46–71.

62. Sandeep Bakshi, "Decoloniality, Queerness and Giddha," in *Decolonizing Sexualities: Transnational Perspectives, Critical Interventions*, ed. Sandeep Bakshi, Suhraiya Jivraj, and Silvia Posocco (Oxford: Counterpress, 2016), 81–99; M. Jacqui Alexander, *Pedagogies of Crossing: Meditations on Feminism, Sexual Politics, Memory, and the Sacred* (Durham, NC: Duke University Press, 2005); Lyndon Kamaal Gill, *Erotic Islands: Art and Activism in the Queer Caribbean* (Durham, NC: Duke University Press, 2018).

63. Arvind Narrain and Vinay Chandran, *Nothing to Fix: Medicalisation of Sexual Orientation and Gender Identity* (New Delhi: Sage Publications India, 2016).

64. Ronak Kapadia, "We're Not Queer, We're Just Foreign: Desi Drags, Disidentifications and Activist Film in New York," *Stanford Undergraduate Research Journal* 4, no. 1 (2005): 1–7.

65. Richard Fung, "Looking for My Penis: The Eroticized Asian in Gay Video Porn," in *Q & A: Queer in Asian America*, ed. David L. Eng and Alice Y. Hom (Philadelphia: Temple University Press, 1998), 115–34.

66. Jason Ritchie, "How Do You Say 'Come Out of the Closet' in Arabic? Queer Activism and the Politics of Visibility in Israel-Palestine," *GLQ* 16, no. 4 (2010): 557–76.

67. Rivera-Servera, *Performing Queer Latinidad*, 176.

68. Christine Bacareza Balance, *Tropical Renditions: Making Musical Scenes in Filipino America* (Durham, NC: Duke University Press, 2016), 4–5.

69. D. Soyini Madison, *Critical Ethnography: Method, Ethics, and Performance* (Thousand Oaks, CA: Sage Publications, 2005), 167.

70. Mallapragada, *Virtual Homelands*.

71. A. Aneesh, *Virtual Migration: The Programming of Globalization* (Durham, NC: Duke University Press, 2006).

72. Carol Upadhya and A. R. Vasavi, eds., *In an Outpost of the Global Economy: Work and Workers in India's Information Technology Industry* (New Delhi: Routledge, 2008).

73. Aneesh, *Virtual Migration*, 76.

74. Amita Baviskar and Raka Ray, *Elite and Everyman: The Cultural Politics of the Indian Middle Classes* (New Delhi: Routledge, 2011), 2.

75. Leela Fernandes, *India's New Middle Class: Democratic Politics in an Era of Economic Reform* (Minneapolis: University of Minnesota Press, 2006), 34.

76. Marta Savigliano, *Angora Matta: Fatal Acts of North-South Translation = Actos Fatales De Traduccion Norte-Sur* (Middletown, CT: Wesleyan University Press, 2003), 144.

77. James Heitzman, *Network City: Planning the Information Society in Bangalore* (New Delhi: Oxford University Press, 2004), 180–81.

78. Aneesh, *Virtual Migration*, 69–70; A. Aneesh, "Negotiating Globalization: Men and Women of India's Call Centers," *Journal of Social Issues* 68, no. 3 (2012): 520.

79. Ara Wilson, *The Intimate Economies of Bangkok: Tomboys, Tycoons, and Avon Ladies in the Global City* (Berkeley: University of California Press, 2004).

80. Ashvin R. Kini, "Diasporic Relationalities: Queer Affiliations in Shani Mootoo's 'Out on Main Street,'" *South Asian Review* 35, no. 3 (2014): 185–202.

81. Heitzman, *Network City*, 79.

82. Xiang Biao, *Global "Body Shopping"* (Princeton, NJ: Princeton University Press, 2011), 283.

83. Marisa D'Melo and Sundeep Sabay, "Betwixt and Between? Exploring Mobilities in a Global Workplace in India," in Upadhya and Vasavi, *Outpost of the Global Economy*.

84. Inderpal Grewal, *Transnational America: Feminisms, Diasporas, Neoliberalisms* (Durham, NC: Duke University Press, 2005), 6; Fernandes, *India's New Middle Class*, 105.

85. As Audrey Yue argues in the case of Australia, these kinds of intimate living conditions between Indian education migrants render them suspicious, queer, and vulnerable to violence. Audrey Yue, "Queer Asian Mobility and Homonational Modernity: Marriage Equality, Indian Students in Australia and Malaysian Transgender Refugees in the Media," *Global Media and Communication* 8, no. 3 (2012): 269–87.

86. Payal Banerjee, "Indian Information Technology Workers in the United States: The H-1B Visa, Flexible Production, and the Racialization of Labor," *Critical Sociology* 32, nos. 2–3 (2006): 425–45.

87. Aneesh, "Negotiating Globalization," 526; Aimee Carrillo Rowe, Sheena Malhotra, and Kim Perez, *Answer the Call: Virtual Migration in Indian Call Centers* (Minneapolis: University of Minnesota Press, 2013), 9, 118.

88. Junaid Akram Rana, *Terrifying Muslims: Race and Labor in the South Asian Diaspora* (Durham, NC: Duke University Press, 2011).

89. Mallapragada, *Virtual Homelands*, 29–31.

90. Carol Upadhya, "Management of Culture and Management through Culture in the Indian Software Outsourcing Industry," in Upadhya and Vasavi, *Outpost of the Global Economy*, 109; Fernandes, *India's New Middle Class*, 97.

91. Lalaie Ameeriar, *Downwardly Global: Women, Work, and Citizenship in the Pakistani Diaspora* (Durham, NC: Duke University Press, 2017).

92. Rowe et al., *Answer the Call*, 11.

93. Aneesh, "Negotiating Globalization," 523.

94. Rowe et al., *Answer the Call*, x.

95. Lisa Lowe, *Immigrant Acts: On Asian American Cultural Politics* (Durham, NC: Duke University Press, 1996), 156.

96. John C. Stallmeyer, "New Silicon Valleys: Tradition, Globalization, and Information-Technology Development in Bangalore, India," *Traditional Dwellings and Settlements Review* 19, no. 2 (2008): 34; Sareeta Amrute, "Proprietary Freedoms in an IT Office: How Indian IT Workers Negotiate Code and Cultural Branding," *Social Anthropology* 22, no. 1 (2014): 101–17.

97. Priya Srinivasan, *Sweating Saris: Indian Dance as Transnational Labor* (Philadelphia: Temple University Press, 2011).

98. Roli Varma, "Transnational Migration and Entrepreneurialism: Indians in the U.S. Technology Sector," *Perspectives on Global Development and Technology* 10, no. 2 (2011): 270–87.

99. Srivastava, *Passionate Modernity*, 3.

100. Sociologist Smitha Radhakrishnan writes about IT professionals produced by the

flexibilization of labor, explaining that they "are not, for the most part, included among the elite transnational capitalist class examined in other studies; rather they are *professionals* for whom the traversing of borders (or the possibility of doing so) is critical to their socialization, belief system, and the expression of cultural belonging to India." Smitha Radhakrishnan, *Appropriately Indian: Gender and Culture in a New Transnational Class* (Durham, NC: Duke University Press, 2011), 17.

101. Nayan Shah, *Stranger Intimacy: Contesting Race, Sexuality, and the Law in the North American West* (Berkeley: University of California Press, 2011).

102. Amy Bhatt, *High-Tech Housewives: Indian IT Workers, Gendered Labor, and Transmigration* (Seattle: University of Washington Press, 2018).

103. Reena Patel, *Working the Night Shift: Women in India's Call Center Industry* (Stanford, CA: Stanford University Press, 2010).

104. Ibid., 43; Amy Bhatt, Madhavi Murty, and Priti Ramamurthy, "Hegemonic Developments: The New Indian Middle Class, Gendered Subalterns, and Diasporic Returnees in the Event of Neoliberalism," *Signs* 36, no. 1 (2010): 130.

105. Some scholars do discuss the "call center couple," centering heterosexual pairing as a possible fulfillment work can provide beyond financial and geographic mobility. Rowe et al., *Answer the Call*, 166; Michiel Baas, "The IT Caste: Love and Arranged Marriages in the IT Industry of Bangalore," *South Asia: Journal of South Asian Studies* 32, no. 2 (2009): 307.

106. Baviskar and Ray, *Elite and Everyman*, 13.

107. Aneesh, *Virtual Migration*, 63; Rowe et al., *Answer the Call*, xi; D'Melo and Sabay, "Betwixt and Between?," 88; Upadhya and Vasavi, *Outpost of the Global Economy*, 35.

108. Zora Neale Hurston, "Folklore and Music," *Frontiers* 12, no. 1 (1991): 184.

109. Rowe et al., *Answer the Call*, 11.

110. Lawrence La Fountain-Stokes, "Queer Diasporas, Boricua Lives: A Meditation on Sexile," *Review: Literature and Arts of the Americas* 41, no. 2 (2008): 299.

111. They are "second cities" not necessarily "second tier" in terms of population, political clout, or economy, but secondary in national urban narratives.

112. Manalansan, "Shadows of Stonewall."

113. Timothy Stewart-Winter, *Queer Clout: Chicago and the Rise of Gay Politics* (Philadelphia: University of Pennsylvania Press, 2016).

114. Alex G. Papadopoulos, "From 'Towertown' to 'Boystown' to 'Girltown': Chicago's Gay and Lesbian Geographies," in *Chicago's Geographies: Metropolis for the 21st Century*, ed. Richard P. Greene, Mark J. Bouman, and Dennis Grammenos (Washington, DC: Association of American Geographers, 2006), 232–41; Christopher Reed, "We're from Oz: Marking Ethnic and Sexual Identity in Chicago," *Environment and Planning D: Society and Space* 21, no. 4 (2003): 425–40; Japonica Brown-Saracino, *A Neighborhood That Never Changes: Gentrification, Social Preservation, and the Search for Authenticity* (Chicago: University of Chicago Press, 2009). Predominantly black queer bars and primarily working-class Latinx queer bars in Chicago's South Side continue to thrive without the clout of neighborhood merchant associations that North Side neighborhoods wield.

115. Padma Rangaswamy, *Namasté America: Indian Immigrants in an American Metropolis* (University Park: Pennsylvania State University Press, 2000), 80; Ishan Ashutosh, "(Re-)Creating the Community: South Asian Transnationalism on Chicago's Devon Avenue," *Urban Geography* 29, no. 3 (2008): 224–45.

116. Rangaswamy, *Namasté America*, 88.

117. Ajay Mehotra, "Pakistanis," Vinay Lal, "Indians," and Amanda Seligman, "Uptown," all in *The Encyclopedia of Chicago*, ed. James R. Grossman, Ann Durkin Keating, and Janice L. Reiff (Chicago: University of Chicago Press, 2004).

118. Kim, "They Aren't That Primitive," 95.

119. Shahani, *Gay Bombay*.

120. Naisargi Dave, *Queer Activism in India: A Story in the Anthropology of Ethics* (Durham, NC: Duke University Press, 2012).

121. Cubbon Park historically divided city and cantonment in colonial Bangalore, and has long been a site for cross-class and interracial/interethnic encounter. Janaki Nair, *The Promise of the Metropolis: Bangalore's Twentieth Century* (New Delhi: Oxford University Press, 2005).

122. Sneha Annavarapu, "'Where Do All the Lovers Go?': The Cultural Politics of Public Kissing in Mumbai, India (1950–2005)," *Journal of Historical Sociology* 31, no. 4 (2018): 405–19.

123. Hemangini Gupta, "No Sleep Till Ban-Galore!!!," *Cityscapes Digital*, last modified May 8, 2013, https://www.cityscapesdigital.net/2013/05/08/no-sleep-till-ban-galore/ (accessed October 13, 2018).

124. When I present research on policing of nightlife in Bangalore, US audiences hear my descriptions as quite fascistic. However, queer Indians experience limitations on their pleasures as part of a larger system of moral policing that they live with every day, a system they manage, evade, and laugh at intuitively. Additionally, US exceptionalism enables a perspective that reads moral policing in India as more brutal than quotidian violence that queer, trans, and ethnic minorities in the United States endure at the hands of society, media, and agents of the state. In Chicago, the horrific vice legislation of the mid-twentieth century that targeted nightlife and dance venues has left its imprint on the city's gay geography, race relations, and the permissions granted to the police to commit violence. Further, systemic violence in India and the United States are coconstitutive; as I've shown in other research, antiblackness in India draws from mediated visions of race in America, and Indian diasporas reproduce caste-based heteronormativity through professional and education migrations. Kareem Khubchandani, "Voguing in Bangalore: Blackness, Femininity, and Performance in Globalized India," *Scholar and Feminist Online* 14, no. 3 (2018); Kareem Khubchandani, "Caste, Queerness, Migration, and the Erotics of Activism," *South Asia Multidisciplinary Academic Journal* 20 (2019).

125. Deborah B. Gould, *Moving Politics: Emotion and Act Up's Fight against AIDS.* (Chicago: University of Chicago Press, 2009); Sara Warner, *Acts of Gaiety: LGBT Performance and the Politics of Pleasure* (Ann Arbor: University of Michigan Press, 2012); David Román, *Acts of Intervention: Performance, Gay Culture, and AIDS* (Bloomington: Indiana University Press, 1998).

126. Susan Leigh Foster, "Choreographies of Protest," *Theatre Journal* 55, no. 3 (2003): 395–412; Anusha Kedhar, "'Hands Up! Don't Shoot': Gesture, Choreography, and Protest in Ferguson," *Feminist Wire*, last modified October 6, 2014, http://thefeministwire.com/2014/10/protest-in-ferguson/ (accessed June 30, 2019).

127. Monisha Das Gupta, *Unruly Immigrants: Rights, Activism, and Transnational South Asian Politics in the United States* (Durham, NC: Duke University Press, 2006), 163.

Chapter 1. B1nary C0des: Undoing Dichotomies at *Heatwave*

1. An earlier version of this chapter appeared as "Cruising the Ephemeral Archives of Bangalore's Queer Nightlife" in *Queering Digital India: Activisms, Intimacies, and Subjectivities* edited by Rohit Dasgupta and Debanuj DasGupta (Edinburgh: Edinburgh University Press, 2018), 72–94.

2. Baviskar and Ray, *Elite and Everyman.*

3. Srivastava, *Passionate Modernity*, 187.

4. Lilian G. Mengesha and Lakshmi Padmanabhan, "Introduction to Performing Refusal / Refusing to Perform," *Women & Performance* 29, no. 1 (2019): 1–8.

5. Radhakrishnan, *Appropriately Indian.*

6. Gautham Reddy, personal communication, February 22, 2011.

7. Pawan Singh, "The TV9 Sting Operation on PlanetRomeo: Absent Subjects, Digital Privacy and LGBTQ Activism," in *Queering Digital India: Activisms, Intimacies, and Subjectivities*, ed. Rohit Dasgupta and Debanuj DasGupta (Edinburgh: Edinburgh University Press, 2018), 132–50.

8. This is one of very few filmic documentations of gay nightlife in India in online circulation. At my first gay party in Bangalore in 2009, when I lifted my camera above the crowd to film joyous screams and cheerful arms during Shakira's "Waka Waka," the DJ's voice asserted over the music, "No photos please. No filming." Privacy was sacred at these parties. However, since the 2018 decriminalization of sodomy, *Heatwave's* organizers have become much less stringent about photography, and they even post images of party attendees on Facebook and Instagram.

9. Abdul K. Rahoof, "Gay Party Busted," *Deccan Chronicle*, https://www.pressreader .com/india/deccan-chronicle/20130903/282394102117178 (accessed October 13, 2018).

10. PUCL-K, *Attacking Pubs and Birthday Parties: Communal Policing by Hindutva Outfits* (Mangalore: People's Union for Civil Liberties Karnataka and Forum Against Atrocities on Women, 2012).

11. Rahoof, "Gay Party Busted."

12. TV5 News, "Pulse Pub Gay Party at Begumpet, Hyderabad," *YouTube*, https:// www.youtube.com/watch?v=k0eGMDqgp7E (accessed October 13, 2018).

13. Radhakrishnan, *Appropriately Indian*, 162.

14. Debashree Mukherjee, "Notes on a Scandal: Writing Women's Film History against an Absent Archive," *BioScope* 4, no. 1 (2013): 10.

15. Ben Crair, "Maniac Killers of the Bangalore IT Department," *Bloomberg Businessweek*, https://www.bloomberg.com/news/features/2017–02-15/maniac-killers-of-the-bangalore-it-department (accessed October 13, 2018).

16. "Infosys Techie Booked under Sec 377 after Wife Filmed His Gay Encounters," https://www.dailymail.co.uk/indiahome/indianews/article-2813556/Infosys-techie-booked-Sec-377-wife-filmed-gay-encounters.html (accessed June 30, 2019).

17. "Techies Reveal Their Colours," *Times of India*, last modified November 28, 2011, http://timesofindia.indiatimes.com/articleshow/10898301.cms (accessed October 13, 2018).

18. Lawrence Cohen, "Song for Pushkin," *Daedalus* 136, no. 2 (2007): 103–15.

19. Ibid.

20. Ibid.; Srivastava, *Passionate Modernity*, 228; Constantine V. Nakassis, *Doing Style:*

Youth and Mass Mediation in South India (Chicago: University of Chicago Press, 2016); Sarah Pinto, "Drugs and the Single Woman: Pharmacy, Fashion, Desire, and Destitution in India," *Culture, Medicine, and Psychiatry* 38, no. 2 (2014): 237–54.

21. Suparna Bhaskaran, *Made in India: Decolonizations, Queer Sexualities, Trans/National Projects* (New York: Palgrave Macmillan, 2004), 79; Ruth Vanita, *Gandhi's Tiger and Sita's Smile: Essays on Gender, Sexuality, and Culture* (New Delhi: Yoda Press, 2005), 84.

22. Paola Bacchetta, "When the (Hindu) Nation Exiles Its Queers," *Social Text* 61 (1999): 141–66.

23. Dave, *Queer Activism in India*, 85.

24. Ibid.; see also Nayan Shah, "Sexuality, Identity, and the Uses of History," in Eng and Hom, *Q & A*, 141–56.

25. Nishant Upadhyay, "Queer Rights, Section 377, and Decolonizing Sexualities." Last modified July 19, 2018, https://decolonizingsexualities.com/2018/07/ (accessed October 12, 2019); and Santhosh Chandrashekhar, "South Asian Queer Politics and the Rise of Homohinduism," presented at "Homonationalism and Pinkwashing" conference at CUNY, New York, April 11, 2013.

26. Aniruddha Dutta, "Section 377 and the Retroactive Consolidation of 'Homophobia,'" in *Law Like Love: Queer Perspectives on Law*, ed. Arvind Narrain and Alok Gupta (New Delhi: Yoda Press, 2011), 162–73.

27. Anjali Arondekar, *For the Record: On Sexuality and the Colonial Archive in India* (Durham, NC: Duke University Press, 2009), 1.

28. Diana Taylor, *The Archive and the Repertoire: Performing Cultural Memory in the Americas* (Durham, NC: Duke University Press, 2003).

29. Arun Saldanha, *Psychedelic White: Goa Trance and the Viscosity of Race* (Minneapolis: University of Minnesota Press, 2007).

30. David Grazian, *On the Make: The Hustle of Urban Nightlife* (Chicago: University of Chicago Press, 2008).

31. Heitzman, *Network City*, 45; Florian Taeube, "The Indian Software Industry: Cultural Factors Underpinning Its Evolution," in *Popular Culture in a Globalised India*, ed. K. Moti Gokulsing and Wimal Dissanayake (London: Routledge / Taylor & Francis Group, 2009), 223–35.

32. Heitzman, *Network City*, 203.

33. M. K. Raghavendra, "Local Resistance to Global Bangalore: Reading Minority Indian Cinema," in Gokulsing and Dissanayake, *Popular Culture*, 15–27.

34. Nair, *Promise of the Metropolis*, 235.

35. Lawrence Liang, "Strangers in a Place They Call Home," *The Hindu*, https://www.thehindu.com/opinion/op-ed/strangers-in-a-place-they-call-home/article3785965.ece (accessed June 30, 2019).

36. Nivedita Menon, "How Natural Is Normal? Feminism and Compulsory Heterosexuality," in Narrain and Bhan, *Because I Have a Voice*, 35; Ritty A. Lukose, *Liberalization's Children: Gender, Youth, and Consumer Citizenship in Globalizing India* (Durham, NC: Duke University Press, 2009), 96.

37. A. Veeramani, "It's 'We' Day," *Daily News and Analysis*, February 14, 2012.

38. Baas, "The IT Caste."

39. Joshua Muyiwa, "Amour the Merrier," *Time Out Bengaluru*, February–March, 2012.

40. Román, *Acts of Intervention*, xxvi–xxvii.
41. Amrute, "Proprietary Freedoms," 103.
42. Hurston, "Folklore and Music," 188.
43. Marta Savigliano, *Tango and the Political Economy of Passion* (Boulder, CO: Westview Press, 1995).
44. Benedicto, *Under Bright Lights*, 95.
45. Meredith McGuire, "'How to Sit, How to Stand': Bodily Practice and the New Urban Middle Class," in *A Companion to the Anthropology of India*, ed. Isabelle Clark-Decès and Christophe Guilmoto (Malden, MA: Wiley-Blackwell, 2011), 115–36.
46. Héctor Carrillo, *The Night Is Young: Sexuality in Mexico in the Time of AIDS* (Chicago: University of Chicago Press, 2002), 116.
47. Lawrence Cohen, "Holi in Banaras and the Mahaland of Modernity," *GLQ* 2, no. 4 (1995): 399–424.
48. On queer mapping practices see Matthew Thomann, "Zones of Difference, Boundaries of Access: Moral Geography and Community Mapping in Abidjan, Côte d'Ivoire," *Journal of Homosexuality* 63, no. 3 (2016): 426–36.
49. Scott Herring, *Another Country: Queer Anti-urbanism* (New York: New York University Press, 2010); Mary L. Gray, *Out in the Country: Youth, Media, and Queer Visibility in Rural America* (New York: New York University Press, 2009).
50. Stallmeyer, "New Silicon Valleys."
51. Amico, "I Want Muscles"; Grant Tyler Peterson, "Clubbing Masculinities: Gender Shifts in Gay Men's Dance Floor Choreographies," *Journal of Homosexuality* 58, no. 5 (2011): 608–25.
52. On this phenomenon in Mumbai see Gupta, "Englishpur *Ki Kothi*," 135; Shahani, *Gay Bombay*, 85.
53. Parmesh Shahani, speaking specifically to a Bombay context, explains that a Malaysian drag troupe was invited to perform at a gay party, but the many local queens were not foreign enough to meet the party's "up market" aspirations. Shahani, *Gay Bombay*, 25.
54. Hartman, *Scenes of Subjection*, 67; Shane Vogel, *Stolen Time: Black Fad Performance and the Calypso Craze* (Chicago: University of Chicago Press, 2018); on queerness and closing time see Shane Vogel, *The Scene of Harlem Cabaret: Race, Sexuality, Performance* (Chicago: University of Chicago Press, 2009), 112.
55. Ila Nagar, "Digitally Untouched: Janana (In)Visibility and the Digital Divide," in Dasgupta and DasGupta, *Queering Digital India*, 97–111.
56. Poorva Rajaram, "I Was Once a Gay Party Enthusiast," *Tehelka*, http://old.tehelka.com/i-was-once-a-gay-party-enthusiast/ (accessed October 13, 2018).
57. Shaka McGlotten, *Virtual Intimacies: Media, Affect, and Queer Sociality* (Albany: State University of New York Press, 2013).
58. Vikram Johri, "From Earth to Planet Romeo," *Business Standard*, https://www.business-standard.com/article/opinion/vikram-johri-from-earth-to-planet-romeo-113011200014_1.html (accessed October 13, 2018).
59. Shanté Paradigm Smalls and Elliott H. Powell, "Introduction," *Black Scholar* 49, no. 1 (2019): 1–5.
60. Rohit K. Dasgupta and Debanuj DasGupta, "Intimate Subjects and Virtual Spaces: Rethinking Sexuality as a Category for Intimate Ethnographies," *Sexualities* 21, nos. 5–6 (2018): 932–50.

61. Bobby Benedicto, "Desiring Sameness: Globalization, Agency, and the Filipino Gay Imaginary," *Journal of Homosexuality* 55, no. 2 (2008): 274–311.

Chapter 2. Dancing against the Law: Critical Moves in Pub City

1. Ritika Nair, "Chin Lung Got a Makeover but the Vibes and Prices Remain Old-School," *Little Black Book*, https://lbb.in/bangalore/chin-lung-restobar/ (accessed October 13, 2018).

2. Shravan Bhat, "Chin Lung: The Worst Bar in Bangalore," *Shravan's Blog*, http://shravanblog.blogspot.com/2012/06/chin-lung-worst-bar-in-bangalore.html (accessed October 13, 2018).

3. Vargas, "Ruminations," 723.

4. Sukhdeep Singh, "Gay Men Attacked in a Bar in Bangalore," *Gaylaxy Magazine*, http://www.gaylaxymag.com/latest-news/gay-men-attacked-in-a-bar-in-bangalore/ (accessed October 13, 2018).

5. Gupta, "No Sleep Till Ban-Galore!!!"

6. PUCL-K, *Attacking Pubs and Birthday Parties*.

7. Vogel, *Scene of Harlem Cabaret*, 23.

8. Chambers-Letson, *A Race So Different*.

9. Jyoti Puri, *Sexual States: Governance and the Struggle over the Antisodomy Law in India* (Durham, NC: Duke University Press, 2016), 10.

10. Elizabeth Son, *Embodied Reckonings: "Comfort Women," Performance, and Transpacific Redress* (Ann Arbor: University of Michigan Press, 2018).

11. Narrain and Gupta, *Law Like Love*, 42.

12. Arvind Narrain and Marcus Eldridge, *The Right That Dares to Speak Its Name: Decriminalising Sexual Orientation and Gender Identity in India* (Bangalore: Alternative Law Forum, 2009), 12.

13. Janaki Nair and Mary. E. John, *A Question of Silence: The Sexual Economies of Modern India* (London: Zed Books, 2000), 24.

14. Puri, *Sexual States*, 5; Ponni Arasu and Priya Thangarajah, "Queer Women and Habeas Corpus in India: The Love That Blinds the Law," *Indian Journal of Gender Studies* 19, no. 3 (2012): 413–35; Nishant Shahani, "Patently Queer: Late Effects and the Sexual Economies of India." *GLQ* 23, no. 2 (2017): 195–220.

15. Narrain and Gupta, *Law Like Love*, xx; Alok Gupta, "The Presumption of Sodomy," in Narrain and Gupta, *Law Like Love*, 115–61.

16. Arondekar, *For the Record*, 69.

17. Narrain and Gupta, *Law Like Love*, xvi; my emphasis.

18. Despite the 2014 NALSA judgment, little infrastructure has developed to redistribute resources for hijras, and the subsequent transgender bills drafted have in fact been quite transphobic. Also, while the Criminal Tribes Act was repealed soon after independence, it functioned as a template for the 2011 Karnataka Police Act 36A, which offers police expansive leeway to detain and harass hijras.

19. Akshay Khanna, "The Social Lives of 377," in Narrain and Gupta, *Law Like Love*, 174–202.

20. Puri, *Sexual States*, 42.

21. Dwaipayan Banerjee, "Writing the Disaster: Substance Activism after Bhopal," *Contemporary South Asia* 21, no. 3 (2013): 241.

22. Matthew Rahaim, *Musicking Bodies: Gesture and Voice in Hindustani Music* (Middletown, CT: Wesleyan University Press, 2012).

23. Eve Kosofsky Sedgwick, "Gosh, Boy George, You Must Be Awfully Secure in Your Masculinity!," in *Constructing Masculinity*, ed. Maurice Berger, Brian Wallis, and Simon Watson (New York: Routledge, 1995), 11–20.

24. Gowri Vijayakumar complicates feminist and queer critiques of utopian "community" by articulating the many valences of the term "community" in Bangalore's gender and sexuality NGO complex. Gowri Vijayakumar, "Collective Demands and Secret Codes: The Multiple Uses of 'Community' in 'Community Mobilization,'" *World Development* 104 (2018): 173–82.

25. Vogel, *Scene of Harlem Cabaret*, 118.

26. Michel de Certeau, *The Practice of Everyday Life*, trans. Steven Rendall (Berkeley: University of California Press, 1984).

27. In October 2011, the Bangalore-based rap duo Two Much released a song called "Two Much Ban-Galore," a manifesto critiquing the ban on live music and dancing, pointing fingers at government corruption and negligence for using the ban to distraction the public from more systemic political issues.

28. N. Bhanutej, "Dance-Bars Spice Up the Night Life in Bangalore," *Week*, November 14, 2004; M. T. Shiva Kumar, "It Is More Than Just Song and Dance," *Hindu*, January 26, 2010.

29. "Dancing Ban: Blame It on Live Bands," *Times of India*, http://timesofindia.indiatimes.com/articleshow/2788616.cms (accessed April 10, 2018).

30. M. K. Madhusoodan, "Bangalore Police Commissioner: We're Enforcing Old Rules, So What's New?," *Daily News and Analysis*, https://www.dnaindia.com/bangalore/interview-bangalore-police-commissioner-we-re-enforcing-old-rules-so-what-s-new-1486638 (accessed April 10, 2014).

31. William Mazzarella, "A Different Kind of Flesh: Public Obscenity, Globalisation and the Mumbai Dance Bar Ban," *South Asia* 38, no. 3 (2015): 483.

32. Anna Morcom, *Illicit Worlds of Indian Dance: Cultures of Exclusion* (Oxford: Oxford University Press, 2013).

33. Some feminist criticism and gay diva worship performs an important nostalgia for the alternative economies, kinship systems, sexualities, and aesthetics of the lost courtesan, but idealistic imaginations of the courtesan potentially miss the desire for emancipation from these systems by oppressed caste devadasis, or alternatively are unable to imagine the evolving sexualities of ongoing devadasi communities. Saleem Kidwai, "Of Begums and Tawaifs: The Women of Awadh," 118–23, in *Women's Studies in India*, edited by Mary John (New Delhi: Penguin, 2008), 118–23; Saleem Kidwai, "The Singing Ladies Find a Voice," *Seminar* 540 (August 2004): 48–54; Ruth Vanita, *Dancing with the Nation: Courtesans in Bombay Cinema* (New York: Bloomsbury Academic, 2018); Veena Talwar Oldenburg, "Lifestyle as Resistance: The Case of the Courtesans of Lucknow," in *Contesting Power: Resistance and Everyday Social Relations in South Asia*, ed. Gyan Prakash and Douglas Haynes (Berkeley: University of California Press, 1991), 23–61; Anjali Arondekar, "Subject to Sex: A Small History of the Gomatak Maratha Samaj," in *South Asian Feminisms: Contemporary Interventions*, ed. Ania Loomba and

Ritty A. Lukose (Durham, NC: Duke University Press, 2012), 244–64; Lucinda Ramberg, *Given to the Goddess: South Indian Devadasis and the Sexuality of Religion* (Durham, NC: Duke University Press, 2014).

34. Other parties were also invested in the revaluation of devadasi practices, such as the subordinate castes pursuing a respectability movement, and men in the devadasi community interested in instating patrilineal rights to property. Amrit Srinivasan, "Reform and Revival: The Devadasi and Her Dance," *Economic and Political Weekly* 20, no. 44 (1985): 1869–76; Srinivasan, *Sweating Saris*; Avanthi Meduri, "Temple Stage as Historical Allegory in Bharatanatyam: Rukmini Devi as Dancer-Historian," in *Performing Pasts: Reinventing the Arts in Modern South India*, ed. Indira Viswanathan Peterson and Devesh Soneji (New Delhi: Oxford University Press, 2008), 133–64; Avanthi Meduri, "Bharatha Natyam—What Are You?," *Asian Theatre Journal* 5, no. 1 (1988): 1–22.

35. Mazzarella, "Different Kind of Flesh," 486.

36. In addition to the dance ban, Bangalore's bars were in a protracted battle with city legislations around the bar's closing time, fixed in 2008 at 11:30 p.m. In 2017, bars were permitted to stay open until 1:00 a.m. on Fridays and Saturdays; however, this boon was then confounded by a ban on selling alcohol within five hundred feet of major highways. In July 2018, bars were given permission to stay open until 1:00 a.m. throughout the week to accommodate the flexibility of neoliberal work life.

37. "Bangalore Put on Mute at 10pm," *Times of India*, August 3, 2013.

38. Vogel, *Scene of Harlem Cabaret*, 112.

39. Morcom, *Illicit Worlds*; Sangita Shresthova, *Is It All about Hips? Around the World with Bollywood Dance* (New Delhi: Sage Publications, 2011), 93.

40. Pallabi Chakravorty, *Bells of Change: Kathak Dance, Women, and Modernity in India* (Kolkata: Seagull Books, 2008); Margaret E. Walker, *India's Kathak Dance in Historical Perspective* (Farnham, Surrey, England: Ashgate Publishing, 2014).

41. Treva Carrie Ellison, "Black Femme Praxis and the Promise of Black Gender," *Black Scholar* 49, no. 1 (2019): 12.

Chapter 3. Desiring Desis: Race, Migration, and Markets in Boystown

1. Nan Alamilla Boyd, *Wide-Open Town: A History of Queer San Francisco to 1965* (Berkeley: University of California Press, 2003); Shalini Shankar, *Desi Land: Teen Culture, Class, and Success in Silicon Valley* (Durham, NC: Duke University Press, 2008).

2. Héctor Carrillo, *Pathways of Desire: The Sexual Migration of Mexican Gay Men* (Chicago: University of Chicago Press, 2017); Lionel Cantú, Nancy A. Naples, and Salvador Vidal-Ortiz, *The Sexuality of Migration: Border Crossings and Mexican Immigrant Men* (New York: New York University Press, 2009).

3. On the multiplicity of claims made to gay neighborhoods see Theodore Greene, "Gay Neighborhoods and the Rights of the Vicarious Citizen," *City & Community* 13, no. 2 (2014): 99–118.

4. Contemporaneous with Towertown in Chicago's North Side was a black ball scene on Chicago's South Side that attracted many white and straight residents from the city's North Side to witness the gender-bending performances of black queers. Drag bars, gay spaces, and sex work had been thriving in Chicago's North Side since the 1930s only a

mile south in Towertown (now known as River North and the Gold Coast) under the protection of organized crime. City-sponsored efforts to "clean up" Towertown led to the displacement of gay residents and clients into Lakeview. While the traffic of white queers from North to South has dwindled, there continues to be vibrant Black and Latinx queer subcultures on Chicago's South Side at venues such as Jeffrey's Pub, Club Escape, and La Cueva. St Sukie De la Croix, *Chicago Whispers: A History of LGBT Chicago before Stonewall* (Madison: University of Wisconsin Press, 2012); David K. Johnson, "The Kids of Fairytown: Gay Male Culture on Chicago's Near North Side in the 1930s," in *Creating a Place for Ourselves*, ed. Brett Beemyn (New York: Routledge, 1997), 97–144; Alex Papadopoulos, "From 'Towertown' to 'Boystown,'" 239; Chad C. Heap, *Slumming: Sexual and Racial Encounters in American Nightlife, 1885–1940* (Chicago: University of Chicago Press, 2009).

5. Reed, "We're from Oz."

6. Brown-Saracino, *Neighborhood That Never Changes,* 37.

7. Summer Kim Lee, "Staying In: Mitski, Ocean Vuong, and Asian American Asociality," *Social Text* 37, no. 1 (2019): 30–31.

8. Pranta Pratik Patnaik, "Bearly Indian: 'Fat' Gay Men's Negotiation of Embodiment, Culture, and Masculinity," in *Masculinity and Its Challenges in India: Essays on Changing Perceptions*, ed. Rohit K. Dasgupta and K. Moti Gokulsing (Jefferson, NC: McFarland, 2014) : 93–105.

9. Andrew J. Brown, "Performing Blackness in the 'Rainbow Nation': Athi-Patra Ruga's The Future White Women of Azania," *Women & Performance* 27, no. 1 (2017): 67–80.

10. Dwight A. McBride, *Why I Hate Abercrombie & Fitch: Essays on Race and Sexuality* (New York: New York University Press, 2005).

11. Johnson, "'Quare' Studies": 7.

12. Roderick Ferguson, *Aberrations in Black: Toward a Queer of Color Critique* (Minneapolis: University of Minnesota Press, 2004).

13. Said, *Orientalism*, 190; Anne Anlin Cheng, *Ornamentalism* (New York: Oxford University Press, 2019), 2.

14. Kumiko Nemoto, *Racing Romance: Love, Power, and Desire among Asian American / White Couples* (New Brunswick, NJ: Rutgers University Press, 2009), 81.

15. Joseph Boone, "Vacation Cruises; or, the Homoerotics of Orientalism," *PMLA* 110, no. 1 (1995): 89–107.

16. Uri McMillan, *Embodied Avatars: Genealogies of Black Feminist Art and Performance* (New York: NYU Press 2015).

17. Russell Leong, ed., *Asian American Sexualities: Dimensions of the Gay and Lesbian Experience* (New York: Routledge, 1996), 8.

18. Gregory Mitchell, *Tourist Attractions: Performing Race and Masculinity in Brazil's Sexual Economy* (Chicago: University of Chicago Press, 2015), 34.

19. Tan Hoang Nguyen, *A View from the Bottom: Asian American Masculinity and Sexual Representation* (Durham, NC: Duke University Press, 2014); Fung, "Looking for My Penis."

20. C. Winter Han, *Geisha of a Different Kind: Race and Sexuality in Gaysian America* (New York: New York University Press, 2015).

21. McBride, *Why I Hate Abercrombie & Fitch.*

22. Peggy Phelan, *Unmarked: The Politics of Performance* (London: Routledge, 1993).

23. Eng-Beng Lim, *Brown Boys and Rice Queens: Spellbinding Performance in the Asias* (New York: New York University Press 2014).

24. Said, *Orientalism*, 7.

25. Mrinalini Sinha, "Giving Masculinity a History: Some Contributions from the Historiography of Colonial India," *Gender & History* 11, no. 3 (2002): 447.

26. Shah, *Stranger Intimacy*, 39.

27. Puar, *Terrorist Assemblages*.

28. Ahmed Afzal, *Lone Star Muslims: Transnational Lives and the South Asian Experience in Texas* (New York: New York University Press, 2015).

29. Cherríe Moraga in *This Bridge Called My Back: Writings by Radical Women of Color*, ed. Cherríe Moraga and Gloria Anzaldúa (New York: Kitchen Table, Women of Color Press, 1983).

30. On interviews as "definitional ceremony" see Barbara G. Myerhoff, *Number Our Days: Culture and Community among Elderly Jews in an American Ghetto* (New York: Meridian, 1994). On interviews as performance and theory, see D. Soyini Madison, "'That Was My Occupation': Oral Narrative, Performance, and Black Feminist Thought," *Text and Performance Quarterly* 13, no. 3 (1993): 213–32; Micaela Di Leonardo, "Oral History as Ethnographic Encounter," *Oral History Review* 15, no. 1 (1987): 1–20; Della Pollock, *Remembering: Oral History Performance* (New York: Palgrave Macmillan, 2005); Cox, *Shapeshifters*, 8.

31. Mitchell, *Tourist Attractions*.

32. GerShun Avilez, "Uncertain Freedom," *Black Scholar* 49, no. 2 (2019): 50–64; E. Patrick Johnson, "'Scatter the Pigeons': Baldness and the Performance of Black Hypermasculinity," in *Blackberries and Redbones: Critical Articulations of Black Hair/Body Politics in Africana Communities*, ed. Regina E. Spellers and Kimberly R. Moffitt (Cresskill: Hampton Press, 2010), 147–56.

33. McBride, *Why I Hate Abercrombie & Fitch*, 122.

34. Hiram Pérez, *A Taste for Brown Bodies: Gay Modernity and Cosmopolitan Desire* (New York: New York University Press, 2015), 2.

35. Davé, *Indian Accents*, 46. Vijay Prashad importantly warns against long-standing fantasies of the acquiescent and hardworking Indian laborer, not only because these generalizations ignore the diversity of migration histories and class positions within South Asian America, but also because they speciously authenticate myths about other migrants and people color as responsible for their own lack of mobility by championing individual success and obscuring systemic barriers. Vijay Prashad, *The Karma of Brown Folk* (Minneapolis: University of Minnesota Press, 2000).

36. David S. Roh, Betsy Huang, and Greta A. Niu, *Techno-Orientalism: Imagining Asia in Speculative Fiction, History, and Media* (New Brunswick, NJ: Rutgers University Press, 2015), 2.

37. Ghalib Shiraz Dhalla, *Ode to Lata: A Novel* (Los Angeles: Really Great Books, 2002).

38. Davé, *Indian Accents*, 52.

39. Johnson, *Appropriating Blackness*.

40. Andil Gosine, "Brown to Blonde at Gay.Com: Passing White in Queer Cyberspace," in *Queer Online: Media Technology & Sexuality*, ed. Kate O'Riordan and David J.

Phillips (New York: Peter Lang, 2007); McGlotten, *Virtual Intimacies*; Sharif Mowlabo-cus, *Gaydar Culture: Gay Men, Technology and Embodiment in the Digital Age* (London: Routledge, 2010).

41. Gayle Rubin, "Thinking Sex: Notes for a Radical Theory of the Politics of Sexuality," in *The Lesbian and Gay Studies Reader*, ed. Henry Abelove, Michèle Aina Barale, and David M. Halperin (New York: Routledge, 1993), 3–44.

42. Anne McClintock, *Imperial Leather: Race, Gender, and Sexuality in the Colonial Context* (London: Routledge, 1995).

43. Mitchell, *Tourist Attractions*.

44. Benedicto, *Under Bright Lights*, 28, 106.

45. Han, *Geisha of a Different Kind*, 130.

46. Benji Hart, "The Anti-blackness of Believing There's No Support for Queerness in the Hood," *Black Youth Project*, http://blackyouthproject.com/anti-blackness-believing-theres-no-support-queerness-hood/ (accessed July 4, 2019).

47. Shah, *Stranger Intimacy*, 271.

48. Gopinath, *Impossible Desires*; Das Gupta, *Unruly Immigrants*; Sunita Sunder Mukhi, *Doing the Desi Thing: Performing Indianness in New York City* (New York: Garland, 2000).

49. Manolo Guzmán, *Gay Hegemony / Latino Homosexualities* (New York: Routledge, 2006), 26.

50. Cynthia Wu, *Sticky Rice: A Politics of Intraracial Desire* (Philadelphia: Temple University Press, 2018), 3.

51. Anita Mannur and Martin Manalansan, "Dude, What's That Smell? The Sriracha Shutdown and Immigrant Excess," *MH Magazine*, last modified January 16, 2014, https://www.fromthesquare.org/dude-whats-that-smell-the-sriracha-shutdown-and-immigrant-excess/ (accessed October 13, 2018).

52. Anita Mannur, *Culinary Fictions: Food in South Asian Diasporic Culture* (Philadelphia: Temple University Press, 2010), 3.

53. Shankar, *Desi Land*. The alternative to FOB-y would perhaps be Sunaina Maira's articulation of "Indo-chic." Sunaina Maira, "Henna and Hip Hop: The Politics of Cultural Production and the Work of Cultural Studies," *Journal of Asian American Studies* 3, no. 3 (2000): 329–69.

54. McClintock, *Imperial Leather*.

55. Ann Cvetkovich, "9-11 Every Day," *Signs* 28, no. 1 (2002): 471–73.

56. Rana, *Terrifying Muslims*.

57. Santhosh Chandrashekar, "Engendering Threat in the Guise of Protection: Orientalism and Sikh Vulnerability," *Journal of Multicultural Discourses* 12, no. 4 (2017): 366–81.

58. Puar, *Terrorist Assemblages*, 83–87.

59. Juana María Rodríguez, "Queer Sociality and Other Sexual Fantasies," *GLQ* 17, nos. 2–3 (2011): 341.

60. Mehammed Amadeus Mack, *Sexagon: Muslims, France, and the Sexualization of National Culture* (New York: Fordham University Press, 2017), 232.

61. See also Sandip Roy, "Curry Queens and Other Spices," in Eng and Hom, *Q & A*, 256–61; Afzal, *Lone Star Muslims*, 129.

62. Colleen Kim Daniher, "Yella Gal: Eartha Kitt's Racial Modulations," *Women & Performance* 28, no. 1 (2018): 16–33; see also Stanley I. Thangaraj, *Desi Hoop Dreams: Pickup Basketball and the Making of Asian American Masculinity* (New York: New York University Press, 2015), 114.

63. Prasant Nukalapati, "Brown and Blue: An Interview with Desi Adult Film Star Vikram Sohan," *Trikone Magazine* 2004, 12.

64. Khubchandani, "Voguing in Bangalore"; Khubchandani, "Terrifying Performances: Black-Brown-Queer Borrowings in Loins of Punjab Presents," *Journal of Asian American Studies* 19, no. 3 (2016): 275–97.

65. Avtar Brah, *Cartographies of Diaspora: Contesting Identities* (London: Routledge, 1996).

66. Lisa Lowe, *The Intimacies of Four Continents* (Durham, NC: Duke University Press, 2015).

67. On shifting identities in migration see chapter 2, "Moving Portraits," in Carlos Ulises Decena, *Tacit Subjects: Belonging and Same-Sex Desire among Dominican Immigrant Men* (Durham, NC: Duke University Press, 2011).

68. Robin Bernstein, *Racial Innocence: Performing American Childhood from Slavery to Civil Rights* (New York: New York University Press, 2011).

69. Rowe et al., *Answer the Call*, 122.

70. Roy, "Curry Queens," 260.

71. McBride, *Why I Hate Abercrombie & Fitch*, 118.

72. Eric C. Wat, "Preserving the Paradox: Stories from a Gay-Loh," in Leong, *Asian American Sexualities*, 73.

73. See also Frantz Fanon, who writes, "Between these white breasts that my wandering hands fondle, white civilization and worthiness become mine." Fanon, *Black Skin, White Masks*, 45.

74. Senthorun Raj, "Asylum and Sexual Orientation," in *The Wiley Blackwell Encyclopedia of Gender and Sexuality Studies* (Malden, MA: Wiley Blackwell, 2016); Chandan Reddy, *Freedom with Violence: Race, Sexuality, and the US State* (Durham, NC: Duke University Press, 2011), 151.

75. Armando García, "The Illegalities of Brownness," *Social Text* 33, no. 2 (2015): 103; my emphasis.

76. Kantara Souffrant, "Circling Dantò's Daughter: Reflections on Lenelle Moïse's Performances of Shamelessness," *Women & Performance* 27, no. 2 (2017): 229–34.

Chapter 4. Slumdogs and Big Chicks: Unsettling Orientations at Jai Ho!

1. C. S. Nagarkatti, "Sense of Liberation Sweeps Indian Gays in US," *India Today*, https://www.indiatoday.in/magazine/international/story/19890228-sense-of-liberation-sweeps-indian-gays-in-us-815816-1989-02-28 (accessed June 30, 2019).

2. Sandip Roy, "How Silicon Valley fostered India's LGBTQ+ movement," LiveMint (last updated August 31, 2019), https://www.livemint.com/mint-lounge/features/how-silicon-valley-fostered-india-s-lgbtq-movement-1567161918842.html (accessed October 12, 2019).

3. He told me that they first named the organization Trikone, but the Bay Area organization was not responsive to his messages, and so he and Viru came up with the name Sangat, meaning "harmony."

4. Seligman, "Uptown."

5. Keely Jones, "Big Chicks, Tweet and the Famous Michelle Fire," *Edgeville Buzz*, http://www.edgevillebuzz.com/news/big-chicks-tweet-and-the-famous-michelle-fire (accessed October 13, 2018).

6. Karen Shimakawa, *National Abjection: The Asian American Body Onstage* (Durham, NC: Duke University Press, 2002), 17.

7. Ahmed, *Queer Phenomenology*.

8. Fintan Walsh, "Queer Performance and the Drama of Disorientation," in Campbell and Farrier, *Queer Dramaturgies*, 324.

9. Purnima Mankekar, *Unsettling India: Affect, Temporality, Transnationality* (Durham, NC: Duke University Press, 2015).

10. Sharon Holland, "Foreword: Home Is a Four-Letter Word," in *Black Queer Studies: A Critical Anthology*, ed. E. Patrick Johnson and Mae Henderson (Durham, NC: Duke University Press, 2005), ix–xiii.

11. Grazian, *On the Make*, 37.

12. Emily Apter, "Acting Out Orientalism: Sapphic Theatricality in Turn-of-the-Century Paris," in Diamond, *Performance and Cultural Politics*, 15–34.

13. Fanon, *Black Skin, White Masks*, 119.

14. See chapter 6, "Stages," in Muñoz, *Cruising Utopia*.

15. In stark contrast to most of the other bars, posters for two weekly parties at Circuit—*Noché Latino* and *Urbano*— featured men of color, shirtless with gold chains, or wearing cowboy hats and large belt buckles, to attract Black and Latinx men. During my fieldwork, the gay neighborhood's inclusive nature came into question as black and Latinx queer and trans youth called out Boystown residents, business owners, and police who were actively privatizing public space in the name of "safety." Orne, *Boystown*; Zachary Blair, "Boystown: Gay Neighborhoods, Social Media, and the (Re)Production of Racism," in *No Tea, No Shade: New Writings in Black Queer Studies*, ed. E. Patrick Johnson (Durham, NC: Duke University Press, 2016), 287–302.

16. Savigliano, *Tango*, 96.

17. Said, *Orientalism*, 100.

18. Michael Moon, "Flaming Closets," *October* 51 (1989): 19–54. See also Amy Haruko Sueyoshi, *Discriminating Sex: White Leisure and the Making of the American "Oriental"* (Urbana: University of Illinois Press, 2018).

19. These Orientalist themes are not limited to South Asian appropriations alone. The 2000 Hotlanta River Expo circuit event was themed *Year of the Dragon* with individual parties named *Shogun, China Doll, Tsunami,* and *Fried Rice.* NBC Asian America, "Tracing the Evolution of Asian-Pacific Islander LGBTQ Nightlife Spaces," *NBC Universal*, last modified June 28, 2018, https://www.nbcnews.com/video/tracing-the-evolution-of-asian-pacific-islander-lgbtq-nightlife-spaces-1264034371628 (accessed October 13, 2018).

20. Sangita Gopal and Sujata Moorti, "Bollywood in Drag: *Moulin Rouge!* and the Aesthetics of Global Cinema," *Camera Obscura* 25, no. 3 (2011): 28–67.

21. Gayatri Gopinath, "Bollywood Spectacles: Queer Diasporic Critique in the After-

math of 9/11," *Social Text* 23, nos. 3–4 (2005); Rajinder Dudrah, *Bollywood: Sociology Goes to the Movies* (New Delhi: Sage Publications, 2006), 119.

22. Michelle's class politics are strongly informed by the community she found working in gay bars in the seventies and eighties, and her own struggles in the industry. She opened her own bar because she realized that in a male-dominated industry she would never be made manager. Though clients from other parts of Chicago came to her new gay bar, she learned from her old-timers that they would come to this very bar, even before she bought it, to pick up trade. Just as desiness preceded us at Big Chicks before *Jai Ho!*, queerness lived there too, in an economically depressed and racially diverse neighborhood, before it was a "gay bar."

23. Brinda Bose and Subhabrata Bhattacharyya, eds., *The Phobic and the Erotic: The Politics of Sexualities in Contemporary India* (Calcutta: Seagull Books, 2007).

24. Sunaina Maira, *Desis in the House: Indian American Youth Culture in New York City* (Philadelphia: Temple University Press, 2002), 12.

25. Thomas F. DeFrantz, "Foreword: Black Bodies Dancing Black Culture—Black Atlantic Transformations," in *Embodying Liberation: The Black Body in American Dance*, ed. Dorothea Fischer-Hornung and Alison D. Goeller (Hamburg: LIT Verlag, 2001), 11.

26. Heap, *Slumming*.

27. Orne, *Boystown*, 74.

28. Martin Manalansan makes a similar argument about the policing of Asian clients in NYC's rice bars. Manalansan, *Global Divas*, 82–84.

29. On being stuck in representation, Christina León writes, "Audiences refuse to recognize minoritarian art as having a form, as constituting a mode of aesthetic rather than only 'ethnic' representation." Christina A. León, "Forms of Opacity: Roaches, Blood, and Being Stuck in Xandra Ibarra's Corpus." *ASAP/Journal* 2, no. 2 (2017): 371.

30. Gopinath, *Impossible Desires*, 29.

31. Sarah Hankins, "So Contagious: Hybridity and Subcultural Exchange in Hip-Hop's Use of Indian Samples," *Black Music Research Journal* 31, no. 2 (2011): 193–208.

32. Gregory Diethrich, "Dancing the Diaspora: Indian Desi Music in Chicago," in *Identity and the Arts in Diaspora Communities*, ed. Thomas Turino and James Lea (Warren, MI: Harmonie Park Press, 2004), 103–15.

33. Geeta Dayal, "Indian Summer," *Sight&Sound*, June 2016.

34. Alice Echols, *Hot Stuff: Disco and the Remaking of American Culture* (New York: W. W. Norton, 2010); Tim Lawrence, "In Defence of Disco (Again)," *New Formations* 58, no. 1 (2006): 128–46; Richard Dyer, "In Defense of Disco," *New Formations* 58, no. 1 (2006): 101–8.

35. Ani Maitra, "Hearing Queerly: Musings on the Ethics of Disco/Sexuality," *Continuum* 25, no. 3 (2011): 375–96.

36. Ajay Gehlawat, "The Construction of 1970s Femininity, or Why Zeenat Aman Sings the Same Song Twice," *South Asian Popular Culture* 10, no. 1 (2012): 51–62; Neepa Majumdar, *Wanted: Cultured Ladies Only! Female Stardom and Cinema in India, 1930s–1950s* (Urbana: University of Illinois Press, 2009).

37. Greene, "Gay Neighborhood," 107.

38. Hollis Griffin, "Your Favorite Stars, Live on Our Screens: Media Culture, Queer Publics, and Commercial Space," *Velvet Light Trap* 62, no. 1 (2008): 15–28.

39. Dudrah, *Bollywood*.

40. Sudhanva Deshpande, "The Consumable Hero of Globalised India," in *Bollyworld: Popular Indian Cinema through a Transnational Lens*, ed. Raminder Kaur and Ajay J. Sinha (New Delhi: Sage Publications, 2005), 186–203; Krupa Shandilya, "Of Enraged Shirts, Gyrating Gangsters, and Farting Bullets: Salman Khan and the New Bollywood Action Film," *South Asian Popular Culture* 12, no. 2 (2014): 111–21.

41. Rahim Thawer, "Did This Drag Queen Go Too Far?," *Huffington Post*, https://www.huffingtonpost.ca/rahim-thawer/drag-toronto_b_2323047.html (accessed October 13, 2018).

42. Helga Borsky, "Toronto's Queen of Comedy Donnarama Performs a Medley of 'Jai Ho' and 'Spice Up Your Life!,'" *YouTube*, last modified January 24, 2011, https://www.youtube.com/watch?v=ALPdMk8gvB8 (accessed October 13, 2018).

43. Bryan Buttler, "Philly Drag Queen Offends with 9/11-Themed Performance. Did She Go Too Far?," *Philadelphia (Metro Corp.)*, https://www.phillymag.com/g-philly/2014/09/17/art-just-plain-offensive/ (accessed October 13, 2018).

44. Shimakawa, *National Abjection*.

45. Ibid., 56.

46. Ann R. David, "Beyond the Silver Screen: Bollywood and Filmi Dance in the UK," *South Asia Research* 27, no. 1 (2007): 5–24; Elizabeth Chacko and Rajiv Menon, "Longings and Belongings: Indian American Youth Identity, Folk Dance Competitions, and the Construction of 'Tradition,'" *Ethnic and Racial Studies* 36, no. 1 (2013): 97–116.

47. Manalansan, *Global Divas*; Héctor Carrillo, "Sexual Migration, Cross-Cultural Sexual Encounters, and Sexual Health," *Sexuality Research & Social Policy* 1, no. 3 (2004): 58–70.

48. Jasbir Puar, "Global Circuits: Transnational Sexualities and Trinidad," *Signs* 26, no. 4 (2001): 1039–65.

49. Michael Warner, *Publics and Counterpublics* (New York: Zone Books, 2002), 120.

50. Muñoz, *Disidentifications*, 189. See also Josephine D. Lee, *Performing Asian America: Race and Ethnicity on the Contemporary Stage* (Philadelphia: Temple University Press, 1997), 7.

51. Ju Yon Kim, *The Racial Mundane: Asian American Performance and the Embodied Everyday* (New York: New York University Press, 2015), 188.

52. Sarah Thornton, *Club Cultures: Music, Media, and Subcultural Capital* (Hanover, NH: University Press of New England, 1996); Jonathan Bollen, "Queer Kinesthesia: Performativity on the Dance Floor," in *Dancing Desires: Choreographing Sexualities on and off the Stage*, ed. Jane Desmond (Madison: University of Wisconsin Press, 2001), 285–314; Buckland, *Impossible Dance*; Xavier Livermon, "Soweto Nights: Making Black Queer Space in Post-apartheid South Africa," *Gender, Place & Culture* 21, no. 4 (2014): 508–25.

53. Thornton, *Club Cultures*, 156; Bollen, "Queer Kinesthesia," 300; Buckland, *Impossible Dance*, 103.

54. Tim Lawrence, "Beyond the Hustle: 1970s Social Dancing, Discotheque Culture, and the Emergence of the Contemporary Club Dancer," in *Ballroom, Boogie, Shimmy Sham, Shake: A Social and Popular Dance Reader*, ed. Julie Malnig (Urbana: University of Illinois Press, 2009), 203.

55. DeFrantz, "Queer Dance," 175.

56. DeFrantz, "Foreword," 13.

57. Falu Pravin Bakrania, *Bhangra and Asian Underground: South Asian Music and the Politics of Belonging in Britain* (Durham, NC: Duke University Press, 2013).

58. Rajinder Dudrah, "British Bhangra Music as Soundscapes of the Midlands," *Midland History* 36, no. 2 (2011): 278–91.

59. Anjali Gera Roy, *Bhangra Moves: From Ludhiana to London and Beyond* (Burlington, VT: Ashgate, 2010); Gayatri Gopinath, "'Bombay, U.K., Yuba City': Bhangra Music and the Engendering of Diaspora," *Diaspora* 4, no. 3 (1995): 303–21; Nicola Mooney, "Aaja Nach Lai [Come Dance]: Performing and Practicing Identity among Punjabis in Canada," *Ethnologies* 30, no. 1 (2008): 103–24.

60. Patricia Nguyen, "Project 0395A.ĐC: Performing Disorientation," *Women & Performance* 29, no. 1 (2019): 91.

61. Maira, *Desis in the House*, 34.

62. Gopinath, *Impossible Desires*, 47.

63. David Román, "Dance Liberation," *Theatre Journal* 55, no. 3 (2003): vii–xxiv.

64. Deidre Sklar, "Reprise: On Dance Ethnography," *Dance Research Journal* 32, no. 1 (2000): 71.

65. Kareem Khubchandani, "Aunty Fever: A Queer Impression," in Croft, *Queer Dance*, 199–204.

66. Camila Bassi, "The Precarious and Contradictory Moments of Existence for an Emergent British Gay Asian Culture," in *New Geographies of Race and Racism*, ed. Claire Dwyer and Caroline Bressey (Aldershot, UK: Ashgate, 2008), 209–22.

67. Croft, *Queer Dance*, 4.

68. Arthur Knight, "Star Dances: African-American Constructions of Stardom, 1925–1960," in *Classic Hollywood, Classic Whiteness*, ed. Daniel Bernardi (Minneapolis: University of Minnesota Press, 2001), 398.

69. Vogel, *Scene of Harlem Cabaret*, 98.

70. José Esteban Muñoz, "'Gimme Gimme This . . . Gimme Gimme That': Annihilation and Innovation in the Punk Rock Commons," *Social Text* 31, no. 3 (116) (2013): 96.

71. George Lipsitz, *How Racism Takes Place* (Philadelphia: Temple University Press, 2011).

72. Bollen, "Queer Kinesthesia," 297.

73. Ibid., 293.

74. Sklar, "Reprise," 77.

75. Queer Coolie, "Review Queer Desi Dance Party: Jai Ho 5!," *Gaysi*, http://gaysi family.com/2010/08/30/review-queer-desi-dance-party-jai-ho-5/ (accessed September 30, 2018).

76. Jill Dolan, *Utopia in Performance: Finding Hope at the Theater* (Ann Arbor: University of Michigan Press, 2005); Muñoz, *Cruising Utopia*.

77. Muñoz, *Cruising Utopia*, 81.

78. Román, "Dance Liberation."

Chapter 5. Snakes on the Dance Floor: Bollywood and Diva Worship

1. An earlier version of this chapter appeared as "Snakes on the Dance Floor: Bollywood, Gesture, and Gender," *The Velvet Light Trap*, Vol. 77 (2016): 69–85.

2. Carrie Noland and Sally Ann Ness, *Migrations of Gesture* (Minneapolis: University of Minnesota Press, 2008), xvii.

3. Carolyn Dinshaw, "Got Medieval?," *Journal of the History of Sexuality* 10, no. 2 (2001): 203.

4. Walcott, "Boyfriends with Clits," 172.

5. Thomas Waugh, "Queer Bollywood, or 'I'm the Player, You're the Naive One': Patterns of Sexual Subversion in Recent Indian Popular Cinema," in *Keyframes: Popular Cinema and Cultural Studies,*, ed. Matthew Tinkcom and Amy Villarejo (London: Routledge, 2001), 280–97; Shohini Ghosh, "False Appearances and Mistaken Identities: The Phobic and the Erotic in Bombay Cinema's Queer Vision," in Bose and Bhattacharyya, *The Phobic and the Erotic*, 417–35; Gayatri Gopinath, "Queering Bollywood: Alternative Sexualities in Popular Indian Cinema," *Journal of Homosexuality* 39, nos. 3–4 (2000): 283–97; Priya Jha, "Lyrical Nationalism: Gender, Friendship, and Excess in 1970s Hindi Cinema," *Velvet Light Trap* 51 (2003): 43–53.

6. Nakassis, *Doing Style*, 184.

7. Alexander Doty, *Making Things Perfectly Queer: Interpreting Mass Culture* (Minneapolis: University of Minnesota Press, 1993).

8. Tejaswini Ganti, *Producing Bollywood: Inside the Contemporary Hindi Film Industry* (Durham, NC: Duke University Press, 2012).

9. Aditi N. Menon-Broker, "A Hall of Mirrors: Repetition and Recycling in Hindi Commercial Cinema" (PhD diss., Northwestern University, 2005).

10. Rodriguez, *Sexual Futures*, 2.

11. Gopinath, "Queering Bollywood"; Jha, "Lyrical Nationalism"; Waugh, "Queer Bollywood."

12. Stacy Ellen Wolf, "'We'll Always Be Bosom Buddies': Female Duets and the Queering of Broadway Musical Theater," *GLQ* 12, no. 3 (2006): 356.

13. Ajay Gehlawat, "The Bollywood Song and Dance, or Making a Culinary Theatre from Dung-Cakes and Dust," *Quarterly Review of Film and Video* 23, no. 4 (2006): 331–40.

14. Lalitha Gopalan, *Cinema of Interruptions: Action Genres in Contemporary Indian Cinema* (New Delhi: Oxford University Press, 2003).

15. Nithin Manayath, "Inhi Logon Ne: Meena Kumari and All That Was Lost with Her," *Big Indian Picture*, last modified March 2013, http://thebigindianpicture. com/2013/03/inhi-logon-ne/ (accessed October 13, 2018).

16. Pallabi Chakravorty, "Moved to Dance: Remix, Rasa, and a New India," *Visual Anthropology* 22, nos. 2–3 (2009): 211–28; Shresthova, *Is It All about Hips?*

17. Ochoa, *Queen for a Day*, 5.

18. In *Ode to Lata*, Ghalib Shiraz Dhalla's Kenyan-Indian protagonist draws on the saccharine melodies of Bollywood playback singer Lata Mangeshkar as he navigates Los Angeles bathhouses and tumultuous affairs. Sixties icon Sharmila Tagore serves as Pakistani-Canadian Fawzia Mirza's muse for both her short film *Queen of My Dreams* and solo play *Me, My Mom, and Sharmila*, which deal with coming out, Islam, and diasporic womanhood. Bay Area–based Anuj Vaidya mixes live performance and film in *Bad Girl with a Heart of Gold* to rescue Helen, the French-Burmese vamp of seventies cinema, from her perpetual death or disappearance from the plot. British Asian theater company Rifco Arts developed and premiered *Miss Meena and the Masala Queens*,

in which the drag queen protagonist is ghosted by Bollywood's premiere tragedienne Meena Kumari. Harjant Gill's short, *Milind Soman Made Me Gay*, overlays the controversies around Soman's nude photoshoot, with his own challenges as a migrant queer. *The Gentleman's Club*, a play devised by Mumbai's Patchwork Ensemble and written by Vikram Phukan, features a drag king who models himself in the soft masculinity of Shammi Kapoor. Hindi film too takes up the queer intimacies between film stars and their fans; in Zoya Akhtar's short, *Sheila Ki Jawaani*, a preteen boy is disciplined for dancing like Katrina Kaif.

19. Rachel Dwyer, "Representing the Muslim: The 'Courtesan Film' in Indian Popular Cinema," in *Jews, Muslims, and Mass Media: Mediating the "Other"*, ed. Tudor Parfitt and Yulia Egorova (London: RoutledgeCurzon, 2005), 78–92; Ranjani Mazumdar, "Desiring Women," in *Bombay Cinema: An Archive of the City* (Minneapolis: University of Minnesota Press, 2007); Geetanjali Gangoli, "Sexuality, Sensuality and Belonging: Representations of the 'Anglo-Indian' and the 'Western' Woman in Hindi Cinema," in Kaur and Sinha, *Bollyworld*, 114–23; Jerry Pinto, *Helen: The Life and Times of an H-Bomb* (New Delhi: Penguin, 2006).

20. Gehlawat, "Construction of 1970s Femininity."

21. Usha Iyer, "Stardom *Ke Peeche Kya Hai*? / What Is behind the Stardom? Madhuri Dixit, the Production Number, and the Construction of the Female Star Text in 1990s Hindi Cinema," *Camera Obscura* 30, no. 3 (2015): 129–59.

22. Wayne Koestenbaum, *The Queen's Throat: Opera, Homosexuality, and the Mystery of Desire* (New York: Poseidon Press, 1993); Brett Farmer, "The Fabulous Sublimity of Gay Diva Worship," *Camera Obscura* 20, no. 2 (2005): 165–95; Jimmy Draper, "'What Has She Actually Done??!': Gay Men, Diva Worship, and the Paratextualization of Gay-Rights Support," *Critical Studies in Media Communication* 34, no. 2 (2017): 130–37.

23. *Camera Obscura* 22, no. 2 (2007); *Camera Obscura* 23, no. 1 (2008).

24. Peter Stoneley, *A Queer History of the Ballet* (London: Routledge / Taylor & Francis Group, 2007).

25. Iyer, "Stardom," 131.

26. Majumdar, *Wanted Cultured Ladies Only*.

27. Amita Nijhawan, "Excusing the Female Dancer: Tradition and Transgression in Bollywood Dancing," *South Asian Popular Culture* 7, no. 2 (2009): 99–112.

28. Maira, *Desis in the House*, 170.

29. Deborah Parédez, *Selenidad: Selena, Latinos, and the Performance of Memory* (Durham, NC: Duke University Press, 2009).

30. Deborah Paredez, "Lena Horne and Judy Garland: Divas, Desire, and Discipline in the Civil Rights Era," *TDR* 58, no. 4 (2014): 107.

31. Anna Morcom, *Hindi Film Songs and the Cinema* (Burlington, VT: Ashgate, 2007).

32. Monika Mehta, "What Is behind Film Censorship? The Khalnayak Debates," in *The Bollywood Reader*, ed. Jigna Desai and Rajinder Dudrah (New York: Open University Press, 2008), 129; see also Tejaswini Ganti, *Bollywood: A Guidebook to Popular Hindi Cinema*, 2nd ed. (London: Routledge, 2013), 79.

33. Shohini Ghosh, "Queer Pleasures for Queer People: Film, Television, and Queer Sexuality in India," in *Queering India: Same-Sex Love and Eroticism in Indian Culture and Society*, ed. Ruth Vanita (New York: Routledge, 2002), 207–21.

34. Amita Nijhawan, "Of Snake Dances, Overseas Brides, and Miss World Pageants: Frolicking through Gurinder Chadha's *Bride and Prejudice*," in *Oxford Handbook of Dance and the Popular Screen*, ed. Melissa Blanco Borelli (Oxford: Oxford University Press, 2014), 387. See also 10:04 in All India Bakchod, "Honest Indian Weddings," *YouTube*, https://www.youtube.com/watch?v=iU6qI92Nt-Q (accessed October 13, 2018).

35. Madison Moore, "Tina Theory: Notes on Fierceness," *Journal of Popular Music Studies* 24, no. 1 (2012): 83.

36. Stacy Wolf, "Wicked Divas, Musical Theater, and Internet Girl Fans," *Camera Obscura* 22, no. 2 (65) (2007): 46.

37. Parédez, "Lena Horne," 105.

38. Joshua Williams, "Going Ape," *Performance Research* 21, no. 5 (2016): 68–77.

39. Lauren Gail Berlant, *The Queen of America Goes to Washington City: Essays on Sex and Citizenship* (Durham, NC: Duke University Press, 1997), 223.

40. Ibid.

41. Ibid.

42. Ganti, *Producing Bollywood*; Morcom, *Illicit Worlds*.

43. Gopinath, *Impossible Desires*; Patricia Uberoi, "Imagining the Family: An Ethnography of Viewing *Hum Aapke Hain Koun*," in Desai and Dudrah, *The Bollywood Reader*, 172–88.

44. On relationships between changing economies, class aspiration, and choreography inside the Shiamak studios see Shresthova, *Is It All about Hips?*

45. Julian Carter, "Jérôme Bel, Swan Lake, and the Alternative Futures of Re-enacted Dance," in Croft, *Queer Dance*, 111.

46. Kaustav Bakshi and Anugyan Nag, "Sridevi, the Dancing Queen and Queer Icon Who Opened Many Doors," *Wire India*, https://thewire.in/film/sridevi-dancing-queen-queer-icon (accessed October 13, 2018).

47. Angela Alghren, "Futari Tomo: A Queer Duet for Taiko," in Croft, *Queer Dance*, 236.

48. Daniel Harris, "The Death of Camp: Gay Men and Hollywood Diva Worship, from Reverence to Ridicule," *Salmagundi* 112 (1996): 166.

49. Parédez, "Lena Horne," 106.

50. Melissa Blanco Borelli, "'¿Y ahora qué vas a hacer, mulata?': Hip Choreographies in the Mexican Cabaretera Film Mulata (1954)," *Women & Performance* 18, no. 3 (2008): 216.

51. Brett Farmer, "Julie Andrews Made Me Gay," *Camera Obscura* 22, no. 2 (65) (2007): 146–48.

52. Brian Herrera, "Evanescence: Three Tales of the Recent Queer Theatrical Past." *Theatre Topics* 26, no. 1 (2016): 47–51.

53. See "Saving' Khmer Classical Dance in Long Beach," in Hamera, *Dancing Communities*.

54. Gloria Anzaldúa, *Borderlands / La Frontera*, 2nd ed. (San Francisco: Aunt Lute Books, 1999), 42.

55. Rahul K. Gairola, *Homelandings: Postcolonial Diasporas and Transatlantic Belonging* (London: Rowman & Littlefield International, 2016); Gopinath, *Impossible Desires*.

56. Anzaldúa, *Borderlands / La Frontera*, 43.

57. David Gere, "29 Effeminate Gestures: Choreographer Joe Goode and the Heroism of Effeminacy," in Desmond, *Dancing Desires*, 349–81.

58. For a similar story about a hijra in India see Jeff Roy, "Translating Hijra into Transgender: Performance and in India's Trans-Communities," *TSQ* 3, nos. 3–4 (2016): 424.

59. Mukhi, *Doing the Desi Thing*.

60. Buckland, *Impossible Dance*, 93.

61. Brian A. Horton, "What's So 'Queer' about Coming Out? Silent Queers and Theorizing Kinship Agonistically in Mumbai," *Sexualities* 21, no. 7 (2018): 1061.

62. Herring, *Another Country*, 125.

63. On the policing of queerness in straight desi spaces see Thangaraj, *Desi Hoop Dreams*.

64. Peterson, "Clubbing Masculinities."

65. David M. Halperin, *How to Be Gay* (Cambridge, MA: Belknap Press of Harvard University Press, 2012), 202.

66. Muñoz, *Cruising Utopia*, 78–81.

67. Joseph Litvak quoted in Sedgwick, *Touching Feeling*, 147.

68. E. Patrick Johnson, "Feeling the Spirit in the Dark: Expanding Notions of the Sacred in the African-American Gay Community," *Callaloo* 21, no. 2 (1998): 399–416; Jeffrey Q. McCune, "Transformance: Reading the Gospel in Drag," in *The Drag Queen Anthology: The Absolutely Fabulous but Flawless Customary World of Female Impersonators*, ed. Steven P. Schacht and Lisa Underwood (New York: Harrington Park Press, 2004), 151–67; Manalansan, *Global Divas*, 136.

69. Dean Spade, "Mutilating Gender," in *The Transgender Studies Reader*, ed. Susan Stryker and Stephen Whittle (New York: Routledge, 2006), 20.

70. Elizabeth Freeman, *Time Binds: Queer Temporalities, Queer Histories* (Durham, NC: Duke University Press, 2010).

71. Sedgwick, *Touching Feeling*, 149.

72. Kathryn Bond Stockton, *The Queer Child, or Growing Sideways in the Twentieth Century* (Durham, NC: Duke University Press, 2009), 3.

Chapter 6. Raw and Uncouth: Class, Region, and Caste at Koothnytz

1. "Koothu" refers to a wide genre of heritage folk performance practices, each one having "koothu" as a suffix. The popularity *dappankoothu* has acquired through cinema has given it precedence as the most visible manifestation of koothu practices.

2. Zoe Sherinian, *Tamil Folk Music as Dalit Liberation Theology* (Bloomington: Indiana University Press, 2014), 14–19; Sharanya Manivannan, "Professional Mourners," *Motherland* 2012: 14–19.

3. Preminda Jacob, *Celluloid Deities: The Visual Culture of Cinema and Politics in South India* (Lanham, MD: Lexington Books, 2009), 92; S. V. Srinivas, *Megastar: Chiranjeevi and Telugu Cinema after N.T. Rama Rao* (Oxford: Oxford University Press, 2009), xix.

4. Zoe Sherinian, "Religious Encounters: Empowerment through Tamil Outcaste Folk Drumming," *Interpretation* 71, no. 1 (2017): 64–79.

5. Amanda Weidman, "Voices of Meenakumari: Sound, Meaning, and Self-Fashioning in Performances of an Item Number," *South Asian Popular Culture* 10, no. 3 (2012): 311.

6. Ibid.

7. Akhil Kang, "Queering Dalit," Tanqeed, last modified October 2016 http://www.tanqeed.org/2016/10/queering-dalit-tq-salon/) (accessed September 6, 2017)

8. Anupama Rao, *The Caste Question: Dalits and the Politics of Modern India* (Berkeley: University of California Press, 2009), 221–22. See also "Dhiren Borisa on Dalit Queerness," *Godrej India Culture Lab*, https://indiaculturelab.org/videos/library/special-events/dhiren-borisa-on-dalit-queerness/ (accessed October 12, 2019).

9. Lucinda Ramberg, "Backward Futures and Pasts Forward: Queer Time, Sexual Politics, and Dalit Religiosity in South India," *GLQ* 22, no. 2 (2016): 229.

10. Marlon M. Bailey, "Black Gay (Raw) Sex," in Johnson, *No Tea, No Shade*, 256.

11. Nguyen, *View from the Bottom*.

12. Maira, *Desis in the House*, 69.

13. Rajyashree Narayanareddy, "Specters of Waste in India's 'Silicon Valley': The Underside of Bangalore's Hi-Tech Economy" (PhD diss., University of Minnesota, 2011).

14. Kaveri Karthik and Gee Ameena Suleiman, "(Trans)Gender and Caste Lived Experience—Transphobia as a Form of Brahminism: An Interview of Living Smile Vidya," *Sanhati*, http://sanhati.com/excerpted/6051/ (accessed October 13, 2018).

15. Surinder S. Jodhka, "Caste & the Corporate Sector," *Indian Journal of Industrial Relations* 44, no. 2 (2008): 192.

16. Gayatri Reddy, *With Respect to Sex: Negotiating Hijra Identity in South India* (Chicago: University of Chicago Press, 2005).

17. Gupta, "*Englishpur Ki* Kothi."

18. Kareem Khubchandani, "Staging Transgender Solidarities at Bangalore's Queer Pride," *TSQ* 1, no. 4 (2014): 517–22.

19. Dhiren Borisa, "Imagined Spaces of Freedom: Negotiating Queer Cartographies of Desires in Delhi" (PhD diss., Jawaharlal Nehru University, New Delhi, 2018); Dasgupta, "Parties, Advocacy, and Activism."

20. Johnson, "Foreword."

21. Benedicto, *Under Bright Lights*, 12.

22. Katyal, *The Doubleness of Sexuality*; Waugh, "Queer Bollywood."

23. Srinivas, *Megastar*, xxix, 147.

24. Horton-Stallings, *Funk the Erotic*, 4.

25. Gopinath, *Unruly Visions,* 30.

26. Anjali Gera Roy, "Black Beats with a Punjabi Twist," *Popular Music* 32, no. 2 (2013): 241–57; Bakrania, *Bhangra and Asian Underground*; Khubchandani, "Terrifying Performances."

27. Lukose, *Liberalization's Children*, 68.

28. Josh Kun, *Audiotopia: Music, Race, and America* (Berkeley: University of California Press, 2005).

29. Aniruddha Dutta, "Nation, Liberalisation and Film Songs: Technology and Hybridisation in Contemporary Hindi Film Music," *Wide Screen* 1, no. 1 (2009): 1–11.

30. Sneha Krishnan, "Bitch Don't Be a Lesbian: Selfies, Selves and Same-Sex Desire," in Dasgupta and DasGupta, *Queering Digital India*, 159.

31. Nakassis, *Doing Style*, 186.

32. Weidman, "Voices of Meenakumari."

33. Hartman, *Scenes of Subjection*, 67; Vogel, *Stolen Time*.

34. Allen, "For 'the Children,'" 252.

35. Michael Herzfeld, *Cultural Intimacy: Social Poetics in the Nation-State*, 2nd ed. (New York: Routledge, 2005).

36. Jacob, *Celluloid Deities*.

37. Weidman, "Voices of Meenakumari."

38. Meena Gopal, "Caste, Sexuality and Labour: The Troubled Connection," *Current Sociology* 60, no. 2 (2012): 222–38.

39. Jenny Rowena, "The 'Dirt' in the Dirty Picture: Caste, Gender and Silk Smitha," *Round Table India*, https://roundtableindia.co.in/index.php?option=com_content&vie w=article&id=5283%253Athe-dirt-in-the-dirty-picture-caste-gender-and-silk-smitha (accessed Monday July 1, 2019).

40. Ramberg, *Given to the Goddess*, 17.

4`. Divya Karthikeyan, "Interview: A Dalit Poet's Explorations into Discrimination and the Female Body," *Wire India*, https://thewire.in/caste/dalit-poet-discrimination-female-body-poetry (accessed October 13, 2018).

41. Anupama Rao, *Gender & Caste* (London: Zed Books, 2005); Shefali Chandra, "The World's Largest Dynasty: Caste, Sexuality and the Manufacture of Indian 'Democracy,'" in *Dialectical Anthropology*, ed. Perry Anderson, Sharmila Rege, and Eleanor Zelliot (Berlin: Springer, 2014), 235.

43. Narrain and Gupta, *Law Like Love*, xiv; Arvind Narrain, "Queering Democracy: The Politics of Erotic Love," in Narrain and Gupta, *Law Like Love*, 19.

44. Karthik and Suleiman, "(Trans)Gender and Caste Lived Experience"; Sumit Baudh, "Invisibility of 'Other' Dalits and Silence in the Law," *Biography* 40, no. 1 (2017): 222–43.

45. Dhrubo Jyoti, "Being a Queer Dalit and the Assertion of Dalit Identities in Pride Marches," *Feminism in India (FII Media)*, https://feminisminindia.com/2017/06/22/ queer-dalit-assertion-pride-marches/ (accessed October 13, 2018).

46. Surya, "The Failed Radical Possibilities of Queerness in India," *RAIOT*, last modified February 4, 2016, http://raiot.in/the-failed-radical-possibilities-of-queerness-in-india/ (accessed October 13, 2018).

47. Tondon, "Exclusionary Masculinities."

48. Dhrubo Jyoti, "Caste Broke Our Hearts and Love Cannot Put Them Back Together," *BuzzFeed*, https://www.buzzfeed.com/dhrubojyoti/will-you-buy-me-a-pair-of-shorts (accessed October 13, 2018); Borisa, "Imagined Spaces of Freedom."

49. Nikhil Rampal, "Gay Modi Fans Can Finally Shut the Liberals Up If Section 377 Is Decriminalised," *The Print*, https://theprint.in/opinion/gay-modi-fans-can-finally-shut-the-liberals-up-if-section-377-is-decriminalised/81762/ (accessed October 13, 2018).

50. Borisa, "Imagined Spaces of Freedom."

51. Kikyo, "The Art of Dappankuthu—the Famous Dance of the Tamilian Commoner," *Rants of a Kitchen Toaster*, last modified July 19, 2008, http://toasters-rant .blogspot.com/2008/07/art-of-dappankuthu-famous-dance-of.html (accessed September 10, 2013).

52. Dinesh Babu, "Dappankuthu—a Form of South Indian Dance," *Maduraiveeran (18,000 RPM)*, https://maduraiveeran.wordpress.com/2008/05/15/dappankuthu-a-form-of-south-indian-dance/ (accessed September 10, 2013).

53. "How to Learn DAPPANKUTHU (Drunken Dance) in 5 Easy Steps," *YouTube*, https://www.youtube.com/watch?v=jW1117aY8A4 (accessed 2017).

54. Wilbur Sargunaraj, "How to Do the Dappankuthu," *YouTube*, last modified December 7, 2017, https://www.youtube.com/watch?v=51Vp2GBBxVY (accessed October 13, 2018).

55. Sherinian, "Religious Encounters," 72–75.

56. Zoe Sherinian, "Drumming Dalit Female Masculinity: Queering Gender in South Asia," presented at "Queer Symposium: Un/desirable Encounters at the Intersections of Race, Class, and Caste," Annual Conference on South Asia (Madison, WI, 2018).

57. Shailaja Paik, "Mangala Bansode and the Social Life of Tamasha: Caste, Sexuality, and Discrimination in Modern Maharashtra," *Biography* 40, no. 1 (2017): 170–98; Sharmila Rege, "The Hegemonic Appropriation of Sexuality: The Case of the Lavani Performers of Maharashtra," *Contributions to Indian Sociology* 29, nos. 1–2 (1995): 23–38; Urmila Sarkar-Munshi, "Another Time, Another Space: Does the Dance Remain the Same?," in *Dance Matters: Performing India*, ed. Pallabi Chakraborty and Nilanjana Gupta (London: Routledge, 2010), 29–39; Rumya S. Putcha, "Gender, Caste, and Feminist Praxis in Transnational South India," *South Asian Popular Culture* 17, no. 1 (2019): 61–79.

58. Srinivas, *Megastar*, 139.

59. Thomas F. DeFrantz, "Unchecked Popularity: Neoliberal Circulations of Black Social Dance," in *Neoliberalism and Global Theatres: Performance Permutations*, ed. Lara D. Nielsen and Patricia A. Ybarra (New York: Palgrave Macmillan, 2012), 128–42.

60. Ibid.

61. Rinaldo Walcott, "Reconstructing Manhood; or, The Drag of Black Masculinity," *Small Axe* 13, no. 1 (2009): 78.

62. Rivera-Servera, *Performing Queer Latinidad*, 196.

63. Ibid., 197.

64. DeFrantz, "Unchecked Popularity," 139.

65. Sumita S. Chakravarty, *National Identity in Indian Popular Cinema, 1947–1987* (Austin: University of Texas Press, 1993).

66. Ramberg, *Given to the Goddess*, 18.

67. Danielle Goldman, *I Want to Be Ready: Improvised Dance as a Practice of Freedom* (Ann Arbor: University of Michigan Press, 2010).

68. Vijeta Kumar, "Sure, You Could Say I Went to a Dalit Women's Conference but Woah It Was a Zingat Party," *Ladies Finger*, http://theladiesfinger.com/dalit-women-conference/ (accessed October 13, 2018).

Conclusion. Strangers in the Night: Curating Nightlife at *Besharam*

1. Muñoz, *Cruising Utopia*, 1.

2. Muñoz, *Cruising Utopia*, 81.

3. Sara Ahmed, *Strange Encounters: Embodied Others in Post-coloniality* (London, Routledge, 2000).

4. Shah, *Stranger Intimacy*, 43.

5. Manning, *Politics of Touch*, xvii.

6. Bobby Benedicto, "Agents and Objects of Death: Gay Murder, Boyfriend Twins, and Queer of Color Negativity," *GLQ* 25, no. 2 (2019): 273–96.

7. Erica Lerner and Cynthia E. Milton, "Introduction: Witness to Witnessing," in *Curating Difficult Knowledge: Violent Pasts in Public Spaces*, ed. Erica Lerner, Cynthia E. Milton, and Monica Eileen Patterson (New York: Palgrave Macmillan, 2001), 1–19; see also Gopinath, *Unruly Visions*, 3.

8. See "Mr. Mesa's Ticket," in Buckland, *Impossible Dance*; Allen, "For 'the Children,'" 255; Ramón Rivera-Servera, "History in Drag: Latina/o Queer Affective Circuits in Chicago," in *Latina/o Midwest Reader*, ed. Omar Valerio-Jimenez and Santiago Vaquera-Vasquez (Urbana: University of Illinois Press, 2017), 185–95.

9. Jennifer Tyburczy, *Sex Museums: The Politics and Performance of Display* (Chicago: University of Chicago Press, 2016), 176.

10. "Creating Space for Straight and Queer: Besharam," *South Asian Generation Next*, http://www.sagennext.com/2012/02/23/creating-space-for-straight-and-queer-besharam-2/ (accessed July 4, 2019).

11. Omme-Salma Rahemtullah, "Bollywood in *Da* Club: Social Space in Toronto's 'South Asian' Community," in *The Magic of Bollywood: At Home and Abroad*, ed. Anjali Gera Roy (New Delhi: Sage Publications, 2012), 250.

12. Taylor, *The Archive and the Repertoire*.

13. Jenna Wortham, "The Joy of Queer Parties: 'We Breathe, We Dip, We Flex,'" *New York Times*, https://www.nytimes.com/2019/06/26/style/queer-party-safe-space.html (accessed July 5, 2019).

14. DeFrantz, "Queer Dance in Three Acts," 179.

15. Justin Torres, "In Praise of Latin Night at the Queer Club," *Washington Post*, https://www.washingtonpost.com/opinions/in-praise-of-latin-night-at-the-queer-club/2016/06/13/e841867e-317b-11e6-95c0-2a6873031302_story.html (accessed October 13, 2018).

16. Buckland, *Impossible Dance*, 47.

Bibliography

Adebayo, Mojisola. "Everything You Know about Queerness You Learnt from Blackness: The Afri-Quia Theatre of Black Dykes, Crips, and Kids." In *Queer Dramaturgies: International Perspectives on Where Performance Leads Queer*, edited by Alyson Campbell and Stephen Farrier, 131–50. London: Palgrave Macmillan UK, 2016.

Adeyemi, Kemi. "Beyond 90°: The Angularities of Black/Queer/Women/Lean." *Women & Performance* 29, no. 1 (2019): 9–24.

Adeyemi, Kemi. "Oliverio Rodriguez's The Last Seduction / La Seducción Fatal (2015–)." *TSQ* 6, no. 2 (2019): 269–73.

Adjepong, Anima. "Invading Ethnography: A Queer of Color Reflexive Practice." *Ethnography* 20, no. 1 (2017): 27–46.

Afzal, Ahmed. *Lone Star Muslims: Transnational Lives and the South Asian Experience in Texas*. New York: New York University Press, 2015.

Ahmed, Sara. *Queer Phenomenology: Orientations, Objects, Others*. Durham, NC: Duke University Press, 2006.

Ahmed, Sara. *Strange Encounters: Embodied Others in Post-coloniality*. London: Routledge, 2000.

Alexander, Bryant Keith. "Standing in the Wake: A Critical Auto/Ethnographic Exercise on Reflexivity in Three Movements." *Cultural Studies—Critical Methodologies* 11, no. 2 (2011): 98–107.

Alexander, M. Jacqui. *Pedagogies of Crossing: Meditations on Feminism, Sexual Politics, Memory, and the Sacred*. Durham, NC: Duke University Press, 2005.

Alghren, Angela. "Futari Tomo: A Queer Duet for Taiko." In *Queer Dance: Meanings and Makings*, edited by Clare Croft, 229–42. New York: Oxford University Press, 2017.

All India Bakchod. "Honest Indian Weddings." *YouTube*. Last modified May 11, 2015. Accessed October 13, 2018. https://www.youtube.com/watch?v=iU6qI92Nt-Q

Allen, Jafari Sinclaire. "For 'the Children' Dancing the Beloved Community." *Souls* 11, no. 3 (2009): 311–26.

Ameeriar, Lalaie. *Downwardly Global: Women, Work, and Citizenship in the Pakistani Diaspora*. Durham, NC: Duke University Press, 2017.

Amico, Stephen. "'I Want Muscles': House Music, Homosexuality and Masculine Signification." *Popular Music* 20, no. 3 (2001): 359–78.

Amrute, Sareeta. "Proprietary Freedoms in an IT Office: How Indian IT Workers Negotiate Code and Cultural Branding." *Social Anthropology* 22, no. 1 (2014): 101–17.

Aneesh, A. "Negotiating Globalization: Men and Women of India's Call Centers." *Journal of Social Issues* 68, no. 3 (2012): 514–33.

Aneesh, A. *Virtual Migration: The Programming of Globalization.* Durham, NC: Duke University Press, 2006.

Annavarapu, Sneha. "'Where Do All the Lovers Go?': The Cultural Politics of Public Kissing in Mumbai, India (1950–2005)." *Journal of Historical Sociology* 31, no. 4 (2018): 405–19.

Anzaldúa, Gloria. *Borderlands / La Frontera.* 2nd ed. San Francisco: Aunt Lute Books, 1999.

Apter, Emily. "Acting Out Orientalism: Sapphic Theatricality in Turn-of-the-Century Paris." In *Performance and Cultural Politics*, edited by Elin Diamond, 15–34. London: Routledge, 1996.

Arasu, Ponni, and Priya Thangarajah. "Queer Women and Habeas Corpus in India: The Love That Blinds the Law." *Indian Journal of Gender Studies* 19, no. 3 (2012): 413–35.

Arondekar, Anjali. *For the Record: On Sexuality and the Colonial Archive in India.* Durham, NC: Duke University Press, 2009.

Arondekar, Anjali. "Subject to Sex: A Small History of the Gomatak Maratha Samaj." In *South Asian Feminisms: Contemporary Interventions*, edited by Ania Loomba and Ritty A. Lukose, 244–64. Durham, NC: Duke University Press, 2012.

Arondekar, Anjali, and Geeta Patel. "Area Impossible: Notes toward an Introduction." *GLQ* 22, no. 2 (2016): 151–71.

Ashutosh, Ishan. "(Re-)Creating the Community: South Asian Transnationalism on Chicago's Devon Avenue." *Urban Geography* 29, no. 3 (2008): 224–45.

Avilez, GerShun. "Uncertain Freedom." *Black Scholar* 49, no. 2 (2019): 50–64.

Baas, Michiel. "The IT Caste: Love and Arranged Marriages in the IT Industry of Bangalore." *South Asia* 32, no. 2 (2009): 285–307.

Babu, Dinesh. "Dappankuthu—a Form of South Indian Dance." *Maduraiveeran (18,000 RPM).* Last modified May 15, 2008. Accessed September 10, 2013. https://maduraiveeran.wordpress.com/2008/05/15/dappankuthu-a-form-of-south-indian-dance/

Bacchetta, Paola. "When the (Hindu) Nation Exiles Its Queers." *Social Text* 61 (1999): 141–66.

Bailey, Marlon M. "Black Gay (Raw) Sex." In *No Tea, No Shade: New Writings in Black Queer Studies*, edited by E. Patrick Johnson, 239–61. Durham, NC: Duke University Press, 2016.

Bailey, Marlon M. *Butch Queens up in Pumps: Gender, Performance, and Ballroom Culture in Detroit.* Ann Arbor: University of Michigan Press, 2013.

Balance, Christine Bacareza. *Tropical Renditions: Making Musical Scenes in Filipino America.* Durham, NC: Duke University Press, 2016.

Bakrania, Falu Pravin. *Bhangra and Asian Underground: South Asian Music and the Politics of Belonging in Britain.* Durham, NC: Duke University Press, 2013.

Bakshi, Kaustav, and Anugyan Nag. "Sridevi, the Dancing Queen and Queer Icon Who Opened Many Doors." *Wire India.* Last modified March 4, 2018. Accessed October 13, 2018. https://thewire.in/film/sridevi-dancing-queen-queer-icon

Bakshi, Sandeep. "Decoloniality, Queerness and Giddha." In *Decolonizing Sexualities: Transnational Perspectives, Critical Interventions*, edited by Sandeep Bakshi, Suhraiya Jivraj and Silvia Posocco, 81–99. Oxford: Counterpress, 2016.

Banerjee, Dwaipayan. "Writing the Disaster: Substance Activism after Bhopal." *Contemporary South Asia* 21, no. 3 (2013): 230–42.

Banerjee, Payal. "Indian Information Technology Workers in the United States: The H-1B Visa, Flexible Production, and the Racialization of Labor." *Critical Sociology* 32, nos. 2–3 (2006): 425–45.

"Bangalore Put on Mute at 10pm." *Times of India*, August 3, 2013, 8.

Bassi, Camila. "The Precarious and Contradictory Moments of Existence for an Emergent British Gay Asian Culture." In *New Geographies of Race and Racism*, edited by Claire Dwyer and Caroline Bressey, 209–22. Aldershot, UK: Ashgate, 2008.

Baudh, Sumit. "Invisibility of 'Other' Dalits and Silence in the Law." *Biography* 40, no. 1 (2017): 222–43.

Baviskar, Amita, and Raka Ray. *Elite and Everyman: The Cultural Politics of the Indian Middle Classes*. New Delhi: Routledge, 2011.

Benedicto, Bobby. "Agents and Objects of Death: Gay Murder, Boyfriend Twins, and Queer of Color Negativity." *GLQ* 25, no. 2 (2019): 273–96.

Benedicto, Bobby. "Desiring Sameness: Globalization, Agency, and the Filipino Gay Imaginary." *Journal of Homosexuality* 55, no. 2 (2008): 274–311.

Benedicto, Bobby. *Under Bright Lights: Gay Manila and the Global Scene*. Minneapolis: University of Minnesota Press, 2014.

Berlant, Lauren Gail. *The Queen of America Goes to Washington City: Essays on Sex and Citizenship*. Durham, NC: Duke University Press, 1997.

Bernstein, Robin. *Racial Innocence: Performing American Childhood from Slavery to Civil Rights*. New York: New York University Press, 2011.

Bhabha, Homi K. *The Location of Culture*. New York: Routledge, 1994.

Bhanutej, N. "Dance-Bars Spice Up the Night Life in Bangalore." *Week*, November 14, 2004.

Bhaskaran, Suparna. *Made in India: Decolonizations, Queer Sexualities, Trans/National Projects*. New York: Palgrave Macmillan, 2004.

Bhat, Shravan. "Chin Lung: The Worst Bar in Bangalore." *Shravan's Blog*. Last modified June 10, 2012. Accessed October 13, 2018. http://shravanblog.blogspot.com/2012/06/chin-lung-worst-bar-in-bangalore.html

Bhatt, Amy. *High-Tech Housewives: Indian IT Workers, Gendered Labor, and Transmigration*. Seattle: University of Washington Press, 2018.

Bhatt, Amy, Madhavi Murty, and Priti Ramamurthy. "Hegemonic Developments: The New Indian Middle Class, Gendered Subalterns, and Diasporic Returnees in the Event of Neoliberalism." *Signs* 36, no. 1 (2010): 127–52.

Biao, Xiang. *Global "Body Shopping"*. Princeton, NJ: Princeton University Press, 2011.

Blair, Zachary. "Boystown: Gay Neighborhoods, Social Media, and the (Re)Production of Racism." In *No Tea, No Shade: New Writings in Black Queer Studies*, edited by E. Patrick Johnson, 287–302. Durham, NC: Duke University Press, 2016.

Blanco Borelli, Melissa. "'¿Y Ahora Qué Vas a Hacer, Mulata?': Hip Choreographies in the Mexican Cabaretera Film Mulata (1954)." *Women & Performance* 18, no. 3 (2008): 215–33.

Boellstorff, Tom. *The Gay Archipelago: Sexuality and Nation in Indonesia*. Princeton, NJ: Princeton University Press, 2005.

Boellstorff, Tom, Mauro Cabral, Micha Cárdenas, Trystan Cotten, Eric A. Stanley, Ka-

Ianiopua Young, and Aren Z. Aizura. "Decolonizing Transgender: A Roundtable Discussion." *TSQ* 1, no. 3 (2014): 419–39.

Bollen, Jonathan. "Queer Kinesthesia: Performativity on the Dance Floor." In *Dancing Desires: Choreographing Sexualities on and off the Stage*, edited by Jane Desmond, 285–314. Madison: University of Wisconsin Press, 2001.

Boone, Joseph. "Vacation Cruises; or, the Homoerotics of Orientalism." *PMLA* 110, no. 1 (1995): 89–107.

Borisa, Dhiren. "Imagined Spaces of Freedom: Negotiating Queer Cartographies of Desires in Delhi." Ph.D. diss., Jawaharlal Nehru University, New Delhi, 2018.

Borisa, Dhiren. "Dhiren Borisa on Dalit Queerness," *Godrej India Culture Lab*, https://indiaculturelab.org/videos/library/special-events/dhiren-borisa-on-dalit-queerness/ (accessed October 12, 2019).

Borsky, Helga. "Toronto's Queen of Comedy Donnarama Performs a Medley of 'Jai Ho' and 'Spice Up Your Life!.'" *YouTube*. Last modified January 24, 2011. Accessed October 13, 2018. https://www.youtube.com/watch?v=ALPdMk8gvB8

Bose, Brinda, and Subhabrata Bhattacharyya. *The Phobic and the Erotic: The Politics of Sexualities in Contemporary India*. Calcutta: Seagull Books, 2007.

Bourdieu, Pierre. *Outline of a Theory of Practice*. Translated by Richard Nice. Cambridge: Cambridge University Press, 1977.

Boyd, Nan Alamilla. *Wide-Open Town: A History of Queer San Francisco to 1965*. Berkeley: University of California Press, 2003.

Bragin, Naomi. "Techniques of Black Male Re/Dress: Corporeal Drag and Kinesthetic Politics in the Rebirth of Waacking/Punkin'." *Women & Performance* 24, no. 1 (2014): 61–78.

Brah, Avtar. *Cartographies of Diaspora: Contesting Identities*. London: Routledge, 1996.

Brown, Andrew J. "Performing Blackness in the 'Rainbow Nation': Athi-Patra Ruga's The Future White Women of Azania." *Women & Performance* 27, no. 1 (2017): 67–80.

Brown-Saracino, Japonica. *A Neighborhood That Never Changes: Gentrification, Social Preservation, and the Search for Authenticity*. Chicago: University of Chicago Press, 2009.

Buckland, Fiona. *Impossible Dance: Club Culture and Queer World-Making*. Middletown, CT: Wesleyan University Press, 2002.

Burns, Lucy Mae San Pablo. *Puro Arte: Filipinos on the Stages of Empire*. New York: New York University Press, 2012.

Butler, Judith. *Bodies That Matter: On the Discursive Limits of "Sex"*. New York: Routledge, 1993.

Buttler, Bryan. "Philly Drag Queen Offends with 9/11-Themed Performance. Did She Go Too Far?" *Philadelphia (Metro Corp.)*. Last modified September 17, 2014. Accessed October 13, 2018. https://www.phillymag.com/g-philly/2014/09/17/art-just-plain-offensive/

Cantú, Lionel, Nancy A. Naples, and Salvador Vidal-Ortiz. *The Sexuality of Migration: Border Crossings and Mexican Immigrant Men*. New York: New York University Press, 2009.

Carrillo, Héctor. *The Night Is Young: Sexuality in Mexico in the Time of AIDS*. Chicago: University of Chicago Press, 2002.

Carrillo, Héctor. *Pathways of Desire: The Sexual Migration of Mexican Gay Men*. Chicago: University of Chicago Press, 2017.

Carrillo, Héctor. "Sexual Migration, Cross-Cultural Sexual Encounters, and Sexual Health." *Sexuality Research & Social Policy* 1, no. 3 (2004): 58–70.

Carter, Julian. "Jérôme Bel, Swan Lake, and the Alternative Futures of Re-enacted Dance." In *Queer Dance: Meanings and Makings*, edited by Clare Croft, 109–23. New York: Oxford University Press, 2017.

Chacko, Elizabeth, and Rajiv Menon. "Longings and Belongings: Indian American Youth Identity, Folk Dance Competitions, and the Construction of 'Tradition.'" *Ethnic and Racial Studies* 36, no. 1 (2013): 97–116.

Chakravarty, Sumita S. *National Identity in Indian Popular Cinema, 1947–1987*. Austin: University of Texas Press, 1993.

Chakravorty, Pallabi. *Bells of Change: Kathak Dance, Women, and Modernity in India*. Kolkata: Seagull Books, 2008.

Chakravorty, Pallabi. "Moved to Dance: Remix, Rasa, and a New India." *Visual Anthropology* 22, nos. 2–3 (2009): 211–28.

Chambers-Letson, Joshua Takano. *A Race So Different: Performance and Law in Asian America*. New York: New York University Press, 2013.

Chambers-Letson, Joshua Takano. *After the Party: A Manifesto for Queer of Color Life*. New York: New York University Press, 2018.

Chandra, Shefali. "The World's Largest Dynasty: Caste, Sexuality and the Manufacture of Indian 'Democracy.'" In *Dialectical Anthropology*, edited by Perry Anderson, Sharmila Rege, and Eleanor Zelliot, 225–38. Berlin: Springer, 2014.

Chandrashekar, Santhosh. "Engendering Threat in the Guise of Protection: Orientalism and Sikh Vulnerability." *Journal of Multicultural Discourses* 12, no. 4 (2017): 366–81.

Chandrashekar, Santhosh. "South Asian Queer Politics and the Rise of Homohinduism." Presented at "Homonationalism and Pinkwashing" conference at CUNY, New York City (April 11, 2013).

Cheng, Anne Anlin. *Ornamentalism*. New York: Oxford University Press, 2019.

Chung, Kelly I. "The Defiant Still Worker: Ramiro Gomez and the Expressionism of Abstract Labor." *Women & Performance* 29, no. 1 (2019): 62–78.

Cohen, Lawrence. "Holi in Banaras and the Mahaland of Modernity." *GLQ* 2, no. 4 (1995): 399–424.

Cohen, Lawrence. "The Kothi Wars: AIDS Cosmopolitanism and the Morality of Classification." In *Sex in Development: Science, Sexuality, and Morality in Global Perspective*, edited by Stacy Leigh Pigg and Vincanne Adams, 269–303. Durham, NC: Duke University Press, 2005.

Cohen, Lawrence. "Song for Pushkin." *Daedalus* 136, no. 2 (2007): 103–15.

Collins, Cory G. "Drag Race to the Bottom? Updated Notes on the Aesthetic and Political Economy of RuPaul's Drag Race." *TSQ* 4, no. 1 (2017): 128–34.

Conquergood, Dwight. *Cultural Struggles: Performance, Ethnography, Praxis*. Edited by E. Patrick Johnson. Ann Arbor: University of Michigan Press, 2013.

Cowie, Claire. "The Accents of Outsourcing: The Meanings of 'Neutral' in the Indian Call Centre Industry." *World Englishes* 26, no. 3 (2007): 316–30.

Cox, Aimee Meredith. *Shapeshifters: Black Girls and the Choreography of Citizenship.* Durham, NC: Duke University Press, 2015.

Crair, Ben. "Maniac Killers of the Bangalore IT Department." *Bloomberg Businessweek.* Last modified February 15, 2017. Accessed October 13, 2018. https://www.bloomberg .com/news/features/2017-02-15/maniac-killers-of-the-bangalore-it-department

"Creating Space for Straight and Queer: Besharam." *South Asian Generation Next.* Last modified February 23, 2012. Accessed July 4, 2019. http://www.sagennext. com/2012/02/23/creating-space-for-straight-and-queer-besharam2/

Croft, Clare, ed. *Queer Dance: Meanings and Makings.* New York: Oxford University Press, 2017.

Cvetkovich, Ann. "9-11 Every Day." *Signs* 28, no. 1 (2002): 471–73.

D'Melo, Marisa, and Sundeep Sabay. "Betwixt and Between? Exploring Mobilities in a Global Workplace in India." In *In an Outpost of the Global Economy: Work and Workers in India's Information Technology Industry*, edited by Carol Upadhya and Aninhalli Rame Vasavi, 76–100. New Delhi: Routledge, 2008.

"Dancing Ban: Blame It on Live Bands." *Times of India.* Last modified February 17, 2008. Accessed April 10, 2018. http://timesofindia.indiatimes.com/articleshow/2788616.cms

Daniher, Colleen Kim. "Yella Gal: Eartha Kitt's Racial Modulations." *Women & Performance* 28, no. 1 (2018): 16–33.

Das Gupta, Monisha. *Unruly Immigrants: Rights, Activism, and Transnational South Asian Politics in the United States.* Durham, NC: Duke University Press, 2006.

Dasgupta, Rohit K. "Parties, Advocacy, and Activism: Interrogating Community and Class in Digital Queer India." In *Queer Youth and Media Cultures*, edited by Christopher Pullen, 265–77. London: Palgrave Macmillan, 2014.

Dasgupta, Rohit K., and Debanuj DasGupta. "Intimate Subjects and Virtual Spaces: Rethinking Sexuality as a Category for Intimate Ethnographies." *Sexualities* 21, nos. 5–6 (2018): 932–50.

Dave, Naisargi. *Queer Activism in India: A Story in the Anthropology of Ethics.* Durham, NC: Duke University Press, 2012.

Davé, Shilpa. *Indian Accents: Brown Voice and Racial Performance in American Television and Film.* Urbana: University of Illinois Press, 2013.

David, Ann R. "Beyond the Silver Screen: Bollywood and Filmi Dance in the UK." *South Asia Research* 27, no. 1 (2007): 5–24.

Dayal, Geeta. "Indian Summer." *Sight&Sound*, June 2016, 50–51.

de Certeau, Michel. *The Practice of Everyday Life.* Translated by Steven Rendall. Berkeley: University of California Press, 1984.

De la Croix, St Sukie. *Chicago Whispers: A History of LGBT Chicago before Stonewall.* Madison: University of Wisconsin Press, 2012.

Decena, Carlos Ulises. *Tacit Subjects: Belonging and Same-Sex Desire among Dominican Immigrant Men.* Durham, NC: Duke University Press, 2011.

DeFrantz, Thomas F. "Foreword: Black Bodies Dancing Black Culture—Black Atlantic Transformations." In *Embodying Liberation: The Black Body in American Dance*, edited by Dorothea Fischer-Hornung and Alison D. Goeller, 11–16. Hamburg: LIT Verlag, 2001.

DeFrantz, Thomas F. "Hip Hop Habitus V.2.0." In *Black Performance Theory*, edited by Thomas F. DeFrantz and Anita Gonzalez, 223—42. Durham, NC: Duke University Press, 2014.

DeFrantz, Thomas F. "Queer Dance in Three Acts." In *Queer Dance: Meanings and Makings*, edited by Clare Croft, 169–81. New York: Oxford University Press, 2017.

DeFrantz, Thomas F. "Unchecked Popularity: Neoliberal Circulations of Black Social Dance." In *Neoliberalism and Global Theatres: Performance Permutations*, edited by Lara D. Nielsen and Patricia A. Ybarra, 128–42. New York: Palgrave Macmillan, 2012.

Delgado, Celeste Fraser, and José Esteban Muñoz. *Everynight Life: Culture and Dance in Latin/O America*. Durham, NC: Duke University Press, 1997.

Desai, Poulomi, and Parminder Sekhon. *Red Threads: The South Asian Queer Connection in Photographs*. London: Millivres Prowler, 2003.

Desai Hidier, Tanuja. *Born Confused*. New York: Scholastic Press, 2002.

Deshpande, Sudhanva. "The Consumable Hero of Globalised India." In *Bollyworld: Popular Indian Cinema through a Transnational Lens*, edited by Raminder Kaur and Ajay J. Sinha, 186–203. New Delhi: Sage Publications, 2005.

Dhalla, Ghalib Shiraz. *Ode to Lata: A Novel*. Los Angeles: Really Great Books, 2002.

Di Leonardo, Micaela. "Oral History as Ethnographic Encounter." *Oral History Review* 15, no. 1 (1987): 1–20.

Diaz, Robert. "Biyuti from Below." *TSQ* 5, no. 3 (2018): 404–24.

Diethrich, Gregory. "Dancing the Diaspora: Indian Desi Music in Chicago." In *Identity and the Arts in Diaspora Communities*, edited by Thomas Turino and James Lea, 103–15. Warren, MI: Harmonie Park Press, 2004.

Dinshaw, Carolyn. "Got Medieval?" *Journal of the History of Sexuality* 10, no. 2 (2001): 202–12.

Dishoom Dishoom. "Ishtyle." *Samosapedia*. Last updated June 29, 2011. Accessed June 30, 2019. http://www.samosapedia.com/e/ishtyle

Dolan, Jill. *Utopia in Performance: Finding Hope at the Theater*. Ann Arbor: University of Michigan Press, 2005.

Doty, Alexander. *Making Things Perfectly Queer: Interpreting Mass Culture*. Minneapolis: University of Minnesota Press, 1993.

Draper, Jimmy. "'What Has She Actually Done??!': Gay Men, Diva Worship, and the Paratextualization of Gay-Rights Support." *Critical Studies in Media Communication* 34, no. 2 (2017): 130–37.

Dudrah, Rajinder. *Bollywood: Sociology Goes to the Movies*. New Delhi: Sage Publications, 2006.

Dudrah, Rajinder. "British Bhangra Music as Soundscapes of the Midlands." *Midland History* 36, no. 2 (2011): 278–91.

Dutta, Aniruddha. "Claiming Citizenship, Contesting Civility: The Institutional LGBT Movement and the Regulation of Gender/Sexual Dissidence in West Bengal, India." *Jindal Global Law Review* 4, no. 1 (2012): 110–41.

Dutta, Aniruddha. "An Epistemology of Collusion: Hijras, Kothis and the Historical (Dis)Continuity of Gender/Sexual Identities in Eastern India." *Gender & History* 24, no. 3 (2012): 825–49.

Dutta, Aniruddha. "Nation, Liberalisation and Film Songs: Technology and Hybridisation in Contemporary Hindi Film Music." *Wide Screen* 1, no. 1 (2009): 1–11.

Dutta, Aniruddha. "Section 377 and the Retroactive Consolidation of 'Homophobia.'" In *Law Like Love: Queer Perspectives on Law*, edited by Arvind Narrain and Alok Gupta, 162–73. New Delhi: Yoda Press, 2011.

Dwyer, Rachel. "Bombay Ishtyle." In *Fashion Cultures: Theories, Explorations and Analysis*, edited by Stella Bruzzi and Pamela Gibson, 178–90. London: Routledge, 2000.

Dwyer, Rachel. "Representing the Muslim: The 'Courtesan Film' in Indian Popular Cinema." In *Jews, Muslims, and Mass Media: Mediating the "Other"*, edited by Tudor Parfitt and Yulia Egorova, 78–92. London: RoutledgeCurzon, 2005.

Dyer, Richard. "In Defense of Disco." *New Formations* 58, no. 1 (2006): 101–8.

Echols, Alice. *Hot Stuff: Disco and the Remaking of American Culture*. New York: W. W. Norton, 2010.

Ellison, Treva Carrie. "Black Femme Praxis and the Promise of Black Gender." *Black Scholar* 49, no. 1 (2019): 6–16.

Fanon, Frantz. *Black Skin, White Masks*. Translated by Richard Philcox. New York: Grove Press, 1967.

Farmer, Brett. "The Fabulous Sublimity of Gay Diva Worship." *Camera Obscura* 20, no. 2 (2005): 165–95.

Farmer, Brett. "Julie Andrews Made Me Gay." *Camera Obscura* 22, no. 2 (2007): 144–53.

Ferguson, Roderick. *Aberrations in Black: Toward a Queer of Color Critique*. Minneapolis: University of Minnesota Press, 2004.

Fernandes, Leela. *India's New Middle Class: Democratic Politics in an Era of Economic Reform*. Minneapolis: University of Minnesota Press, 2006.

Fortuna, Victoria. "A Dance of Many Bodies: Moving Trauma in Susana Tambutti's La Puñalada." *Performance Research* 16, no. 1 (2011): 43–51.

Foster, Susan. "Pygmalion's No-Body and the Body of Dance." In *Performance and Cultural Politics*, edited by Elin Diamond, 133–54. New York: Routledge.

Freeman, Elizabeth. *Time Binds: Queer Temporalities, Queer Histories*. Durham, NC: Duke University Press, 2010.

Fung, Richard. "Looking for My Penis: The Eroticized Asian in Gay Video Porn." In *Q & A: Queer in Asian America*, edited by David L. Eng and Alice Y. Hom, 115–34. Philadelphia: Temple University Press, 1998.

Gairola, Rahul K. *Homelandings: Postcolonial Diasporas and Transatlantic Belonging*. London: Rowman & Littlefield International, 2016.

Gangoli, Geetanjali. "Sexuality, Sensuality and Belonging: Representations of the 'Anglo-Indian' and the 'Western' Woman in Hindi Cinema." In *Bollyworld: Popular Indian Cinema through a Transnational Lens*, edited by Raminder Kaur and Ajay J. Sinha, 114–23. New Delhi: Sage Publications, 2005.

Ganti, Tejaswini. *Bollywood: A Guidebook to Popular Hindi Cinema*. 2nd ed. London: Routledge, 2013.

Ganti, Tejaswini. *Producing Bollywood: Inside the Contemporary Hindi Film Industry*. Durham, NC: Duke University Press, 2012.

García, Armando. "The Illegalities of Brownness." *Social Text* 33, no. 2 (2015): 99–120.

Geertz, Clifford. "Deep Play: Notes on the Balinese Cockfight." *Daedalus* 101, no. 1 (1972): 1–37.

Gehlawat, Ajay. "The Bollywood Song and Dance, or Making a Culinary Theatre from Dung-Cakes and Dust." *Quarterly Review of Film and Video* 23, no. 4 (2006): 331–40.

Gehlawat, Ajay. "The Construction of 1970s Femininity, or Why Zeenat Aman Sings the Same Song Twice." *South Asian Popular Culture* 10, no. 1 (2012): 51–62.

Gere, David. "29 Effeminate Gestures: Choreographer Joe Goode and the Heroism of Effeminacy." In *Dancing Desires: Choreographing Sexualities on and off the Stage*, edited by Jane Desmond, 349–81. Madison: University of Wisconsin Press, 2001.

Ghosh, Shohini. "False Appearances and Mistaken Identities: The Phobic and the Erotic in Bombay Cinema's Queer Vision." In *The Phobic and the Erotic: The Politics of Sexualities in Contemporary India*, edited by Brinda Bose and Subhabrata Bhattacharyya, 417–35. Calcutta: Seagull Books, 2007.

Ghosh, Shohini. "Queer Pleasures for Queer People: Film, Television, and Queer Sexuality in India." In *Queering India: Same-Sex Love and Eroticism in Indian Culture and Society*, edited by Ruth Vanita, 207–21. New York: Routledge, 2002.

Gill, Lyndon Kamaal. *Erotic Islands: Art and Activism in the Queer Caribbean*. Durham, NC: Duke University Press, 2018.

Goldman, Danielle. *I Want to Be Ready: Improvised Dance as a Practice of Freedom*. Ann Arbor: University of Michigan Press, 2010.

Gopal, Meena. "Caste, Sexuality and Labour: The Troubled Connection." *Current Sociology* 60, no. 2 (2012): 222–38.

Gopal, Sangita, and Sujata Moorti. "Bollywood in Drag: *Moulin Rouge!* and the Aesthetics of Global Cinema." *Camera Obscura* 25, no. 3 (2011): 28–67.

Gopalan, Lalitha. *Cinema of Interruptions: Action Genres in Contemporary Indian Cinema*. New Delhi: Oxford University Press, 2003.

Gopinath, Gayatri. "Bollywood Spectacles: Queer Diasporic Critique in the Aftermath of 9/11." *Social Text* 23, nos. 3–4 (2005): 157–69.

Gopinath, Gayatri. "'Bombay, U.K., Yuba City': Bhangra Music and the Engendering of Diaspora." *Diaspora* 4, no. 3 (1995): 303–21.

Gopinath, Gayatri. *Impossible Desires: Queer Diasporas and South Asian Public Cultures*. Durham, NC: Duke University Press, 2005.

Gopinath, Gayatri. "Queering Bollywood: Alternative Sexualities in Popular Indian Cinema." *Journal of Homosexuality* 39, nos. 3–4 (2000): 283–97.

Gopinath, Gayatri. *Unruly Visions: The Aesthetic Practices of Queer Diaspora*. Durham, NC: Duke University Press, 2018.

Gosine, Andil. "Brown to Blonde at Gay.Com: Passing White in Queer Cyberspace." In *Queer Online: Media Technology & Sexuality*, edited by Kate O'Riordan and David J. Phillips, 139–53. New York: Peter Lang, 2007.

Gould, Deborah B. *Moving Politics: Emotion and Act Up's Fight against Aids*. Chicago: University of Chicago Press, 2009.

Gray, Mary L. *Out in the Country: Youth, Media, and Queer Visibility in Rural America*. New York: New York University Press, 2009.

Grazian, David. *On the Make: The Hustle of Urban Nightlife*. Chicago: University of Chicago Press, 2008.

Greene, Theodore. "Gay Neighborhoods and the Rights of the Vicarious Citizen." *City & Community* 13, no. 2 (2014): 99–118.

Grewal, Inderpal. *Transnational America: Feminisms, Diasporas, Neoliberalisms*. Durham, NC: Duke University Press, 2005.

Griffin, Hollis. "Your Favorite Stars, Live on Our Screens: Media Culture, Queer Publics, and Commercial Space." *Velvet Light Trap* 62, no. 1 (2008): 15–28.

Gupta, Alok. "*Englishpur Ki Kothi*." In *Because I Have a Voice: Queer Politics in*

India, edited by Arvind Narrain and Gautam Bhan, 123–42. New Delhi: Yoda Press, 2005.

Gupta, Alok. "The Presumption of Sodomy." In *Law Like Love: Queer Perspectives on Law*, edited by Arvind Narrain and Alok Gupta, 115–61. New Delhi: Yoda Press, 2011.

Gupta, Hemangini. "No Sleep Till Ban-Galore!!!" *Cityscapes Digital*. Last modified May 8, 2013. Accessed October 13, 2018. https://www.cityscapesdigital.net/2013/05/08/no-sleep-till-ban-galore/

Guzmán, Joshua Javier, and Christina A. León. "Cuts and Impressions: The Aesthetic Work of Lingering in Latinidad." *Women & Performance* 24, no. 3 (2015): 261–76.

Guzmán, Manolo. *Gay Hegemony / Latino Homosexualities*. New York: Routledge, 2006.

Halberstam, Jack. *In a Queer Time and Place: Transgender Bodies, Subcultural Lives*. New York: New York University Press, 2005.

Halberstam, Jack. *The Queer Art of Failure*. Durham, NC: Duke University Press, 2011.

Halperin, David M. *How to Be Gay*. Cambridge, MA: Belknap Press of Harvard University Press, 2012.

Hamera, Judith. *Dancing Communities: Performance, Difference and Connection in the Global City*. London: Palgrave Macmillan UK, 2007.

Han, C. Winter. *Geisha of a Different Kind: Race and Sexuality in Gaysian America*. New York: New York University Press, 2015.

Hankins, Sarah. "'I'm a Cross between a Clown, a Stripper, and a Streetwalker': Drag Tipping, Sex Work, and a Queer Sociosexual Economy." *Signs* 40, no. 2 (2015): 441–66.

Hankins, Sarah. "So Contagious: Hybridity and Subcultural Exchange in Hip-Hop's Use of Indian Samples." *Black Music Research Journal* 31, no. 2 (2011): 193–208.

Harris, Daniel. "The Death of Camp: Gay Men and Hollywood Diva Worship, from Reverence to Ridicule." *Salmagundi* 112 (1996): 166–91.

Hart, Benji. "The Anti-blackness of Believing There's No Support for Queerness in the Hood." *Black Youth Project*. Last modified September 20, 2017. Accessed July 4, 2019. http://blackyouthproject.com/anti-blackness-believing-theres-no-support-queerness-hood/

Hartman, Saidiya V. "The Belly of the World: A Note on Black Women's Labors." *Souls* 18, no. 1 (2016): 166–73.

Hartman, Saidiya V. *Scenes of Subjection: Terror, Slavery, and Self-Making in Nineteenth-Century America*. New York: Oxford University Press, 1997.

Heap, Chad. *Slumming: Sexual and Racial Encounters in American Nightlife, 1885–1940*. Chicago: University of Chicago Press, 2009.

Hebdige, Dick. *Subculture: The Meaning of Style*. London: Methuen, 1979.

Heitzman, James. *Network City: Planning the Information Society in Bangalore*. New Delhi: Oxford University Press, 2004.

Herrera, Brian. "Evanescence: Three Tales of the Recent Queer Theatrical Past." *Theatre Topics* 26, no. 1 (2016): 47–51.

Herring, Scott. *Another Country: Queer Anti-urbanism*. New York: New York University Press, 2010.

Herzfeld, Michael. *Cultural Intimacy: Social Poetics in the Nation-State*. 2nd ed. New York: Routledge, 2005.

Hoad, Neville Wallace. *African Intimacies: Race, Homosexuality, and Globalization*. Minneapolis: University of Minnesota Press, 2007.

Holland, Sharon. "Foreword: Home Is a Four-Letter Word." In *Black Queer Studies: A Critical Anthology*, edited by E. Patrick Johnson and Mae Henderson, ix–xiii. Durham, NC: Duke University Press, 2005.

hooks, bell. *Black Looks: Race and Representation*. Boston: South End Press, 1992.

Horton, Brian A. "The Queer Turn in South Asian Studies? or 'That's Over & Done Queen, On to the Next.'" *QED* 5, no. 3 (2018): 165–80.

Horton, Brian A. "What's So 'Queer' about Coming Out? Silent Queers and Theorizing Kinship Agonistically in Mumbai." *Sexualities* 21, no. 7 (2018): 1059–74.

Horton-Stallings, LaMonda. *Funk the Erotic: Transaesthetics and Black Sexual Cultures*. Urbana: University of Illinois Press, 2015.

Hudson, Dale. "Undesirable Bodies and Desirable Labor: Documenting the Globalization and Digitization of Transnational American Dreams in Indian Call Centers." *Cinema Journal* 49, no. 1 (2009): 82–102.

Hurston, Zora Neale. "Folklore and Music." *Frontiers* 12, no. 1 (1991): 182–98.

Iyer, Usha. "Stardom *Ke Peeche Kya Hai*? / What Is behind the Stardom? Madhuri Dixit, the Production Number, and the Construction of the Female Star Text in 1990s Hindi Cinema." *Camera Obscura* 30, no. 3 (2015): 129–59.

Jacob, Preminda. *Celluloid Deities: The Visual Culture of Cinema and Politics in South India*. Lanham, MD: Lexington Books, 2009.

Jha, Priya. "Lyrical Nationalism: Gender, Friendship, and Excess in 1970s Hindi Cinema." *Velvet Light Trap* 51 (2003): 43–53.

Jodhka, Surinder S. "Caste & the Corporate Sector." *Indian Journal of Industrial Relations* 44, no. 2 (2008): 185–93.

Johnson, David K. "The Kids of Fairytown: Gay Male Culture on Chicago's Near North Side in the 1930s." In *Creating a Place for Ourselves*, edited by Brett Beemyn, 97–144. New York: Routledge, 1997.

Johnson, E. Patrick. *Appropriating Blackness: Performance and the Politics of Authenticity*. Durham, NC: Duke University Press, 2003.

Johnson, E. Patrick. "Feeling the Spirit in the Dark: Expanding Notions of the Sacred in the African-American Gay Community." *Callaloo* 21, no. 2 (1998): 399–416.

Johnson, E. Patrick. "Foreword." In *From Bourgeois to Boojie: Black Middle-Class Performances*, edited by Vershawn Ashanti Young and Bridget Harris Tsemo, xiii–xxii. Detroit: Wayne State University Press, 2011.

Johnson, E. Patrick. "'Quare' Studies, or (Almost) Everything I Know about Queer Studies I Learned from My Grandmother." *Text and Performance Quarterly* 21, no. 1 (2001): 1–25.

Johnson, E. Patrick. "'Scatter the Pigeons': Baldness and the Performance of Black Hypermasculinity." In *Blackberries and Redbones: Critical Articulations of Black Hair/Body Politics in Africana Communities*, edited by Regina E. Spellers and Kimberly R. Moffitt, 147–56. Cresskill: Hampton Press, 2010.

Johri, Vikram. "From Earth to Planet Romeo." *Business Standard*. Last modified January 29, 2013. Accessed October 13, 2018. https://www.business-standard.com/article/opinion/vikram-johri-from-earth-to-planet-romeo-113011200014_1.html

Jones, Keely. "Big Chicks, Tweet and the Famous Michelle Fire." *Edgeville Buzz*. Last modified February 11, 2014. Accessed October 13, 2018. http://www.edgevillebuzz.com/news/big-chicks-tweet-and-the-famous-michelle-fire

Jyoti, Dhrubo. "Being a Queer Dalit and the Assertion of Dalit Identities in Pride Marches." *Feminism in India (FII Media)*. Last modified June 22, 2017. Accessed October 13, 2018. https://feminisminindia.com/2017/06/22/queer-dalit-assertion-pride-marches/

Jyoti, Dhrubo. "Caste Broke Our Hearts and Love Cannot Put Them Back Together." *BuzzFeed*. Last modified February 28, 2018. Accessed October 13, 2018. https://www.buzzfeed.com/dhrubojyoti/will-you-buy-me-a-pair-of-shorts

Kang, Akhil. "Queering Dalit." Tanqeed. Last modified October 2016. Accessed September 6, 2017. http://www.tanqeed.org/2016/10/queering-dalit-tq-salon/

Kapadia, Ronak. "Up in the Air and on the Skin: Drone Warfare and the Queer Calculus of Pain." In *Critical Ethnic Studies: A Reader*, edited by Nadia Elia, David M. Hernández, Jodi Kim, Shana L. Redmon, Dylan Rodríguez, and Sarita Echavez See, 360–75. Durham, NC: Duke University Press, 2016.

Kapadia, Ronak. "We're Not Queer, We're Just Foreign: Desi Drags, Disidentification, and Activist Film in New York." *Stanford Undergraduate Research Journal* 4, no. 1 (2005): 1–7.

Karthik, Kaveri, and Gee Ameena Suleiman. "(Trans)Gender and Caste Lived Experience—Transphobia as a Form of Brahminism: An Interview of Living Smile Vidya." *Sanhati*. Last modified January 26, 2013. Accessed October 13, 2018. http://sanhati.com/excerpted/6051/

Karthikeyan, Divya. "Interview: A Dalit Poet's Explorations into Discrimination and the Female Body." *Wire India*. Last modified July 16, 2017. Accessed October 13, 2018. https://thewire.in/caste/dalit-poet-discrimination-female-body-poetry

Katyal, Akhil. *The Doubleness of Sexuality: Idioms of Same-Sex Desire in Modern India*. New Delhi: New Text, 2016.

Kedhar, Anusha. "Flexibility and Its Bodily Limits: Transnational South Asian Dancers in an Age of Neoliberalism." *Dance Research Journal* 46, no. 1 (2014): 23–40.

Kedhar, Anusha. "'Hands Up! Don't Shoot': Gesture, Choreography, and Protest in Ferguson." *Feminist Wire*. Last modified October 6, 2014. Accessed June 30, 2019. http://thefeministwire.com/2014/10/protest-in-ferguson/

Khanna, Akshay. "The Social Lives of 377." In *Law Like Love: Queer Perspectives on Law*, edited by Arvind Narrain and Alok Gupta, 174–202. New Delhi: Yoda Press, 2011.

Khubchandani, Kareem. "Aunty Fever: A Queer Impression." In *Queer Dance: Meanings and Makings*, edited by Clare Croft, 199–204. New York: Oxford University Press, 2017.

Khubchandani, Kareem. "Caste, Queerness, Migration, and the Erotics of Activism." *South Asia Multidisciplinary Academic Journal* 20 (2019). https://journals.openedition.org/samaj/5118

Khubchandani, Kareem. "Staging Transgender Solidarities at Bangalore's Queer Pride." *TSQ* 1, no. 4 (2014): 517–22.

Khubchandani, Kareem. "Terrifying Performances: Black-Brown-Queer Borrowings in *Loins of Punjab Presents*." *Journal of Asian American Studies* 19, no. 3 (2016): 275–97.

Khubchandani, Kareem. "Voguing in Bangalore: Blackness, Femininity, and Performance in Globalized India." *Scholar and Feminist Online* 14, no. 3 (2018). http://sfonline.barnard.edu/feminist-and-queer-afro-asian-formations/voguing-in-bangalore-desire-blackness-and-femininity-in-globalized-india/

Kidwai, Saleem. "Of Begums and Tawaifs: The Women of Awadh." In *Women's Studies in India: A Reader*, edited by Mary John, 118–23. New Delhi: Penguin, 2008.

Kidwai, Saleem. "The Singing Ladies Find a Voice." *Seminar* 540 (August 2004): 48–54.

Kikyo. "The Art of Dappankuthu—the Famous Dance of the Tamilian Commoner." *Rants of a Kitchen Toaster.* Last modified July 19, 2008. Accessed September 10, 2013. http://toasters-rant.blogspot.com/2008/07/art-of-dappankuthu-famous-dance-of.html

Kim. "They Aren't That Primitive Back Home." In *Lotus of Another Color: An Unfolding of the South Asian Gay and Lesbian Experience,* edited by Rakesh Ratti, 92–97. Boston: Alyson Publications, 1993.

Kim, Ju Yon. *The Racial Mundane: Asian American Performance and the Embodied Everyday.* New York: New York University Press, 2015.

Kim Lee, Summer. "Staying In: Mitski, Ocean Vuong, and Asian American Asociality." *Social Text* 37, no. 1 (2019): 27–50.

Kini, Ashvin R. "Diasporic Relationalities: Queer Affiliations in Shani Mootoo's 'Out on Main Street.'" *South Asian Review* 35, no. 3 (2014): 185–202.

Knight, Arthur. "Star Dances: African-American Constructions of Stardom, 1925–1960." In *Classic Hollywood, Classic Whiteness,* edited by Daniel Bernardi, 386–414. Minneapolis: University of Minnesota Press, 2001.

Koestenbaum, Wayne. *The Queen's Throat: Opera, Homosexuality, and the Mystery of Desire.* New York: Poseidon Press, 1993.

Kondo, Dorinne K. *About Face: Performing Race in Fashion and Theater.* New York: Routledge, 1997.

Krishnan, Sneha. "Bitch Don't Be a Lesbian: Selfies, Selves and Same-Sex Desire." In *Queering Digital India: Activisms, Intimacies, and Subjectivities,* edited by Rohit Dasgupta and Debanuj DasGupta, 151–64. New York: Oxford University Press, 2018.

Kumar, Vijeta. "Sure, You Could Say I Went to a Dalit Women's Conference but Woah It Was a Zingat Party." *Ladies Finger.* Last modified December 25, 2017. Accessed October 13, 2018. http://theladiesfinger.com/dalit-women-conference/

Kun, Josh. *Audiotopia: Music, Race, and America.* Berkeley: University of California Press, 2005.

Kwan, SanSan. "Performing a Geography of Asian America: The Chop Suey Circuit." *TDR* 55, no. 1 (2011): 120–36.

La Fountain-Stokes, Lawrence. "Queer Diasporas, Boricua Lives: A Meditation on Sexile." *Review: Literature and Arts of the Americas* 41, no. 2 (2008): 294–301.

Lal, Vinay. "Indians." In *The Encyclopedia of Chicago,* edited by James R. Grossman, Ann Durkin Keating and Janice L. Reiff, 410. Chicago: University of Chicago Press, 2004.

Lawrence, Tim. "Beyond the Hustle: 1970s Social Dancing, Discotheque Culture, and the Emergence of the Contemporary Club Dancer." In *Ballroom, Boogie, Shimmy Sham, Shake: A Social and Popular Dance Reader,* edited by Julie Malnig, 199–215. Urbana: University of Illinois Press, 2009.

Lawrence, Tim. "In Defence of Disco (Again)." *New Formations* 58, no. 1 (2006): 128–46.

Lee, Josephine D. *Performing Asian America: Race and Ethnicity on the Contemporary Stage.* Philadelphia: Temple University Press, 1997.

León, Christina A. "Forms of Opacity: Roaches, Blood, and Being Stuck in Xandra Ibarra's Corpus." *ASAP/Journal* 2, no. 2 (2017): 369–94.

Leong, Andrew. "The Pocket and the Watch: A Collective Individualist Reading of Japanese American Literature." *Verge: Studies in Global Asias* 1, no. 2 (2015): 76–114.

Leong, Russell. *Asian American Sexualities: Dimensions of the Gay and Lesbian Experience*. New York: Routledge, 1996.

Lerner, Erica, and Cynthia E. Milton. "Introduction: Witness to Witnessing." In *Curating Difficult Knowledge: Violent Pasts in Public Spaces*, edited by Erica Lerner, Cynthia E. Milton, and Monica Eileen Patterson, 1–19. New York: Palgrave Macmillan, 2001.

Levine, Martin P., and Michael S. Kimmel. *Gay Macho: The Life and Death of the Homosexual Clone*. New York: New York University Press, 1998.

Liang, Lawrence. "Strangers in a Place They Call Home." *The Hindu*. Last modified July 1, 2016. Accessed June 30, 2019. https://www.thehindu.com/opinion/op-ed/strangers-in-a-place-they-call-home/article3785965.ece

Lim, Eng-Beng. *Brown Boys and Rice Queens: Spellbinding Performance in the Asias*. New York: New York University Press 2014.

Lipsitz, George. *How Racism Takes Place*. Philadelphia: Temple University Press, 2011.

Livermon, Xavier. "Soweto Nights: Making Black Queer Space in Post-apartheid South Africa." *Gender, Place & Culture* 21, no. 4 (2014): 508–25.

Lowe, Lisa. *Immigrant Acts: On Asian American Cultural Politics*. Durham, NC: Duke University Press, 1996.

Lowe, Lisa. *The Intimacies of Four Continents*. Durham, NC: Duke University Press, 2015.

Lukose, Ritty A. *Liberalization's Children: Gender, Youth, and Consumer Citizenship in Globalizing India*. Durham, NC: Duke University Press, 2009.

Mack, Mehammed Amadeus. *Sexagon: Muslims, France, and the Sexualization of National Culture*. New York: Fordham University Press, 2017.

Madhusoodan, M. K. "Bangalore Police Commissioner: We're Enforcing Old Rules, So What's New?" *Daily News and Analysis*. Last modified December 27, 2010. Accessed April 10, 2014. https://www.dnaindia.com/bangalore/interview-bangalore-police-commissioner-we-re-enforcing-old-rules-so-what-s-new-1486638

Madison, D. Soyini. "Co-performative Witnessing." *Cultural Studies* 21, no. 6 (2007): 826–31.

Madison, D. Soyini. *Critical Ethnography: Method, Ethics, and Performance*. 2nd ed. Thousand Oaks, CA: Sage Publications, 2005.

Madison, D. Soyini. "Dressing Out-of-Place: From Ghana to Obama Commemorative Cloth on the USAmerican Red Carpet." In *African Dress: Fashion, Agency, Performance*, edited by Karen Tranberg Hansen and D. Soyini Madison, 217–29. London: Bloomsbury, 2013.

Madison, D. Soyini. "'That Was My Occupation': Oral Narrative, Performance, and Black Feminist Thought." *Text and Performance Quarterly* 13, no. 3 (1993): 213–32.

Maira, Sunaina. *Desis in the House: Indian American Youth Culture in New York City*. Philadelphia: Temple University Press, 2002.

Maira, Sunaina. "Henna and Hip Hop: The Politics of Cultural Production and the Work of Cultural Studies." *Journal of Asian American Studies* 3, no. 3 (2000): 329–69.

Maitra, Ani. "Hearing Queerly: Musings on the Ethics of Disco/Sexuality." *Continuum* 25, no. 3 (2011): 375–96.

Majumdar, Neepa. *Wanted: Cultured Ladies Only! Female Stardom and Cinema in India, 1930s–1950s*. Urbana: University of Illinois Press, 2009.

Malhotra, Sheena. "Finding Home in a Song and a Dance: Nation, Culture, Bollywood."

In *Race/Gender/Class/Media 3.0*, edited by Gail Dines and Jean Humez, 71–77. Los Angeles: Sage Publications, 2009.

Mallapragada, Madhavi. *Virtual Homelands: Indian Immigrants and Online Cultures in the United States*. Urbana: University of Illinois Press, 2014.

Manalansan, Martin F., IV. *Global Divas: Filipino Gay Men in the Diaspora*. Durham, NC: Duke University Press, 2003.

Manalansan, Martin F., IV. "In the Shadows of Stonewall: Examining Gay Transnational Politics and the Diasporic Dilemma." *GLQ* 2, no. 4 (1995): 425–38.

Manalansan, Martin F., IV, Anita Mannur, and Robert Ji-Song Ku. *Eating Asian America: A Food Studies Reader*. New York: New York University Press, 2013.

Manalansan, Martin F., IV, Chantal Nadeau, Richard T. Rodríguez, and Siobhan B. Somerville. "Queering the Middle: Race, Region, and a Queer Midwest." *GLQ* 20, nos. 1–2 (2014): 1–12.

Manayath, Nithin. "Inhi Logon Ne: Meena Kumari and All That Was Lost with Her." *Big Indian Picture*. Last modified March 2013. Accessed October 13, 2018. http://thebig indianpicture.com/2013/03/inhi-logon-ne/

Manivannan, Sharanya. "Professional Mourners." *Motherland* 2012: 14–19.

Mankekar, Purnima. *Unsettling India: Affect, Temporality, Transnationality*. Durham, NC: Duke University Press, 2015.

Manning, Erin. *Politics of Touch: Sense, Movement, Sovereignty*. Minneapolis: University of Minnesota Press, 2007.

Mannur, Anita. *Culinary Fictions: Food in South Asian Diasporic Culture*. Philadelphia: Temple University Press, 2010.

Mannur, Anita, and Martin Manalansan. "Dude, What's That Smell? The Sriracha Shutdown and Immigrant Excess." *MH Magazine*. Last modified January 16, 2014. Accessed October 13, 2018. https://www.fromthesquare.org/dude-whats-that-smell-the-sriracha-shutdown-and-immigrant-excess/

Mazumdar, Ranjani. *Bombay Cinema: An Archive of the City*. Minneapolis: University of Minnesota Press, 2007.

Mazzarella, William. "A Different Kind of Flesh: Public Obscenity, Globalisation and the Mumbai Dance Bar Ban." *South Asia* 38, no. 3 (2015): 481–94.

McBride, Dwight A. *Why I Hate Abercrombie & Fitch: Essays on Race and Sexuality*. New York: New York University, 2005.

McClintock, Anne. *Imperial Leather: Race, Gender, and Sexuality in the Colonial Contest*. New York: Routledge, 1995.

McCune, Jeffrey Q. "Transformance: Reading the Gospel in Drag." In *The Drag Queen Anthology: The Absolutely Fabulous but Flawless Customary World of Female Impersonators*, edited by Steven P. Schacht and Lisa Underwood, 151–67. New York: Harrington Park Press, 2004.

McGlotten, Shaka. *Virtual Intimacies: Media, Affect, and Queer Sociality*. Albany: State University of New York Press, 2013.

McGuire, Meredith. "'How to Sit, How to Stand': Bodily Practice and the New Urban Middle Class." In *A Companion to the Anthropology of India*, edited by Isabelle Clark-Decès and Christophe Guilmoto, 115–36. Malden, MA: Wiley-Blackwell, 2011.

McMillan, Uri. *Embodied Avatars: Genealogies of Black Feminist Art and Performance* (New York: NYU Press 2015).

Meduri, Avanthi. "Bharatha Natyam—What Are You?" *Asian Theatre Journal* 5, no. 1 (1988): 1–22.

Meduri, Avanthi. "Temple Stage as Historical Allegory in Bharatanatyam: Rukmini Devi as Dancer-Historian." In *Performing Pasts: Reinventing the Arts in Modern South India*, edited by Indira Viswanathan Peterson and Devesh Soneji, 133–64. New Delhi: Oxford University Press, 2008.

Mehotra, Ajay. "Pakistanis." In *The Encyclopedia of Chicago*, edited by James R. Grossman, Ann Durkin Keating, and Janice L. Reiff, 596. Chicago: University of Chicago Press, 2004.

Mehta, Monika. "What Is behind Film Censorship? The Khalnayak Debates." In *The Bollywood Reader*, edited by Jigna Desai and Rajinder Dudrah, 122–33. New York: Open University Press, 2008.

Mengesha Lilian G., and Lakshmi Padmanabhan. "Introduction to Performing Refusal / Refusing to Perform." *Women & Performance* 29, no. 1 (2019): 1–8.

Menon, Jisha. "Calling Local / Talking Global: The Cosmo-Politics of the Call-Center Industry." *Women & Performance* 23, no. 2 (2013): 162–77.

Menon, Jisha. *The Performance of Nationalism: India, Pakistan, and the Memory of Partition*. Cambridge: Cambridge University Press, 2013.

Menon, Jisha. "Queer Selfhoods in the Shadow of Neoliberal Urbanism." *Journal of Historical Sociology* 26, no. 1 (2013): 100–19.

Menon, Nivedita. "How Natural Is Normal? Feminism and Compulsory Heterosexuality." In *Because I Have a Voice: Queer Politics in India*, edited by Arvind Narrain and Gautam Bhan, 33–39. New Delhi: Yoda Press, 2005.

Menon-Broker, Aditi N. "A Hall of Mirrors: Repetition and Recycling in Hindi Commercial Cinema." PhD diss., Northwestern University, 2005.

Merabet, Sofian. "Disavowed Homosexualities in Beirut." *Middle East Report* 230 (2004): 30–33.

Minning, Heidi. "Qwir-English Code Mixing in Germany: Constructing a Rainbow of Identities." In *Speaking in Queer Tongues*, edited by William Leap and Tom Boellstorff, 46–71. Urbana: University of Illinois Press, 2004.

Mitchell, Gregory. *Tourist Attractions: Performing Race and Masculinity in Brazil's Sexual Economy*. Chicago: University of Chicago Press, 2015.

Moon, Michael. "Flaming Closets." *October* 51 (1989): 19–54.

Mooney, Nicola. "Aaja Nach Lai [Come Dance]: Performing and Practicing Identity among Punjabis in Canada." *Ethnologies* 30, no. 1 (2008): 103–24.

Moore, Madison. *Fabulous: The Rise of the Beautiful Eccentric*. New Haven: Yale University Press, 2018.

Moore, Madison. "Tina Theory: Notes on Fierceness." *Journal of Popular Music Studies* 24, no. 1 (2012): 71–86.

Moraga, Cherríe, and Gloria Anzaldúa. *This Bridge Called My Back: Writings by Radical Women of Color*. 2nd ed. New York: Kitchen Table, Women of Color Press, 1983.

Morcom, Anna. *Hindi Film Songs and the Cinema*. Burlington, VT: Ashgate, 2007.

Morcom, Anna. *Illicit Worlds of Indian Dance: Cultures of Exclusion*. Oxford: Oxford University Press, 2013.

Mowlabocus, Sharif. *Gaydar Culture: Gay Men, Technology and Embodiment in the Digital Age*. London: Routledge, 2010.

Mukherjee, Debashree. "Notes on a Scandal: Writing Women's Film History against an Absent Archive." *BioScope: South Asian Screen Studies* 4, no. 1 (2013): 9–30.

Mukhi, Sunita Sunder. *Doing the Desi Thing: Performing Indianness in New York City.* Asian Americans. New York: Garland Pub., 2000.

Muñoz, José Esteban. *Cruising Utopia: The Then and There of Queer Futurity.* New York: New York University Press, 2009.

Muñoz, José Esteban. *Disidentifications: Queers of Color and the Performance of Politics.* Minneapolis: University of Minnesota Press, 1999.

Muñoz, José Esteban. "Ephemera as Evidence: Introductory Notes to Queer Acts." *Women & Performance* 8, no. 2 (1996): 5–16.

Muñoz, José Esteban. "'Gimme Gimme This . . . Gimme Gimme That': Annihilation and Innovation in the Punk Rock Commons." *Social Text* 31, no. 3 (2013): 95–110.

Muyiwa, Joshua. "Amour the Merrier." *Time Out Bengaluru*, February–March 2012, 17–21.

Myerhoff, Barbara G. *Number Our Days: Culture and Community among Elderly Jews in an American Ghetto.* New York: Meridian, 1994.

Naficy, Hamid. *An Accented Cinema: Exilic and Diasporic Filmmaking.* Princeton, NJ: Princeton University Press, 2001.

Nagar, Ila. "Digitally Untouched: Janana (In)Visibility and the Digital Divide." In *Queering Digital India: Activisms, Intimacies, and Subjectivities*, edited by Rohit Dasgupta and Debanuj DasGupta, 97–111. Edinburgh: Edinburgh University Press, 2018.

Nagarkatti, C. S. "Sense of Liberation Sweeps Indian Gays in US." *India Today.* Last modified February 28, 1989. Accessed June 30, 2019. https://www.indiatoday.in/magazine/international/story/19890228-sense-of-liberation-sweeps-indian-gays-in-us-815816-1989-02-28

Nair, Janaki. *The Promise of the Metropolis: Bangalore's Twentieth Century.* New Delhi: Oxford University Press, 2005.

Nair, Janaki, and Mary E. John. *A Question of Silence: The Sexual Economies of Modern India.* London: Zed Books, 2000.

Nair, Ritika. "Chin Lung Got a Makeover but the Vibes and Prices Remain Old-School." *Little Black Book.* Last modified January 28, 2017. Accessed October 13, 2018. https://lbb.in/bangalore/chin-lung-restobar/

Nakassis, Constantine V. *Doing Style: Youth and Mass Mediation in South India.* Chicago: University of Chicago Press, 2016.

Narayanareddy, Rajyashree. "Specters of Waste in India's 'Silicon Valley': The Underside of Bangalore's Hi-Tech Economy." PhD diss., University of Minnesota, 2011.

Narrain, Arvind. "Queering Democracy: The Politics of Erotic Love." In *Law Like Love: Queer Perspectives on Law*, edited by Arvind Narrain and Alok Gupta, 3–23. New Delhi: Yoda Press, 2011.

Narrain, Arvind, and Vinay Chandran. *Nothing to Fix: Medicalisation of Sexual Orientation and Gender Identity.* New Delhi: Sage Publications India, 2016.

Narrain, Arvind, and Marcus Eldridge. *The Right That Dares to Speak Its Name: Decriminalising Sexual Orientation and Gender Identity in India.* Bangalore: Alternative Law Forum, 2009.

Narrain, Arvind, and Alok Gupta, eds. *Law Like Love: Queer Perspectives on Law.* New Delhi: Yoda Press, 2011.

NBC Asian America. "Tracing the Evolution of Asian-Pacific Islander LGBTQ Nightlife Spaces." *NBC Universal.* Last modified June 28, 2018. Accessed October 13, 2018. https://www.nbcnews.com/video/tracing-the-evolution-of-asian-pacific-islander-lgbtq-nightlife-spaces-1264034371628

Nemoto, Kumiko. *Racing Romance: Love, Power, and Desire among Asian American / White Couples.* New Brunswick, NJ: Rutgers University Press, 2009.

Newton, Esther. "My Best Informant's Dress." *Cultural Anthropology* 8, no. 1 (1993): 3–23.

Nguyen, Patricia. "Project 0395A.ĐC | Performing Disorientation." *Women & Performance* 29, no. 1 (2019): 88–94.

Nguyen, Tan Hoang. *A View from the Bottom: Asian American Masculinity and Sexual Representation.* Durham, NC: Duke University Press, 2014.

Nijhawan, Amita. "Excusing the Female Dancer: Tradition and Transgression in Bollywood Dancing." *South Asian Popular Culture* 7, no. 2 (2009): 99–112.

Nijhawan, Amita. "Of Snake Dances, Overseas Brides, and Miss World Pageants: Frolicking through Gurinder Chadha's *Bride and Prejudice.*" In *Oxford Handbook of Dance and the Popular Screen,* edited by Melissa Blanco Borelli, 378–91. Oxford: Oxford University Press, 2014.

Noland, Carrie, and Sally Ann Ness. *Migrations of Gesture.* Minneapolis: University of Minnesota Press, 2008.

Nukalapati, Prasant. "Brown and Blue: An Interview with Desi Adult Film Star Vikram Sohan." *Trikone Magazine* 2004, 12.

Ochoa, Marcia. *Queen for a Day: Transformistas, Beauty Queens, and the Performance of Femininity in Venezuela.* Durham, NC: Duke University Press, 2014.

Oldenburg, Veena Talwar. "Lifestyle as Resistance: The Case of the Courtesans of Lucknow." In *Contesting Power: Resistance and Everyday Social Relations in South Asia,* edited by Gyan Prakash and Douglas Haynes, 23–61. Berkeley: University of California Press, 1991.

Orne, Jason. *Boystown: Sex & Community in Chicago.* Chicago: University of Chicago Press, 2017.

Paik, Shailaja. "Mangala Bansode and the Social Life of Tamasha: Caste, Sexuality, and Discrimination in Modern Maharashtra." *Biography* 40, no. 1 (2017): 170–98.

Papadopoulos, Alex G. "From 'Towertown' to 'Boystown' to 'Girltown': Chicago's Gay and Lesbian Geographies." In *Chicago's Geographies: Metropolis for the 21st Century,* edited by Richard P. Greene, Mark J. Bouman, and Dennis Grammenos, 232–41. Washington, DC: Association of American Geographers, 2006.

Parédez, Deborah. "Lena Horne and Judy Garland: Divas, Desire, and Discipline in the Civil Rights Era." *TDR* 58, no. 4 (2014): 105–19.

Parédez, Deborah. *Selenidad: Selena, Latinos, and the Performance of Memory.* Durham, NC: Duke University Press, 2009.

Patel, Reena. *Working the Night Shift: Women in India's Call Center Industry.* Stanford, CA: Stanford University Press, 2010.

Patel, Shailja. *Migritude.* New York: Kaya Press, 2010.

Patnaik, Pranta Pratik. "Bearly Indian: 'Fat' Gay Men's Negotiation of Embodiment, Culture, and Masculinity." In *Masculinity and Its Challenges in India: Essays on Changing Perceptions,* edited by Rohit K. Dasgupta and K. Moti Gokulsing, 93–105. Jefferson, NC: McFarland, 2014.

Pawar, Yogesh. "Cracks Surface in LGBTQI Community." *DNA India.* Last modified

January 28, 2017. Accessed September 30, 2018. http://www.dnaindia.com/mumbai/report-cracks-surface-in-lgbtqi-community-2296830

Pérez, Hiram. *A Taste for Brown Bodies: Gay Modernity and Cosmopolitan Desire*. New York: New York University Press, 2015.

Peterson, Grant Tyler. "Clubbing Masculinities: Gender Shifts in Gay Men's Dance Floor Choreographies." *Journal of Homosexuality* 58, no. 5 (2011): 608–25.

Phelan, Peggy. *Unmarked: The Politics of Performance*. London: Routledge, 1993.

Pinto, Jerry. *Helen: The Life and Times of an H-Bomb*. New Delhi: Penguin, 2006.

Pinto, Sarah. "Drugs and the Single Woman: Pharmacy, Fashion, Desire, and Destitution in India." *Culture, Medicine, and Psychiatry* 38, no. 2 (2014): 237–54.

Pollock, Della. "Failing." *Communication and Critical/Cultural Studies* 4, no. 4 (2007): 441–44.

Pollock, Della. *Remembering: Oral History Performance*. New York: Palgrave Macmillan, 2005.

Powell, Elliott H. "Unmastered: The Queer Black Aesthetics of Unfinished Recordings." *Black Scholar* 49, no. 1 (2019): 28–39.

Prashad, Vijay. *The Karma of Brown Folk*. Minneapolis: University of Minnesota Press, 2000.

Puar, Jasbir Kaur. *Terrorist Assemblages: Homonationalism in Queer Times*. Durham, NC: Duke University Press, 2007.

Puar, Jasbir Kaur. "Global Circuits: Transnational Sexualities and Trinidad." *Signs* 26, no. 4 (2001): 1039–65.

PUCL-K. *Attacking Pubs and Birthday Parties: Communal Policing by Hindutva Outfits*. Mangalore: People's Union for Civil Liberties Karnataka and Forum Against Atrocities on Women, 2012.

Puri, Jyoti. *Sexual States: Governance and the Struggle over the Antisodomy Law in India*. Durham, NC: Duke University Press, 2016.

Putcha, Rumya S. "Gender, Caste, and Feminist Praxis in Transnational South India." *South Asian Popular Culture* 17, no. 1 (2019): 61–79.

Quazi, Suman. "I Am a Heterosexual Indian Girl Who Went to a Gay Party." *News Yahoo*. Last modified May 30, 2017. Accessed September 30, 2018. https://sg.news.yahoo.com/i-am-a-heterosexual-indian-girl-who-went-to-a-gay-120936996.html

Queer Coolie. "Review Queer Desi Dance Party: Jai Ho 5!" *Gaysi*. Last modified August 30, 2010. Accessed September 30, 2018. http://gaysifamily.com/2010/08/30/review-queer-desi-dance-party-jai-ho-5/

Radhakrishnan, Smitha. *Appropriately Indian: Gender and Culture in a New Transnational Class*. Durham, NC: Duke University Press, 2011.

Raghavendra, M. K. "Local Resistance to Global Bangalore: Reading Minority Indian Cinema." In *Popular Culture in a Globalised India*, edited by K. Moti Gokulsing and Wimal Dissanayake, 15–27. London: Routledge / Taylor & Francis Group, 2009.

Rahaim, Matthew. *Musicking Bodies: Gesture and Voice in Hindustani Music*. Middletown, CT: Wesleyan University Press, 2012.

Rahemtullah, Omme-Salma. "Bollywood in *Da* Club: Social Space in Toronto's 'South Asian' Community." In *The Magic of Bollywood: At Home and Abroad*, edited by Anjali Gera Roy, 234–53. New Delhi: Sage Publications, 2012.

Rahoof, Abdul K. K. "Gay Party Busted." *Deccan Chronicle*. Last modified September 3, 2013. Accessed October 13, 2018. https://www.pressreader.com/india/deccan-chronicle/20130903/282394102117178

Raj, Senthorun. "Asylum and Sexual Orientation." In *The Wiley Blackwell Encyclopedia of Gender and Sexuality Studies*. Malden, MA: Wiley Blackwell, 2016.

Rajaram, Poorva. "I Was Once a Gay Party Enthusiast." *Tehelka*. Last modified April 23, 2011. Accessed October 13, 2018. http://old.tehelka.com/i-was-once-a-gay-party-enthusiast/

Ramberg, Lucinda. "Backward Futures and Pasts Forward: Queer Time, Sexual Politics, and Dalit Religiosity in South India." *GLQ* 22, no. 2 (2016): 223–48.

Ramberg, Lucinda. *Given to the Goddess: South Indian Devadasis and the Sexuality of Religion*. Durham, NC: Duke University Press, 2014.

Rampal, Nikhil. "Gay Modi Fans Can Finally Shut the Liberals Up If Section 377 Is Decriminalised." *The Print*. Last modified July, 2018. Accessed October 13, 2018. https://theprint.in/opinion/gay-modi-fans-can-finally-shut-the-liberals-up-if-section-377-is-decriminalised/81762/

Rana, Junaid Akram. *Terrifying Muslims: Race and Labor in the South Asian Diaspora*. Durham, NC: Duke University Press, 2011.

Rangaswamy, Padma. *Namasté America: Indian Immigrants in an American Metropolis*. University Park: Pennsylvania State University Press, 2000.

Rao, Anupama. *The Caste Question: Dalits and the Politics of Modern India*. Berkeley: University of California Press, 2009.

Rao, Anupama. *Gender & Caste*. London: Zed Books, 2005.

Ratnam, Dhamini. "The Party Must Go On." *HT Media*. Last modified June 17, 2016. Accessed September 30, 2018. https://www.livemint.com/Leisure/iim5VoD6CBsWLVMGb5I1tJ/The-party-must-go-on.html

Ratti, Rakesh. *A Lotus of Another Color: An Unfolding of the South Asian Gay and Lesbian Experience*. Boston: Alyson Publications, 1993.

Reddy, Chandan. *Freedom with Violence: Race, Sexuality, and the US State*. Durham, NC: Duke University Press, 2011.

Reddy, Gayatri. *With Respect to Sex: Negotiating Hijra Identity in South India*. Chicago: University of Chicago Press, 2005.

Reddy, Vanita. *Fashioning Diaspora: Beauty, Femininity, and South Asian American Culture*. Philadelphia: Temple University Press, 2016.

Reed, Christopher. "We're from Oz: Marking Ethnic and Sexual Identity in Chicago." *Environment and Planning D: Society and Space* 21, no. 4 (2003): 425–40.

Rege, Sharmila. "The Hegemonic Appropriation of Sexuality: The Case of the Lavani Performers of Maharashtra." *Contributions to Indian Sociology* 29, nos. 1–2 (1995): 23–38.

Rivera, Sylvia. "Queens in Exile, the Forgotten Ones." In *GenderQueer: Voices from beyond the Sexual Binary*, edited by Joan Nestle, Clare Howell, and Riki Wilchins, 67–85. Los Angeles: Alyson Publications, 2002.

Ritchie, Jason. "How Do You Say 'Come Out of the Closet' in Arabic? Queer Activism and the Politics of Visibility in Israel-Palestine." *GLQ* 16, no. 4 (2010): 557–76.

Rivera-Servera, Ramón H. "History in Drag: Latina/o Queer Affective Circuits in Chicago." In *Latina/o Midwest Reader*, edited by Omar Valerio-Jimenez and Santiago Vaquera-Vasquez, 185–95. Urbana: University of Illinois Press, 2017.

Rivera-Servera, Ramón H. *Performing Queer Latinidad: Dance, Sexuality, Politics*. Ann Arbor: University of Michigan Press, 2012.

Roach, Joseph R. *Cities of the Dead: Circum-Atlantic Performance*. New York: Columbia University Press, 1996.

Rodríguez, Juana María. "Queer Sociality and Other Sexual Fantasies." *GLQ* 17, nos. 2–3 (2011).

Rodríguez, Juana María. *Sexual Futures, Queer Gestures, and Other Latina Longings*. New York: New York University Press, 2014.

Roh, David S., Betsy Huang, and Greta A. Niu. *Techno-Orientalism: Imagining Asia in Speculative Fiction, History, and Media*. New Brunswick, NJ: Rutgers University Press, 2015.

Román, David. *Acts of Intervention: Performance, Gay Culture, and AIDS*. Bloomington: Indiana University Press, 1998.

Román, David. "Dance Liberation." *Theatre Journal* 55, no. 3 (2003): vii–xxiv.

Rowe, Aimee Carrillo, Sheena Malhotra, and Kim Perez. *Answer the Call: Virtual Migration in Indian Call Centers*. Minneapolis: University of Minnesota Press, 2013.

Rowena, Jenny. "The 'Dirt' in the Dirty Picture: Caste, Gender and Silk Smitha." *Round Table India*. Last modified June 17, 2012. Accessed July 1, 2019. https://roundtableindia.co.in/index.php?option=com_content&view=article&id=5283%253Athe-dirt-in-the-dirty-picture-caste-gender-and-silk-smitha

Roy, Anjali Gera. *Bhangra Moves: From Ludhiana to London and Beyond*. Burlington, VT: Ashgate, 2010.

Roy, Anjali Gera. "Black Beats with a Punjabi Twist." *Popular Music* 32, no. 2 (2013): 241–57.

Roy, Jeff. "Translating Hijra into Transgender: Performance and in India's Trans-Communities." *TSQ* 3, nos. 3–4 (2016): 412–32.

Roy, Sandip. "Curry Queens and Other Spices." In *Q & A: Queer in Asian America*, edited by David L. Eng and Alice Y. Hom, 256–61. Philadelphia: Temple University Press, 1998.

Roy, Sandip. "How Silicon Valley fostered India's LGBTQ+ movement," *LiveMint* Last updated August 31, 2019). Accessed October 12, 2019. https://www.livemint.com/mint-lounge/features/how-silicon-valley-fostered-india-s-lgbtq-movement-1567161918842.html.

Rubin, Gayle. "Thinking Sex: Notes for a Radical Theory of the Politics of Sexuality." In *The Lesbian and Gay Studies Reader*, edited by Henry Abelove, Michèle Aina Barale, and David M. Halperin, 3–44. New York: Routledge, 1993.

Said, Edward W. *Orientalism*. New York: Pantheon Books, 1978.

Saldanha, Arun. *Psychedelic White: Goa Trance and the Viscosity of Race*. Minneapolis: University of Minnesota Press, 2007.

Sandhu, Arti. *Indian Fashion: Tradition, Innovation, Style*. London: Bloomsbury Academic, 2015.

Sangarasivam, Yamuna. "Researcher, Informant, 'Assassin,' Me." *Geographical Review* 91, nos. 1–2 (2001): 95–104.

Sargunaraj, Wilbur. "How to Do the Dappankuthu." *YouTube*. Last modified December 7, 2017. Accessed October 13, 2018. https://www.youtube.com/watch?v=51Vp2GBBxVY

Sarkar-Munshi, Urmila. "Another Time, Another Space: Does the Dance Remain the Same?" In *Dance Matters: Performing India*, edited by Pallabi Chakraborty and Nilanjana Gupta, 29–39. London: Routledge, 2010.

Savigliano, Marta. *Angora Matta: Fatal Acts of North-South Translation = Actos Fatales De Traduccion Norte-Sur*. Middletown, CT: Wesleyan University Press, 2003.

Savigliano, Marta. *Tango and the Political Economy of Passion*. Boulder, CO: Westview Press, 1995.

Sedgwick, Eve Kosofsky. "Gosh, Boy George, You Must Be Awfully Secure in Your Masculinity!" In *Constructing Masculinity*, edited by Maurice Berger, Brian Wallis, and Simon Watson, 11–20. New York: Routledge, 1995.

Sedgwick, Eve Kosofsky. *Touching Feeling: Affect, Pedagogy, Performativity*. Durham, NC: Duke University Press, 2003.

Seligman, Amanda. "Uptown." In *The Encyclopedia of Chicago*, edited by James R. Grossman, Ann Durkin Keating, and Janice L. Reiff, 847–48. Chicago: University of Chicago Press, 2004.

Sengupta, Durga M. "I Am Not a Hijra: A Damaging Offensive Transgender India Photo Campaign." *Catchnews*. Last modified August 19, 2016. Accessed June 30, 2019. http://www.catchnews.com/gender-and-sex/i-am-not-a-hijra-a-damaging-offen sive-transgender-india-photo-campaign-1471618717.html

Shah, Nayan. "Sexuality, Identity, and the Uses of History." In *Q & A: Queer in Asian America*, edited by David L. Eng and Alice Y. Hom, 141–56. Philadelphia: Temple University Press, 1998.

Shah, Nayan. *Stranger Intimacy: Contesting Race, Sexuality, and the Law in the North American West*. Berkeley: University of California Press, 2011.

Shahani, Nishant. "Patently Queer: Late Effects and the Sexual Economies of India." *GLQ* 23, no. 2 (2017): 195–220.

Shahani, Parmesh. *Gay Bombay: Globalization, Love and (Be)Longing in Contemporary India*. Thousand Oaks, CA: Sage Publications, 2008.

Shandilya, Krupa. "Of Enraged Shirts, Gyrating Gangsters, and Farting Bullets: Salman Khan and the New Bollywood Action Film." *South Asian Popular Culture* 12, no. 2 (2014): 111–21.

Shankar, Shalini. *Desi Land: Teen Culture, Class, and Success in Silicon Valley*. Durham, NC: Duke University Press, 2008.

Sherinian, Zoe. "Drumming Dalit Female Masculinity: Queering Gender in South Asia." Presented at "Queer Symposium: Un/desirable Encounters at the Intersections of Race, Class, and Caste." Annual Conference on South Asia, Madison, WI, 2018.

Sherinian, Zoe. "Religious Encounters: Empowerment through Tamil Outcaste Folk Drumming." *Interpretation* 71, no. 1 (2016): 64–79.

Sherinian, Zoe. *Tamil Folk Music as Dalit Liberation Theology*. Bloomington: Indiana University Press, 2014.

Shimakawa, Karen. *National Abjection: The Asian American Body Onstage*. Durham, NC: Duke University Press, 2002.

Shiva Kumar, M. T. "It Is More Than Just Song and Dance." *Hindu*, January 26, 2010.

Shresthova, Sangita. *Is It All About Hips? Around the World with Bollywood Dance*. New Delhi: Sage Publications, 2011.

Singh, Pawan. "The TV9 Sting Operation on PlanetRomeo: Absent Subjects, Digital Privacy and LGBTQ Activism." In *Queering Digital India: Activisms, Intimacies, and Subjectivities*, edited by Rohit Dasgupta and Debanuj DasGupta, 132–50. Edinburgh: Edinburgh University Press, 2018.

Singh, Sukhdeep. "Gay Men Attacked in a Bar in Bangalore." *Gaylaxy Magazine*. Last modified March 9, 2014. Accessed October 13, 2018. http://www.gaylaxymag.com/latest-news/gay-men-attacked-in-a-bar-in-bangalore/

Sinha, Mrinalini. *Colonial Masculinity: The "Manly Englishman" and the "Effeminate Bengali" in the Late Nineteenth Century*. Manchester: Manchester University Press, 1995.

Sinha, Mrinalini. "Giving Masculinity a History: Some Contributions from the Historiography of Colonial India." *Gender & History* 11, no. 3 (2002): 445–60.

Sklar, Deidre. "Reprise: On Dance Ethnography." *Dance Research Journal* 32, no. 1 (2000): 70–77.

Smalls, Shanté Paradigm, and Elliott H. Powell, "Introduction." *Black Scholar* 49, no. 1 (2019): 1–5.

Son, Elizabeth. *Embodied Reckonings: "Comfort Women," Performance, and Transpacific Redress*. Ann Arbor: University of Michigan Press, 2018.

Souffrant, Kantara. "Circling Dantò's Daughter: Reflections on Lenelle Moïse's Performances of Shamelessness." *Women & Performance* 27, no. 2 (2017): 229–34.

Spade, Dean. "Mutilating Gender." In *The Transgender Studies Reader*, edited by Susan Stryker and Stephen Whittle, 315–32. New York: Routledge, 2006.

Srinivas, S. V., *Megastar: Chiranjeevi and Telugu Cinema after N.T. Rama Rao*. Oxford: Oxford University Press, 2009.

Srinivasan, Amrit. "Reform and Revival: The Devadasi and Her Dance." *Economic and Political Weekly* 20, no. 44 (1985): 1869–76.

Srinivasan, Priya. *Sweating Saris: Indian Dance as Transnational Labor*. Philadelphia: Temple University Press, 2011.

Srivastava, Sanjay. *Passionate Modernity: Sexuality, Class, and Consumption in India*. New Delhi: Routledge, 2007.

Stallmeyer, John C. "New Silicon Valleys: Tradition, Globalization, and Information-Technology Development in Bangalore, India." *Traditional Dwellings and Settlements Review* 19, no. 2 (2008): 21–36.

Stewart-Winter, Timothy. *Queer Clout: Chicago and the Rise of Gay Politics*. Philadelphia: University of Pennsylvania Press, 2016.

Stockton, Kathryn Bond. *The Queer Child, or Growing Sideways in the Twentieth Century*. Durham, NC: Duke University Press, 2009.

Stoler, Ann Laura. *Carnal Knowledge and Imperial Power: Race and the Intimate in Colonial Rule*. Berkeley: University of California Press, 2002.

Stoneley, Peter. *A Queer History of the Ballet*. London: Routledge / Taylor & Francis Group, 2007.

Strey, Jacquelyn P. "Queerness's Domain? Queer Negotiations, Utopian Visions and the Failures of Heterotopias in Bangalore." In *Urban Utopias: Excess and Expulsion in Neoliberal South Asia*, edited by Tereza Kuldova and Mathew A. Varghese, 247–67. Cham, Switzerland: Palgrave Macmillan 2017.

Sueyoshi, Amy Haruko. *Discriminating Sex: White Leisure and the Making of the American "Oriental"*. Urbana: University of Illinois Press, 2018.

Surya. "The Failed Radical Possibilities of Queerness in India." *RAIOT*. Last modified February 4, 2016. Accessed October 13, 2018. http://raiot.in/the-failed-radical-possibilities-of-queerness-in-india/

Taeube, Florian. "The Indian Software Industry: Cultural Factors Underpinning Its Evolution." In *Popular Culture in a Globalised India*, edited by K. Moti Gokulsing and Wimal Dissanayake, 223–35. London: Routledge / Taylor & Francis Group, 2009.

Taylor, Diana. *The Archive and the Repertoire: Performing Cultural Memory in the Americas*. Durham, NC: Duke University Press, 2003.

"Techies Reveal Their Colours." *Times of India*. Last modified November 28, 2011. Accessed October 13, 2018. http://timesofindia.indiatimes.com/articleshow/10898301.cms

Thangaraj, Stanley I. *Desi Hoop Dreams: Pickup Basketball and the Making of Asian American Masculinity*. New York: New York University Press, 2015.

Thawer, Rahim. "Did This Drag Queen Go Too Far?" *Huffington Post*. Last modified February 17, 2013. Accessed October 13, 2018. https://www.huffingtonpost.ca/rahim-thawer/drag-toronto_b_2323047.html

Thomann, Matthew. "Zones of Difference, Boundaries of Access: Moral Geography and Community Mapping in Abidjan, Côte d'Ivoire." *Journal of Homosexuality* 63, no. 3 (2016): 426–36.

Thornton, Sarah. *Club Cultures: Music, Media, and Subcultural Capital*. Hanover, NH: University Press of New England, 1996.

Tondon, Vishal. "Exclusionary Masculinities: Exploring Caste, Class, and Gender Bias in Urban Indian Gay Men." *Café Dissensus*. Last modified May 15, 2017. Accessed October 13, 2018. https://cafedissensus.com/2017/05/15/exclusionary-masculinities-exploring-caste-class-and-gender-bias-in-urban-indian-gay-men/

Torres, Justin "In Praise of Latin Night at the Queer Club." *Washington Post*. Last modified June 13, 2016. Accessed October 13, 2018. https://www.washingtonpost.com/opinions/in-praise-of-latin-night-at-the-queer-club/2016/06/13/e841867e-317b-11e6-95c0-2a6873031302_story.html

TV5 News. "Pulse Pub Gay Party at Begumpet, Hyderabad." *YouTube*. Last modified September 1, 2013. Accessed October 13, 2018. https://www.youtube.com/watch?v=k0eGMDqgp7E

Tyburczy, Jennifer. *Sex Museums: The Politics and Performance of Display*. Chicago: University of Chicago Press, 2016.

Uberoi, Patricia. "Imagining the Family: An Ethnography of Viewing *Hum Aapke Hain Koun*." In *The Bollywood Reader*, edited by Jigna Desai and Rajinder Dudrah, 172–88. New York: Open University Press, 2008.

Upadhya, Carol. "Management of Culture and Management through Culture in the Indian Software Outsourcing Industry." In *In an Outpost of the Global Economy: Work and Workers in India's Information Technology Industry*, edited by Carol Upadhya and Aninhalli Rame Vasavi, 76–100. New Delhi: Routledge, 2008.

Upadhya, Carol, and A. R. Vasavi, eds. *In an Outpost of the Global Economy: Work and Workers in India's Information Technology Industry*. New Delhi: Routledge, 2008.

Upadhyay, Nishant. "Queer Rights, Section 377, and Decolonizing Sexualities." *Decolonizing Sexualities,* Last modified July 19, 2018. Accessed October 12, 2019. https://decolonizingsexualities.com/2018/07/

Vaid-Menon, Alok. "Imp Queen and the Perpetually Problematic Erasure of Trans Drag Queens." *Them: Condé Nast*. Last modified September 29, 2018. Accessed October 13, 2018. https://www.them.us/story/imp-queen-trans-drag-queens

Valentine, David. *Imagining Transgender: An Ethnography of a Category*. Durham, NC: Duke University Press, 2007.

Vanita, Ruth. *Dancing with the Nation: Courtesans in Bombay Cinema*. New York: Bloomsbury Academic, 2018.

Vanita, Ruth. *Gandhi's Tiger and Sita's Smile: Essays on Gender, Sexuality, and Culture*. New Delhi: Yoda Press, 2005.

Vargas, Deborah R. "Ruminations on *Lo Sucio* as a Latino Queer Analytic." *American Quarterly* 66, no. 3 (2014): 715–26.

Varma, Roli. "Transnational Migration and Entrepreneurialism: Indians in the U.S. Technology Sector." *Perspectives on Global Development and Technology* 10, no. 2 (2011): 270–87.

Veeramani, A. "It's 'We' Day." *Daily News and Analysis*, February 14, 2012, 4.

Vijayakumar, Gowri. "Collective Demands and Secret Codes: The Multiple Uses of 'Community' in 'Community Mobilization.'" *World Development* 104 (2018): 173–82.

Vogel, Shane. *The Scene of Harlem Cabaret: Race, Sexuality, Performance*. Chicago: University of Chicago Press, 2009.

Vogel, Shane. *Stolen Time: Black Fad Performance and the Calypso Craze*. Chicago: University of Chicago Press, 2018.

Vora, Kalindi. "Limits of 'Labor': Accounting for Affect and the Biological in Transnational Surrogacy and Service Work." *South Atlantic Quarterly* 111, no. 4 (2012): 681–700.

Walcott, Rinaldo. "Boyfriends with Clits and Girlfriends with Dicks: Hip Hop's Queer Future." *Palimpsest* 2, no. 2 (2013): 168–73.

Walcott, Rinaldo. "Reconstructing Manhood; or, The Drag of Black Masculinity." *Small Axe* 13, no. 1 (2009): 75–89.

Walker, Margaret E. *India's Kathak Dance in Historical Perspective*. Farnham, Surrey, England: Ashgate Publishing, 2014.

Walsh, Fintan. "Queer Performance and the Drama of Disorientation." In *Queer Dramaturgies: International Perspectives on Where Performance Leads Queer*, edited by Alyson Campbell and Stephen Farrier, 313–29. New York: Palgrave Macmillan, 2015.

Warner, Michael. *Publics and Counterpublics*. New York: Zone Books, 2002.

Warner, Sara. *Acts of Gaiety: LGBT Performance and the Politics of Pleasure*. Ann Arbor: University of Michigan Press, 2012.

Wat, Eric C. "Preserving the Paradox: Stories from a Gay-Loh." In *Asian American Sexualities: Dimensions of the Gay and Lesbian Experience*, edited by Russell Leong, 71–81. New York: Routledge, 1996.

Waugh, Thomas. "Queer Bollywood, or 'I'm the Player, You're the Naive One': Patterns of Sexual Subversion in Recent Indian Popular Cinema." In *Keyframes: Popular Cinema and Cultural Studies,*, edited by Matthew Tinkcom and Amy Villarejo, 280–97. London: Routledge, 2001.

Weidman, Amanda. "Voices of Meenakumari: Sound, Meaning, and Self-Fashioning in Performances of an Item Number." *South Asian Popular Culture* 10, no. 3 (2012): 307–18.

Williams, Joshua. "Going Ape." *Performance Research* 21, no. 5 (2016): 68–77.

Wilson, Ara. *The Intimate Economies of Bangkok: Tomboys, Tycoons, and Avon Ladies in the Global City*. Berkeley: University of California Press, 2004.

Wolf, Stacy. "'We'll Always Be Bosom Buddies': Female Duets and the Queering of Broadway Musical Theater." *GLQ* 12, no. 3 (2006): 351–76.

Wolf, Stacy. "Wicked Divas, Musical Theater, and Internet Girl Fans." *Camera Obscura* 22, no. 2 (2007): 39–71.

Wortham, Jenna. "The Joy of Queer Parties: 'We Breathe, We Dip, We Flex." *New York Times.* Last modified June 26, 2019. Accessed July 5, 2019. https://www.nytimes.com/2019/06/26/style/queer-party-safe-space.html

Wu, Cynthia. *Sticky Rice: A Politics of Intraracial Desire.* Philadelphia: Temple University Press, 2018.

Yue, Audrey. "Queer Asian Mobility and Homonational Modernity: Marriage Equality, Indian Students in Australia and Malaysian Transgender Refugees in the Media." *Global Media and Communication* 8, no. 3 (2012): 269–87.

Index